D1524263

Imagining Our Americas

A book in the series

Radical Perspectives

A *Radical History Review* book series

Series editors:

Daniel J. Walkowitz, New York University

Barbara Weinstein, New York University

Imagining Our Americas

Toward a Transnational Frame

Edited by Sandhya Shukla and Heidi Tinsman

Duke University Press   *Durham and London*   **2007**

© 2007 Duke University Press

All rights reserved

Printed in the United States of America on acid-free paper ∞

Typeset in Minion and Officina by Tseng Information Systems, Inc.

Library of Congress Cataloging-in-Publication Data

appear on the last printed page of this book.

Contents

About the Series

History, as radical historians have long observed, cannot be severed from authorial subjectivity, indeed from politics. Political concerns animate the questions we ask, the subjects on which we write. For over thirty years the *Radical History Review* has led in nurturing and advancing politically engaged historical research. Radical Perspectives seeks to further the journal's mission: any author wishing to be in the series makes a self-conscious decision to associate her or his work with a radical perspective. To be sure, many of us are struggling with the issue of what it means to be a radical historian in the early twenty-first century, and this series provides some signposts for what we judge to be radical history. It offers innovative ways of telling stories from multiple perspectives; comparative, transnational, and global histories that transcend conventional boundaries of region and nation; works that elaborate on the implications of the postcolonial move to "provincialize Europe"; studies of the public in and of the past, including those that consider the commodification of the past; histories that explore the intersection of identities such as gender, race, class, and sexuality with an eye to their political implications and complications. Above all, this book series seeks to create an important intellectual space and discursive community to explore the very issue of what constitutes radical history. Within this context, some of the books published in the series may privilege alternative and oppositional political cultures, but all will be concerned with the way power is constituted, contested, used, and abused.

In *Imagining Our Americas*, a disciplinarily diverse group of scholars boldly intervenes in the growing debate over the longstanding segmentation of academic knowledge into Latin American Studies and U.S. American Studies and the consequent inclination to rethink "American Studies" in hemispheric terms. The editors take as their point of departure José Martí's famous protest in the essay "Our America" against the monopolization of the term by U.S. Americans, as well as his prescient recognition of the inseparability of political and cultural developments throughout the hemisphere. Their pluralization of Martí's phrase, however, reflects an awareness of the imbricated nature of knowledge and identities in these two "areas" and an insistence that the historically constructed differences in power, politics, and culture cannot be erased through an academic sleight of hand. The editors note at the outset that the paradoxes of globalization and empire—the "accelerated migration of goods and peoples" alongside deepening inequalities—compel us to rethink conventional categories of knowledge, but also recognize the differing stakes involved in the retention or rejection of certain categories. Hence, if scholars in U.S. American studies have much more readily responded to postmodern invocations of the global and the transnational over the national, for Latin American scholars' "modernist conceptualizations of state-formation and national liberation have had a special urgency."

The thirteen essays that follow the stimulating introduction vividly demonstrate what we gain if we simultaneously cross, and even question, the epistemological border/barrier between U.S. America and Latin America while not losing sight of the inequalities that have made that division meaningful in myriad contexts. We gain new insights into the formation and destabilization of racial identities by considering the circulation of racist discourses and discourses about race among the United States, Mexico, and Cuba, instead of analyzing racial identities in a strictly national context. We encounter cases of national identities forged by the loss of national autonomy, making evident the transnational processes that produce the national imaginary. And we are moved to rethink the very contours of the Americas as "Western Hemisphere" in essays that cogently argue for the inclusion of Hawaii and the Philippines in "Our Americas." Thoughtful, provocative, and profoundly interdisciplinary, this volume offers persuasive evidence for refusing to allow even well-surveyed boundaries to become reified into barriers that block critical thinking or political innovation.

Acknowledgments

A big collective project produces correspondingly large frustrations and pleasures. Striving, as we have, to produce a real dialogue between Latin American studies and U.S. American studies has entailed navigating among diverse interests, many of them fervent and well developed, others tentative and anticipatory. The administrative challenge (and periodic drudgery) to produce a coherent work, however, has been eased greatly by the construction of a community of interlocutors, of authors, readers, commentators, and reviewers. It may not be that this community can easily be captured by a category—of those who work on, or are committed to, "Americas" inquiry—but the names we mention here should at least trace some of the productive intellectual currents we swam as we put together this book.

First, the shape of this book emerged from a set of conversations enabled by the work of our coedited special issue of the *Radical History Review*, "Our Americas: Political and Cultural Imaginings." We would like to thank the contributors to that volume: Néstor García Canclini, Martin Hopenhayn, Rossana Reguillo, Arturo Arias, Ian Lekus, John D. Blanco, Aimee Carrillo Rowe, María Josefina Saldaña-Portillo, Aisha Khan, Paul Giles, Salah D. Hassan, Patricio del Real, Carlos E. Bojorquez Urzaiz, Enrique C. Ochoa, Ian Christopher Fletcher, Diana Paton, John Beck, Gemma Robinson, and Kate Masur. Other scholars who supported that project with encouragement, readings, and reviews deepened our thoughts about the Americas, and we are grateful to them; they include Lauren Derby, Julio Moreno, Karen Flint, Teresa Meade, Pete Sigal, Lisa Brock, Doug Haynes, Van Gosse, Jim O'Brien, Sharmila Sen, Karen Sotiropoulos, Vicente Diaz, Duane Corpis, Susan Gosse, Iona Man-Cheong, Yvonne Lasalle, Gary Okihiro, Claudia Milian, Raul Fernández, and Paul Bové. Martin Woessner, Ernest Ialongo, and Chia Yin Hsu, at the *Radical History Review* office at the time, ensured that the journal was published. The editorial collective of the *Radical History Review* has supported every stage of this project (vague idea, journal theme, book project) with both hard work and political-intellectual inspiration. Barbara Weinstein and Daniel Walkowitz, editors of the *Radical Perspectives* book series, encouraged us to expand on what appeared in "Our Americas." We also thank the Council of Editors of Learned Journals; their award of "Best Special Issue of 2004" gave this book (and us) a necessary shot in the arm.

The staff of Duke University Press has been very supportive of this book. Our editor Valerie Millholland has become legendary in the field of Latin American studies, not least because she sees the potential of a range of projects and diligently follows so many of them through. Miriam Angress has been extremely helpful in getting everything done fast, and has been gracious in the process. Two extremely insightful readers for the press bravely read the manuscript through twice (unpaginated the first time!) and offered detailed suggestions that profoundly shaped the current form of the book. We thank Vicki Ruiz and Sally Stern for their advice about the cover. We are grateful to Malaquias Montoya for allowing us to reproduce his remarkable work, and to Lezlie Salkowitz-Montoya for organizing this. We are most appreciative of Brian Karl's fine work on the index.

We would like to end with some words about friendship and collegiality, and their juncture, which lies at the heart of the conception and execution of this volume. We were incredibly fortunate to attend Yale graduate school together. As part of a larger interdisciplinary cohort, whose field of activity as often spanned the union movement at Yale (which included the Graduate Employees and Students Organization) and drinks at the Anchor as it did the classes we sometimes (but not always) took together, we found that our critical tools compelled conversations across departments and regional specialties. Having landed as we did in rather different disciplinary spaces, we have since remarked how unique, and special, that border crossing was. But happily, personal intimacies have a life of their own and diverge from professional theaters of activity. Our continuing friendship has produced the desire to talk across the limits of our own fields and, in the end, made the difficult work of scholarly collaboration possible. In that vein, we thank our partners Thomas Klubock and Erik Kongshaug for supporting this, and all other, endeavors. And finally, this project has had an odd simultaneity with another one, beginning in earnest when two of our children were about to be born. To them, Kiran and Noel, and to Arlo, future citizens of the world, we offer our hopes that thinking beyond the nation, and being connected to others, will always be possible.

Introduction: Across the Americas

Heidi Tinsman and Sandhya Shukla

Late into the first decade of the twenty-first century, we are witnesses to, indeed participants in, a more profound sense of global connection and a more acute experience of national and regional division than world history has perhaps ever presented. Accelerated migrations of goods and peoples proceed alongside the execution of regional and imperial wars and deepened international and intranational inequalities. These are the paradoxes of globalization and empire at our front door, at every world citizen's door. It seems that political and academic inquiries into the nature of distinct global communities and into what constitutes historical ruptures and continuities are all in some basic way concerned with how, analytically, we will work out the apparent contradictions of connection and division.

Twinned imperatives, to contend with contemporary globalization's intensity and to understand globality's historical depth, shape any exploration of nation and empire. Locating such efforts in the geographical and imaginative possibilities of *region* is one way to introduce important questions of time and space into deeply politicized debates about how nation-states and their peoples relate to one another. The Americas, as a political, economic, social, and spatial formation not of recent origin, animate global paradoxes in a number of powerful ways.[1] From the perspective of the United States, we look out into a fog of ironies. Latino Americans are now the nation's largest ethnic minority, and many estimate that by 2020, a full 20 percent of the U.S. population will be Latino. Latino majorities already exist in a number of southwestern cities and will increase regardless of attempts to stem that tide with new immigration regulations. Importantly, these populations are extraordinarily heterogeneous: they comprise U.S. citizens over more than one generation, children of documented and undocumented migrants, and those migrants themselves, from Mexico, Central and South America, and the Caribbean, from a range of class backgrounds. The population as a whole defies attempts to make political generalizations and confounds the use of established models for inclusion (or exclusion). These demographic shifts have fashioned a broad and renewed public questioning about the nature of belonging and citizenship. The border, always a vexed topic in national imaginings and territorial stakes, acquires the status of anxious preoccupation for all of us. How can it be crossed, how is it patrolled, how has it become a site of racial anxiety in the "war on terror," how does it matter?

The border between the United States and Latin America — most seriously there, and so frequently transgressed — demands our attention at the time when other borders, arguably, are being broken down. This border's constitution gives us a window onto the Americas that we seek to explore in this book. Latino political power in the United States, fresh fruit on U.S. dinner tables in the middle of January: today's Americas are quotidian realities. But the Americas have long existed through connections of politics and culture dating back several centuries, and especially marked in the last hundred years. The question, of course, is how to define the Americas. On the one hand, policymakers tout the "free market" and hold up trade alliances and other forms of cooperation between the United States and Latin America, all to boost the Americas as a superior instance of globalization's production and consumption circuits. On the other, there is the distinctly regional flavor of trade and cultural agreements positioned against the United States, between Brazil and Chile, through Central America, and developing new possibilities of Pacific flows. And as we write, Latin America boasts a bevy of left-leaning political leaders — Luiz Ignácio Lula da Silva of Brazil, Nestor Kirchner of Argentina, Michelle Bachelet of Chile, Evo Morales of Bolivia — with others in the wings, whose programs revive, indeed rely on, Latin American cooperation in the face of U.S. desires to dominate the hemisphere. The end to the Washington consensus on Latin America (and a particular vision of the Americas) resounds in Hugo Chavez's offering cut-rate heating oil to poor communities in the northeastern United States, not to mention his enduring alliance with Cuba's Fidel Castro.

Many groups, and many interests, then, lay claim to the Americas and increasingly seek to derive social, economic, or political meaning from the regional formation that crosses so many divides yet leaves others intact. With this collection of essays, we willingly join that race. As humanistic scholars based in the United States academy, we suggest that now, more than ever, it seems urgent for scholars here to offer vigorous critiques of how regional and national categories of difference and dichotomy are politically generated. Inevitably, this is a question, we assert, about the global politics of disciplines and regions. It is in the fertile ground of such an inquiry that our own collaboration — of scholars, colleagues, and friends from, as it were, different sides of the aisle, U.S. American studies and Latin American studies, and also anthropology and history — has taken shape.

Recent geopolitical events that express connections, divisions, and flows do give the contradictions of the Americas a dramatic shape and content. But the existence of Guantanamo — within Cuba geographically, but maintained by the United States militarily — or Colombia's export of flowers and Chile's providing grapes to the United States might be seen less as specifically iconic of contemporary globalization, and more as terrifying reminders of banana republics: political-economic arrangements that spawned horrific violence and disenfranchisement for a range of workers and citizens. So this book emerges from a sense of the contemporary that is deeply steeped in the past. More precisely, it is the result of our efforts to debate the newness of today's global crisis alongside the limits and possibilities of how the academy organizes world regions and produces historical, literary, and ethnographic knowledge about such places. Our conversation first took formal shape in a special issue of the *Radical History Review* in which we proposed that the topic of the Americas might provide a space for rethinking histories of imperialism, nation, and area while at the same time outlining the full necessity of interdisciplinary ways of thinking.[2] In the present volume, we elaborate such ideas much further, suggesting how the Americas might constitute a new interdisciplinary field. This introduction aspires to provide a theoretical road map for thinking about where such an endeavor might take us, about what questions and tools are implied in such work, as well as about the multiple traditions on which an interdisciplinary Americas scholarship must rest and build. The chapters that follow, in turn, each in some way engage with a central aspect of the larger, ongoing challenge that *Imagining Our Americas* invites.

Like many other transnational projects—from those stressing geopolitical cooperation to those seeking greater cultural integration among societies and nations in the continental mass that extends from southern Chile and Argentina to northern Canada—we find in José Martí's seminal essay "Our America" (1891) special inspiration for collecting exciting new work highlighting the cultural and political crossings of the term "the Americas" and the experiences of living and thinking in and through the region of the Americas. The figure of Martí has come to serve as a kind of shorthand for a formation that integrates "Latin America" and "the United States." And because Martí was a radical Cuban voice for national independence and an opponent of U.S. hemispheric domination, he can animate a version of union that is more inherently anti-imperialist and critical of capitalist development than "the Americas" one finds in neoliberal tracts of international relations and U.S. foreign policy manuals.

When Martí wrote, "The scorn of our formidable neighbor, who does not know us, is the greatest danger for our America; and it is imperative that our neighbor know us, and know us soon, so she shall not scorn us, for the day of the visit is at hand,"[3] he conjured up an impending imperial confrontation that would transform the political (and social) development of what were at that time the young republics (and enduring colonies) descended from Iberian empires. Of course he was right, in a more profound way than he could recognize at the time; North American invasions of, and interventions in, Latin America and the Caribbean did indeed soon come to pass and became routinized as a feature of life in the region. The pursuit of knowledge of the other, from the standpoint of the United States, took various forms, ranging from the development of anthropological obsessions in the early twentieth century to the initiation of formal "areas" of study in post-1940s Cold War educational programs. From and through Latin America, the United States was comprehended through intimate forms of contact, both exploitative and generative. Yet Martí's anxiety that the neighbors do not really "know" one another still resonates, as irreconcilable political divides between North and South obscure the persistent crossings that define this, as any, regional formation. The challenge, then, for this project is to at once deeply probe the cultural and political nature of an imbricated Americas, and at the same time remain attuned to the broader context that has produced hostilities, inequality, and acute division.

During a time of reinvigorated U.S. militarism abroad, most notable today in Iraq and Afghanistan, we suggest that it does scholars some good to dwell on the particulars of alternative paradigms, of a transnational relationship that on the one hand has been profoundly structured by imperialism and on the other has given rise to political and cultural formations that may undermine the calcified boundaries between nation-states, those formations that are the ironic consequences of the operations of that imperialism. This is to say, in an age where the oppositions between East and West (which the late Edward Said so compellingly explained through his model of "Orientalism") are acquiring renewed energy in the U.S. popular and political imagination and yet being relegated to a safe distance away from our shores, it is more crucial than ever to examine the structuring dilemmas of imperial relationships that constitute the "front" and "back" yards of the Americas. These categories, elaborated most fully through U.S. Cold War projects in Latin America, prefigured and now help sustain the dichotomies of modern versus backward, democracy versus authoritarianism, and freedom versus terrorism at work in the United States' current "Middle East crisis."[4]

How, precisely, might we do the work of thinking across the nation, to construct a politically and intellectually rigorous formation of the Americas? In fact there are three subquestions here, one about newly conceiving objects of study, a second about devising theoretical maps, and a third about the materials that are rendered in such moves. That multifaceted inquiry forms the heart of this collection of essays, which we suggest represent important new directions in a field that we come to from different perspectives. As scholars who are each situated in Latin American studies and U.S. American studies, we have seen the boundaries of our methods and topics break down. In some respects, the relief is to be found not simply in some kind of ideal middle ground, some inclusive Americas that encompasses North America, Latin America, and the Caribbean, but in the very maneuvers that make it possible to conceive of any formation that acknowledges the necessary transnational dynamics that create it and the national forces that militate against it. That formation, of region or area, must also recognize its limits: surely the Philippines and Hawaii might, and should, be considered part of the Americas, but wherein the extensions of the Pacific and the Atlantic worlds?

This idea of the Americas, then, as a transnational and transregional formation defined across the notion of nation-states as well as against the central organizing principle of a North-South dichotomy, does more than reproduce the bounded space of area studies shaped by the Cold War. While perhaps perversely the Americas does take *area* as its object, in this rendition, it works to conceive of nation and region in new and politicized ways, to resist the facile blending of distinct areas of the world that underlies the much-touted agreements of economic globalization. We are interested not so much in "comparative history"—the side-by-side examination of different "countries"—but in the experiences, imaginaries, and histories of interaction. These spaces of dialogue, linkage, conflict, domination, and resistance take shape across, or sometimes outside, the confines of national and regional borders and sensibilities and therefore allow for new epistemologies. Shared problematics, then, rather than a common geography, colonizing power, or language, might define an "Americas" inquiry that radically de-privileges the never fully inclusive Anglo-Iberian axis around which area studies currently constructs American "regions."

In challenging the analytical primacy of the nation, thinking across the Americas illuminates how many of the most significant social formations that mark the Americas' various regions and states were profoundly nonnational in character: diverse and complex indigenous societies, European conquest and colonization, African slavery, Enlightenment-based independence movements and republic-building projects, mass (im)migrations, populist welfare states, Cold War political cultures, neoliberal economies, to name but a few. Our goal is not to declare historical differences—or the power of nation-states in creating these differences—irrelevant; nor do we simply compel commonalities. Rather, we propose the need to think about how social formations such as colonization or migration are propelled by historical forces beyond the nation, as well as how they take their distinct shapes within transnational and transregional processes. Our work to develop a concept of the Americas, then, is to wrestle seriously with the importance of the global for contemporary scholarship that is historical at its very core.

Field Paradigms

The intervention of *Imagining Our Americas*, to simultaneously critique the boundary effects (not to mention political repercussions) of area studies topics and reimagine the space of a "region," emerges from a variety of specific institutional locales, each with its own complicated, and often troubled, history. We do not claim either to be the first to utilize the Americas as an object of inquiry or to be doing such work in a vacuum.[5] Americas work in the humanities and more humanistic social sciences has pushed beyond a concern with the trade and formal concerns of a geopolitical formation to consider literary cultures and transnational connections that live beyond the nation-state. But that work, frankly, often evolves from one side of the border, to reach into an Other space without a sustained mastery of multiple locales. What would it mean to strive for a concept of the Americas that considers the United States and Latin America, Canada and the Caribbean, along with their histories, cultures, and political formations, to be similarly generative and influential, in a sort of *relation*? Even beginning to answer that question entails the elaboration of a more careful history of the components of the dialogue.

First we must necessarily engage with the scholarly paradigms of Latin American studies and U.S. American studies. Cold War formations both, these two fields emerged at a moment when the United States could not help but understand itself as embedded in a broader world of cultural crossings, if on a superior footing. Annexed to the specter of communism was the hypermodern sensibility of progress: cultural, political, and economic. Thus the origins of U.S. American studies are not separate from the nation-state's elaboration of curricula and scholarship on "Western civilization," an entity of purportedly unique human achievement that would be a model for aspiring non-NATO countries. In turn, Latin American studies began as an initiative to measure Latin America's capacity for U.S.-style capitalist democracy and military trustworthiness. It is worth remembering, though, that such modernization paradigms were not imagined by their creators as means to invade peoples around the world, however foundational many such paradigms were for the very real and widespread forms of oppression perpetrated by U.S. foreign policy. Rather, the disciplines of area studies were born as liberal solutions to global difference and inequality, and they aspired to shape the "developing world" in an altruistic manner. The ambitions and effects of area studies, as was true of all U.S. Cold War projects, varied hugely around the world, and it may be difficult to compare area studies in Latin America, say, and Asia, without deep contextualization and qualification.[6] Yet if the work that emerged under the rubric of area studies had productive consequences, they lay in the proliferation of deep knowledges about places that had been understudied within the U.S. academy. This is to say that the richness of the field of Latin American studies results directly from U.S. postwar aspirations for hemispheric dominance and the awareness that this required knowing one's neighbors much better. U.S. American studies, too, developed closely with the ideological imperatives of building and maintaining U.S. political and cultural hegemony.[7]

Neither U.S. American studies nor Latin American studies was ever a mere tool of empire. Like the broader Cold War from which they emerged, area studies were politically contested and generated radical traditions that profoundly critiqued forms of domination. It was precisely U.S. American studies' self-assigned responsibility to map the specificity of cultural traditions in the United States that, in the aftermath of the social movements of the 1960s, helped make the field a hospitable space to work through pathbreaking paradigms for thinking about difference and inequality, including ethnic studies, feminist and queer theory, and Marxist-oriented cultural studies. But even earlier, scholars in U.S. American studies came to questions of "exceptionalism" in not always politically predictable ways. So too, in Latin American studies, the forced generalizations about what Latin America shared and how it differed from Europe and the United States often intentionally critiqued legacies of colonialism and imperialism, several decades before the contemporary contemplation of the "transnational." Many such critiques hailed from intellectual circles within the Latin American Left, where, for example, area studies categories energized dependency theory's famous indictment of Latin America's systematic underdevelopment by the developed world. And in the aftermath of the Cuban Revolution, "Latin America as the Third World" imagined an international solidarity and moral alternative distinct from either superpower. While such paradigms flatly rejected the proposition that the United States might provide a model for Latin America's advance, they retained the area studies notion of Latin America's regional specificity as well as the fantasy of national modernization. Such homegrown reformulations of the Latin American, in turn, inspired within U.S. academic circles an outpouring of scholarship explicitly aligned with Latin American national-revolutionary struggles or, at the least, strongly sympathetic to Latin American aspirations for political, economic, and cultural sovereignty. This last incarnation of Latin American studies has been particularly long-lived, producing an array of highly nuanced scholarship that privileges the idea that local and national histories unfold within wider hemispheric or international matrices of inequality, conflict, and contingent alliance.

So we have at this historical moment the benefit of over fifty years of knowledge about areas and fields, processed within debates about the politics of the global. Yet regardless of the diverse and sometimes oppositional ends for which area studies' arguments could be mobilized, their constitution of Latin America and the United States as historically juxtaposed had the effect of homogenizing and essentializing the internal dynamics of each area in relation to the other. In the case of U.S. American studies, this reinforced the tendency to look at processes taking place only within the borders of the United States (or its eventual borders). Even the most sophisticated examinations of difference and power — the many superb U.S. American histories of race, gender, or labor, for example — have too frequently been narrated as implicitly unique to the U.S. American experience or have unfolded in ways that only obliquely reference how social relations in the United States were connected to processes of dominance and exchange abroad. Latin American studies has suffered from somewhat the opposite problem. On the one hand, it has strained to identify the unique historical "traditions" that justify membership within the term "Latin"; and at the same time, the field has had difficulty discussing Latin American difference in ways that avoid implications of imitation or deviation from North Atlantic models. Like U.S. American studies, Latin American studies has been concerned with establishing narratives of national experience — what is specific to Chile, Mexico, or Cuba — but its paradigms have overwhelmingly focused on questions of political economy and national political culture, themes that talk back to enduring accusations of underdevelopment. In contrast to U.S. American studies, Latin American studies less often prioritized dynamics of racial, gender, or sexual difference except in anthropological studies of "the ethnic" — indigenous and African practices that, almost by definition, seemed outside or marginal to histories of "the nation." Despite an outpouring of Latin Americanist feminist scholarship over the last two decades, gender and sexuality are only just now becoming widely accepted as indispensable to all social analysis.

Many differences between U.S. American studies' and Latin American studies' discussions of the nation emerge from the internal logic of area studies and the geopolitics that produced such categories. At times, Latin American studies' greater emphasis on sketching a more singular national experience flowed directly from the way the Cold War (and U.S. and European policy before 1945) deeply compromised the sovereignty of Latin American states, calling into question their national fitness. U.S. American studies never needed to first defend the existence of the United States as a nation, even if the discipline was passionately critiquing the inequalities and exclusions on which such a concept was based. Given how infrequently assumptions of national exceptionalism are examined in many works of U.S. American studies, one could argue that many explorations of multicultural difference actually rely on an implied goal of eventual inclusion in U.S. national formations.

A productive tension might also exist between studies of "region" in Latin America and studies of "national space" in the United States, different focuses that in part reflect unequal and interconnected relationships to modernity. Not that Latin America has been only partially modern and the United States more fully so, but that — at least since the mid-nineteenth century — the modernity of many Latin American countries has been constituted partly through a denial of national autonomy, itself related to the way U.S. self-understandings of national autonomy and consequent modernity have been premised on ever-growing dominion within "its" hemisphere. More immediately, since the Cold War, these different and related trajectories of modernity have shaped area studies through the impact of the diverse social movements emerging from Latin America and the United States. In the United States, struggles for civil rights or against particular foreign policies always spoke most directly to issues of citizen empowerment, equality, and diversity within an already given nation. In Latin America, by contrast, leftist revolutionary struggles and pro-democracy movements grappled with how to take over (or take back) nation-states and wrest more economic control from "outsiders." We might say that the consequent result of these differences is that, within Latin American studies circles, modernist conceptualizations of state formation and national liberation have had a special urgency that they have often lacked in U.S. American studies, where the object of study was far less frequently "the state" or "national liberation," even when one was writing critically about "the nation."

It is also true that the solidarities forged between scholars and social movements in Latin America and Latin American studies articulated critical pan-regionalisms that offered a different set of economic, political, and cultural possibilities than the repressive imagined communities of the U.S. nation. The pan–Latin Americanism that area studies perhaps unwittingly bolstered, then, was of a politically charged nature and was an intellectual formation that disputed the hegemony of a variety of reactionary political projects. Ironically, it may have been in the cultural consequences of a Cold War–originated Latin American studies that one could find the logic of all sorts of challenges. These insights should urge us to resist the temptation to flatten the multiple trajectories of area studies into a singular, coherent project of rule. Likewise, we would do well to avoid collapsing the differences between all renditions of area studies, such as those in and of South Asia, East Asia, or Africa. And, finally and straightforwardly, it seems crucial to acknowledge that a great deal of what we in the U.S. academy know about Latin America is the consequence of area studies. It seems necessary to say both that area studies has too often falsely presented language or quasi-ethnographic detail as representative of bounded national cultures *and* that area studies projects have generated contestations that in turn produced different frameworks and understandings that could no longer remain invisible.[8]

Two relatively recent developments in U.S. American studies also have some bearing on these questions. The first is the emphasis within the field (and its institutions) on "difference." U.S. American studies has long been extremely sympathetic to, and perhaps even annexing of, developments in African American studies, Chicano and Latino studies, and Asian American studies, each of which has interrogated the ethnicized and racialized cultures that make up the nation-state. So too, feminist studies' and queer theory's critiques of the gendered and sexualized politics shaping national subjectivity and other communities have found a comfortable perch in U.S. American studies. Diversity, more generally, then, has not been seen as antithetical to the "America" that the field of U.S. American studies constructed; very much to the contrary. This cuts two ways, opening up inquiry and perhaps capturing it within familiar narratives of "America" that elide fracturing conflicts of the nation-state. Turning a skeptical eye to that compatibility, of nation and difference, that is surprisingly nonexistent within more traditional disciplinary spaces, we might ask whether accounting for difference within the U.S. American nation has done little more than prop up the nation, affirm its mythologies of itself, and project unity in the face of extraordinary incoherence.[9] Many feminist and queer scholars, too, in their work on gender and sexuality, have addressed how gender and sexuality reveal the porousness of national borders and the exclusions of citizenship. The model of ethnic, gendered, and sexualized culture should stand in a critical relationship to the U.S. American nation, not simply as an outgrowth or a composite part of the whole.

There have been more recent critiques of "America" within U.S. American studies that operate exclusively under the sign of the transnational.[10] In particular, there is a move to understand the social formations of migrants and other racialized peoples across multiple nation-states and regions. This has inspired scholars to resituate America in a global framework, in which other nations or imperial projects play a role in the U.S. national-cultural space. Transnational formation has also enabled a fuller discussion of U.S. empire within U.S. American studies, to much good effect, including the 1993 collection *Cultures of United States Imperialism*, edited by Amy Kaplan and Donald Pease.[11] And more recently there has been an efflorescence of works that take the charge of that collection, to integrate questions of empire into a study of the nation, seriously.[12]

Yet even throughout that important new work in U.S. American studies there is a glaring absence of the appearance and thick description of other places in the world, not just as specters or victimized objects but as actors, producers, and sources within transnational circuitry.[13] Recent books on empire may do the important work of explaining in detail the role of the United States in the world, but they do so, often, without the cultural or linguistic fluency of those acted-upon sites that would help us understand the depth of impact and the possibilities for resistance.[14] We must ask here whether U.S. American studies can truly understand the imbrication of cultures that transnational exchanges produce, without the fine detail of national formations other than those of the United States. Even more to the point, an interconnected world produces more than the national formations themselves; it produces cultural, political, and social encounter that contains the possibility of something new. This is to say that our interest here in this book is not simply to juxtapose work from U.S. American studies and Latin American studies, nor is it to compare and contrast scholarship, but to develop a theoretical paradigm that can produce an argument about the relationship of areas of the world and the knowledges produced in, through, and out of them. If this project uses a vocabulary of encounter that may rehearse a sense of the Americas and Europe as embodying contrasting visions of time and space, it also reinscribes it in more dynamic global historical formations, such that no site can be wholly untouched by the other.[15]

Many of the ongoing differences between U.S. American studies and Latin American studies flow from the way these fields have differently responded to the vibrant critiques of modernist paradigms launched since the early 1980s by poststructuralist and postcolonial theories. We might say that whereas U.S. American studies more readily accommodated poststructuralism's rejection of the unified subject and postcolonialism's unveiling of Enlightenment conceptual binaries, Latin American studies was initially more resistant to such ideas, or at least more selective about how they were used. U.S. American studies, because of its interest in questions of culture and the imaginary, became a particularly receptive place for the new interdiscipline of "cultural studies" — a field with origins in Britain, in the Marxist traditions of the Birmingham school, and in the United States with particular affinities to literature. Imported debates about social theory, the place of ethnic and racial formation in challenging "national culture," and the role of the popular in developing new ideas about the social, as well as constructing audiences to experience the traffic in intellectual and political ideas across the borders of the ivory tower, inspired in U.S. American studies a sense of self-critique and self-reflection and have in turn provided a model for recent transnational academic developments—a model that is not unrelated to trends toward studying empire and transnational cultures within U.S. American studies.[16] That model's structure might be resurrected here, too, for our own inquiry that seeks to produce intellectual and political exchanges among many kinds of "Americanists."

This is not to suggest that Latin American studies was entirely opposed to, or outside, the intellectual agenda set by the poststructuralist-postcolonial move. On the contrary, recent histories of Latin American *mestizaje* and racial hybridity, diaspora and migration, gender and sexuality, as well as a new attention to the transnational nature of Latin American political and popular culture, all speak to the ways that Latin American studies as area studies has been transformed in response to these newer paradigms.[17] Certain disciplines, such as literature and women's studies, engaged with poststructuralist-postcolonialist concepts from the beginning.[18] So too did particular national academic circles; for example, intellectuals in Brazil and Argentina "discovered" Foucault and Lacan at the same moment as their counterparts in U.S. American studies. Nonetheless it is difficult to resist the notion that Latin American studies as a whole has lagged in its consideration of issues of heterogeneity, representation, exclusions, discursive power, and the inherent instability of the nation. Even a cursory glance at the comparative offerings of recent meetings of the Latin American Studies Association and the American Studies Association reveals a significant, if narrowing, divergence precisely along these lines. Yet the very notion of "lag" points to an epistemological politics within U.S. American studies that many Latin Americanists have found worrisome: namely, they asked, was it not peculiar that "nation" could be jettisoned as an object of privileged study in U.S. American (and European) circles at precisely the moment when the achievement of greater sovereignty vis-à-vis the United States and Europe seemed on the horizon, if not at hand, among former colonies and "spheres of influence" elsewhere in the world? The post–Cold War geopolitics of permeable national markets under the benign umbrella of U.S. neoliberalism and military supremacy made this all the more troubling. But adding to the confusion was the fact that many postcolonialist paradigms, in particular, were being formulated largely within progressive circles, often by people of color or so-called "third world intellectuals in the first world," who fully shared the staunch criticism leveled by many within Latin American studies against colonialism and imperialism. So surely the poststructuralist move was something other than a plot to defang Latin Americanist critiques of political and economic inequality. But then why did politically like-minded folks appear to be on such opposite conceptual sides?

One debate that generated particular mutual suspicion was the discussion over the future place of Marx. Poststructuralism had especially criticized Marxism for its rigid subordination of analytical narratives to the story of class within capitalism and for its failure to satisfactorily consider culture and language as fundamental and independent apparatuses of power. In its most polemical stance, poststructuralism tended to suggest that Marxism—as a body of thought steeped in Enlightenment notions of linear progress and unified subjectivities—might be nonrecuperable for scholarly and political projects aimed at overthrowing universalist categories. The response to such a proposition (including unfair caricatures of the proposition) by many within Latin American studies was a mixture of bewilderment and hostility. Indeed, a great deal was at stake in calling Marxism, and materialist frameworks more broadly, into question. After all, Marxist theory of various strains had long provided some of the most compelling conceptual frameworks in Latin American studies and had been central to Latin American studies' theoretical radicalism and oppositional politics.[19] Dependency theory, as well as the far more nuanced histories of colonialism and imperialism that followed, drew in creative ways from Marxian notions of capitalism as a world-historical process and the centrality of colonies or hinterlands to capitalist profit.[20] Of equal importance were Marxian notions of "class" as a relationship between human divisions of labor, and of "the state" as a site of political struggle among classes, or among momentary coalitions of classes.[21]

But Marxist-oriented Latin American studies have not always ignored culture. On the contrary, Marxist paradigms were prevalent in much of the pioneering work by anthropologists on indigenous societies and urban migration,[22] while the models provided by E. P. Thompson and other British Marxists for writing "history from below" inspired a generation of labor history that emphasized the everyday activities and the worldviews of peasants, slaves, and workers.[23] Since the mid-1980s, the revival of Antonio Gramsci's writing on hegemony has generated a virtual explosion of Latin Americanist scholarship on labor, popular culture, and state formation.[24] As was true of Gramsci's appeal to other intellectual circles—in particular, South Asian subaltern studies and British cultural studies—a focus on the relationship between state power and the cultural manufacture of consent, and its contestation, seemed especially helpful to scholars who were rethinking why so often "the masses" seemed to support authoritarian projects that seemed counter to "their interests." More fundamentally, the turn to history from below and the study of cultural hegemony generated a radical revision of orthodox Marxist paradigms. In particular, the political lives of peasants (as distinct from industrial workers) moved to center stage, and considerations of capitalist imperialism became more nuanced accounts of simultaneously overlapping and conflicting orientations of foreign and national business interests and governments.[25] The scholarship of the contributors to the volume *Close Encounters of Empire: Writing the Cultural History of U.S.–Latin American Relations*, edited by Gilbert Joseph, Catherine LeGrand, and Ricardo Salvatore, critically revised presumptions about U.S. cultural and economic control in Latin America and, along with the work of other scholars, gestured strongly toward the need for transnational histories that took Latin American influence on U.S. actors seriously.[26] There has also been an increasing attention by Latin Americanists to social and cultural formations that lie outside, or are opposed to, the arena of national political economy. Questions about indigenous and peasant resistance to national independence movements and revolutionary struggles as something other than "reactionary" became increasingly urgent.[27]

Not coincidentally, Latin American studies has more recently produced its own contributions to postcolonial and subaltern studies.[28] Innovative works in colonial history and literature have emphasized the importance of Enlightenment binaries and fantasies to the politics of possession.[29] And various writers took on some of these questions textually, and through a variety of cultural formations.[30] New studies in political culture have stressed the volatile heterogeneity of ideology and the limits of dominance.[31] Especially important work on transnational culture has taken on questions of consumption and hybridity: those that illuminate the very contradictions of the "global" network that constructs regional affiliations like the Americas. Néstor García Canclini's seminal text *Hybrid Cultures* has provided, if not a model, then certainly a language for understanding the postmodern cultural spaces where "first" and "third" worlds inevitably meet.[32] However, the extent to which Canclini's discussion of hybridity has been widely cited may also obscure the powerful cautionary notes that this and all his works have sounded about romanticizing cultural work that is embedded in the specific inequalities of late capitalism, and the ways that Latin American autonomy threatens to become compromised in the process. In many ways, this very problem is one that is central to any paradigm like that of the Americas that seeks to build a field of cooperation, for the particularities and, especially, the power dynamics threaten to become flattened out. The interests of a United States that makes claims to a more expansive "America" and an "America" that José Martí posed as a bulwark against North American imperialism may not be so easily massaged into a harmonious dialogue. The disconnect between those Americas must underwrite any claims, most of all our own, to organize solidaristic forms of knowledge.[33]

Theorizing the Global

Imagining Our Americas builds on, and also departs from, a variety of conversations that have sought to critically situate paradigms of the nation-state and area studies "regions." In retheorizing continental formation, we can stress the interconnected nature of North and South power relations. Historical understandings of the United States must be shaped by careful studies of empire, and Latin America may be seen, too, to impact the United States. Borderland studies, which has powerfully interrogated the fluid encounters and identities delineating the spaces between Mexico and the United States, in particular, is one such model for thinking through the place of the Latin American in the United States.[34] But we might push this still further, beyond the figure of "the Latino" or "the immigrant," to address even wider zones of dialogue. How, for instance, did the Haitian Revolution shape U.S. or Canadian political culture, or how did notions of racial hybridity officially promoted in Brazil and Mexico challenge racial formations to the North? Perhaps, in these moves, we can not only reverse the top-down view of imperialism as a one-way process of North-South domination but also construct the gaze from a number of standpoints. Here ethnic and feminist studies have much more to add than simply proposing new topics for the mix. These interdisciplinary projects have posited a set of subjectivities around "difference" that make all overarching frameworks—nation, region, empire—much more porous, contested, and in the process of becoming constituted. As such, the United States, Latin America, and the Caribbean, not to mention a range of geographical possibilities within, become formations rather than fixed entities. Latin American nations as well as the U.S. nation are thus built more through fractures (of race, class, gender, sexuality) than shared interests. To put one example bluntly: Latin America or its component nations can no longer inhabit the space of the "ethnic" but must be subjected to analyses of ethnic formation. Nor can the "Latino/Latina" stand in for all the complex dynamics of imperialism and the history of capitalist development that has made the "America" of the United States.

If one of the main impulses of an Americas paradigm is to see transnational processes of domination, another powerful ambition, political as well as historical, is to locate instances of transnational solidarity against those dominations. Histories of slave rebellion, indigenous resistance, labor radicalism, feminism, abolition, socialism, revolution, or anti-imperialist projects, for example, all gain enormously from analytical approaches that privilege transregional forces and influences across borders. Beyond stressing the internationalism or transnationalism of these solidarities, an Americas paradigm may also reveal how very American they often were—resistances and counterhegemonic projects that linked people with shared regional subjectivities vis-à-vis their opponents, for example, uprooted African slaves against European masters; American Creoles against Spanish rulers; or defenders of the Mexican, Cuban, and Nicaraguan revolutions against U.S. foreign policy.

And yet, while we widen the lens to view transnationality more fully, we remain aware of the various historical projects, of slavery, of state formation, of social movements, that have been articulated nationally. The nation-state and nationalism have shaped all forms of modern cultural and social life throughout the United States and Latin America just as they have around the world. How to reconcile that fact with other developments across national borders is a central dilemma for a range of interpretive moments, like that of the Americas. And, relatedly, alongside connections within and across the Americas there has been disjuncture. Whether the Americas, then, is a fragmented or integrated entity is a question that should be accorded some degree of flexibility. Thinking in terms of the Americas enables us to think across nation while also always referencing and investigating the specificity of the multiple nations that have given the Americas their distinct and changing forms. Indeed, understanding transnational processes of imperialism or of emancipatory struggle often demands attention to the nation as the concrete site, goal, or experience of such processes. Likewise, because "nations" are often the objects of imperial politics or emancipatory struggles, thinking in terms of nation helps keep postcolonial theories (and we could also say theories of the Americas) from becoming ahistorical or collapsing different dynamics into one another. There are reasons to distinguish between the more colonialist activities of the United States in Hawaii, the Philippines, or Puerto Rico and U.S. military and economic imperialism in the Southern Cone, not to mention European colonialism and U.S. imperialism.

Much of the recent literature on transnationalism has pointed to the fluid and mobile nature of cultural formations that have mediated increasingly integrated capitalist markets and labor migrations. Especially important in this debate has been the recognition of how "local" and "global" dynamics thoroughly inform one another, as well as of how capitalist expansion and globalization generate new forms of difference and hybridity, rather than simple homogenization. But to a fault, this scholarship has overwhelmingly focused on the twentieth century (and the late twentieth century at that), unwittingly suggesting that transnational (or, more appropriately, transregional) dynamics were less relevant at earlier points in time. While not refuting the intensity of more recent global formations, we argue for a more historical sensibility—not only a consideration of earlier transregional or transnational connections, but also an interrogation of how arguments about the past are mobilized to underwrite theories about more contemporary moments.

Recent discussions in world history seem especially relevant here. Often located within the analytical domain of political economy, new work in world history has reinvigorated older materialist debates about the origins and expansion of capitalism and the centrality of European colonialism and imperialism to modernity.[35] Many such arguments, it is worth noting, drew partial inspiration from Latin Americanist dependency scholars such as Fernando Henrique Cardoso and André Gunder Frank, who helped shape the conceptual language for Immanuel Wallerstein's famous "world systems analysis" that posited global exploitative relations between "metropolitan cores" and "peripheries."[36] But more recent scholarship, especially that by historians of Asia and Africa, has worked to challenge the strong Eurocentrism of world history's central plot about the West's action on "the rest."[37] Kenneth Pomeranz's comparative work about the profound congruence between eighteenth-century China and England has radically upended the idea that industrialization and its spread were ever inevitably "European" phenomena.[38] This underscores the crucial challenge of exploring historical contingencies, conflicts, even accidents, and calls on us to question whose history stands as the norm. Dipesh Chakrabarty, too, rethinks colonial and postcolonial cultural formations through a decentering of European paradigms for thought and influence, turning to "translate" not only cultural or linguistic difference but varied (and often opposed) historical experiences of capitalism and modernity.[39] If Chakrabarty's conclusions betray that famous "linguistic turn," his concerns also reflect the Marxist underpinnings of South Asian subaltern studies, which we might conceive of as a militant area challenge to area studies paradigms.[40]

One can imagine similar reversals being helpful in any juxtaposition of

"Latin American" and "North American" histories. This is not an invitation to utopian speculation but an insistence that we formulate questions that scrutinize the winner's terms and not begin the story at its end. Revisiting Wallerstein's notion of world system through a postcolonialist lens, Walter Mignolo argues that sixteenth- and seventeenth-century colonialism in the Americas (especially by Spain and Portugal) provided the genesis for Western modernity, and that the Americas were imagined as Europe's extension rather than as a place of radical alterity.[41] It is only with the formation of national republics, amid Iberia's decline as a world power, that "Latin America" comes to inhabit a more ambiguous place vis-à-vis "the West" — not as Oriental Other but as stepchild and malformed version of its Anglophone sibling to the north. The Americas, then, offer something different to postcolonial narratives of the colonizing West and its colonized Other; historical and regional-local specificity can revise theoretical frameworks in important ways. A number of scholars, too, have emphasized the importance of granting particular agency and creativity to "subalterns," such as the indigenous, Creole, or slave, who did not emerge as victors in, or authors of, the story of the Latin American nation.[42]

Unorthodox reorderings of place and time have enabled many powerful critiques of colonialism and modernity. Paul Gilroy's seminal work on the now-paradigmatic black Atlantic, for example, constructed a new spatiality, in the words of Gilles Deleuze and Félix Guattari, a "rhizomatic" space of encounter. Here diaspora emerged as a formation to permit dialogue and conversation; there is disjuncture and difference, and yet a space for a collectivity to emerge.[43] But how striking that Gilroy should have elaborated a sensibility about the black Atlantic without drawing our attention to the crossings into and through Latin America, where the trade in African slaves was largest and most enduring. Partly this has to do with an emphasis on the Anglophone black diaspora, but the problem exposes the more general limits of the linguistic-based singularities of a variety of scholarly projects. We might ask, too, whether even the wonderful theoretical possibilities of a black diaspora structured by exchanges between the United States, Africa, and England would be interrogated and challenged by views from the south. Transnational blackness may, for example, have a different relationship to the state when we look at the case of Nicaragua in Edmund T. Gordon's work, where Creoleness was a relatively more empowered site for negotiating local identity.[44] The point here may be less about inclusion and expansiveness, and more about distinct maps of racial and ethnic formation that do not easily translate. And just as we cannot easily graft models of U.S.

ethnic-racial formation onto Brazil's mythical "racial democracy" or Mexico's "Cosmic Race," so too might we resist the temptation to recycle the categories of difference. It may be that thinking difference transnationally, through a paradigm of the Americas in which U.S. empire figures so prominently, would create both lasting connections among disenfranchised peoples as well as surprising renditions of mixture.

Interdisciplinary Americas

Our ambition to propose a body of work that moves across established boundaries of nation and region also necessarily strives to move across the borders of scholarly disciplines. We retain a belief in engaged disciplinary perspectives on the politics of economy, the everyday of ethnography, and the textuality of any given imaginary, and yet we argue that these can be interesting only if we conceive of what we do in new ways and commit ourselves to deeper inquiries into time, space, and meaning. Despite today's significant cross-pollination among disciplines — social history's debt to cultural anthropology and vice versa, literature's revitalization by critical theory, and the like — the allure of disciplinary work is precisely that it is disciplined, rigorously focused on questions of time (the past, the present, and the future), and spatially situated in a place, text, or community. In our thinking about the Americas, we insist on a notion of "the historical," not as a truth claim or background facts about specified places but as vital arguments about which pasts matter, what categories are employed to discuss the past, and how the past is mobilized in arguments about the present. The historical perspective that interests us, then, is discursive, representational, and lived, and its interdisciplinarity entails not merely a fusion of multiple disciplinary techniques but their use to interrogate how questions are asked and meanings are generated. The Americas as an interdisciplinary inquiry is at once integrated and made up of deeply dissonant parts and as such can be understood only through a theory that takes the constructed imaginary of a transnational space, and its national components, seriously. Just as the geography produced through the rubric of "the Americas" calls attention to the very formation of "nations" and "regions," so interdisciplinary epistemology emphasizes the intellectual forms in which knowledges of areas have been created.

Feminist and queer studies may offer particular lessons here, as they have managed to walk the fine line of the interdisciplinary, navigating critical conceptions of history as well as global-local tensions, with admirable finesse. This is precisely because that work has *needed* to be theoretical, questioning the categories and how they have been constructed in hegemonic narrative, and political, dedicated to liberation on both personal and public levels.[45] And thus those paradigms help us think about transnational and world-historical processes in ways that speak directly to any project on the Americas. The centrality of gender and sexuality to European colonialism, not only as a metaphor for the politics of dominance and subordination but as concrete material organizations of power, including ideologies and practices of race, centrally sustains colonial projects both "within" Europe and "abroad." And much new scholarship has given substantial consideration to non-European and pre-Iberian conquest empires, which nicely cuts against the tendency to focus on "Western influence" or conflate "imperialism" with "European and U.S. expansion."

Importantly, too, the best of feminist and queer studies avoids essentialization by explicitly critiquing conceptualizations of "community," not only and especially "national communities" but also alternatives to the nation, including ethnic, religious, and diasporic communities. These too are structured by gender- and sexuality-based hierarchies and exclusions. As Inderpal Grewal and Caren Kaplan noted in their edited collection on transnationalism and feminism, it is stunning that analyses of gender and sexuality have been almost entirely absent from many of the most celebrated scholarly examples of postcolonial cultural studies and globalization.[46] Such omission in world-historical projects has, as Ulrike Strasser observed, flowed partly from the tension between the meta-narratives of global paradigms and feminist and queer theories' long-standing criticism of "the big story" for rendering gendered and sexual subjectivities invisible, irrelevant, or at best secondary.[47] But it is precisely feminism's and queer theory's close attention to the local and specific that offers particular guidance for newly thinking about transnational and world dynamics. Following Gayatri Spivak's feminist reformulation of subaltern studies, we might see all subjectivities (individual or group) as perpetually relational and "irretrievably heterogeneous."[48] Similarly, we might embrace Grewal and Kaplan's notion of "scattered hegemonies" as a way to think across the transnational persistence, yet vast diversity and historical specificity, of gender and sexuality as sites of domination and resistance.

Inevitably our notion of an interdisciplinary Americas runs into the vexed issue of comparison: of nations, regions, literatures, languages, and, less literally but perhaps most importantly, ways of inhabiting the world. In the field of comparative literature there have been admirable attempts to use different languages and literatures alongside one another, to confront, contest, and compare one another, in a utopian manner. But as Rey Chow notes of these projects: "Because language as such tends to be viewed as a neutral fact, seldom is it pointed out in discussions of comparative literature that languages and cultures rarely enter the world stage and encounter one another on an equal footing."[49] Within the Americas that we put forward as an analytic, we face a similar problem, that despite the important goal of bringing cultures, social formations, and projects from Latin America, the Caribbean, and North America into contact, the relations of inequality make not only for varied access to a language that might be common but also for sensibilities that are at times deeply incompatible, untranslatable, as it were. Precisely because of the different political meanings of the nation across region, theoretical work on hybridity, the porousness of borders, and even the borderlands have uneven articulations across this formation we have produced as "the Americas."

In large part, our inquiry brings into sustained focus the dilemma of canons. This is to say that the historical events and documents, novels and other artifacts of the imaginary, and ethnographic moments and sociological "data" considered to make "Latin America" (or its countries) or the "United States" might be interrogated for both their representativeness and their explanatory power. Román de la Campa notes, quite importantly, that regional categories, most especially those of "other" places, can play a curious role in the construction of knowledge in the U.S. academy.[50] That tension may be addressed by what John Muthyala has proposed, for a broader view of the Americas, in "a critical pan-American localism that acknowledges the global dimensions of its contestatory and revisionary impulses."[51] Discovery, conquest, wars, social upheavals, then, all become necessarily more than nation-defining; their articulation to the global asks us to question local iterations of experience. The Iberian empires that have so defined Latin America cannot remain obscured from the historical narratives of the United States; cultural and political flows establish deeper dialogues between and among various sites of the Americas that we develop here. Likewise the literary imaginary of the Americas arrays magical realism alongside pastoral writing, retaining the special power that each of those discursive modes might have for a landscape, a history, or a community, but also questioning how it is that reading and writing experiences that employ border-crossing skills would transport particularized textual strategies out of their place and time.

Those new interpretive modes might have real impact on how we think about disciplines.[52] If the object of the Americas asks us to consider how the past is mobilized within questions of social and political concern, we must move away from a notion of history as necessarily implying a linear chronology. Requiring a deep understanding of multiple national-cultural spaces, Americas work develops methodologies for multi-sited ethnography and sensibilities about what an anthropology of mobility could look like. And the Americas, as well, should destabilize the presumption of national literatures and implore us to see novels and other texts as global in their purview, and in the codes and signs of their production. The work of the essays collected here is precisely to do that difficult work of interpreting across areas of the world and fields of study. The historical "region" that emerges, then, is simultaneously geographic, cultural, and political.

The essays collected here provide an entree into that broader conversation about the Americas. None of them alone does the work of putting together North and South, history and literature, domination and resistance, but they all in some way question boundaries that have been drawn within and between U.S. American studies and Latin American studies and their regional objects. They range widely but do not cover all possibilities. Canada's relative marginality within both U.S. American studies and Americas studies, unfortunately, is mirrored in the offerings here. Yet, taken as a whole, this volume fundamentally speaks across conventional notions of American areas and challenges us to rethink categories of difference and discipline.

Several essays take representation seriously, subjecting any facile conception of literary practice to intense historical scrutiny and reading beyond origins or roots in place. While some essays employ close textual analysis to make their points, others emphasize detailed social histories. Some pieces here choose to illuminate chaotic cultural formations of empire through corresponding plays with narrative structure. There is necessarily some labor that is demanded of the reader to move from one approach to another, but that is partly the point. An interdisciplinary paradigm of the Americas emerges from the sum of its parts and thus requires a particular kind of openness to hear multiple epistemological voices. To be plainer, perhaps, we hope that Marxist historians and poststructuralist literary critics, and scholars in Latin American studies and U.S. American studies, will read one another's work, because they may be engaged in projects that would be well served by some kind of dialogue.

We are asked by the essays collected here not only to expand our canon of representational forms but to rethink the correspondences that have become second nature to us, and, ultimately, to think about transnational politics and culture in new ways. Harilaos Stecopoulos, in "Up from Empire: James Weldon Johnson, Latin America, and the Jim Crow South," takes a paradigmatic national-race writer, James Weldon Johnson, and resituates him and his work in the hemispheric connections (and divides) that this book as a whole strives to elaborate. Just because Johnson embodied insurgent racial politics at home did not mean that he would necessarily oppose benevolent U.S. imperialism abroad. And his cultural work in the service of imperialism, not only his writings of popular musicals but also his position as U.S. consul to Venezuela, betrayed a complex and critical patriotism that was the result of powerful regional divides between North and South, and the loyalties that inhered, of the period. John D. Blanco's "Bastards of the Unfinished Revolution: Bolívar's Ismael and Rizal's Martí at the End of the Nineteenth Century" presents a different pairing, contrasting visions of anticolonial struggle in Cuba and the Philippines embodied in the respective writings of two literary giants and national heroes, José Martí and José Rizal. Blanco underscores that at the time these contemporaries wrote, both Rizal and Martí located their homelands within a broader "Spanish American" heritage; yet in just a few decades, the Philippines would all but disappear from conceptually belonging to the region of "Latin America." Blanco ponders how this vanishing, along with Rizal's and Martí's disagreements, emanated from differing resolutions of, and possibilities for, anticolonial liberalism. And Caroline Levander, in "Confederate Cuba," explores how Cuban race relations have been central to U.S. imperial aspirations as well as to U.S. domestic politics since the early nineteenth century. Levander argues that Cuban racial formations both enabled and disrupted U.S. national fantasies of imperial mastery, a thesis that strongly suggests the porous and mutually constituted nature of "domestic" and "foreign" dynamics.

Susan Najita shifts our attention to Hawaii, an area that sits somewhat uneasily in conventional interpretations of what and where the Americas are, showing, indeed, how Hawaii's transnational cultural production following the islands' annexation by the United States might newly illuminate region, empire, and race. In "Pleasure and Colonial Resistance: Translating the Politics of Pidgin in Milton Murayama's *All I Asking for Is My Body*," Najita discusses how pidgin language developments of Japanese, Hawaiian, and English functioned as a way for nisei to critique Hawaii's plantation labor systems as well as the Japanese family's hierarchies of gender, generation, and race. She suggests that the local production of transnational "immigrant" identities may at times flow as much from the relinquishing of diasporic and familial commitments as from a sense of displacement from homeland. Nicholas Turse's "Experimental Dreams, Ethical Nightmares: Leprosy, Isolation, and Human Experimentation in Nineteenth-Century Hawaii" signals the material effects of an imperialism that hardly respects the boundaries that "area" disciplines may have reified. He explores the production of leprosy as a "tropical disease" delineating colonialist boundaries between U.S.-European authority and native subjugation, *haole* whites and indigenous Hawaiians, civilized and primitive, healthy and sick, and effectively documents the aggressive enforcement of segregated leper colonies by U.S. authorities following Hawaii's incorporation as a U.S. territory. Also addressing the "Asia Pacific" as an occasion to rethink the deep cultural contradictions of living transnationally through a global capitalist framework is Rob Wilson's essay "Tracking the 'China Peril' along the U.S. Pacific Rim: Carpetbaggers, Yacht People, 1.2 Billion Cyborg Consumers, and the Bamboo Gang, Coming Soon to a Neighborhood Near You!" Wilson's, Turse's, and Najita's Pacific Rim gives this collection an important comparative dimension and also effectively puts the brakes on any contentment we may feel about the expansion of national-regional categories. Much of the Americas proper borders the Pacific and yet disassociates itself from various "Asian" formations. At the same time there are significant efforts within neoliberal political cultures of South America, especially, to follow in the footsteps of Pacific Rim economies. Wilson takes up the ambivalent future that Asian worlds represent by looking closely at fantasy projections of what he calls "neo-Orientalisms" in and of films like *Lost in Translation* and recent contemporary political moments, all of which sit rather comfortably with security apparatuses of the U.S. nation-state.

Another group of essays critically considers the concept of mobility. Michelle Stephens rethinks Atlantic history's production of indigeneity in "Uprooted Bodies: Indigenous Subjects and Colonial Discourses in Atlantic American Studies." Using Leslie Marmon Silko's novel *Almanac of the Dead*, Stephens argues for seeing the indigenous through paradigms like the polycultural that foreground movement rather than rootedness or stasis. This results in an important new way to imagine the historical-cultural connections that have made the Americas, not only from outside but also from within. Rachel Adams provides a bridge from the paradigms of the black Atlantic to those of borderland studies to explicate several histories of African American presence in Mexico and Chicano communities in her essay "Blackness Goes South: Race and Mestizaje in Our America." Beyond recovery, Adams's work wonderfully illustrates how rethinking histories of race outside the (official) national narrative reveals the very constitutive nature of national borders and racial or ethnic communities. Ian Lekus, in "Queer Harvests: Homosexuality, the U.S. New Left, and the Venceremos Brigades to Cuba," recounts the deeply moving but equally troubled history of U.S. gay and lesbian solidarity with the Cuban Revolution. While the emerging U.S. gay rights movement saw its own aspirations for liberation and equality mirrored in the promises of a new Cuba, widespread homophobia among both Students for a Democratic Society and the revolutionary government worked to silence and ultimately exclude U.S. homosexuals from international work as well as to abet the quashing and persecution of nonheterosexual identifications within Cuba.

The Cold War has been a subject of sustained focus for new work on the Americas. Rebecca M. Schreiber, in "Dislocations of Cold War Cultures: Exile, Transnationalism, and the Politics of Form," provides an interesting, if compelled, instance of cultural work situated in the Americas during that period. Schreiber discusses how African American artists and writers who deliberately chose exile in the rich context of Mexico developed hybrid work that must be understood through movement and circuits of influence that ultimately challenge the boundedness of national cultures. And Alyosha Goldstein, in "The Attributes of Sovereignty: The Cold War, Colonialism, and Community Education in Puerto Rico," explores how U.S. foreign policy ideas about community and development played out in the context of hemispheric ambitions in and of Puerto Rico.

What does it mean when cultural forms migrate? is a question posed by Héctor Fernández L'Hoeste in "All Cumbias, the Cumbia: The Latin Americanization of a Tropical Genre." Providing a comparative discussion of the diverse ways that *cumbia*, a musical genre that emerged first in Colombia, is incorporated into the "national music traditions" not only of Colombia but also of Argentina, Peru, and Mexico, Fernández L'Hoeste pays particular attention to the diverse racial and class meanings that cumbia assumes as it moves transnationally to create distinct national cultures.

And with an eye to our ambivalent political futures, Victor Bascara, in " 'Panama Money': Reading the Transition to U.S. Imperialism," reads dangerous moments of transition within U.S. imperialism through Paule Marshall's literary work and life. In Marshall's imaginary, the building of the Panama Canal becomes a flash point for understanding not only the future geopolitical connectivity between Latin America, more formally defined, and North America, but also the cultural crossings that would produce new subjects who live transnationally and ambivalently. With such cultural occasions, Bascara's essay and others also help us read the narrative of globalization back into the past, as much for historical specificity as for ways to think about our violently transnational present.

Ultimately these essays collectively suggest that confronting globalization is only one way of rethinking what we have come to call the Americas. Whether we consider them to be productive or destructive, the connections across various countries in Latin America, North America, and the Caribbean (and the Philippines and Hawaii) prompt a reconsideration of our very object of study. Region, area, and continent are all bounded categories that by their very natures set up limits to be crossed and perhaps transgressed. If our conclusions, from scholars based in the U.S. academy, seem at one moment to have a particularist emphasis, they must also point to comparisons with other places in the world and gesture at other organizing principles for associated knowledges. This is to ask whether, in fact, "the Americas" are either really that different from "Asia" or "the Middle East" or are constructed so discretely, apart from other regions. We invite, indeed insist on, conversation about the extent to which our ideas are shared, or are in dialogue, in the spirit of work toward a more productive, and perhaps utopian, sense of the global.

Notes

1   In this essay, we intentionally shift between references to singular and plural forms of the Americas, alternately indicating a singular Americas paradigm and the plural territorial spaces/nations of the Americas. That the Americas might serve both as a conceptual framework and as multiple geographical sites of study is, we argue, a productive tension.

2   "Our Americas: Political and Cultural Imaginings," special issue of *Radical History Review* 89 (spring 2004), edited by Sandhya Shukla and Heidi Tinsman. We especially thank the contributors to this journal issue: Néstor García Canclini, Martin Hopenhayn, Rossana Reguillo, Arturo Arias, Ian Lekus, John D. Blanco, Aimee Carrillo Rowe, María Josefina Saldaña-Portillo, Aisha Khan, Paul Giles, Salah D. Hassan, Patricio del Real, Carlos E. Bojorquez Urzaiz, Enrique C. Ochoa, Ian Christopher Fletcher, Diana Paton, John Beck, Gemma Robinson, and Kate Masur.

3   José Martí, "Our America" (1891), in *The America of José Martí: Selected Writings of José Martí, translated from the Spanish*, ed. Juan de Onis (New York: Funk and Wagnalls, 1954), 149–50.

4   See Greg Grandin, *Empire's Workshop: Latin America, the United States, and the Rise of the New Imperialism* (New York: Metropolitan Books, 2006).

5   Other important examples of work on the Americas include Matthew C. Gutmann,

Féliz V. Matos Rodríguez, Lynn Stephen, and Patricia Zavella, eds., *Perspectives on Las Américas: A Reader in Culture, History, and Representation* (Oxford: Blackwell, 2003); Neil Larsen, *Determinations: Essays on Theory, Narrative and Nation in the Americas* (New York: Verso, 2001); Jeffrey Belnap and Raúl Fernández, eds., *José Martí's "Our America": From National to Hemispheric Cultural Studies* (Durham: Duke University Press, 1998); Paul Giles, *Virtual Americas: Transnational Fictions and the Transatlantic Imaginary* (Durham: Duke University Press, 2002); María Josefina Saldaña-Portillo, *The Revolutionary Imagination in the Americas and the Age of Development* (Durham: Duke University Press, 2003); and José E. Limon, *American Encounters: Greater Mexico, the United States, and the Erotics of Culture* (Boston: Beacon Press, 1998).

6   Masao Miyoshi and H. D. Harootunian, for example, make a number of important observations about area studies in the introduction to their collection *Learning Places: The Afterlives of Area Studies* (Durham: Duke University Press, 2002), but their experiences are largely of the projects as they took shape in East Asia. The case in Latin America, as we shall see, offers a different sort of picture.

7   Paul Bové, in "Can American Studies Be Area Studies?" in Miyoshi and Harootunian, *Learning Places*, 206–30, makes an argument for the sustained separation of the cultural effects of American studies projects from the operations of the U.S. nation-state. In large part, our move to take the U.S. state seriously is precisely to address that disconnect.

8   On area studies, see also David L. Szanton, ed., *The Politics of Knowledge: Area Studies and the Disciplines* (Berkeley: University of California Press, 2004).

9   See Lisa Lowe, *Immigrant Acts: On Asian American Cultural Politics* (Durham: Duke University Press, 1996), 9.

10   On transnationalism, also see *Towards a Transnational Perspective on Migration: Race, Class, Ethnicity and Nationalism Reconsidered*, ed. Nina Glick Schiller, Linda Basch, and Cristina Szanton Blanc (New York: New York Academy of Sciences, 1992); and Linda Basch, Nina Glick Schiller, and Cristina Szanton Blanc, *Nations Unbound: Transnational Projects, Postcolonial Predicaments, and Deterritorialized Nation-States* (New York: Gordon and Breach, 1994).

11   Amy Kaplan and Donald E. Pease, eds., *Cultures of United States Imperialism* (Durham: Duke University Press, 1993). John Carlos Rowe's edited volume *Postnationalist American Studies* (Berkeley: University of California Press, 2000) has also productively opened up many of these questions.

12   For example, Melani McAlister, *Epic Encounters: Culture, Media and U.S. Interests in the Middle East, 1945–2000* (Berkeley: University of California Press, 2001); Laura Briggs, *Reproducing Empire: Race, Sex, Science and U.S. Imperialism in Puerto Rico* (Berkeley: University of California Press, 2003).

13   Jane C. Desmond and Virginia R. Dominguez forecasted this problem over fifteen years ago in "Resituating American Studies in a Critical Internationalism," *American Quarterly* 48, no. 3 (1990): 475–90.

14   An example of this tendency is Mary Renda's book *Taking Haiti: Military Occupa-*

tion and the Culture of U.S. Imperialism (Chapel Hill: University of North Carolina Press, 2001), which quite wonderfully uses U.S. documents to analyze and critique imperial ventures in Haiti but deals very little with Haitian sources or discourses from the Caribbean.

15   In a sense, then, we take both the power of the critical framework that Tzvetan Todorov develops in *The Conquest of America*, trans. Richard Howard (Norman: University of Oklahoma Press, 1999), originally published in French in 1982, and also the criticisms of the dichotomized cultures that underwrite his analysis (for example, Deborah Root, "The Imperial Signifier: Todorov and the Conquest of Mexico," *Cultural Critique* 9 [Spring 1988]: 197–219), seriously.

16   See Graeme Turner, *British Cultural Studies: An Introduction* (London: Unwin-Hyman, 1990); and Joel Pfister, "The Americanization of Cultural Studies," *Yale Journal of Criticism* 4.2 (1991): 199–229.

17   For example, Richard Graham, ed., *The Idea of Race in Latin America, 1870–1940* (Austin: University of Texas Press, 1990); Nancy Stepan, *The Hour of Eugenics: Race, Gender, and Nation in Latin America* (Ithaca: Cornell University Press, 1991); Jeffrey Gould, *To Die in This Way: Nicaraguan Indians and the Myth of Mestizaje, 1880–1965* (Durham: Duke University Press, 1998); Eileen Findlay, *Imposing Decency: The Politics of Sexuality and Race in Puerto Rico, 1870–1920* (Durham: Duke University Press, 1999); Marisol de la Cadena, *Indigenous Mestizos: The Politics of Race and Culture in Cuzco, Peru* (Durham: Duke University Press, 2000); Nancy P. Appelbaum, Anne S. Macpherson, and Karin Rosemblatt, eds., *Race and Nation in Modern Latin America* (Chapel Hill: University of North Carolina Press, 2003).

18   For example, Irene Silverblatt, *Moon, Sun, and Witches: Gender Ideologies and Class in Inca and Spanish Peru* (Princeton: Princeton University Press, 1987); Jean Franco, *Plotting Women: Gender and Representation in Mexico* (New York: Columbia University Press, 1988); Ana María Alonso, *Thread of Blood: Colonialism, Revolution, and Gender on Mexico's Northern Frontier* (Tucson: University of Arizona Press, 1995); Karin Alejandra Rosemblatt, *Gendered Compromises: Political Cultures and the State in Chile, 1920–1950* (Chapel Hill: University of North Carolina Press, 2000); Sueann Caulfield, *In Defense of Honor: Sexual Morality, Modernity, and Nation in Early Twentieth Century Brazil* (Durham: Duke University Press, 2000); Daniel James, *Dona Maria's Story: Life History, Memory, and Political Identity* (Durham: Duke University Press, 2000); Ileana Rodriguez, *House/Garden/Nation: Space, Gender and Ethnicity in Post-colonial Latin American Literatures by Women*, trans. Robert Carr (Durham: Duke University Press, 2004).

19   Important early examples in Marxist histories of Latin America include Stanley Stein, *Vassouras, a Brazilian Coffee County, 1850–1900: The Role of Planter and Slave in a Changing Plantation Society* (Cambridge: Harvard University Press, 1957); John Womack, *Zapata and the Mexican Revolution* (New York: Alfred Knopf, 1968); Florencia Mallon, *Defense of Community in Peru's Central Highlands: Peasant Struggle and Capitalist Transition, 1860–1940* (Princeton: Princeton University Press, 1983); Barbara Weinstein, *The Amazon Rubber Boom, 1850–1920* (Stanford: Stanford Uni-

versity Press, 1983); Walter LaFeber, *Inevitable Revolutions: The United States in Central America* (New York: W. W. Norton, 1984); Sidney Mintz, *Sweetness and Power: The Place of Sugar in Modern History* (New York: Penguin, 1985). For more about the relationship between Marxist theory and U.S. American studies, see Michael Denning, "'The Special American Conditions': Marxism and American Studies," in *American Quarterly* 38 (1986): 356–80.

20 Certainly the most important models of Latin American studies for any future transnational work are the many superb studies of imperialism and global political economy. For example, Thomas Miller Klubock, *Contested Communities: Class, Gender and Politics in Chile's El Teniente Copper Mine, 1904–1951* (Durham: Duke University Press, 1998); Steven C. Topik and Allen Wells, eds., *The Second Conquest of Latin America: Coffee, Henequen, and Oil during the Export Boom, 1850–1930* (Austin: University of Texas Press, 1998); Aviva Chomsky, *West Indian Workers and the United Fruit Company, 1870–1940* (Baton Rouge: Louisiana State University Press, 1996); Emilia Viotti da Costa, *Crowns of Glory, Tears of Blood: The Demerara Slave Rebellion of 1823* (New York: Oxford University Press, 1994); Jonathan Brown, *Oil and Revolution in Mexico* (Berkeley: University of California Press, 1992).

21 Peter Winn, *Weavers of Revolution: The Yarur Workers and Chile's Road to Socialism* (New York: Oxford University Press, 1986); John D. French, *The Brazilian Workers' ABC: Class Conflict and Alliances in Modern Sao Paulo* (Chapel Hill: University of North Carolina Press, 1992); Barbara Weinstein, *Social Peace in Brazil: Industrialists and the Remaking of the Working-Class in Brazil, 1920–1964* (Chapel Hill: University of North Carolina Press, 1996); Julio Pinto, *Trabajos y rebeldías en la pampa salitrera: El ciclo del salitre y la reconfiguración de las identidades populares* (Santiago: Universidad de Santiago, 1998); Anne Farnsworth-Alvear, *Dulcinea in the Factory: Myths, Morals, Men and Women in Colombia's Industrial Experiment, 1905–1960* (Durham: Duke University Press, 2000); Elizabeth Quay Hutchison, *Labors Appropriate to Their Sex: Gender, Work, and Politics in Urban Chile, 1900–1930* (Durham: Duke University Press, 2001).

22 In anthropology see Kay B. Warren, *The Symbolism of Subordination: Indian Identity in a Guatemalan Town* (Austin: University of Texas Press, 1978); June Nash, *We Eat the Mines and the Mines Eat Us: Dependency and Exploitation in Bolivian Tin Mines* (New York: Columbia University Press, 1979); Michael Taussig, *The Devil and Commodity Fetishism in South America* (Chapel Hill: University of North Carolina Press, 1980); Steve J. Stern, *Peru's Indian Peoples and the Challenge of the Spanish Conquest: Huamanga to 1640* (Madison: University of Wisconsin Press, 1982).

23 E. P. Thompson, *The Making of the English Working Class* (New York: Vintage, 1963); Stuart Hall, *The Politics of Thatcherism* (London: Lawrence and Wishart, 1983); Hall, *The Hard Road to Renewal: Thatcherism and the Crisis of the Left* (London: Verso, 1988); Stuart Hall and Martin Jacques, eds., *New Times: The Changing Face of Politics in the 1990s* (London: Verso, 1990).

24 For example, Daniel James, *Resistance and Integration: Peronism and the Argentine Working Class, 1946–1976* (New York: Cambridge University Press, 1988); William

Roseberry, *Anthropologies and Histories: Essays in Culture, History, and Political Economy* (New Brunswick: Rutgers University Press, 1989); Gilbert Joseph and Daniel Nugent, eds., *Everyday Forms of State Formation: Revolution and the Negotiation of Rule in Modern Mexico* (Chapel Hill: University of North Carolina Press, 1994), Matthew C. Gutmann, *The Meaning of Macho: Being a Man in Mexico City* (Berkeley: University of California Press, 1996); Greg Grandin, *The Blood of Guatemala: A History of Race and Nation* (Durham: Duke University Press, 2000).

25   Alan Knight, *The Mexican Revolution*, 2 vols. (New York: Cambridge University Press, 1986); Catherine LeGrand, *Frontier Expansion and Peasant Protest in Colombia, 1850–1936* (Albuquerque: University of New Mexico Press, 1986); John Tutino, *From Insurrection to Revolution in Mexico: Social Bases of Agrarian Violence, 1750–1940* (Princeton: Princeton University Press, 1986).

26   Gilbert Joseph, Catherine LeGrand, and Ricardo Salvatore, eds., *Close Encounters of Empire: Writing the Cultural History of U.S.-Latin American Relations* (Durham: Duke University Press, 1998).

27   Mary Roldán, *Blood and Fire: La Violencia in Anitoquia Colombia, 1946–1953* (Durham: Duke University Press, 2002); Eric VanYoung, *The Other Rebellion: Popular Violence, Ideology, and the Mexican Struggle for Independence, 1810–1821* (Stanford: Stanford University Press, 2001).

28   See, for example, Florencia Mallon, "The Promise and Dilemma of Subaltern Studies: Perspectives from Latin American History," *American Historical Review* 99, no. 5 (December 1994): 1491–1515; Claudio Lomnitz, "Barbarians at the Gate? A Few Remarks on the Politics of the 'New Cultural History of Mexico,'" *Hispanic American Research Review* 79, no. 2 (May 1999): 367–83; Ileana Rodriguez, *The Latin American Subaltern Studies Reader* (Durham: Duke University Press, 2001).

29   Peter Hulme, *Colonial Encounters: Europe and the Native Caribbean, 1492–1797* (London: Routledge, 1986); Inga Clendinnen, *Ambivalent Conquests: Maya and Spanish in Yucatán, 1517–1570* (Cambridge: Cambridge University Press, 1987); Walter Mignolo, *The Darker Side of the Renaissance: Literacy, Territoriality, and Colonization* (Ann Arbor: University of Michigan Press, 1995); Patricia Seed, *Ceremonies of Possession in Europe's Conquest of the New World* (Cambridge: Cambridge University Press, 1995); Peter Sigal, *From Moon Goddesses to Virgins: The Colonization of Yucatecan Mayan Sexual Desire* (Austin: University of Texas Press, 2000).

30   See Ana Del Sarto, Alicia Rios, and Abril Trigo, eds., *The Latin American Cultural Studies Reader* (Durham: Duke University Press, 2004).

31   See Florencia Mallon, *Peasant and Nation: The Making of Post-colonial Mexico and Peru* (Berkeley: University of California Press, 1995); Steve J. Stern, *The Secret History of Gender: Women, Men, and Power in Late Colonial Mexico* (Chapel Hill: University of North Carolina Press, 1995); Fernando Coronil, *The Magical State: Nature, Money, and Modernity in Venezuela* (Chicago: University of Chicago Press, 1997); Sarah C. Chambers, *From Subjects to Citizens: Honor, Gender, and Politics in Arequipa, Peru, 1780–1854* (University Park: Pennsylvania State University Press, 1999).

32   Néstor García Canclini, *Hybrid Cultures: Strategies for Entering and Leaving Modernity* (Minneapolis: University of Minnesota Press, 1995).

33   George Yúdice, *The Expediency of Culture: Uses of Culture in the Global Era* (Durham: Duke University Press, 2001); Fredric Jameson, *Postmodernism, or The Cultural Logic of Late Capitalism* (Durham: Duke University Press, 1991).

34   For example, Gloria Anzaldúa, *Borderlands/La Frontera: The New Mestiza* (San Francisco: Aunt Lute Books, 1987); Ramon Gutierrez, *When Jesus Came the Corn Mothers Went Away: Sexuality and Marriage in Colonial Mexico* (Palo Alto: Stanford University Press, 1991); José David Saldívar, *Border Matters: Remapping American Cultural Studies* (Berkeley: University of California Press, 1997); Scott Michaelson and David E. Johnson, eds., *Border Theory: The Limits of Cultural Politics* (Minneapolis: University of Minnesota Press, 1997); Carl Gutierrez Jones, *Rethinking the Borderlands: Between Chicano Culture and Legal Discourse* (Berkeley: University of California Press, 1995); Vicki Ruiz and Virginia Sánchez Korrol, eds., *Latina Legacies: Identity, Biography, and Community* (New York: Oxford University Press, 2005). Also see the journal entitled *Nepantla: Views from the South* (Duke University Press).

35   Eric R. Wolf, *Europe and the People without History* (Berkeley: University of California Press, 1982); Fernand Braudel, *The Wheels of Commerce* (New York: Harper and Row, 1982); Immanuel Wallerstein, *The Modern World System* (New York: Academic Press, 1974); Wallerstein, *The Capitalist World Economy* (Cambridge: Cambridge University Press, 1979).

36   Fernando Henrique Cardoso, *Dependencia y desarrollo en América Latina: Ensayo de interpretación sociológica* (Mexico City: Siglo XXI, 1969); André Gunder Frank, *Capitalism and Underdevelopment in Latin America* (New York: Monthly Review Press, 1967).

37   Frederick Cooper et al., *Confronting Historical Paradigms: Peasants, Labor, and the Capitalist World System in Africa and Latin America* (Madison: University of Wisconsin Press, 1993); Roy Bin Wong, *China Transformed: Historical Change and the Limits of European Experience* (Ithaca: Cornell University Press, 1997); Prasenjit Duara, "Transnationalism and the Challenge to National Histories," in *Rethinking American History in a Global Age*, ed. Thomas Bender (Berkeley: University of California Press, 2002).

38   Kenneth Pomeranz, *The Great Divergence: Europe, China, and the Making of the Modern World Economy* (Princeton: Princeton University Press, 2000).

39   Dipesh Chakrabarty, *Provincializing Europe: Postcolonial Thought and Historical Difference* (Princeton: Princeton University Press, 2000).

40   The intersections between world history and transnational studies have been the central topic of a resident scholars seminar entitled "Historical Problematics of Gender, Sexuality, and the Global," co-convened by Ulrike Strasser and Heidi Tinsman at the University of California Humanities Research Institute in the fall of 2006.

41   Walter Mignolo, *Local Histories/Global Designs: Coloniality, Subaltern Knowledges, and Border Thinking* (Princeton: Princeton University Press, 2000).

42   Joanne Rappaport, *Cumbe Reborn: An Andean Ethnography of History* (Chicago: University of Chicago Press, 1994); and Rappaport, *The Politics of Memory: Native Historical Interpretation in the Colombian Andes* (Cambridge: Cambridge University Press, 1990).

43   Paul Gilroy, *The Black Atlantic: Modernity and Double Consciousness* (Cambridge: Harvard University Press, 1993).

44   Edmund T. Gordon, *Disparate Diasporas: Identity and Politics in an African-Nicaraguan Community* (Austin: University of Texas Press, 1998).

45   Examples abound. See Elizabeth Spellman, *Inessential Woman: Problems of Exclusion in Feminist Thought* (Boston: Beacon Press, 1988); Anne McClintock, *Imperial Leather: Race, Gender, and Sexuality in the Colonial Contest* (New York: Routledge, 1995); Anne McClintock, Aamir Mufti, and Ella Shohat, eds., *Dangerous Liaisons: Gender, Nation, and Postcolonial Perspectives* (Minneapolis: University of Minnesota Press, 1997); Jacqui Alexander and Chandra Mohanty, eds., *Feminist Genealogies, Colonial Legacies, Democratic Futures* (New York: Routledge, 1997); Lauren Berlant, ed., *Intimacy* (Chicago: University of Chicago Press, 2000); Ann Laura Stoler, *Carnal Knowledge: Race and the Intimate in Colonial Rule* (Berkeley: University of California Press, 2002).

46   Inderpal Grewal and Caren Kaplan, eds., *Scattered Hegemonies: Postmodernity and Transnational Feminist Practices* (Minneapolis: University of Minnesota Press, 1994).

47   See Ulrike Strasser and Heidi Tinsman, "Engendering World History," *Radical History Review* 92 (winter 2005).

48   Gayatri Chakravorty Spivak, *A Critique of Postcolonial Reason: Toward a History of the Vanishing Present* (Cambridge: Harvard University Press, 1999).

49   Rey Chow, "The Old/New Question of Comparison in Literary Studies: A Post-European Perspective," *English Literary History* 72, no. 2 (2004): 289–311.

50   Roman de la Campa, *Latin Americanism* (Minneapolis: University of Minnesota Press, 1991).

51   John Muthyala, "Reworlding America: The Globalization of American Studies," *Cultural Critique* 47 (winter 2001): 99.

52   Gayatri Chakravorty Spivak, *Death of a Discipline* (New York: Columbia University Press, 2003).

Up from Empire

James Weldon Johnson, Latin America,

and the Jim Crow South

Harilaos Stecopoulos

At one point in James Weldon Johnson's *The Autobiography of an Ex-Colored Man* (1912), the titular protagonist overhears an argument between a white Union army veteran and a white Texan.[1] Overtly about the Civil War, the debate also comments on another type of division, one not of national but of hemispheric dimensions. The Union veteran, invoking the contemporary condition of Latin America, proclaims: "Can you imagine . . . what would have been the condition of things eventually if there had been no war, and the South had been allowed to follow its course? Instead of one great, prosperous country with nothing before it but the conquest of peace, a score of petty republics, as in Central and South America, wasting their energies in war with each other or in revolutions" (339–40). His interlocutor responds by rejecting not only the veteran's investment in national integrity but also the need for nations altogether. "'Well,' replied the Texan, 'anything—no country at all—is better than having niggers over you'" (340). If the Texan states that "anything" "is better" than "black power," the Union veteran suggests that anything is better than allowing the United States to degenerate into a collection of what O. Henry would dub "banana republics," a situation tantamount to having "no country at all."[2] For the soldier of the Grand Army of the Republic, the idea of slipping into the Latin American way of life represents something far worse than the danger of black insurgency iterated repeatedly by the Texan.

To be sure, the veteran seems interested in the deplorable state of Latin America only as an example of what Union victory spared the United States; he does not comment on turn-of-the-century U.S. policy in the region and refers to U.S. imperialism only through the euphemistic phrase "the conquest of peace." Yet the 1912 publication date of Johnson's novel invites us to read the old soldier's words in light of the "big stick" diplomacy that characterized U.S. relations with its southern neighbors. Between 1898 and 1914, the United States intervened militarily in Cuba, Puerto Rico, the Dominican Republic, Honduras, Mexico, and Nicaragua even as U.S. banks and businesses assumed control of national economies in these and other Latin American nations.[3] When we place the Union veteran's statement in the context of contemporary U.S. imperialism south of the border, the implications of his extravagant historical analogy grow palpable: the U.S. government stands in much the same relation to an unruly South and Central America at the close of the nineteenth century as it did to a disordered and insurgent "Dixie" forty years before.[4] The problem of a rebellious U.S. South had demanded a violent Yankee response; the current disorder of the hemispheric South seems to require another type of northern intervention.

The narrator of *The Autobiography of an Ex-Colored Man* does not comment on the larger meaning of this historical analogy, but James Weldon Johnson devoted serious thought to the relationship of the national and the hemispheric North-South divides in his richly varied public writings. And he did so in a manner that often seems to echo the Union veteran's argument. Eager to link the federal administration of the domestic South with U.S. intervention abroad, Johnson had few problems supporting the new U.S. imperialism so long as the party of Lincoln articulated that expansionist vision. His diplomatic work suggests as much. A staunch Republican, author of the campaign song "You're Alright Teddy," Johnson transformed himself into a gunboat diplomat, winning the post of U.S. consul to Puerto Cabello, Venezuela, in 1906. His subsequent assignment as consul to Corinto, Nicaragua, would make manifest his role in the burgeoning U.S. empire. In 1912, Johnson would defend U.S. interests in Nicaragua during the civil conflict between president Adolfo Díaz and the rebel leader Luis Mena, a contest that pitted a conservative dictator against a peasant insurgent. Eager to preserve Díaz's pro-U.S. regime, Johnson not only convinced the rebels to refrain from invading Corinto but also facilitated the landing and deployment of U.S. military forces. In July 1912, several thousand Marines landed in Nicaragua and soon routed the insurgent forces; government executioners dispatched Mena, and U.S. financiers quietly took control of the central Nicaraguan bank. Johnson's rhetorical skill and logistical intelligence played a vital role in suppressing the peasant rebellion and setting the stage for a military and fiscal U.S. presence in Nicaragua that would last well into the twentieth century. With respect to U.S. expansion in the Americas, Johnson seemed to accept the principle underlying Theodore Roosevelt's corollary to the Monroe Doctrine (1904): the idea that the United States had the right to intervene in the affairs of other American nations when those unstable states endangered the common good of the hemisphere.[5]

Johnson was not alone among African Americans in supporting the new U.S. empire. As Kevin Gaines has reminded us, prominent African Americans such as Booker T. Washington, Edward E. Cooper, and Pauline Hopkins supported U.S. imperialism in the late 1890s, and some black intellectuals would continue to defend U.S. policy into the new century.[6] While these figures would support U.S. expansionism for any number of reasons—patriotic ideals, a belief in the idea of the civilizing mission, personal ambition—many convinced themselves of the rightness of empire for a distinctly practical reason: a need for some sense of prophylactic connection to the white power elite. With the elimination of vestigial Reconstruction in the late 1880s came an increase in black disenfranchisement and white racist violence throughout much of the nation, but particularly in the South. In 1906, the year Johnson began working for the consular service, sixty-two black men and women were lynched in the region, and one of the worst white racist riots of the era erupted in Atlanta.[7] These episodes of lethal white violence vivified the more quotidian forms of white racism endured by African Americans in the U.S. South. A willingness to identify with and support the Republican Party, the party of Emancipation and Reconstruction, seemed to offer some protection, however minor, from the threats of regional white supremacy. And the African American investment in the Republican vision of federal policy and power extended to the new imperialism of the era.[8] For all its obvious reliance on white supremacist discourse, for all its cruelty to people of color abroad, in the eyes of some blacks the new empire held forth the prospect of bonding more tightly to Washington in a terrible time. Not only did serving the new Republican empire entitle some

African American soldiers to receive military training and carry guns—a fact that sparked no end of confrontations throughout the Southeast—but it also confirmed the black bourgeoisie's sense of metropolitan superiority to both the underdeveloped U.S. South and the seemingly uncivilized spaces of U.S. expansion. During a time of pronounced and savage white supremacy, in other words, U.S. imperialism seems to have offered some members of the black bourgeoisie a sense of "northernness" and a concomitant feeling of civilized belonging.

That the fantasy of an imperial reconstruction of the African American demanded considerable ethical compromise on the part of contemporary black intellectuals goes without saying. The vexed relationship between dreams of enfranchisement and nightmares of complicity proved a heavy burden for even the most sensitive and articulate of these figures. It should hardly come as a surprise that Johnson—talented and opportunistic, well aware that African American success often depended on the patronage of powerful white men—would do the empire's work. Yet even as he endorsed U.S. imperialism and defended U.S. interests in Nicaragua, Johnson also expressed considerable anxiety over the nation's new expansionist policies and their potential consequences for African Americans. Evidence of concern about this issue appears early in his literary career. Johnson's poem "The Colored Sergeant" (1898) rebuts Theodore Roosevelt's charge that black soldiers performed poorly on San Juan Hill, and his libretto to the unproduced opera *Tolosa* (1899) satirizes the U.S. annexation of Pacific islands. A critique of U.S. expansion would continue to inform Johnson's work well into the new century and his work for the State Department. He would criticize Roosevelt again in the lyrics to a song from the unproduced play *The Presidente and the Yellow Peril*: "We'll nail the 'big stick' to the wall / and round it will drape / No streamers red white and blue / But ordinary crepe"; and he would complain to Booker T. Washington that Jim Crow racism made the United States unpopular among the dark-skinned populations of the Caribbean and South America—a position that would inform his forceful speech "Why Latin Americans Dislike the United States" (1913). Long before he indicted the U.S. occupation of Haiti in his essays for the *Nation*, Johnson recognized and critiqued the problem of empire.

Such a delicate, not to say uncomfortable, balancing act would be for some intellectuals a largely private affair, but in Johnson's case, literary ambition and racial politics inspired an unusual commentary on his conflicted relationship to empire: not an essay, lecture, or polemic, but the novel with which we began: *The Autobiography of an Ex-Colored Man*. A narrative that chronicles the mainly domestic adventures of an African American musician who eventually passes for white, *The Autobiography* seems to have little if anything to do with the new U.S. expansionism that emerged, large and rapacious, with the sinking of the USS *Maine*. While critics have read the novel in light of myriad issues — publication history, the unreliable narrator, African American music, the representation of male sexuality, and, of course, the vexed question of racial passing — they have never considered how *The Autobiography* might speak to the contemporary question of empire.[9] Such an occlusion will come as no surprise to readers familiar with scholarship on African American literature and culture. With few exceptions, most critics tend to read black texts in exclusively national terms, the odd reference to African roots notwithstanding. Yet as Brent Edwards and Michelle Stephens have recently reminded us, the diasporic range of black literary culture demands more of a transnational approach — one sensitive to both the hemispheric and transatlantic orientations of African America.[10] The case of *The Autobiography* well illustrates this point, for Johnson interwove his diplomatic responsibilities and his literary efforts. Johnson wrote much of the novel during a U.S. diplomatic assignment to Puerto Cabello, Venezuela, and received news of its publication while working with the marines in Nicaragua. Even as he defended and promoted U.S. empire, in other words, Johnson generated an account of a man torn between black and white, between racial solidarity and bourgeois opportunism, between domestic struggle and imperial reward. In *The Autobiography*, Johnson queries the idea that U.S. expansion will offer African Americans the opportunity to claim their citizenship and civil rights; he does so by engaging subtly, but significantly, with a constellation of themes that denote the range and complexity of fin de siècle U.S. expansion: the politics of the Cuban independence movement, the globalization of black popular music, Wall Street's exploitation of Latin America. That he weaves his commentary on empire through a story of acquisitiveness and weakness suggests the degree to which imperial temptations appear only to be critiqued.

In what follows, I argue that Johnson critically imagines the racial passer and the imperialist of color as linked figures: both abandon the potential glories of racial struggle for the thin possibility of recognition by the white status quo; both attempt to remake themselves at the expense of black people throughout the Americas. Johnson critiques the notion that U.S. imperialism will afford African Americans the chance to bond with the nation-state and thus avoid racist oppression, particularly in the South. The picaresque titular character escapes the tyranny of the South not through trickery or resistance but by exploiting foreign people of color. Each time he ventures southward, the ex-colored man ends up in a difficult, if not perilous, situation that is eased or resolved through his manipulation of Latin Americans. A virtual (Latin American) South provides him with the comforts he cannot locate in the Jim Crow South or anywhere in the United States. Indeed, the ex-colored man's ability to jettison the terrifying problems of the regional for the colonialist compensations of the hemispheric informs, indeed helps render successful, his life as a racial passer. U.S. imperialism thus not only seduces African Americans into believing that colonialism will offer them all they have been denied at home; empire also lures African Americans away from a sense of hemispheric racial and political identity through much the same strategy. Little wonder, then, that Johnson's turn to anti-imperialist politics coincided with his transformation of the NAACP through grassroots organizational work in the South. By the second decade of the new century, Johnson had recognized that empire must be combated in a tandem fashion, at home and in the world.

History Travels with the Seas

A native of Jacksonville, Florida, Johnson experienced the geographic proximity of Latin American society and culture from childhood onward. His father taught him Spanish; he developed friendships with Cuban American cigar factory owners and workers; and most importantly, his family hosted a visiting Cuban student, Ricardo Ponce. Ponce and Johnson became great friends, attending both high school and college together. As Johnson writes in his memoir *Along This Way*, there grew "between us a strong bond of companionship; and what was, perhaps, more binding, the bond of [the Spanish] language" (63). One cannot overestimate the importance of this Cuban connection to Johnson's linked conceptions of race, space, and community. The Latin presence within "Dixie" would offer him a third term with which to better negotiate his relationship to the U.S. region for much of his life. For Johnson, the black-white divide could never completely encapsulate the U.S. South. At the same time, his early sensitivity to his region's hemispheric connections would also inform his vision of Latin America. He would draw on, and respond to, this formative exposure to Cuban American culture repeatedly in his future experiences in Venezuela and Nicaragua. His adult understanding of U.S. policy in the Americas would emerge from his youthful exposure to a hybridized, if still violently white supremacist, U.S. South.

Johnson was hardly unusual in linking what Deborah Cohn has called "the two souths."[11] As Cohn, Edouard Glissant, George Handley, Kirsten Gruesz, and others have argued, blacks and whites of the U.S. South had for centuries maintained a variety of connections to Latin America.[12] In his book *Faulkner, Mississippi*, Glissant reminds us that such disparate phenomena as cherry wood furniture, piquant cuisine, vibrant dance, and the literary figure of the black female servant bind together the cultures of the U.S. South, the Caribbean, and parts of Central and South America. For Glissant this connection stems from these nations' shared history of colonialism, slavery, racism, and poverty. As he puts it with respect to the legacy of New World plantation culture, "The same architecture, furniture, and rows of slave shacks, the same instruments of torture are found everywhere in the old slave order. . . . History travels with the seas."[13] The nineteenth- and early-twentieth-century record of this relationship presents us with ample evidence of the myriad crossings and exchanges that constitute a seaborne history: the celebration of Cuban poetry in the newspapers of antebellum New Orleans, William Walker's ill-fated attempt to reproduce U.S. southern culture in Mexico and Nicaragua, black Cubans' migration to the U.S. South after the abolition of slavery, the manipulative presence of Alabaman Samuel Zemurray's United Fruit Company throughout Central and South America. No less than the Mexico–southwest U.S. contact zone, the southeast border exists as a site of dynamic encounters between black, white, and Latin, between master and slave, between capital and labor.

As his memoir *Along This Way* affirms, at an early age Johnson experienced firsthand the value of his Latin American connections. At one point in the narrative, Johnson and his Cuban friend Ricardo Ponce manage to retain their seats in the first-class compartment of a segregated train because the conductor overhears them speaking Spanish and misidentifies them as Latin American visitors. As Johnson puts it, "As soon as the conductor heard us speaking a foreign language, his attitude changed" (65). In another train scene from *Along This Way*, Johnson receives a warm welcome from a group of white men after they realize he can help them understand Cuban society in the wake of the Spanish-American War. They even pause to admire and examine his authentic Panama hat—an object that seems to validate Johnson's Latin American origin (88). Johnson punctuates his narration of these autobiographical episodes with a tag line that captures perfectly the fluctuating meaning of black identity in the turn-of-the-century United States: "In such situations any kind of Negro will do; provided he is not one who is an American citizen." Johnson makes clear that "Negroes" who seem Latin American "will do" far better than any others in the Jim Crow South. He would later make this point more explicitly in "The Absurdity of American Prejudice" (1922): "There are many instances of prejudice being laid aside when it was thought or known that the colored person concerned was a Cuban, or a South American" (48). Johnson would have recognized that exoticism alone did not explain the success of his Latin passing. Adopting a Latin American identity momentarily liberated the black U.S. citizen from the oppressiveness of the U.S. South not only because that alternate black identity was alien or exotic but also because the hemispheric South represented an alluring space of economic and political opportunity for the New South.[14] Whatever their feelings about the mixed-race populations south of the border, U.S. southern capitalists viewed Latin America as a new market for the region's burgeoning textile industry—not to mention as a potential source of cheap labor.[15]

Yet every manipulation of identity demands something of the subject in question, and Johnson's Latino masquerade is no exception. While we might assess the performative meaning of Johnson's Latino act in the U.S. South in terms of a nascent and necessarily complex solidarity with Latin Americans against white U.S. racism and imperialism, an equally valid reading of these masquerades suggests the power plays of U.S. empire. By passing for Latino to momentarily improve his position in the white supremacist South, Johnson engages in his own version of the imperial aggression so tantalizing to white Americans, north and south. Even as Johnson experienced a brief thrill of liberation by dazzling provincial southern whites with his Latin American ways, this moment of freedom from Jim Crow stood in tension with a U.S. expansionist regime eager to appropriate things Latin for far less commendable reasons. We see but a hint of this appetitive impulse in the white train passengers' desire for information about Cuba: "The preacher asked me about conditions in Cuba . . . concerning which I had a good deal of information" (89). Johnson's willingness to appropriate a Latin American identity for his own domestic purposes points to his future interest in pursuing imperial ambitions south of the border. His Latino act in the Jim Crow South at once challenges and supports the white hegemony of an expansionist United States.

Johnson would stage a very different type of Latino performance years later when serving as U.S. consul in Corinto, Nicaragua, during an attempted coup d'état. If he had played the exotic Latin outsider in the U.S. South, he would play the faux native informant for the U.S. military in the Latin American context. In a contemporary letter to his wife Grace Nail Johnson, he describes the relationship between his appropriation of "Latinness" and his new connection to a powerful white U.S. admiral:

> I shall have to tell you in order to make you know how fine Admiral Southerland's treatment of me has been. I don't mean any more patting on the back as a very nice *colored* man [emphasis in original]; but recognizing me in the fullest degree as a man and officer. I am called into every consultation with him and his staff. He takes no important step or action without asking my opinion and advice. In dealing with communications from the rebels he has even asked I always sit near him. . . . I feel sure that I have measured up to his estimate of me.
>
> Another thing with reference to the Admiral—the day after arriving here he issued a general order to all the American forces occupying Corinto, and in that order he commanded that the consul was to receive the same naval honors as those accorded to officers of the fleet; so whenever I pass, the men on duty come to "present arms" and I salute. A little thing, but it means a great deal. He never sends me back from the flag ship except in his "barge," which is, in fact, a luxurious little steam yacht. But, as I intimated in the first part of my letter, I've been through enough to merit these little honors.[16]

Johnson claims to have good reason to dwell so long on these "little honors" elsewhere in the letter. He was at this point in his diplomatic career striving for a better post, preferably one in France, and the approval of an influential admiral held great value for him. Yet even if we acknowledge these career aspirations, we must still ponder the meaning of a letter that links Johnson's knowledge of Nicaragua with his newfound status among the white U.S. military brass. On the face of it, the many gestures of respect offered by the Admiral demonstrate that Johnson had indeed escaped the stereotype of the "very nice *colored* man" in his position as U.S. consul. Yet as the letter suggests, he has received the recognition due "a man and officer" only because he has taken on the role of Latin America expert—of knowledgeable "local"—for the U.S. admiral and his staff. Fluent in Spanish, familiar with Nicaragua, knowledgeable about the rebels, Johnson has the counterinsurgency expertise needed by the U.S. military; as he boasts to his wife in the letter, "I *know* this revolution from A to Z." By giving the U.S. military an insider's perspective on Nicaragua and its political turmoil, Johnson is able to indulge in a fantasy of enfranchisement. His special relationship to the Latin world has enabled him to shift from subaltern black subject to a white admiral's valued confidante.[17]

Yet the letter by no means presents us with an unqualified celebration of this exchange. When Johnson comments that he has "been through enough to merit these little honors," he connects his arduous, not to say ethically questionable, work on behalf of U.S. empire to the special recognition he receives from the white naval officer. He further suggests his unease with the appropriation of a Latin identity by segueing from a discussion of his role in suppressing the rebellion of Luis Mena and his peasant allies to a comment on Johnson's newly published narrative of racial passing, *The Autobiography of an Ex-Colored Man*. He queries his wife about the reviews the book has received — "so the *Crisis* has not yet reviewed my book," he comments — and discusses the novel's chances in the literary marketplace. These questions evince Johnson's ambition; thrilled at his new success on the diplomatic front, he demands news of further achievement in the world of letters. Yet the problem of the color line cuts across these two fields of endeavor, linking his pleasure over the admiral's attention with Johnson's desire to be recognized by W. E. B. Du Bois's new journal. Johnson's exploitation of Latino identity in the imperial context cannot help but recall the vexed issue of racial passing that informs his narrative. When we read the line "whenever *I pass*, the men on duty come to 'present arms' and I salute" (italics mine), it is difficult indeed not to consider that Johnson senses a certain disturbing connection between his work on behalf of U.S. empire and the machinations of his literary protagonist. Inasmuch as Johnson's new "white" privileges are predicated on the value of his Latin connections to the military, he too is a "passer." And the contingent nature of this masquerade unsettles him. Whatever Johnson's hope that U.S. expansion will allow him to exist in a space where he can assume the prerogatives of full U.S. citizenship, both the letter and the passing novel to which the letter refers register the impossibility of this dream. *The Autobiography* stands, as we shall see, as an African American diplomat's uneasy commentary on his position between a white imperial elite, a black U.S. population, and Latin America; with its tale of an African American man's anxiety over an abandoned racial identity, this classic literary work tells a related story of an African American man's concern about the acquisition of imperial privilege.

Going South

Early in *The Autobiography*, Johnson connects the struggles of people of color in
the Caribbean to the struggles of African Americans in a manner that belies any
notion that African Americans might exploit foreign people of color in support
of U.S. policy. While attending his grammar school graduation in a Connecticut town, the novel's protagonist listens to his African American friend "Shiny"
deliver Wendell Phillips's 1861 lecture "Toussaint L'Ouverture"—an abolitionist hagiography of the Haitian leader that celebrates his opposition to European colonialism and New World white racism. The "magical" experience of
listening to Shiny read this celebration of Toussaint L'Ouverture before a mainly
white audience causes the ex-colored man to undergo something of a racial
epiphany. "I could talk of nothing else with my mother except my ambitions
to be a great man, a great colored man, to reflect credit on the race and gain
fame for myself" (291–92). In these lines, the ex-colored man adopts a new perspective on his racial identity. If he had been horrified to learn of his blackness
a few pages before—"Mother, am I white? Are you white?" he asks tearfully
after being labeled black by his teacher (280)—listening to Shiny's rendition of
"Toussaint" has inspired the ex-colored man to accept a new racial identity with
pride. Shiny's passionate articulation of the great Haitian's accomplishments
gives the main character a new perspective on the race question throughout the
Americas.[18] Nothing could seem further from the Union veteran's dismissive
treatment of the republics south of the United States with which we began.

In having the ex-colored man identify Toussaint L'Ouverture as a model for
African American political action, Johnson reminds us that black U.S. citizens
have often invoked the famed Haitian revolutionary as a model for black social
and political action. Yet Johnson's titular protagonist responds to the example
of Toussaint in a distinctly personal manner. Ignorant of racial realities, shel-
tered and sensitive, the ex-colored man views Toussaint as a guide for reclaiming a familial legacy and finding his own triumphant way. Rather than inspire
the ex-colored man to struggle against white oppression in the United States,
the example of the Caribbean leader leads the deracinated hero to seek out
his potentially successful connection to southern black society. The ex-colored
man prefaces his experience listening to Shiny recite "Toussaint L'Ouverture"
with an account of how conversations with his mother made him curious about
U.S. southern culture: "What she told me interested and even fascinated me,
and, what may seem strange, kindled in me a strong desire to see the South"

(290). Johnson's protagonist has ample reason to be curious. After all, the ex-colored man has only recently learned that he is "the child of . . . unsanctioned love" between his Georgia-born mother and a wealthy and nameless southern white man (290). While the bitterly racist customs and laws of the region demand that they resettle in the North and leave the white southern father to marry "a young lady of a . . . great Southern family," the ex-colored man still feels an understandable, if impossible, desire to recover his place of origin (290).

By imaginatively traveling south of the U.S. border with the help of Shiny's performance of "Toussaint," the ex-colored man thinks he has found his way back to his natal zone; the invocation of a hemispheric southern hero will help Johnson's protagonist come to terms, however temporarily, with his own deeply problematic U.S. southern legacy. Or so it seems. Yet we soon discover that the protagonist will experience little more than the ugly facts of racism. His trip into the U.S. South represents less an imaginative rewriting of southern genealogies and geographies than a frightening incarceration in the prison house of his past. On his train trip south, the ex-colored reflects unfavorably on the unkempt fields and poverty-ridden housing he sees along the route. His arrival in Atlanta confirms his growing distaste for the region. Atlanta offends him aesthetically—too "big," too "dull"—and somatically: his lodging and food prove barely tolerable (294–96). To compound matters, his bankroll, the money with which he planned to pay tuition fees, is stolen during his first night in town. The South provides our protagonist with no opportunity to bond with black people, let alone aspire to the status of a latter-day Toussaint L'Ouverture. Rather than constituting a site of redefined origins, of a new heroic black identity, the South suggests nothing more than a life of poor diet, bad accommodations, ugly scenery, and confining, not to say racially divided, living spaces. The ex-colored man leaves the city squashed into the dirty space of a porter's laundry closet; his filthy entombment allegorizes the horror of a region that seems as stultifying as it is segregated (300).

The Cuban Question

Given his experience in the South, one would expect the ex-colored man to reverse direction and in time-honored African American fashion find his way to the allegedly liberated spaces of the North. Yet Johnson sends his hero further south; the ex-colored man flees Atlanta to find himself in a Jacksonville Cuban American community strongly identified with the Cuban independence

movement. The sign of L'Ouverture returns here dressed in Cuban revolutionary garb—an inadvertent reminder that the image of the Toussaint-affirming
Wendell Phillips graced the office wall of the Cuban patriot José Martí. This very
different southern community embraces the protagonist from the first. The ex-
colored man's Cuban American landlord not only finds him work as a tobacco
stripper in a cigar factory but also teaches him Spanish, thus offering our displaced character a chance to assume a new linguistic and social identity: "I was
able in less than a year to speak like a native," the ex-colored man soon boasts
(303). Before long, his language skills and general competence enable him to
move from the lowly job of tobacco stripper to the esteemed position of factory
lector—a role in which he reads from, and comments on, novels, newspapers,
and magazines for the benefit of the Cuban émigrés toiling around him (303).
The protagonist's ability to "go" Cuban within the confines of the U.S. South
speaks powerfully to the complex elasticity of both the region and the nation.
The presence of an anti-imperialist Cuban American community in northern
Florida suggests the commendable heterogeneity of the U.S. South despite its
stringent Jim Crow codes. Yet the existence of this Cuban pocket in Dixie also
testifies to the ability of the southeastern United States to absorb and exploit
persons and populations from proximate nations, regardless of their politics.
The pluralism evidenced may presage a future transformation of social relations in the U.S. South, but it also denotes how dominant white southerners
hijack identities and cultures in the service of future expansion south of the
border.[19]

This is not to deny the subversive politics of the Cuban American community in *The Autobiography*, particularly with respect to questions of race. The
Cuban American world of cigar manufacturing seems to stand in counterpoint
to the racial segregation that the ex-colored man experiences elsewhere in the
U.S. South for one important reason: its fierce identification with the radical political and social ideals of the anticolonialist Cuban independence movement.
In the Cuban world of cigar manufacturing, "the color line is not drawn" (301);
race does not seem to signify as a problem; blacks and whites work side by side
as equals. To be sure, racism did exist in the Cuban American cigar factory, as it
existed in Cuban America and in Cuba itself; the persistence in Cuban society
of the *raza de color*, a rule that differentiated between whites and all people of
color, rendered Cuban racial politics disturbingly similar to the binary racial-
ism of the turn-of-the-century United States.[20] Yet as Johnson may well have
known given his long-standing relationship with Cuban Americans, during the

independence movement at the turn of the century, issues of race and racism were suppressed in favor of a new, supposedly colorblind Cuban nationalism.[21] Whether underground in Cuba or displaced in the United States, members of the anti-imperialist independence movement strove to live up to the inspirational words of the Cuban political leader José Martí. "There can be no racial animosity, because there are no races," Martí preached to his fellow Cubans in "Our America." "The soul, equal and eternal, emanates from the bodies of various shapes and colors. Whoever foments and spreads antagonism and hate between the races, sins against humanity."[22] A hint of Martí's utopian racial vision for the independence movement materializes in *The Autobiography* when Johnson has the ex-colored man's Cuban landlord recite the names of both black and white military leaders central to the cause: "the Gomezes, both the white one and the black one . . . Maceo and Bandera" (303).[23] This list interweaves black heroes with white, gesturing, if only briefly, toward the liberated racial ideal of the cause. By invoking the interracial nature of the Cuban independence movement in the Jacksonville context, Johnson links the egalitarian race relations of the cigar factory to an anti-imperial social movement. The fight against empire south of the border, in other words, has an important — if inchoate — relationship to the African American struggle against segregation in the United States. From Toussaint to Maceo, the heroes of Caribbean independence movements seem capable of giving African Americans new forms with which to contest life under Jim Crow, forms that affirm national struggle even as they suggest new transnational alliances of color. The Cuban American radicals of Jacksonville are from this perspective a thorn in the side of the monster — Martí's gothic appellation for the large and terrifying nation to the north.[24]

Given the inspiring racial ideal represented by the Cuban Americans, one cannot help but note that the remaining pages of the novel's Jacksonville chapter make no further commentary on the utopian dimensions of the Cuban fight against Spanish colonialism. The ex-colored man never again mentions the idea of an egalitarian racial dynamic or the Cuban independence movement, though his job as factory lector would have required him to comment publicly on these and other pressing political issues.[25] The ex-colored man understands his job as lector in far more possessive and individualistic terms; he values the salary and the freedom from manual labor. As he will later explain while working once again as a cigar roller in New York, "making cigars became more and more irksome to me; perhaps my more congenial work as a 'reader' had unfitted me for work at the table" (319). In effect, he treats his job in the politically charged space of the cigar factory as little more than a well-paying gig. The radical politics of Cuban America mean little to him.

This turn away from the Cuban Americans is typical of Johnson's insecure and chameleonic protagonist; like many picaresque characters, he abandons identities and friendships as swiftly as he acquires them. At the same time, however, his meandering ways take on a very different meaning from that which we might identify in the narrative movements of a Moll Flanders or a Dean Moriarty. The often emancipatory meaning of travel in African American letters — in slave narratives, great migration stories, and ethnic rediscovery tales — invites us to read the ex-colored man's abrupt swerve from a politically idealistic community in a rather negative light. After all, when the ex-colored man abandons the Cuban Americans, he does not strive to find his place in the mythic black South he had envisioned ever since his epiphanic response to the performative invocation of Toussaint L'Ouverture. Instead he criticizes the black lumpenproletariat, condescends to the black working class, and identifies smugly with the black bourgeoisie (305–8). The very impulse to reify the black social hierarchy of Jacksonville stands in marked opposition to the Cuban American utopian spirit. Even as the Cuban Americans fight imperialism and reimagine race relations, Johnson has his nameless protagonist abandon their company to find a place in the most exclusive social scene in black Jacksonville. The open embrace of the Cuban Americans becomes the closed circle of the black middle class.

Johnson seems to suggest through this narrative movement that the exchange of communities does not so much testify to the protagonist's racial solidarity as reveal the extent of his elitism. What complicates any interpretation of the protagonist's shift from Cuban American to black bourgeois Jacksonville is Johnson's own membership in the middle class, not to mention his own delicate relationship with Latin American politics and New Negro ambitions.[26] The latter issue warrants our attention. If the ex-colored man drew social and economic sustenance from his well-paid position as lector in the Cuban American cigarmaking community, it seems clear that Johnson generated social capital from his role as U.S. consul in the turbulent societies of Venezuela and Nicaragua. As Johnson's biographer Eugene Levy has pointed out, "a position as a consular official, unlike that of a songwriter, was of unquestioned respectability."[27] Johnson's courtship of, and marriage to, Grace Nail, daughter of the affluent New York businessman John Nail, may have benefited from Johnson's emerging status as a U.S. State Department official. He would meet Grace Nail in 1901 and marry her in 1910, when his future prospects in the State Department seemed bright. To put it another way, Johnson's success as a black bourgeois resulted in part from his willingness to exploit Latin America in the name of U.S. empire—to represent U.S. interests, serve admirals, and suppress unwanted coups. Johnson never suggests anything of the sort in his work, yet we may speculate that the decision to contrast his protagonist's Cuban American experience with his ascendancy of the black social hierarchy—not the least of which is an impending marriage to a genteel black woman—reveals some recognition of the relationship between exploiting Latin America and becoming a black bourgeois success. If Johnson could not address this disturbing conjunction of state violence and black ambition directly, he could gesture toward the problem in his fictional autobiography.

The Empire Rag

Such arguments must remain at the level of speculation. What is clear is that Johnson devoted important sections of *The Autobiography* to examining the relationship of U.S. globalism to black success and, more specifically, black cultural success. If he couldn't focus openly on the connection between the black bourgeoisie and national expansion, he could take up the issue of black achievement and U.S. empire via a commentary on the accomplished musical career he had abandoned for the consul assignment in Venezuela. Johnson saw in the burgeoning U.S. empire a chance to reimagine the relationship of black U.S. music to the nation and the world. He often asserted that a globally hegemonic black culture would generate black acceptance not only abroad but, more importantly, at home. *The Autobiography* makes the appeal of this imperial conception of black culture manifest just before the ex-colored man discovers that an economic crisis in the Cuban American cigar factory has led to the termination of his job as lector. Not only does the ex-colored man disparage the achievements of Native Americans, the first target of European imperialism in the hemisphere—in his view, "all of the Indians between alaska and patagonia haven't done as much" as African Americans (310)—but he also affirms the triumphs of African American culture by celebrating them in a distinctly imperialist manner.[28] The anti-imperial lesson of the Cuban American political movement seems to have been lost on him; he sees only the possibilities of an ever-expansionist American dream. Surveying some of the more prominent forms of black southern popular culture—the cakewalk, the Uncle Remus stories, the Jubilee songs, and ragtime—the ex-colored man soon focuses on ragtime as a sign of U.S. global power that accrues to black as well as white Americans. "No one who has traveled can question the *world-conquering* influence of ragtime," boasts the ex-colored man (309; italics mine). The worldwide success of a black popular music suggests to him not the capacity for African Americans to develop new interracial and international connections—with Cubans, with "Indians"—but rather the ability of African Americans to play an important role in the burgeoning U.S. empire. The new era of U.S. hegemony will at once reflect and promote the globalization of black U.S. music.[29]

Johnson would reiterate his protagonist's infatuation with an expansionist image of black music well into the 1920s. Consider Johnson's description of black musical achievement in "American Music" (1916): "While [white] American composers have been making fair and mediocre copies of German, Italian, and French compositions, American Negro music in its triumphant march has swept the world" (287). In this reading, black music has more in common with U.S. imperial achievement than white music; of all Americans, only black musicians can outdo the Europeans and win global fame for U.S. culture. Likewise, Johnson argues in the preface to *The Book of American Negro Poetry* (1922) that ragtime "is the one artistic production by which America is known the world over. It has been all-conquering. Everywhere it is hailed as 'American music' " (x). As does the ex-colored man's term "world-conquering," so Johnson's choice of "all-conquering" registers the link between ragtime and U.S. imperialism—a connection the writer makes more explicit elsewhere in the preface: "[Ragtime] has become the popular medium for our national expression musically. And who can say that it does not express the blare and jangle and the surge, too, of our national spirit?" (xv). Johnson's use of aggressive ("blare") and expansionist ("surge") nouns captures the sense in which he imagines ragtime to embody a new bond between an imperial United States and a rising black U.S. culture.

Now, to be sure, Johnson was hardly the only U.S. citizen, black or white, to imagine that ragtime might play a constitutive role in a new expansionist version of U.S. public culture. From the early days of blackface minstrelsy, black music had facilitated the formation of a national popular culture.[30] What did change was the increasing acceptance of a "raced" national-popular culture by various portions of the state and its allied institutions. During the rise of the new U.S. imperialism in the fin de siècle, black music came to play an even more visible role in official military and mainstream nationalist cultures than ever before. Ragtime's appearance in the late 1890s—whether in Tom Turpin's

"Harlem Rag" (1897) or in Joplin's "Maple Leaf Rag" (1898) — coincided with the Spanish-American War, a fact not lost on the writers of songs such as "Get Off of Cuba's Toes," "Panama Rag," and "Philippine Rag." Ragtime would play an even more important role in the premier form of musical jingoism of the era: brass band music. John Philip Sousa's Afro-Latino number "El Capitan" would be played on the deck of Admiral Dewey's flagship in Manila Harbor; the brass band maestro would subsequently market ragtime to the Europeans and publish his own Hawaiian — that is to say, colonialist — ragtime number, "Hu-la, Hu-la Cakewalk," in 1901. His expansionist appropriation of ragtime would be emulated by the U.S. Marine Corps Band in their version of "Maple Leaf Rag" in 1906 and by Arthur Pryor's "Triumph of Old Glory," a patriotic rag for his military band, in 1907. When Johnson describes ragtime in terms of triumphant marches and "the blare and jangle of national spirit," he reminds us that fin de siècle black music traveled to global fame with the help of the U.S. military. The seductive appeal of this notion looms large: if U.S. empire and black music can work together for national glory, then one can believe in the enfranchisement of African Americans during a time of growing global power.

Global North and U.S. South

For all its representation of black music as world conquering, however, *The Autobiography* stands apart from Johnson's frequent affirmations of a global black culture. Focused on the travels and travails of the ragtime-playing protagonist, the novel constitutes the one major text in which Johnson troubles the expansionist image of black music he found so appealing. The global allure of black popular sounds leads the titular character to expect financial and professional rewards that never materialize. Upon leaving Jacksonville, the ex-colored man learns how to play ragtime in a New York gambling house; before long he has fallen under the sway of a white millionaire patron who takes him to Europe as a personal musician and companion. The shift in the novel's geography from the north-south axis of the coastal United States (Connecticut, Atlanta, Jacksonville, New York) to a decidedly north Atlantic orientation (New York, London, Paris, Amsterdam, Berlin) might suggest that our antihero has left both the hemispheric and the U.S. South behind — that, in effect, the novel has shifted to a new emphasis on the global North. Yet the net result of the European tour suggests otherwise. The South — as both problem and opportunity — shadows the protagonist during his northern travels.

Johnson first makes this evident by having the ex-colored man see his bio-

logical white southern father and white southern half-sister at the Paris Opera
—a traumatic experience that sends the musician running from the hall (328–
29). This geographic orientation emerges even more importantly for our purposes in the German portion of the ex-colored man's grand tour when his internationalist claims of black musical triumph are challenged and his relationship
to the U.S. South redefined. During a performance in Berlin, the protagonist's
demonstration of ragtime, the "new American music," ends disastrously: "Before there was time for anybody to express an opinion on what I had done, a
big, bespectacled, bushy-headed man rushed over, and, shoving me out of the
chair, exclaimed: 'Get up, Get up!' He seated himself at the piano, and, taking
the theme of my ragtime, played it through first in straight chords; then varied
and developed it through every known musical form. I sat amazed. I had been
turning classic music into ragtime, a comparatively easy task; and this man had
taken ragtime and made it classic" (332). In shoving the ex-colored man off the
piano bench and classicizing ragtime, this parody of a classically trained German musician ("bespectacled, bushy-headed") offers an allegory of how black
music could easily be pushed from the world stage. The scene reveals ragtime
less as world conquering, less as the musical soundtrack to the American century, than as a cultural form that must still contend with challenges from more
established cultural and political contenders, the Europeans. Whatever the success of ragtime as a popular music, indeed, whatever the success of the United
States as an imperial power, the Europeans still seem to rule the global roost.[31]

One would expect the ex-colored man to react angrily to such boorish behavior and defend the music he represents abroad. Yet he does not take offense
at the German's actions. Instead our ever-materialistic protagonist understands
this moment of displacement as an imperial wake-up call, if one rendered
in cultural terms. In Jacksonville, the protagonist learned how to exploit the
Cuban American scene to bankroll his accession to black bourgeois society; in
Berlin, the capital of the most renowned musical nation in Europe, he receives
an oblique hint at how he might exploit black southern music to foster his attempt at becoming a serious composer. Rather than anger him, the German
musician inspires the ex-colored man to think of how he might expropriate
black U.S. folk music for the purpose of writing serious musical compositions.
"I could think of nothing else. I made up my mind to go back into the very
heart of the South, to live among the people, and drink in my inspiration firsthand. I gloated over the immense amount of material I had to work with, not
only modern rag-time, but also the old slave songs—material which no one had

yet touched" (471). The protagonist claims that the encounter with the boorish German had helped him recognize "the way of carrying out the ambition [he] had formed when a boy," yet the desire to gloatingly steal the folk rhythms and melodies of the black rural people for his own professional ambitions hardly corresponds to his earlier desire to bring "honour and glory to the Negro race." The ex-colored man no longer seeks inspiration from the likes of Toussaint L'Ouverture; instead he seeks to colonize the black musical cultures of the Deep South for his own personal gain. Visiting the global North has not so much informed the ex-colored man of the imbalance between white and black, North and South, as it has offered him a salutary reminder of what his experience in Jacksonville had already begun to teach him: that the South is ripe with economic and professional opportunity. His willingness to exploit even the slave songs—those testaments to suffering and resistance—suggests his mercenary vision. When the ex-colored man informs his white patron that he will not be accompanying him to global southern locales such as Egypt and Japan, he does not so much deny himself the colonial pleasures of those lands as assert his right to grab his own colonialist rewards in a more familiar southern space.

This lesson not only corrects the dream of U.S. global conquest through ragtime; it reverses it, as well. Instead of a black southern cultural product colonizing the world—instead of ragtime marching triumphantly across the globe—the black South becomes the site of colonization itself. Imagining the world of culture and the culture of the world in black imperial terms has not linked the ex-colored man to his mother's people in a glorious manner; instead it has separated him from them. Black culture and black people now constitute the object, not the subject, of the ex-colored man's global vision. Johnson thus describes the ex-colored man's behavior in the rural South in aggressively ethnographic terms—"gathering material for work, jotting down in my note-book themes and melodies . . . trying to catch the spirit of the Negro in his relatively primitive state" (345). Our hero's willingness to continue identifying with the urban black bourgeoisie during this primitivist undertaking only suggests how the lesson in cultural expropriation received in Berlin helps him negotiate the linked hierarchies—geographic (Europe and the United States), racial (white and black), class (black bourgeoisie and black folk)—that inform his imperial dreams.

Our hero works hard at his ethnographic task, yet Johnson sends him from the South without any of the cultural riches he had come to retrieve. His trip to the hinterland exposes him not only to the oratorical passion and musical power of the black folk but also to the vicious white scourge that haunts this culturally abundant landscape: lynching. Toward the end of his time in Georgia, the ex-colored man watches local whites burn a black man alive—a sight so terrible that it serves to reorient his relationship to the region yet again. While the confrontation with the German musician had inspired the protagonist to return to the U.S. South, the lynching destroys this dream. The ex-colored man finds himself at an impasse with respect to the region of his birth; he no longer wants to go forth as an emissary of black southern music, but he cannot pursue a colonial relationship with such a terrifying, if musically rich, part of the country. His crisis forces him to step back and for the first time ponder his relationship not to the South but to the nation that tacitly endorses the region's notorious racist violence. Whatever his former pride in being an African American who can represent the imperial drive of a "raced" United States, the brute horror of lynching alienates him from both race and nation: "A great wave of humiliation and shame swept over me. Shame that I belonged to a race that could be so dealt with; and shame for my country, that it, the greatest example of democracy to the world, should be the only civilized, if not the only state on earth, where a human being would be burned alive" (352). The aural power of ragtime no longer sutures this African American to an expansionist United States; the glorious "blare" and "surge" of black popular music has given way to the terrible screams of the black victims of white mob murder.

Given the two challenges the ex-colored man endures during the latter part of the novel—the German's shove, the terrible scene of lynching—it should come as no surprise that he feels compelled to reassess his sense of self. The impasse results in a moment of crisis wherein the protagonist realizes he can no longer bear a black U.S. identity and decides to become a racial passer, or as he puts it: "I would change my name, raise a mustache, and let the world take me for what it would. . . . It was not necessary for me to go about with a label of inferiority pasted across my forehead" (353). The ex-colored man's choice to pass seems on the face of it a direct reaction to the lynching he has just witnessed. Yet perhaps we should see this action in more complicated terms as his response to a long-term inability to negotiate a successful, not to say profitable, relationship to his mother's South—the region he associates with his blackness. Characterized by theft, discomfort, rejection, and terror, the ex-colored man's increasingly tense engagements with the culture and the society of the region have all failed. His only successful experience in the U.S. South depended on the kindness and openness of the Cuban Americans and their independence movement, a group from which he separates himself. The dream of a return to the black southern natal zone—the dream that first took shape during his graduation—has grown increasingly impossible.

The ex-colored man's sense of national belonging evaporates as well. He does not suggest that he will replace his lost southern connection with a renewed tie to Connecticut—the site of his schooling and happiest years. He does not celebrate New England as he did earlier. Instead he describes his decision to pass as an action analogous to immigration: "I argued that to forsake one's race to better one's condition was no less worthy an action than to forsake one's country for the same purpose" (353). The ex-colored man's account of his arrival in New York only reinforces this sense of him as someone with no preexisting connection to the United States, black or white, southern or northern: "When I reached New York, I was completely lost. I could not have felt more a stranger had I been suddenly dropped into Constantinople. I knew not where to turn or how to strike out" (353). Disregarding his earlier connection to the city, the ex-colored man constructs New York as an alien world—a place as strange as that most exotic of metropoles, Constantinople. His usual talents seem to have abandoned him; he is isolated, jobless, bereft of resources. Passing for white has not linked our hero more tightly to a secure sense of U.S. citizenship; it has instead placed him beyond a sense of U.S. belonging as completely as it has placed him beyond a sense of black southern connection. Even as he works to establish a new life for himself in New York, he insists on imagining himself as forever marginal to the nation proper.

To be sure, the ex-colored man mourns the loss of national connection far less than he does his loss of black identity. And with good reason. However much he might appear a failed cosmopolite, as Ross Posnock has argued, this marginal man also proves successful at reconstructing himself as a successful imperialist.[32] Contrary to his protests that passing has nothing to do with ambition, the ex-colored man is indeed looking "for a larger field of action and opportunity" (353), not so much for the cosmopolitan as for the financial rewards. He understands full well that however lonely and isolated he may be, his new world beyond race, region, and nation is a world uniquely well suited to imperial profiteering. His odd and dislocated relationship to white and black New York stands in inverse proportion to his capacity to function as an imperial subject. He suggests as much when he explains that the initial loneliness he experienced in New York evaporated after he developed a relationship with a New York investment house pursuing South American possibilities:

I kept my eyes open, watching for a chance to better my condition. It finally came in the form of a position with a house which was at the time establishing a South American department. My knowledge of Spanish was, of course, the principal cause of my good luck; and it did more for me: it placed me where the other clerks were practically put out of competition with me. I was not slow in taking advantage of the opportunity to make myself indispensable to the firm. (354–55)

Of course, given the preceding emphasis on the ex-colored man's extranational position, one might say that he is already "placed" "where the other clerks" in this department cannot compete with him. Like the investment house itself, situated in New York but eager to exploit financial opportunities south of the border, the ex-colored man recognizes the rich potential of being at once inside and outside the nation. To be sure, he emphasizes how it is his knowledge of Spanish, not his sense of alienation as a racial passer, that renders him "indispensable to the firm." Yet as we have already seen in the Cuban American sequence of the novel—not to mention Johnson's experience as U.S. consul during the Nicaraguan coup—knowing Spanish, demonstrating knowledge of Latin American society, can serve as a profitable form of identity manipulation; it can allow the African American, or at least the light-skinned African American, to somehow escape the prison house of the one-drop rule. Within the contemporary imperial context, the ex-colored man's racial passing and his sociolinguistic connection to South America inform one another to his seeming financial and social advantage. If the ex-colored man was once at least tangentially related to the radical politics of the Cuban independence movement—a movement opposed to both Spanish and U.S. empire—he now represents the very forces of imperial greed and colonial rapacity his Cuban landlord would have decried.

The ex-colored man has indeed found the "endless territory" he desired as a young southern boy (274); the dream of an infinite expanse that originates in a Georgia garden materializes in the ever-expanding hemispheric spaces of the U.S. empire. The challenge of the Cuban Americans, the imperial failure of ragtime, the terrors of lynching: all of these manifestations of what we might call the southern Real are replaced by a South that exists only in terms of investments and financial statements. Johnson signals the connection between rampant northern greed and the ex-colored man's access to the South when he emphasizes that the protagonist procures the investment house position only after he has been infected with the money fever.[33] South America has become, in effect, a virtual South — the only sort of South this character can exploit without having to take a stand on the problem of the color line, the only sort of South that can bolster his life as a racial passer.

By including the closing lament over his failure to achieve the great works of a race man, we see Johnson both critiquing his protagonist's decision to pass and indicting his willingness to exploit others in a vain attempt to satisfy his money fever. To pass for white in the end is not only to betray his African American roots and the ongoing black struggle for justice but also to trade on his hemispheric southern connection as a means of ensuring that his racial passing succeeds within the United States. His new identity depends on the exploitation of Latin America, and that expropriation in turn suggests the transnational costs of black U.S. collaboration with the white imperial elite. If the protagonist has sold his birthright for a mess of pottage, perhaps we should see that birthright not simply as a connection to black U.S. society but in larger terms as a tie to a more hemispheric community of color, one that transcends national and linguistic boundaries. The ex-colored man is no longer African *American* in the fullest and most contentious sense of the word.[34]

Coda

Less than a year after *The Autobiography* was published, Johnson resigned his consular post in Corinto because of the new Wilson administration's refusal to promote him or, indeed, any African American. Johnson's work on behalf of the U.S. empire in Latin America had not been enough to win over an administration that promoted an even more overt white supremacist ideology than that of its Republican predecessor. Johnson would use his anger over a frustrated diplomatic career to fuel a new political career in the NAACP, but he would also draw on his fury to begin crafting a more explicit critique of the relationship between white southern racism and U.S. imperialism.[35]

Three weeks after leaving the State Department, he delivered a speech entitled "Why Latin America Dislikes the United States." In this speech, Johnson does his best to downplay the importance of national feeling by pointing out that Latin Americans have more to fear from the hemispheric spread of U.S. white supremacy than they do from U.S. designs on their land. For Johnson, imperialism is not so much a matter of territorial control; it is a matter of racial discourse. Citing the Latin American media's obsession with the high incidence of lynching in the United States, Johnson argues that many brown-skinned Latin Americans worry about the dangerous potential of white U.S. racism to infect other parts of the hemisphere. Even Latin American intellectuals such as Manuel Ugarte, the Argentine known for passionate anti-imperialist polemics, fear "not that southern republics will lose their independence to the United States, but that they will fall under the bane of American prejudice, a process which he has without doubt, observed going on slowly but surely in Cuba, Puerto Rico, and Panama" (197). In this response to Wilson and, indeed, all U.S. hemispheric imperialists, Johnson rejects the fiction of a civilizing mission and argues instead that U.S. expansion had led to nothing less than the deterioration of culture and society throughout the Americas. Johnson suggests a perspective directly opposed to that of the fictional Union soldier with which we began. If the Union veteran suggests that the United States is superior to the Latin republics because it has solved its own southern problem, Johnson argues to the contrary that not only does the United States' southern problem persist, but it is being exported to the very countries the United States is supposed to help.

Johnson would reiterate this point seven years later when he indicted the U.S. occupation of Haiti: "The mere idea of white Mississippians going down to civilize Haitians and teach them law and order would be laughable except for the fact that the attempt is actually being made to put the idea into execution" (251). The United States did not constitute some ordered North to the chaotic South but instead represented the degree to which the domestic South could render an entire nation unjust, prejudiced, and violently oppressive. By reading the U.S. empire through a southern regional lens, Johnson managed to articulate publicly a critique he had woven into the subtext of his passing novel. The "Dixiefication" of the White House undermined the Roosevelt corollary that Johnson had once found so appealing.

Notes

Many people have helped improve this essay. Thanks are due to Bluford Adams, Matt Brown, Corey Creekmur, Kathleen Diffley, Claire Fox, Eric Lott, Tom Lutz, John Carlos Rowe, Sandhya Shukla, Heidi Tinsman, and, above all, Kathy Lavezzo.

1   James Weldon Johnson, *The Autobiography of an Ex-Colored Man*, in *The Selected Writings of James Weldon Johnson*, vol. II, ed. Sondra K. Wilson (1912; New York: Oxford University Press, 1995). Hereafter cited in the text.

2   William Sydney Porter (O. Henry) introduced the offensive term "banana repub-

lic" in *Cabbages and Kings* (1904), a linked short story collection that takes Central America as its subject.

3   I have learned a great deal about "big stick diplomacy," "dollar diplomacy," and other manifestations of early-twentieth-century U.S. imperialism in the hemisphere from Scott Nearing, *Dollar Diplomacy: A Study in American Imperialism* (New York: B. W. Huebsch and Viking Press, 1925); Richard H. Collin, *Theodore Roosevelt's Caribbean: The Panama Canal, the Monroe Doctrine, and the Latin American Context* (Baton Rouge: Louisiana State University Press, 1990); and Peter Smith, *Talons of the Eagle: Dynamics of U.S.-Latin American Relations: Dynamics of the U.S.-Latin American Relations* (New York: Oxford University Press, 2000).

4   We should note that this argument inverts the more typical scholarly understanding of the relationship between the Civil War and turn-of-the-century imperialism. Richard Hofstader, Christopher Lasch, Michael Rogin, and others have argued that in the eyes of many white Americans, north and south, the conquest of Cuba, Puerto Rico, and the Philippines provided an opportunity to defuse lingering sectional tensions through a common investment in empire.

5   We should also note that Johnson refrained from any public critique of the brutal U.S. campaign in the Philippines. For important insights on Johnson and imperialism, see William E. Gibbs, "James Weldon Johnson: A Black Perspective on 'Big Stick' Diplomacy," *Diplomatic History* 8 (1984): 329–47; and Lawrence J. Oliver, "James Weldon Johnson's *New York Age* Essays," in *Critical Essays on James Weldon Johnson*, ed. Lawrence J. Oliver and Kenneth Price (New York: G. K. Hall). For biographical material on Johnson, I rely on Eugene Levy's useful book *James Weldon Johnson: Black Leader, Black Voice* (Chicago: University of Chicago Press, 1971); and Johnson's autobiography *Along This Way* (New York: Viking, 1933), hereafter cited in the text.

6   See "Black Americans' Racial Uplift Ideology as 'Civilizing Mission': Pauline E. Hopkins on Race and Imperialism," in *Cultures of United States Imperialism*, ed. Amy Kaplan and Donald Pease (Durham: Duke University Press, 1993), 436–38.

7   Johnson himself barely escaped lynching by Florida National Guardsmen in 1901.

8   For more work on the turn-of-the-century African American response to U.S. imperialism, see Willard B. Gatewood, *Black Americans and the White Man's Burden* (Urbana: University of Illinois Press, 1975); George P. Marks, ed., *The Black Press Views American Imperialism* (New York: Arno, 1971); Brenda Plummer, *Rising Wind: Black Americans and U. S. Foreign Affairs, 1935–1960* (Chapel Hill: University of North Carolina Press, 1996; and Amy Kaplan, "Black and Blue on San Juan Hill," in *Cultures of United States Imperialism*, ed. Amy Kaplan and Donald Pease (Durham: Duke University Press, 1993), 219–36.

9   The one partial exception is Eugene Levy's brief interpretation of *The Autobiography* in his biography of Johnson. Briefly put, Levy argues that the *café con leche* racial dynamic of Venezuela disturbed Johnson inasmuch as it seemed to offer mestizos or mulattoes full citizenship at the cost of claiming a black identity (see Levy, 110–12). Among the many articles on *The Autobiography*, I have found the

following to be most useful: Neil Brooks, "On Becoming an Ex Man: Postmodern Irony and the Extinguishing of Certainties in *The Autobiography of an Ex-Colored Man*," *College Literature* 22, no. 3 (1995): 17–29; Cheryl Clarke, "Race, Homosocial Desire, and 'Mammon' in Autobiography of an Ex-Coloured Man," in *Professions of Desire: Lesbian and Gay Studies in Literature*, ed. George E. Haggerty and Bonnie Zimmerman (New York: Modern Language Association of America, 1995), 84–97; Eugenia W. Collier, "The Endless Journey of an Ex-Coloured Man," *Phylon* 32 (1971): 365–73; Robert E. Fleming, "Irony as a Key to Johnson," *American Literature* 43 (1971): 83–96; Samira Kawash, "*The Autobiography of an Ex-Coloured Man*: (Passing for) Black Passing for White," in *Passing and the Fictions of Identity*, ed. Elaine Ginsberg (Durham: Duke University Press, 1996), 59–74; David Levering Lewis, "Dr. Johnson's Friends: Civil Rights by Copyright during Harlem's Mid-Twenties," *Massachusetts Review* 20 (1979): 501–19; Jennifer L. Schulz, "Restaging the Racial Contract: James Weldon Johnson's Signatory Strategies," *American Literature* 74, no. 1 (2002): 31–58; Joseph T. Skerrett Jr., "Irony and Symbolic Action in James Weldon Johnson's *The Autobiography of an Ex-Coloured Man*," *American Quarterly* 32 (1980): 540–58; and Kenneth W. Warren, "Troubled Black Humanity in *The Souls of Black Folk* and *The Autobiography of an Ex-Colored Man*," in *The Cambridge Companion to American Realism and Naturalism: Howells to London*, ed. Donald Pizer (Cambridge: Cambridge University Press, 1995), 263–77.

10 See Brent Edwards, *The Practice of Diaspora* (Cambridge: Harvard University Press, 2003); and Michelle Stephens, *Black Empire* (Durham: Duke University Press, 2005).

11 See Deborah Cohn, *History and Memory in the Two Souths* (Nashville: Vanderbilt University Press, 1999), 3.

12 See, for example, Cohn, *History and Memory in the Two Souths*; George Handley, *Postslavery Literatures in the Americas* (Charlottesville: University Press of Virginia, 2000); and Edouard Glissant, *Faulkner, Mississippi* (New York: Farrar, Straus and Giroux, 1999).

13 Glissant, *Faulkner, Mississippi*, 29.

14 To be sure, a black Latino subject would seem far less exotic in Florida or in coastal Alabama or Mississippi than he would in Virginia.

15 White southern textile manufacturers also looked to China and the Far East as a growing market for their products. This southern interest in Asia helps explain why white southern politicians were among the most passionate proponents of the proposed Panama Canal—the waterway that would expedite sea travel from the Atlantic United States to Pacific Asia. For an important overview of this topic, see Tennant S. McWilliams, *The New South Faces the World* (Baton Rouge: Louisiana State University Press, 1988).

16 The letter, dated August 31, 1912, may be found in the James Weldon Johnson Archive at the Beinecke Library, Yale University.

17 Johnson's delight over the attentions of Admiral Southerland echoes his better-known relationship to Dr. Thomas Osmond Summers, an affluent white eccentric

who hired Johnson as a secretary in Jacksonville. That both of these white-black relationships find their fictional analogue in the ex-colored man's erotically charged relationship to the white millionaire suggests the extent to which Johnson conceived of interracial male friendship as somehow always already queer.

18   The ex-colored man's excited response to Shiny's invocation of Toussaint L'Ouverture looks ahead to Johnson's passionate description of the black Haitian leader Henry Christophe in *Along This Way*. See Mary Renda, *Taking Haiti: Military Occupation and the Culture of U.S. Imperialism* (Chapel Hill: University of North Carolina Press, 2001), 193–94, for an interesting interpretation of Johnson's investment in Christophe.

19   Timothy Brennan has argued that the tradition of U.S. liberal pluralism owes a great debt to Latin American Creole culture and society. See "Cosmo-Theory," *South Atlantic Quarterly* 100, no. 3 (2002): 125–62.

20   For a fascinating examination of racial politics in late-nineteenth-century Cuba, see Ada Ferrer, *Insurgent Cuba: Race, Nation, and Revolution* (Chapel Hill: University of North Carolina Press, 1999).

21   "The cigarworkers in Florida not only provided political support to launch the PRC [the Cuban Revolutionary Party]," writes the historian Louis Perez, "they also supplied the financial base to sustain its activities through the full six years of its existence." See *Jose Marti in the United States: The Florida Experience* (Tempe: Arizona State University Center for Latin American Studies, 1995), 4. Johnson suggests as much when he characterizes the ex-colored man's landlord as "a prominent member of the Jacksonville junta" responsible for collecting money "to buy arms and ammunition for the insurgents" (302).

22   Martí, "Our America," in *Our America: Writings on Latin America and the Struggle for Cuban Independence*, trans. Elinor Randall, Juan de Onis, and Roslyn Held Foner, ed. Philip S. Foner (New York: Monthly Review Press, 1977), 93–94.

23   The ex-colored man's landlord does not mention Martí, but this seems to have more to do with his passion for the overtly military leaders of the movement than with a particular political point. While indispensable to the Cuban independence struggle, Martí was celebrated for his intellectual contribution, not his military prowess.

24   There is a tragic irony to Johnson's invocation of Cuban racial idealism in the year 1912, for this date witnessed the slaughter of former black Cuban independence fighters by their white comrades.

25   Lectors were often the source of radical political education in Latin American factories; their role as public readers placed them in the position of teacher and potential leader, with enormous implications for the creation and maintenance of oppositional social movements.

26   While we must heed Joseph Skerrett and not collapse the distinction between character and creator, we must also register the important parallels between biography and novel. See Skerrett, "Irony and Symbolic Action in James Weldon Johnson's *The Autobiography of an Ex-Colored Man,*" *American Quarterly* 32 (1980): 540–58.

27   Levy, *James Weldon Johnson* (Chicago: University of Chicago Press, 1971), 107.

28   Johnson also critiques the place of Native Americans in the creation of an indigenous popular culture in his *New York Age* editorial "American Music" (1916). He
writes, "When [skilled musicians] have striven to be original they have gone to
Indian themes and legends, but here they have worked sterile soil." Johnson seems
to find the Native American a potential competitor to the throne of U.S. cultural
originality.

29   The ex-colored man expounds on the global power of ragtime in an effort to
counter contemporary white U.S. critiques of the musical form. Ragtime was, as
the protagonist puts it, a cultural form that "originated in the questionable resorts
about Memphis and St. Louis" — and thus represented to many Americans of the
era the most disreputable aspect of the Jim Crow South (314). See Edward Berlin,
Ragtime (Berkeley: University of California Press, 1980), for an important history
of the reception of the musical form.

30   For an important argument about the relationship of black music and the U.S. national popular, see Eric Lott, *Love and Theft* (New York: Oxford University Press,
1993).

31   Paul Gilroy and Brent Edwards have each offered acute "black Atlanticist" readings
of this scene. My reading tends to diverge from both of theirs in emphasizing the
relationship between the imperial implications of the German's dismissive action
and the regional denouement of the encounter. See Paul Gilroy, *The Black Atlantic* (Cambridge: Harvard University Press, 1993), 130–32; and Brent Edwards, *The
Practice of Diaspora* (Cambridge: Harvard University Press, 2003), 40–43.

32   Ross Posnock, *Color and Culture* (Cambridge: Harvard University Press, 1998), 76.
Tom Lutz also engages with the cosmopolitanism of the ex-colored man in *Cosmopolitan Vistas* (Ithaca: Cornell University Press, 2004), 123–27.

33   As Johnson would himself argue in his articles on the U.S. occupation of Haiti,
New York banks and investment houses both exploited and provoked U.S. military
domination south of the border from the turn of the century well into the 1930s.

34   As Michael Hanchard has written, "U.S. blacks lie at the vortex of conquest and
decimation. And so does the hyphen between 'African' and 'American.'" See "Identity, Meaning, and the African American," in *Dangerous Liaisons: Gender, Nation,
and Postcolonial Perspectives*, ed. Anne McClintock et al. (Minneapolis: University
of Minnesota Press, 1997), 230–39.

35   For an important assessment of Johnson's critique of white southern racism, see
Lawrence J. Oliver, "James Weldon Johnson's *New York Age* Essays on *The Birth
of a Nation* and the 'Southern Oligarchy,'" *South Central Review* 10, no. 4 (winter
1993): 1–17.

Bastards of the Unfinished Revolution

Bolívar's Ismael and Rizal's Martí at the
End of the Nineteenth Century

John D. Blanco

Acabarán como el padre—contestó Elías en voz baja—; cuando la
desgracia ha marcado una vez una familia, todos los miembros tienen
que perecer; cuando el rayo hiere un árbol, todo lo reduce a cenizas.

["They will end up like their father," Elías answered in a low voice. "Once
misfortune has marked a family, all its members must perish; like a bolt of
lightning that wounds a tree, reducing everything to ashes."]

—José Rizal, *Noli me tangere*

The title of my essay aims to highlight two important themes in the late colonial
literature of Cuba and the Philippines at the end of the nineteenth century, embodied in the figure of a bastard son or daughter in various novels and poems.
The first theme is the recovery of a lost legacy, patrimony, or the intimation of
fate, which reconfigures the ethical and political decisions of the colonial subject on the eve of revolution. The second is the bastard's anomalous identity,
which prefigures the colonial subject's abandonment by the society that engendered the colonial condition, but also gives her or him the relative freedom to
break with the familial or paternalistic past by criticizing it and announcing the
advent of historical self-assertion in the colonial world. Certainly these themes
frame the central tensions in the most important Cuban novel of the nineteenth
century, *Cecilia Valdés* (1882), but they also provide the central metaphor to
the Cuban patriot and lawyer José Martí's early collection of poems *Ismaelillo*
(1882), dedicated to his son. Across the Atlantic Ocean, not many years afterward, Dr. José Rizal, colonial expatriate of the Philippine archipelago (and soon
to be national martyr and hero), produced his two novels *Noli me tangere* (Do

Not Touch Me) and *El filibusterismo* (Will to Subversion), around a woman whose bastard origins catalyze the hero's unjust persecution and recourse to revolution against the Spanish colonial government.

In each of these instances, the tension between the necessary rediscovery of a lost patrimony and the necessary negation of that patrimony in order to take control of one's individual destiny under colonialism frames a crucial confrontation in the making of the modern world. That was the confrontation between two contesting inheritors of the economic and political upheavals in Europe and the Americas throughout the early nineteenth century: on the one hand, modern imperialism as an international policy; and on the other, the recuperation of Simón Bolívar's anticolonial thought in the Spanish colonial world. One of the most dramatic manifestations of this confrontation at the end of the nineteenth century, the 1898 war with Spain, resulted in the U.S. occupation of Cuba, as well as the takeover of Puerto Rico, the Philippines, and Guam between 1898 and 1912. In doing so, the United States extended its territorial sovereignty by might across the Pacific and the Gulf of Mexico and set an astonishing precedent for military invasions and interventions in other countries throughout the twentieth century.[1] Less known, however, is the way in which the discourse of late liberal, anticolonial revolution continued to serve as a suppressed archive open to cultural elaboration and transformation in both countries up to the present.

Central to this archive are the works of José Rizal and José Martí. Indeed, one may go so far as to say that no conception or discussion of national consciousness in the Philippines and Cuba is possible without somehow identifying the place of these two men in their respective countries or citing the stirring words of their literary and political writings. Both shared a series of ghostly parallels. They were both colonial expatriate intellectuals born in two of Spain's last colonies to survive the Latin American wars of independence (the Philippines and Cuba); both began their careers optimistic about the future of Spanish republicanism but grew disenchanted with the politics of colonial reform; both foresaw in their writings the demise of colonial rule but also the shadow of modern imperialism in their respective regions; and both died as national martyrs to the anticolonial revolutionary movement, with Martí leading an expeditionary force in the 1895 Cuban War of Independence, and Rizal being executed by firing squad for his alleged involvement in the 1896 Filipino revolution.[2] Both consorted at one time or another with the same Spanish political leaders advocating an end to colonial rule; both also had occasion to witness and document the combination of economic power and economic inequality that put the United States in a position of contesting hegemony with the older European nations.[3] Finally, the historical memory of both became an object of political debate in the construction of a national pedagogy for state consolidation in the 1940s and 1950s era of postwar decolonization (and, in Cuba's case, national revolution). Yet for all their overlaps and intersecting itineraries across Spain and the United States—the soon-to-be-past and soon-to-be-present colonial empires at the end of the nineteenth century—the two men never met, and virtually never mentioned each other in the entire corpus of their respective writings.

In the pages that follow, I account for the lost affinities between the Philippines and the Spanish Caribbean through an analysis of these two writers, particularly their common search and questioning of intellectual patrimonies, which were buried or redirected by the advent of U.S. imperialism at the turn of the century. The specific case I treat at length is the common engagement of Rizal and Martí with the thought of Simón Bolívar, to the degree that both Rizal and Martí saw themselves as the problematic inheritors of an unfinished project that began with the Latin American wars of independence in 1810. By juxtaposing the different interpretations of both national heroes at the end of the nineteenth century, I arrive at a more general analysis of Rizal's Filipinas and Martí's "Nuestra América" as narratives that do not so much assert the existence of an "imagined community" (to borrow a phrase from Benedict Anderson) as they ceaselessly announce their future possibility. In doing so, both elicit the task of critically reflecting on the specifically anticolonial character of the late liberal or "romantic" revolutions in Cuba and the Philippines.

I believe that an understanding of such a task contributes to a larger investigation of the concept and literature of the Americas, characterized by the contradictory inheritance of European and American liberalism, the creation of new constituencies around the question of U.S. imperialism, and the imagination and investment of these constituencies in alternative visions of modernity. At present, as the United States overruns yet another country on the spurious claims of national security and territorial integrity, a recuperation of these visions for the subjects and victims of that violence seems both necessary and appropriate.

In attempting to distinguish the late-nineteenth-century political revolutions from their predecessors, Eric Hobsbawm takes up the difficult task of isolating various features of nationalism that exercised some impact on most national movements between 1880 and 1914. These include the expansion of the understanding of nationhood as constituting "any body of people considering themselves a 'nation' . . . which, in the last instance, meant the right to a separate sovereign independent state for their territory," as well as an increasing reliance on ethnicity and language for the articulation of nationhood.[4] For already established nation-states in Europe, as well as the United States, Hobsbawm adds a third feature, "a sharp shift to the right of the nation and flag, for which the term 'nationalism' was actually invented in the last decade(s) of the nineteenth century."[5]

This somewhat schematic historicization of "second-generation nationalisms" nevertheless provides us with an initial point of departure for inserting the theme of patrimony as a way of outlining the matrices of Martí's and Rizal's works and their importance to us today. Yet in elaborating his criteria for what he would later identify as "the age of empire," Hobsbawm fails to highlight the *mutually determining* aspect of these three features: the degree to which the expression of nationhood, for example, was an anticipation of, and defense *against*, the emergence of modern imperialism, or the way in which international legitimacy and right became a central issue between the imperialist powers and leaders like José Rizal and José Martí at the end of the nineteenth century. This mutually determining characteristic frames the particular angle toward the general historical problematic in which I want to situate the works of both thinkers. It also helps to account for the invisibility of the Philippines and Latin America to each other in the twentieth century.

Latin America's intellectuals have always maintained a respectful distance from the Philippines, for both obvious and less obvious reasons. After Mexico gained its independence from Spain in 1821, the jurisdiction of Spanish sovereignty over the Pacific archipelago transferred from Mexico to Madrid. The colonial archipelago thenceforth became part of a floating constellation that included Cuba and Puerto Rico, although the latter two shone more brightly in the eyes of Spain for the profits both islands reaped from the sugar plantations and the slave trade.[6] Other factors responsible for the invisibility of Filipinas in Latin American studies may include geographical distance, our own ambivalence toward the study of Filipino literature in Spanish, and most notably the fact that the Philippines was seized by the United States between 1898 and 1912 in the midst of the islands' national revolution against Spain.

The U.S. intervention in Spain's former colonies reoriented the cultural reception and understandings of the revolutions in Cuba and the Philippines in subtle but significant ways. For one thing, it cut short any developing relations between Filipino and Spanish Caribbean intellectuals and revolutionaries, particularly during the latter half of the nineteenth century and particularly the 1896 Filipino revolution. Throughout the 1880s, Filipino *ilustrados*, or European-educated intellectuals, had lobbied with Cuban expatriates in Spanish political parties and Masonic lodges to abolish colonial rule.[7] At the close of the first phase of the Filipino revolution (1896–97), the revolutionary government in exile corresponded with the Puerto Rican statesman Ramón Emeterio Betances for the purpose of developing mutual ties of solidarity and support for the liberation of both archipelagoes of the Atlantic and Pacific Oceans. Beyond the foreclosure of this conversation, however, was the sudden reorientation of both revolutionary movements to confront a country whose imperialist designs seemed both self-contradictory and ambivalent. For Cuba, formal independence belied de facto U.S. military and economic rule. Across the Pacific, the compromises of various elite ilustrados and the drastic casualties of the Philippine-American War (between 500,000 and 1 million) together facilitated the U.S. takeover of the Philippines, with the proviso that national independence would succeed a brief transition period of "colonial tutelage."

The historical emphasis of the 1898 U.S. war with Spain over the independence movements in both countries has thus served to obscure a proper analysis of the late colonial condition in Cuba and the Philippines, as well as a larger understanding of the Philippines in the context of the anticolonial revolutionary movements in Latin America, in at least two ways. In the U.S. historiography of the period, the Philippines and the Spanish Caribbean became quickly absorbed into a larger narrative of U.S. expansion beginning with the decimation of the Native American population and the seizure of Mexican land in 1846, and culminating in the creation of a trans-Pacific "island empire" at the turn of the century. In an early statement advocating such a project, Charles Morris wrote in 1899: "We have primitive populations to civilize, indolent populations to stimulate, hostile populations to pacify, ignorant populations to educate, oppressed populations to lift into manhood and teach the principles of liberty and the art of self-government."[8]

Yet Latin American responses to 1898 also served to excise the Philippines from an understanding of its own modernity, built around either the question of a southern continental republic (Simón Bolívar); a nascent Western hemispheric "Americanism" that would succeed the barbarism of old Europe

(Domingo F. Sarmiento); the linguistic and cultural affiliation with Spain (Andrés Bello and Rubén Darío); or the threat of a growing U.S. interest in territorial and economic expansion (José Martí and José Enrique Rodó).[9] Particularly after the U.S. seizure of northern Mexico in 1846, projections of national and regional modernity became characterized by a simultaneous comparison to, and differentiation from, North America. The career of the Cuban abolitionist José Antonio Saco, for example, illustrated a decisive shift in the almost unconditional emulation of U.S. modernity by thinkers such as Sarmiento in the early nineteenth century, to a reconsideration of the unfulfilled possibility of constitutional republicanism in Cuba.[10] Another example is the Chilean writer and journalist Francisco Bilbao's reflections on the Mexican-American War, in which he portrays the North-South division in the Americas as a series of oppositions, with Latin America prioritizing the "social to the individual, beauty to wealth, justice to power, art to commerce, poetry to industry, philosophy to texts, pure spirit to measurement, duty to interest."[11] These oppositions certainly impacted José Martí's observations on the rise of U.S. imperialism, captured in his famous essay "Nuestra América" (1893).[12] They also provided the basis for José Enrique Rodó's Latin American cultural aesthetic, or *arielismo*, and Rubén Darío's critique of North American *calibanismo* in their respective essays "Ariel" and "El triunfo de Calibán" (both published in 1900).

Both the adulation and dismissal of North American modernity, however, still tied many Latin American intellectuals to a negative project of conceiving a future Latin America in the eyes of its "other," that is, either along the lines of the European metropolis or in response to the U.S. expansion of its hegemony across the Western Hemisphere and the Pacific Ocean. As Angel Rama has pointed out, the emergence of the modern intellectual, or *letrado*, in Latin America nevertheless failed to address the colonial relationship between city and province, metropolis and colony, lettered and unlettered: divisions that resulted in the further isolation of the masses from political life and representation.[13] Speaking generally, one of the driving forces behind the political fashioning of Latin American modernity for the writers of the late nineteenth century—rationalization in the Weberian sense, but also the assertion of national sovereignty, the art of good government, the implantation of an enlightened pedagogy, et cetera—consisted in a differentiating operation that distinguished "our" Latin America from either Europe or the America of the North, as a way of specifying the challenges of supervening the destructive force of advanced capitalism and a corresponding modern U.S. hegemony. "Nuestra América" thus served not only to assert a cultural claim to the territory, "from the Bravo to the Magallanes!" in Martí's words, against the history of U.S. aggression and aggrandizement in Mexico. It also served to call for a reevaluation of the constitutional experiments that had resulted in almost a century of internecine warfare and the rise of tyranny among the new Latin American republics, and the acceleration or intensification of colonial dichotomies in an avowedly postcolonial order.[14]

The preceding summary of responses to the onset of U.S. imperialism in Latin America and the Caribbean at the turn of the century does not pretend to be exhaustive. It merely serves to highlight the marginal place of Rizal, the Philippines, and in many ways the polyglot Caribbean archipelago as well, with respect to the formation of modern Latin American thought, posed in the terms of the North-South axis. As Cuba's invisible twin, the Philippines fought a war of independence against a weak colonial empire, only to be overrun by the interests of the modern United States. And like Puerto Rico, the Philippines became what was known as an unincorporated territory of the United States — pieces of property recognized by the powerful nations as belonging to the United States, but territories whose inhabitants were nevertheless deprived of constitutional representation, landownership on the mainland, even basic civil rights.[15] Yet set apart from both political representation in the United States and cultural representation in the projections of both U.S. and Latin American modernity, the social and cultural affinities between the Philippines and the Spanish Caribbean, known to the nineteenth-century colonial expatriates from the Philippines, Puerto Rico, and Cuba in Spain, are overshadowed by the discourses of Pan-Americanism and Latin Americanism, which crystallized in the luminous pages of Martí's "Nuestra América."

In the analysis that follows, I want to rescue Rizal's imagined patrimony with the fate of Latin American republics in the age of European and U.S. colonial empires. Second, I want to use this analysis to reflect on the role of the aesthetic in the development of anti-imperial Filipino insular nationalism after Rizal's death, on the one hand, and the affirmation of a Latin Americanism founded on the success of the Cuban Revolution, on the other. If a figure like José Martí comes down to us as a cultural inheritor the "Hispano-American enigma" that began with the wars of independence under Simón Bolívar, in what way does Rizal become akin to Bolívar's Ismael — a lost and illegitimate son of a problem defined specifically as "American"? How does this legacy inform Rizal's aesthetic project through the figure of Simoun — a kind of cynical parody of Cuba's Martí in Rizal's *El filibusterismo*? Finally, what are the implications of this project for revisiting the ambivalent bases of Martí's own Latin Americanism?

The title of Rizal's second (and more ideologically explicit) novel, *El filibusterismo*, references a strange word, *filibustero*, first used in Dutch and English to refer to banditry (*fraybüter*, freebooter) in the late sixteenth century, before entering Spanish in the seventeenth century as the word for pirate, particularly in the Caribbean and Philippine Islands. *The Oxford English Dictionary* records the politicization of the word "filibuster" in the late nineteenth century, when it began to connote the "violation of international law, for the purpose of revolutionizing certain states in Central America and the Spanish West Indies," particularly Cuba and Puerto Rico. In Spanish, *filibusterismo* became synonymous with sedition, a crime that was punishable by imprisonment and deportation without any recourse to due process of law. Particularly in the decade following the 1872 uprising in Cavite province of the Philippines, such arbitrary proceedings relied on the license of the colonial government to perpetuate a state of exception in the Philippines, founded on the administration of special laws distinct from those of the Spanish metropolis.[16]

For Rizal, the arbitrary exposure of any colonial subject accused of being a filibustero to the force of law under colonial sovereignty became a case symptom of tyrannical rule: "All those, in a word, who among normal civilized people are considered good citizens, friends of progress and enlightenment, in the Philippines are *filibusteros*, enemies of order, and, like lightning rods, attract on stormy days wrath and calamities."[17] Yet the incongruity of the word's immediate investiture with the force of law in the colony, in which the presumption of guilt might befall any given member of the colonial population simply by public accusation, became the germinal seed of Rizal's first novel, *Noli me tangere*. In a stirring monologue, the protagonist Crisóstomo Ibarra diagnoses the "social cancer" of colonial society, in which a perpetual disavowal of the due process of law effectively forces the colonial subject to resort to the very sedition he or she is presumed to propagate:

> ¡Ellos me han abierto los ojos, me han hecho ver la llaga y me fuerzan a ser criminal! Y pues que lo han querido, seré filibustero, pero verdadero filibustero; llamaré a todos los desgraciados, a todos los que dentro del pech sienten latir un corazón. . . . Nosotros, durante tres siglos, les tendemos la mano, les pedimos amor, ansiamos llamarlos nuestros hermanos. ¿Cómo

nos contestan? Con el insulto y la burla, negándonos hasta la cualidad de seres humanos. ¡No hay Dios, no hay esperanzas, no hay humanidad; no hay más que el derecho de la fuerza!

[They have opened my eyes, made me see the cancer, and they force me to be a criminal! And since they want it thus, I *will* be a filibustero, but a true filibustero; I will call on all the disenfranchised, all those who feel within their breasts a beating heart. . . . For three centuries, we have extended our hand, asked from them love, longed to call them our brothers. How do they answer us? With insults and mockery, denying us even the status of human beings. There is no God, no hope, no humanity; nothing more than the right of force!][18]

Rizal extends this train of thought in *El filibusterismo* by establishing a sinister connection between the secret return of Crisóstomo Ibarra to the archipelago after thirteen years of exile, and his adventures in the Americas (particularly Cuba) as both a freebooter and financier of sedition and countersedition. Under the significant pseudonym of Simoun, Ibarra succeeds in raising money, arms, and the spirit of vengeance against Spain, all of which would impel and sustain a revolutionary movement long enough to wipe out the traces of colonial oppression and build a constitutional order.

The Filipino writer and national artist Nick Joaquin calls attention to Ibarra's pseudonym Simoun to render explicit Rizal's reference to the history of the Latin American revolutions.[19] Joaquin begins with the following question: if Rizal himself was considered to belong to the social status or caste of native subaltern or *indio* in colonial society, why did he make the agent of historical change in his two novels (Simoun) a Creole? Joaquin's answer becomes one of the main theses of his work: according to Joaquin, from the history of struggles in Latin America led by Creoles in the early nineteenth century, Rizal looked to the figure of the Creole for the emergence of Filipino politics. For Joaquin, Rizal "knew that Spain was overthrown in America by the various uprisings of the Creoles there (Bolívar, San Martín, Iturbide). . . . During Rizal's youth, it looked as if what had happened in America would happen in the Philippines. . . . So, when Rizal wrote his novels, he was writing about an actual movement, and writing to animate it. . . . He was chronicling the Creole revolution in the Philippines."[20] Joaquin recounts various episodes in nineteenth-century Philippine history to substantiate his thesis: the advocacy for native rights by the self-styled "Conde Filipino" during the early years of the Spanish Constitution

(1812–14 and 1820–23); the attempted coup of the colonial government by the Novales brothers in 1822, one of whom proclaimed himself "emperor" (after Iturbide) for a day; and the Creole leadership of Father José Burgos in the defense of native secular priests against the accusations of the Spanish friars. For the colonial expatriates of Rizal's time, the Latin American wars of independence remained a living legacy for Spain's remaining colonies, even as Rizal's compatriots lobbied for the eradication of colonial special laws and the granting of various civil liberties to the colonial population.

Simoun's connection to the Americas, however, extends beyond the identification with the Creole legacy. When the character is first introduced in Rizal's novel, he speaks "with a strange accent, a mixture of English and South American." One of Simoun's new acquaintances balks at the ruthless audacity of the protagonist's opinions, which become labeled as "Yankee": "He [Simoun] doubtless believes that [the native Filipinos] we are dealing with [are] redskins."[21] The mixed association of Simoun with freebooters, Yankee frontiersmen, and Latin American Creoles, in any event, cues the reader to examine the colonial question in the Philippines through the lens of the Americas, particularly the frontier between its privileged and disenfranchised sectors. The latter, in Rizal's mind, are composed of the natives, criminals, and failed leaders of the past generation whose decimation or defeat left a lesson for Simoun to study and resolve.

While the overlap may seem incongruous from a strict historical interpretation of the dichotomy between elite and native groups during the Latin American wars of independence, Simoun projects their partial identification as a way of distinguishing the present revolution from the past:

> Pedís igualdad de derechos, españolizacion de vuestras costumbres y no veís que lo que pedís es la muerte, la destruccion de vuestra nacionalidad, la aniquilacion de vuestra patria, la consagracion de la tiranía! . . . Pedís españolizacion y no palideceis de vergüenza cuando os la niegan! Y aunque os la concedieran ¿qué quereis? Qué vais á ganar? Cuando más feliz, país de pronunciamientos, país de guerras civiles república de rapaces y descontentos como algunas repúblicas de la América de Sur!

> [You ask for equal rights, Hispanization of your customs, and you don't see that what you are asking for is death, the destruction of your nationality, the annihilation of your native land, the consecration of tyranny! . . . You ask for Hispanization and you don't cringe with shame when they deny

it to you! And even if they did, what do you want? What will you gain? The joy of being a country of executive decrees, a country of civil wars, a republic of looters and wretches like some republics of South America?][22]

On the surface, Simoun's Machiavellianism seems to go entirely against the libertarian ideals of his namesake — Simón Bolívar, who dedicated his life and work to the success of Latin American independence from Spain. Yet the Filipino Creole Simoun, who turns against the legacy of his historical agency in the cycle of American revolutions, nevertheless retraces a suppressed chapter in the narrative of North and Latin American independence: the fate of its indigenous populations. It was this division between an increasingly restless Hispanized Creole and mestizo elite minority and a large population of native subalterns whose opinion on national liberation was either nonexistent or entirely unknown that both elicited and foreclosed any favorable analogy between the American wars of independence and the imminent Filipino revolution. To borrow a phrase from W. E. B. Du Bois, Rizal was burdened with the "double-consciousness" of an educated member belonging to a marginalized and historically oppressed caste — the *indios*.[23] Perhaps it should come as no surprise that Rizal was capable of both radicalizing the movement for colonial reforms based in Spain, led predominantly by Creoles and Spanish Chinese mestizos, and toward the end of his life opposing the emergence of national revolution — a movement that he had inspired.[24]

Curiously, Rizal's Simoun, who represented the author's disenchantment with the romantic ideal of republican revolution, unwittingly resurrects the oft-forgotten reflections of Simón Bolívar on the future of an independent Latin America. After all, it was Bolívar who first ruled out the possibility of instituting a constitutional republic on a continent that had spent three centuries under Spanish colonial sovereignty. In Bolívar's letters written from Jamaica in 1815, the supreme commander poses the question that Rizal would confront almost a century later: "¿Se puede concebir que un pueblo recientemente desencadenado se lance a la esfera de la libertad, sin que, como a Icaro, se le deshagan las alas y recaiga en el abismo?" (Can one conceive a recently unshackled people capable of launching itself into the sphere of freedom, without its wings falling apart, like Icarus, only to fall again into the abyss?).[25] Behind this powerful question lies the source of Bolívar's legacy as an intellectual forebear of the 1896 Filipino revolution, as well as the Cuban War of Independence, for Bolívar had to summon the courage and probity to reflect on and criticize the wars of independence in the very momentum of their trajectory.

Rizal's interpretation of Bolívar's question thus anticipates a central theme of the recent scholarship by the Indian Subaltern Studies Collective (I am thinking in particular of Ranajit Guha's *Elementary Aspects of the Peasant Insurgency*): how does the early postcolonial subject go beyond a momentary negation or reversal of the colonial order if the only basis for a national community is a common outrage against a common oppressor?[26] And should the attempt to institute the principles of natural law and democracy in Latin America's new republics fail (as Rizal would believe), what would occupy their place? What symbol could stand in the face of such disenchantment? Readers of Rizal's *El filibusterismo* will hear these same concerns echoed in one of the novel's final soliloquies: "¿A qué la independencia si los esclavos de hoy serán los tiranos de mañana? Y lo serán sin duda porque ama la tiranía quien se somete á ella!" (What is the point of independence if the slaves of today will be the tyrants of tomorrow? And they will be, without a doubt, because he who submits himself to tyranny desires it!).[27]

If we follow this thread as a guide through the labyrinth of Rizal's indictment of liberal revolution at the end of the nineteenth century, *El filibusterismo* underlines the abyss separating the Latin American (and Spanish) project of enlightened republicanism in the earlier part of the century from its disenchantment as it lapsed into the hypocrisy of late colonial rule. If Rizal set out in his first novel to fashion an aesthetic ideal and foundational fiction for the origins of an emergent Filipino nation, he ends his second novel with a profoundly anti-aesthetic gesture. That was the failure of the liberal American revolutions to definitively guarantee a model of self-government that would improve the state of the colony. Rizal's abandonment of this ideal in the short term bore bitter fruit: barely a generation after Rizal's death, Filipinos had already forgotten they were once a part of Latin America. As a fitting emblem of this distance, Rizal's novels are no longer read in Spanish.[28]

In *La expresión americana* José Lezama Lima describes the "terrifying complex of the American [mind]," which applies equally to José Rizal and José Martí: "This is the seed of the American's terrifying complex: believing that one's expression has not reached the level of form, but remains a difficult problem, in need of resolution."[29]

If we isolate Rizal's analysis and critique of Simón Bolívar's legacy, a number of points make a comparison and contrast with Martí's vision of "Nuestra América" fruitful for distinguishing the specificity of the anticolonial movements in the Philippines and Cuba at the end of the nineteenth century. Similar to Rizal, from the outset Martí's projection of the Cuban Revolution (now known as the War of Independence) took as its point of departure a reflection on the legacies of romantic revolution as the means to modern self-assertion and historical agency—the rights of the individual, the agency of the will, the universal legitimacy of the national republic as state. As Martí said elsewhere, "This is not the revolution of anger. It is the revolution of reflection."[30] Both men questioned the possibility of "importing" a model for democratic republicanism from outside the country, whether it meant Hispanization or Americanization for Rizal's character Simoun or the European and U.S. revolutions for Martí. These objections notwithstanding, however, both also recognized that disenchantment with both liberal and radical doctrines of revolution and democracy did not diminish the emancipatory potential of constituting a people who would possess the knowledge and legitimacy to govern themselves and no other. As we will see, it is significant that both writers drew on the figure of the Native American—and with it, the question of the American frontier—as the point of departure for developing their evaluations of the futures of their respective countries.

Are we looking, then, at merely a second-generation case of "imagining community"? Benedict Anderson's well-known reflections on the spread of modern nationalism in the Americas may serve as a point of departure for analyzing the peculiar character of Martí's Cuban nationalism and Latin Americanism, if only because their misapplication to the late-nineteenth-century Americas inadvertently underlines the conceptual foundations of Martí's America.[31] Focusing on the early cosmopolitanism of the North and South American Creoles as the basis for national movements, Anderson isolates the decisive influences in the shaping of the American revolutions. In doing so, he downplays the Spanish revolution against Napoleon in 1812 and the influence of Enlightenment ideas and chooses to emphasize instead the negatively derived "shared fatality of trans-Atlantic birth" that engendered a Creole consciousness.[32] In Anderson's account, the Creole—caught between his exclusion from the metropole and the fear of subaltern mobilization—drew from his bureaucratization under Spanish absolutism, along with the rise of newspapers, opportunities to develop his consciousness of a common connectedness with other Creole pioneers. In contrast, the "general development of capitalism and technology in the late eighteenth century and the 'local' backwardness of Spanish capitalism" led to the failure of Latin Americanism to construct a continental nation-state (or federation) in the nineteenth century.[33]

Doubtless this dialectical account of the coming to consciousness of Europe's "others" as the basis for a new identity, however idealized, applies when one regards a very general outline for Creole class consolidation (and its failure) in Bolívar's revolution. In the Philippines, too, one may argue that a perceived "peninsular Spanish envy" on the part of the Philippine-born Creoles accounted for Spanish fears of revolution throughout the nineteenth century.[34] Still, the implicit Hegelianism in Anderson's account omits a different model for understanding the national project in the Americas *after* the initial consolidation of the thirteen colonies, in which Martí's "Nuestra América" inscribes itself as successor and inheritor. It would be difficult to characterize this American "nation" in the terms Anderson sets forth — "imagined as limited and sovereign" — insofar as it is predicated on the imagination of unlimited expansion and the resulting deadlock between conflicting claims to national and cultural sovereignty. A cursory glance at the novels of James Fenimore Cooper, or Frederick Jackson Turner's "The Significance of the Frontier in American History" (1893), bears this thesis out. In these texts, one sees neither a negatively derived conception of "shared fatality of trans-Atlantic birth," nor the abstract recognition of "homogeneous empty time" fostered by the newspaper industry, the realist novel, increased travel and communications, and other agents of the secularizing process. In contrast, these texts dwell almost entirely on the sustained contact, negotiation, and conflict with that element designated as the frontier:

> Now, the frontier is the line of most rapid and effective Americanization. The wilderness masters the colonist. It finds him a European in dress, industries, tools, modes of travel, and thought. It takes him from the railroad car and puts him in the birch canoe. It strips off the garments of civilization and arrays him in the hunting shirt and the moccasin. It puts him in the log cabin of the Cherokee and Iroquois and runs an Indian palisade around him. Before long he has gone to planting Indian corn and plowing with a sharp stick; he shouts the war cry and takes the scalp in orthodox Indian fashion. In short, at the frontier the environment is at first too strong for the man. He must accept the conditions which it furnishes or perish, and so he fits himself into the Indian clearings and follows the Indian trails.
>
> Little by little he transforms the wilderness, but the outcome is not the old Europe, not simply the development of Germanic germs, anymore

than the first phenomenon was a case of reversion to the Germanic mark. The fact is, that here is a new product that is American.[35]

The frontier mutually and reciprocally redefines, sustains, and reconstitutes the conflicts and complicities between the agents of "civilization" and "barbarism" at the heart of any national imagining in the nineteenth century, whether such a nation extends from the conception of tribe, literate public sphere, civil society, confederation, or other form.

In these and other works, the constitution of a people exceeds and often opposes its representation in the state: if anything, the American frontier demands an ongoing practice of responding to the *absence* of a "limited and sovereign" community. Dependent to a large degree on the flows of immigration and slavery, the individuation of capital accumulation made possible by the expanding American frontier, and the counterassertion of autochthonous claims to territory and human dignity along the frontier or contact zone, any such assertion of national community always begins by unraveling at the seams.[36] Turner's "The Problem of the West" studies this problem: if the United States upholds any sense of nationhood or national community in the nineteenth century, it stems neither from the U.S. Constitution nor from the culture of the thirteen colonies that penned it. Rather, Americanism arises from the ebb and flow of two opposing forces: the projection of "infinite" expansion westward, with its ad hoc creation of rough democracy, lynch law, and the practical sense of securing one's immediate welfare on the frontier; and a corresponding amplification and reinsertion of those values developed in the West, into the eastern cities and into the very heart of the U.S. Constitution.[37] As Turner makes clear, the men of the western frontier even reach a point of challenging and usurping or transforming the Europeanized respect for the law and traditional institutions that define the early democratic republicanism of the United States. Not surprisingly, his shining examples are Andrew Jackson and Abraham Lincoln — men of the West who redefined the East by internalizing the experience of the frontier at the highest seat of executive power.

And in what may be considered the foundational text in the project to conceive a specifically Latin American literature, Domingo F. Sarmiento's *Facundo* — significantly subtitled *Civilización o barbarie* (Civilization or Barbarism) — Sarmiento makes a similar claim regarding the demise of the Argentine republic under the provincialism of its gaucho *caudillo*, or boss leaders. Sarmiento's compelling narrative, which predates and in many ways anticipates Turner's, describes the outlaw culture engendered by the Argentine pampa, embodied in ruthless figures like Facundo Quiroga, which gradually penetrated the institutions of the early republic to occupy the very seat of power under the populist dictator Juan Manuel Rosas (1835–52). Of course, Sarmiento freely associated his own reflections on the "barbarization of civilization" with the novels of James Fenimore Cooper; moreover, Sarmiento's excessive identification with the United States ("Let us be the United States!") remained an enduring theme in his life as president of the second Argentine republic and as a writer and statesman. The point, rather, is to illustrate Sarmiento's and Turner's admiration for, and fascination with, the transculturation and negotiation of cultural and colonial difference that formed the central element in the concept of the Americas. While both Sarmiento's and Turner's Americanism, like nationalism, undertook the task of constituting a people, both showed how "the people" was from the beginning itself a liminal concept, embodied in figures like Facundo and Natty Bumpo, the pioneering Yankee. These bastards of civilization create their respective nations through their contact with the frontier: a liminal experience that pushes the frontier back even as it incorporates or interiorizes its "barbaric" other in the reconstruction of the self.[38]

This detour into an admittedly general comparative sketch of an Americanism that Martí's "Nuestra América" attempts to historicize serves to highlight at least two aspects of Martí's unique approach to the anticipated revolution for independence in Cuba.[39] The first is that, unlike his contemporary José Rizal, Martí's revolution was predicated on not only the singular constitution of a Cuban people but also the singular modern history of *attempting* to constitute a people in the Americas, and a corresponding redemption of its failures in *both* North and South America. This is why (and this is the second point) whereas Rizal sees the exhaustion of a historical process without resolution or redemption, Martí understands the lack of resolution to be constitutive of the very concept of "Our America." The failed transcendence of Rizal's Simoun, then, must give way to an immanent reflection and modification of the idea of America, for the sake of America's very existence as an idea. I will elaborate on each of these two points briefly.

One of the central questions posed by "Nuestra América" is about the relationship between its two objects of critique. Martí devotes the greater part of his essay to the first, the collapse of Latin American republicanism, due to the inappropriate importation of foreign models of government for a singular Latin American nature and people:

La incapacidad no está en el país naciente, que pide formas que se le aco-
moden y grandeza útil, sino en los que quieren regir pueblos originales,
de composición singular y violenta, con leyes heredadas de cuatro siglos
de práctica libre en los Estados Unidos, de diecinueve siglos de monarquía
en Francia. . . . El gobierno ha de nacer del país. El espíritu del gobierno
ha de ser del país. La forma del gobierno ha de avenirse a la constitución
propia del pais.

[The incapacity lies not in the emerging country, which demands forms
that are appropriate to it and a greatness that is useful, but in the leaders
who try to rule unique nations, of a singular and violent composition, with
laws inherited from four centuries of free practice in the United States and
nineteen centuries of monarchy in France. . . . The government must be
born from the country. The spirit of the government must be the spirit of
the country. The form of the government must be in harmony with the
country's natural constitution.][40]

The second object of critique concerns the threat of U.S. economic and military expansion, which reappears in the Pan-American conferences to adjust the
silver standard of currency in Latin America to the gold standard in the United
States: "Es la hora próxima en que se le acerque, demandando relaciones ínti-
mas, un pueblo emprendedor y pujante que la desconoce y la desdeña" (The
hour is near when [our America] will be approached by an enterprising and
forceful nation that will demand intimate relations with her and yet does not
know her and disdains her). A number of times throughout the essay, Martí
disparages both the culture and government of the United States that supports
and propagates the policy of U.S. expansionism. For example, the reference to
"those who, under the protection of a criminal tradition, would tear the land
asunder and wrest it from the defeated brother" has often been ascribed to the
U.S. seizure of Mexican land in the 1848 Mexican-American War.[41] Elsewhere
Martí openly indicts North America for "drown[ing] its own Indians in blood
and . . . going from more to less!" and later cites North America's "vengeful and
sordid masses, [and] its tradition of conquest."[42]

Yet in recent scholarship, the careful pairing of "Nuestra América" with
Martí's decades-long career as a U.S. correspondent for newspapers in Mexico,
Venezuela, Argentina, and other Latin American countries illustrates that the
two objects of critique are in fact one.[43] Point for point, the future of Latin
America appears as the negative relief of the failures of democracy in North

America. Where North America has exterminated its Native American population, Latin America would have to depend on it: "Los gobernadores en las
repúblicas de indios, aprenden indio" (The rulers of Indian republics are learning *how to be Indian*).[44] Whereas the U.S. South had built its economy on slavery
and racial discrimination, Latin America would have to accept all races equally:
"Si la república no abre los brazos a todos y adelanta con todos, muere la república" (If the republic does not open its arms to all and include all in its
progress, it dies).[45] And whereas the prosperity of North America has prevailed
through its "unbridled passion and ambition," Martí announces a confederation of Latin American nations that are bound by love: "Cansados del odio
inútil, de la resistencia del libro contra la lanza, de la razón contra el cirial, de
la ciudad contra el campo . . . se empieza, como sin saberlo, a probar el amor"
(Weary of useless hatred, of the struggle of the book against the sword, reason
against the altar candle, city against countryside . . . we are beginning, almost
unknowingly, to try love).[46]

The second central question posed by "Nuestra América" is its "imagined
community." The insistent grammatical use of the present progressive in Martí's
text — "Le está naciendo a América, en estos tiempos reales, el hombre real"
(There is being born in America, in these real times, the real man) or "Se va
salvando América" (America is being saved) — conveys a testamentary quality
to "Nuestra América" whose relationship to the aesthetic imagination is ambiguous.[47] One can almost imagine Martí as a TV correspondent uttering the
words "right here and right now, history is being made," a history whose sin-
gularity defies aesthetic representation. On the one hand, then, instead of an
"imagined community," Martí never ceases to announce a community that has
yet to be imagined, or that cannot be imagined except in the day-to-day practice of criticizing the myopia of older imagined communities and "creating" a
form of government specific to the country's "natural elements." On the other
hand, the relentless devaluation in "Nuestra América" of past attempts at political representation aims to reestablish critique as being immanent in any project
of representation, political or aesthetic, as *precisely* the politics and aesthetics of "Our America." Martí's reflection on the history of Americanism, and
his (anti-) aesthetic expressionism, are therefore of a piece. In both, the emergent idea of Spanish American republicanism and the creation of a pan–Latin
American nation grows out of an ongoing reflection on, and affirmation of, a
form of knowledge that precedes and exceeds its representation. It is in this
affirmation of the outside that the flawed form of government breaks down

and makes certain, "impossible" forms of inclusion possible: in Martí's words, "absolute ideas, in order not to collapse over an error of form, must be expressed in relative forms."

The following example from "Nuestra América" illustrates the intersection between the republican legacy and the anti-aesthetic project:

> Estos países se salvarán, porque . . . le está naciendo, en estos tiempos reales, el hombre real.
>
> Éramos una vision, con el pecho de atleta, las manos de petrimetre y la frente del niño. Éramos una máscara, con los calzones de Inglaterra, el chaleco parisiense, el chaquetón de Norte América y la montera de España. El indio, mudo, nos daba vueltas alrededor, y se iba al monte . . . a bautizar sus hijos. El negro, oteado, cantaba en la noche la música de su corazón, sólo y desconocido, entre las olas y las fieras. El campesino, el creador, se revolvía, ciego de indignación, contra la ciudad desdeñosa, contra su criatura.
>
> [*These countries will be saved*, because . . . in these real times, *there is being born* in America the real man.
>
> *We were a vision*, with an athlete's breast, a dandy's hands, and a child's brow. We were dressed in costume, with shoes from England, a Parisian vest, a frock coat from North America, and a bicorn from Spain. The indio, mute, gave us a once-over and fled to the mountain . . . to baptize his children. The Negro, terrified, sang the music of his heart in the night, alone, unknown to all, between the waves and the wild. The field hand, the creator, turned his back, blind with indignation, on the disdainful city, on his creature.] [48]

Modern aesthetic transformation here does not begin or end with the assertion of racial synthesis or cultural identity. On the contrary, it reproduces in narrative the time of regression (*"These countries will be saved . . . there is being born. . . . We were a vision . . ."*) and allegorizes the decomposition of identity (represented by the mix-and-match of clothes from different countries). But when the parti-colored, disjointed image reflects, folds back on itself, sees itself not as a movement from the future to the past but rather from the past to the future (*"We were a vision . . . there is being born. . . . These countries will be saved . . ."*), the clothes come off, so to speak, and the "real man" announced by Martí steps forth. "Real," in this instance, refers to an event whose existence can be understood only in the present, that is, as a practice of subordinating the historical past and the aesthetic vision of the future to the needs and desires of a *possible* people, a possible community.

Walter Benjamin would call this image a dialectical one: it takes a variety of objects out of their original contexts and time periods and places them in sudden juxtaposition with one another. In a flash, the pageant of history is flattened into the "now of its recognisability. . . . The redemption which can be carried out in this way and in no other is always to be won out of the perception of that which is being irretrievably lost."[49] For an instant, moving backward and moving forward in time become identical. It is here that the remembrance of Bolívar's campaign, the melancholy contemplation of failed or perverted revolutions, and the future of Cuba coincide. And the fatal aspect of Martí's intellectual patrimony, the patrimony of what Martí calls "nuestras repúblicas dolorosas de América" (our sorrowful Latin American republics), is transformed into the critical practice of transforming the terms of patrimony itself.[50]

It is here that the question of Cuba's future caps the reversals of North and Latin American republicanism and serves as the keystone to a new politics and aesthetics. Indeed, one may go so far as to say that in order for questions of racial difference, the threat of U.S. annexation, and the history of past revolutions to be resolved in Martí's Cuba, Cuba *itself* would have to become the aesthetic answer to racial difference, U.S. imperialism, and Bolívar's legacy. In other words, the question of Cuba's political future became for Martí the aesthetic answer to the future of Latin America. The elusive aspect of Martí's Cuban nationalism is that the investment in its necessity comes not from Cuba itself but from "Our America" as it *might* or *ought to be*. How else can one explain Martí's otherwise delirious statement toward the end of his life, penned on the same day he signed the famous "Montechristi Manifesto" for Cuban independence: "The free Antilles will save the independence of our America and the presently compromised and deplorable honor of Anglo-Saxon America, and perhaps accelerate and fix the equilibrium of the world"?[51] If there was a future to democratic thought in the Americas, Martí saw the aesthetics of Cuban independence as the condition of its possibility. This aesthetic proceeds by ceaselessly performing its death to make possible the birth of politics.

In contrasting Rizal's and Martí's frames for evaluating Bolívar's republicanism, one can see that while Rizal emphasizes the need to acknowledge the closing of a historical epoch and its impossible application to the Philippines, Martí begins with the opposite premise: how can Cuba insert itself into a past of which it played no part, so as to transform that past into an ongoing redemptive narrative? "Nuestra América" was his solution. Cuba's most remarkable characteristic was thus not its past but its futurity: a virtual nation that would provide the opportunity to substantiate the lie Martí explicitly relates in "Nuestra América": "There is no conflict between races, because there are no races."

How specifically does this aesthetic anticipate a concrete political program? Such a question will continue to be a source of speculation and at times disaffection for readers of Rizal and Martí as the Philippines and Cuba entered a new era under the sway of U.S. domination. It is interesting to note, for example, that scholars in both Philippine and Latin American studies remain deeply divided on the use and abuse of Rizal and Martí as names and bodies of writing used to legitimate sometimes opposed ideologies.[52] For now, I simply want to contribute to a deeper understanding of how Rizal's and Martí's divergent ideas on revolution nevertheless betray a common concern regarding the relationship of aesthetics to the role of critique in the projection and institution of a postcolonial constitutional order.

When the Filipino national hero Rizal found the idea of romantic revolution to be at odds with the systematic task of teaching a heterogeneous and divided population how to foreclose the threat of postrevolutionary tyranny, he took the unpopular decision to turn against that aesthetic, condemning it as the mystification of a long-term problem. Perhaps it was this decision that contributed to the relegation of Rizal's novel to minor status as a Spanish and Latin American literary text. Minor literature is characterized not by the ethnic status of the writer but by the compromised autonomy of the aesthetic vision. In the end, the minor text must relinquish (one is tempted to say "defy") even its provisional (aesthetic) authority to transcend or surpass the historical circumstances that limit and define it, even as it embarks on a line of flight to ultimately sidestep or escape its negative interpellation.[53]

This judgment can also be applied to Martí, with the exception that he succeeds in demonstrating the "failure" of the liberal political and aesthetic project as a necessary part of the project itself. Without this lens of critical history, the genealogy of Americanism would be incapable of mitigating the catastrophic effects of an unbridled North American modernization. As later Cuban writers such as Alejo Carpentier, José Lezama Lima, and Roberto Fernández Retamar were to reaffirm, the postcolonial bastard can only move forward in time by moving simultaneously back, recollecting the glass shards of its broken beauty into a mosaic that subordinates the unity of the aesthetic vision to the dignity of the heterogeneous fragment. Such were the reflections of a late-nineteenth-century modernity from below as the juggernaut of a triumphant U.S. imperialism quickly rolled across the Pacific Ocean and southward to Central America, the Caribbean, and the Panama Canal in the early years of the twentieth century.

Notes

1   One can, of course, argue that the history of U.S. expansion across the continent itself set a precedent for overseas expansion. For a partial list of U.S. military interventions in other countries since 1890, see http://www.zmag.org/list2.htm.

2   For the best-known biographies on each of the national heroes, see Jorge Mañach, *José Martí, el Apostól* (1933; Havana: Editorial de Ciencias Sociales, 1990); and León Ma. Guerrero, *The First Filipino: a Biography of José Rizal* (Manila: National Historical Institute, 1963).

3   The question of U.s. hegemony appears in a variety of José Martí's correspondence to Latin American newspapers throughout the 1880s and 1890s, which fall under his proposed title for a collection of U.S. chronicles, *Escenas norteamericanas*; see *Obras completas*, vols. 9–12 (Havana: Editorial de las Ciencias Sociales, 1975) (hereafter cited as *OC*); as well as "La Conferencia Monetaria de las Repúblicas de América: La revista ilustrada, Nueva York may 1891," in *OC*, vol. 6, 157–72. For Rizal's reflections on the United States, see José Rizal, "Filipinas dentro de cien años" (part 4), in *La Solidaridad*, vol. 2 (Pasig City: Fundación Santiago, 1996), 30–39; and *Publicaciones de la Comisión Nacional del Centenario de José Rizal, Escritos de José Rizal*, vol. 1, *Diarios y memorias* (Manila: Comisión Nacional del Centenario de José Rizal, 1961), 226.

4   Eric Hobsbawm, *Nations and Nationalism since 1780: Program, Myth, Reality* (Cambridge: Cambridge University Press, 1990), 102.

5   Ibid.

6   This was reflected in the representation of Cuba and Puerto Rico in the Spanish Cortes after 1871, while the Philippines would have to wait to be admitted until 1893. By then, Rizal had already been exiled to the island of Dapitan for two years, in which time the revolutionary society, or Katipunan, led by Andres Bonfiacio, had begun to attract members.

7   See John Schumacher, *The Propaganda Movement, 1880–1895: The Creators of a Filipino Consciousness, the Makers of Revolution* (Quezon City: Ateneo de Manila University Press, n.d. [1972]), 51–53, 155.

8   Charles Morris, *Our Island Empire* (New York: R. H. Whitten, 1899), vi.

9   The point of departure for these observations is the work of Julio Ramos; see *Divergent Modernities of Latin America: Culture and Politics in the Nineteenth Century*, trans. John Blanco (Durham: Duke University Press, 2001). For a discussion of the

impact of North American modernity as a point of departure for mapping out the future(s) of Latin American identity, see the discussions of Domingo Faustino Sarmiento, Argentine writer and president of the republic, in Mary Louise Pratt, *Imperial Eyes: Travel Writing and Transculturation* (London: Routledge, 1992), 189–93.

10   José Antonio Saco, *Contra la anexión*, ed. Fernando Ortiz (Havana: S.A. Cultural, 1928).

11   Quoted in Ramos, *Divergent Modernities*, 150.

12   The following quotations of this essay are taken from José Martí, "Nuestra América," in *OC*, vol. 6, 15–23. An English translation of this essay appears as an appendix to Ramos, *Divergent Modernities*.

13   This is one of the main theses behind Angel Rama's sketch of the "politicized polis" at the end of the nineteenth century; see *La ciudad letrada* (Hanover: Ediciones del Norte, 1984), 105–33.

14   In juxtaposition to Martí's ethico-political concern over the question of national state consolidation in Cuba, José Enrique Rodó's "Ariel" and Darío's overtly political writings focused on the cultivation of a pan-Latinist cosmopolitan aesthetic, which saw the American continent as the very embodiment of the struggle between opposed linguistic and cultural identities. For Rodó, the Americas represented no less than the divergence between the inhumanity of gross materialism ("nordomanía") and the "impenetrable chamber" ("la estancia impenetrable") of aesthetic subjectivity and integrity or wholeness; see *Ariel: Liberalismo y jacobinismo* (1900; Mexico City: Editorial Porrúa, 1991), 15–16. With the triumph of the Mexican Revolution in 1910, Mexican minister of culture José Vasconcelos would echo Rodó's emphasis on the contemplation of aesthetic finality or integrity as both a defining characteristic of a redeemed "cosmic race" and the overcoming of contradictions brought about by Latin America's uneven reception of modern institutions. See *La raza cósmica* (1948; Mexico City: Espasa-Calpe Mexicana, 1992), esp. 37–53 (part 3).

15   See Efrén Rivera Ramos, "The Legal Construction of American Colonialism: The Insular Cases (1901–1922)," *Revista Jurídica Universidad de Puerto Rico* 65, no. 2 (1996): esp. 240–61.

16   See Schumacher, *Propaganda Movement*, 40–42.

17   Ibid., 42.

18   José Rizal, *Noli me tangere* (Madrid: Ediciones de Cultura Hispánica, 1992), 555. Unless otherwise noted, all translations from the Spanish are mine.

19   Nick Joaquin, "Why Was the Rizal Hero a Creole?" in *A Question of Heroes* (1977; Manila: National Bookstore, 1981).

20   Joaquin, *A Question of Heroes*, 73–74.

21   Ibid., 6, 8.

22   José Rizal, *El filibusterismo* (Manila: National Historical Society, 1993), 47.

23   W. E. B. Du Bois, *The Souls of Black Folk* (1903; New York: Signet Classic, 1995), 3.

24   A recent contribution to the debate on Rizal's position vis-à-vis the revolution is Floro Quibuyen's *A Nation Aborted: Rizal, American Hegemony, and Philippine Nationalism* (Quezon City: Ateneo de Manila University Press, 1999).

25   *Simón Bolívar: Escritos politicos* (Madrid: Alianza Editorial, 1979), 76.

26   Ranajit Guha, *Elementary Aspects of the Peasant Insurgency in Colonial India* (Delhi: Oxford University Press India, 1983); see in particular the chapter entitled "Reversals."

27   Rizal, *El filibusterismo*, 284.

28   See Benedict Anderson, "Hard to Imagine?" in *The Spectre of Comparisons* (London: Verso, 1998), 235–62. Since the passing of the Rizal bill in 1946, Rizal's novels are mandatory reading in secondary education. In accordance with the dual lingua franca of English and "Filipino" promulgated in the post-Commonwealth (1936) constitution, the novels are taught in English and Tagalog. For a summary of the lingua franca in the Philippines, see Romeo V. Cruz, "Ang Nasyonalismo at Wika," in *Mga Piling Diskurso sa Wika at Lipunan*, ed. Pamela C. Constantino and Monico M. Atienza (Quezon City: University of the Philippines Press, 1996), 3–9.

29   José Lezama Lima, *La expresión americana* (Madrid: Alianza Editorial, 1969), 27.

30   Martí, *OC*, vol. 3, 107.

31   Benedict Anderson, *Imagined Communities: Reflections on the Origin and Spread of Nationalism* (London: Verso, 1991), esp. 47–65, 80–82.

32   Ibid., 57–58, 63.

33   Ibid., 63.

34   Two important examples of this thought can be found in Manuel Pizarro's account of the state of the colony in 1812. See "State of the Philippines in 1810," in *The Philippine Islands*, ed. Emma Blair and James Robertson, vol. 51 (Cleveland: Arthur Clarke, 1907); and Sinibaldo de Mas, *Informe secreto de Sinibaldo de Mas* (Manila: Historical Conservation Society, 1963), 17–27.

35   Frederick Jackson Turner, "The Significance of the Frontier in American History" in *The Frontier in American History* (1893; New York: Dover, 1996); see http://xroads.virginia.edu/~hyper/turner/ (accessed on 29 September 2006).

36   Indeed, one may extend this critique to all countries with a colonial history. In different ways, Homi Bhabha, Partha Chatterjee, and Carol Hau have underlined this perpetually "unfinished" character of the nation. See Bhabha, "DissemiNation: Time, Narrative, Etc.," in *Nation and Narration* (London: Routledge, 1990), 290–322; Chatterjee, "Whose Imagined Community?" in *The Nation and Its Fragments* (Princeton: Princeton University Press, 1993), 3–13; and Hau, *Necessary Fictions: Philippine Literature and the Nation, 1946–1980* (Quezon City: Ateneo de Manila University Press, 2000).

37   Turner, "The Problem of the West," in *The Frontier in American History*, chap. 7. One may argue that the highly interpretive, perhaps "Western" (re)reading of the Constitution allowed for hybrid categories, such as the doctrine of territorial incorporation, to reconcile and account for the contradictions between imperial conquest and the prohibition against "taxation without representation."

38   See Ricardo Piglia, "Notas sobre Facundo," *Punto de Vista* 3, no. 8 (1980).

39   It is important to highlight the continental stretch of Martí's reading public: in his career as a journalist, he wrote in English and Spanish for both North and South

American newspapers, often underlining his liminal position with respect to both reading publics to authenticate his unique interpretation of events. For a discussion of this strategy, see Julio Ramos's analysis of Martí's chronicle "Coney Island," in *Divergent Modernities*, 210–13. An English translation of Martí's essay appears as appendix 3 to the volume.

40   Martí, *OC*, vol. 6, 16–17.

41   Ibid., 15.

42   Ibid., 16, 21.

43   See Susanna Rotker, *The American Chronicles of José Martí: Journalism and Modernity in Spanish America*, trans. Jennifer French and Katherine Semler (Hanover, N.H.: University Press of New England, 2000).

44   Martí, *OC*, vol. 6, 21.

45   Ibid., 20.

46   Ibid.

47   Ibid.

48   Ibid. (italics mine).

49   Walter Benjamin, "Central Park," *New German Critique* 34 (winter 1985). Like Benjamin, Martí's allegorical impulse reflected his perception of modernity as a perpetual state of emergency or exception, which undermined the very possibility of democratic republicanism, on the one hand, and aesthetic representation, on the other. The signature essay that reflects Martí's recourse to allegory as a self-effacing, self-dismantling aesthetic is his "Prólogo al Poema del Niágara" (translated as "Prologue to the Poema del Niágara," in Ramos, *Divergent Modernities*, appendix 2).

50   Martí, *OC*, vol. 6, 18.

51   José Martí, "Carta a Federico Martínez Carvajal," in *Sus mejores páginas* (Mexico City: Editorial Porrúa, 1985), 74.

52   In the case of Rizal, Renato Constantino's critique of Rizal as a useful tool for U.S. imperialism at the turn of the century still generates controversy in present scholarship. See "Veneration without Understanding," in *Dissent and Counter-Consciousness* (Manila: Renato Constantino, 1970), 125–45;, Nick Joaquin, *A Question of Heroes*, 73–74; and Floro Quibuyen, *A Nation Aborted: Rizal, American Hegemony, and Philippine Nationalism* (Quezon City: Ateneo de Manila University Press, 1999). In the case of Martí, Cuban president Fidel Castro's invocation of Martí as the father of the Cuban Revolution is well known; less known is Angel Rama's critique of Latin Americanism as an ideology that served to further marginalize oppressed and unrepresented sectors of the continent's population from political life. See Fidel Castro, quoted in Ramón Eduardo Ruíz, *Cuba: The Making of a Revolution* (New York: W. W. Norton, 1970), 58; and Angel Rama, *La ciudad letrada*, 125.

53   The basis for these reflections is Gilles Deleuze and Félix Guattari's discussion of "major" and "minor" uses of language in *A Thousand Plateaus*, trans. Brian Massumi (Minneapolis: University of Minnesota Press, 1982), 105–6.

Confederate Cuba

Caroline Levander

"At a time when the U.S. faces very real terrorist threats in the Middle East and elsewhere, the administration's absurd and increasingly bizarre obsession with Cuba is more than just a shame, it's a dangerous diversion from reality." So says Senator Max Baucus, Democrat of Montana and ranking member of the Finance Committee, in response to the Bush administration's use of military aircraft to help American broadcasters reach Cuba and the increase of money for Cuban critics of Fidel Castro's government.[1] Despite its recent resurgence in U.S. international policy, this "bizarre obsession" with Cuba is not new but has a history of almost two hundred years. Charting such a history, I want to suggest, not only reframes familiar accounts of U.S. national involvement with Cuba that tend to see the legal institution of the 1902 Platt Amendment as an affirmation and extension of U.S. democratic ideals, but just as importantly delineates Cuba's ongoing, current imaginative significance for a nation intent on using the threat of terrorism to justify the increase of international dominance unsanctioned by nongovernmental organizations. By focusing on Cuba's constitutive importance to nineteenth-century U.S. expansionism, this essay uncovers new motivations, meanings, and dynamics behind American intervention in Cuba; develops new avenues for linking the history of race with the history of empire; and suggests new ways of thinking about the recent increase in U.S. imperial activity. To excavate the mutual interdependencies that have long shaped domestic policies within the United States and foreign policies in Cuba, I will assess, first, how U.S. regions that were resistant to northern abolition, like the South, turned to Cuba to enact a program of insurgent white supremacy; second, how Cuba's struggle for national independence articulated an opposing vision of an antiracist nation that was threatening to the racial politics driving both the antebellum South and legal decisions like *Dred Scott v. Sanford* (1857) and the postbellum United States and legal decisions like *Plessy v. Ferguson* (1896); and, third, how Cuban debates about race filtered north—how, in other words, black Americans critiqued U.S. policies in Cuba that, they recognized, reproduced and justified the U.S. federal policies underpinning the rise of race hate in the postbellum South.[2] Immanuel Wallerstein has argued that the emergence of the modern capitalist world system created "a new peripheral region" that stretches from "northeast Brazil to Maryland." By bringing Cuba's relation to the Confederacy into focus, I hope to place the South in a hemispheric context that complicates rather than flattens its northern as well as southernmost borders. Furthermore, analyzing the interplay between the South as the center of U.S. domestic racial policies and Cuba as the locus of the nation's emerging imperial logic puts pressure on the boundary separating the foreign and the domestic, revealing their mutual, constitutive dependencies—dependencies all too often obscured by the rise of U.S. imperialism in the twentieth century.[3]

In excavating the United States' rich ongoing dialogue with Cuba both before and after World War II, I want to suggest that Cuba disrupts as well as enables national fantasies of imperial mastery that, as George W. Bush reminds us, remain alive and well. While there have been significant changes in the nature of U.S. foreign policy over the last hundred years, this analysis emphasizes points of continuity rather than rupture. By reaching back before the Cold War to consider Cuba's political importance to the United States, we can see that the enduring obsession of the United States with Castro is not only a sign of the Cold War's ongoing relevance in a post-1989 U.S. imaginary,[4] but also the most recent occasion of Cuba's protracted importance in U.S. national culture.[5] In other words, if U.S. intervention in Cuba has traditionally been viewed as one of the events that signaled the emergence of the United States on the world stage, Cuba's reemerging significance at times of U.S. imperial aggression and instability suggests the necessity of putting Cuba, rather than the United States, at the center of American cultural and political analysis. Doing so shows us not only the United States' historical impact on Cuba but, conversely, Cuba's crucial transnational impact on U.S. culture—be it Confederate pro-slavery culture or the African American intellectual culture of W. E. B. Du Bois and other African American men of letters. An examination of the long history and ongoing conceptual centrality of Cuba's racial politics to the smooth functioning of the U.S. imperial machinery, therefore, reveals the founding importance of racial inequality to the logic that naturalizes and therefore enables the United States to export its idea of freedom and liberty worldwide.

Daring Ambitions

"Cuba is the great western slave mart of the world—the great channel through which slaves are imported annually into the United States," Martin Delany wrote in 1849.[6] Delany's observation was echoed by many others in the antebellum period, particularly those, like Frederick Douglass, who were concerned about the increasing power of the U.S. slaveholding constituency in Washington. Indeed, Douglass expressed grave concern that "the slaveholding part" of the United States desired to annex Cuba to increase the South's representative power in the White House.[7]

I begin my analysis by taking seriously Delany's and Douglass's recognition of Cuba's centrality to U.S. southern slave states. Approaching the U.S. South not from the usual vantage point of its relation with the increasingly abolitionist states to the north but from the vantage point of the South's dependence on the slaveholding regions to its own south reveals the Confederacy's location within, and dependency on, a hemispheric framework—a framework that elucidates the complex interdependencies existing between slaveholding Spanish American nations like Cuba and the United States. While scholars have examined the history of slave institutions and slave rebellions in the United States and in Cuba and Brazil, there has been scant comparative work that approaches these institutions as interlocking and mutually constituting phenomena. Such a hemispheric approach reveals that U.S. abolition and emancipation are the outgrowth not only of national but also of hemispheric cultural and literary forces that reach across national boundaries to shape pro- and antislavery literature. Moreover, such an approach elucidates how an alternative if short-lived nation like the Confederacy displaced onto outlying geographic regions like Cuba its own unique position within the United States. Just as the freedom and liberty of the new United States were predicated on a simultaneous opposition to, and ownership of, the U.S. South, so too was the Confederacy's goal of assuming a "separate and equal" national status dependent on colonizing southern slave-holding territories like Cuba—territories that had their own multivalent histories of colonization. Locating within these hemispheric dimensions writings on the U.S. South—be it the writings of Frederick Douglass and Martin Delany or of southern apologists like Lucy Holcombe Pickens and Loreta Velazquez—therefore reveals the complex and protracted interchange between American nations about slavery, reframing our understanding of U.S. slave literature by showing it to be the outgrowth not only of black-white, U.S. North–South conflicts but also of a series of mutually constituting hierarchies involving *criollos*, mestizos, and Negroes across the hemisphere.

As nineteenth-century political commentators consistently noted, Cuba was the target not only of turn-of-the-century U.S. imperial outreach but, earlier in the century, of southern leaders' plan to "found a gigantic tropical slave empire" that would outstrip and finally conquer the "free republic" to the north.[8] As such, Cuba aligns U.S. imperialism with southern separatism, revealing a complex, and often occluded, history of intervening sectional, regional, and national interests underpinning U.S.-Cuban relations throughout the nineteenth century. Indeed, the term "manifest destiny" was used, as Oliver Morton recalls, to describe not only U.S. westward expansion but also the "daring ambition" of southern leaders, writers, adventurers, and filibusters to "liberate" Cuba from its "despotic oppressor," Spain.[9] As the prominent nineteenth-century political economist J. E. Cairnes argued, the "Southern party since 1820 had as its leading idea, its paramount aim, almost its single purpose . . . to extend slavery, and to achieve power by extending it."[10] In his 1862 lecture "The Revolution in America," Cairnes therefore contended that "the Seminole War, the annexation of Texas, the war with Mexico, and the filibustering attempts on Cuba and Central America over the previous half-century were all about Southern aggression." John Stuart Mill agreed with Cairnes that the U.S. South's increasing dual commitments to separatism and expansionism were the direct result of "American slavery [which] depended on a perpetual extension of its field and must go on barbarizing the world more and more" if it were to survive. "Set[ting] themselves up, in defiance of the rest of the world, to do the devil's work," the South needed to expand if it wanted to flourish as an independent agricultural entity, and so it must necessarily "propagate [its] national faith at the rifle's mouth in Mexico, Central America, and Cuba" were it to succeed in forming an separate nation.[11] Modeled on the Republic of Texas's territorial aggression, this essentially separate South, in the minds of political philosophers from Mill to Cairnes to Frederick Law Olmsted, was therefore led by southern slave owners who, as Olmsted contended, explicitly "wished to expand their holdings." "Moved by romantic excitements and enthusiasm" and "inflamed by senseless appeals to their patriotism and their combativeness," these southern slave owners specifically targeted slaveholding territories outside their sphere, such as Cuba, because in "annexing Cuba they might secure larger estates and make use of much cheaper [Cuban] land and labor."[12]

Declaring that the goal of antebellum southern filibustering expeditions to Cuba was not only to acquire more land and "to conquer the Spaniard" but to give Cuba the liberty and freedom that only the South could truly represent and defend, the southern novelist Lucy Holcombe Pickens advocated for an imperial South by identifying Cuba as the South's own "southern territory."[13] Recognizing Cuba as "the fairest child of southern waters," Pickens asserted in *The Free Flag of Cuba* (1854) that all true "sons of Washington" were obligated to "liberate the degraded children of tyranny" from Cuba's "despotic oppressor"—Spain (60). Declaring that the goal of Narciso López's 1851 filibustering expedition to Cuba was to give "the bright child of the waves" the liberty that only the South could truly represent and defend, Pickens—like those from Louisiana, Mississippi, Texas, and Florida who created the Order of the Lone Star and mounted a "Lone Star Expedition" to invade Cuba—advocated for an imperial South by relying on the racial logic that the North seemed to be abandoning with its commitment to abolition. "Free[ing] the beauteous child" from the "dark oppressors" who made "so many *slaves*" of their subjects (124), according to Pickens, would bestow "the greatest amount of good to our race" and to the young southern nation that supposedly embodied, upheld, and extended it (117–18). In so doing, Pickens's fictional account of López's expedition to Cuba revealed the South to be an ambitious imperial enterprise that imagined, and often undertook, a series of expansionist projects aimed at proving its racial superiority by absorbing new territory. As these accounts of a rival Confederate nation remind us, the idea of manifest destiny was a hotly contested right, facilitating not only the expansion of the United States but the creation of other young nations, like the Confederacy, that attempted to lay successful claim to the expansionist agenda too often associated exclusively with the United States.

The "vast populous empire" that Pickens predicted the South would establish in "South America and Mexico" became the joint project of a number of southern writers, adventurers, and filibusters before, during, and after the Civil War, who, like Pickens, argued for expansionist undertakings such as creating the 1854 Republic of Sonora, founding a "Universal Republic" with the Confederacy as capital, and invading Cuba.[14] A minority of southerners, such as W. Gilmore Simms, believed that "bringing the State of Cuba" under the control of "the people of our Southern States" while separating from the United States was a mistake, and that there would "be time enough to think of adding Cuba to our domain when we ourselves are rendered secure . . . from the perpetual annoyance of abolition."[15] However, most southerners believed that Cuba offered an enticing opportunity for wealth, territory, and influence. As Samuel Walker argued in his 1854 article "Cuba and the South," "the question of Cuba . . . is of momentous import to the people of this Union . . . and to the South."[16] Arguing for the need to "acquire Cuba as we acquired Texas," Walker contended that "the safety of the South is to be found only in the extension of its peculiar institutions, and the security of the Union in the safety of the South — toward the equator." "The great beauty of our system of governance," according to Walker, "is in its power of expansion," and Cuba was a "southern question demanding the consideration of the people of the south and south-west" precisely because the people "of the north are antagonistic to the institution of slavery" (3). Once "assimilated to our own in their government, what a splendid prospect of commercial eminence opens to the South!" Walker concluded. Thus according to southern separatists like Walker and Evans, the Confederacy not only constituted a separate nation that upheld the white supremacy threatened by U.S. abolitionist zeal, but also testified to its national vitality and promise by undertaking to expand its domain to include a Cuba that was being threatened by British abolitionists much like the U.S. South was being threatened by U.S. antislavery advocates. Indeed, after the abolition of the slave trade in the British empire, Cuba became the primary location where the Atlantic slave trade continued on a large scale, and therefore Cuba became a beleaguered fortress where white planters attempted to protect slavery from British abolitionists who went to Cuba to superintend new slave policy.

Not only did the Confederacy look South to Cuba to expand its influence, but many slave-owning Cubans, conversely, aligned themselves with the Confederacy in their efforts to uphold slavery in the face of British opposition. As the subtitle of her 1876 Civil War narrative stipulates, Loreta Janeta Velazquez identifies herself as both a "Cuban woman and a Confederate soldier."[17] Throughout her account of her experiences as a Cuban resident and then a cross-dressing Confederate soldier, Velazquez reiterates that she is "a Cuban and a true Southern sympathizer" (502). Her movement between Cuba and the Confederacy throughout the narrative reinforces her desire to imagine an independent Cuba aligned with an independent South. Velazquez and Cuban members of groups such as the Club de la Habana, who actively pursued Cuban annexation to the United States, hoped that such an alliance would create a new transnational southern slaveocracy in which the Confederacy and Cuba would jointly maintain a colonial fantasy of white privilege through black slave labor.[18]

Yet not all Cubans applauded Cuba's and the Confederacy's joint commitment to upholding slavery. Widely recognized as "the most perfect picture of Cuban slavery that has ever been given to the world," Juan Francisco Manzano's "Life and Poems of a Cuban Slave" was written at the request of the British abolitionist Richard Madden, who arrived in Cuba in 1835 as superintendent of liberated Africans and was identified by the Cuban slaveholding elite as a person "whose opinions and conduct were dangerous to the safety of the island of Cuba" because of his efforts to press for an end to slavery in Cuba.[19] The only extant Spanish American slave narrative, Manzano's text determined the direction in which Cuban antislavery commentary would unfold. Madden translated the text into English and included it in the antislavery portfolio that he presented to the General Anti-slavery Convention in Britain. This portfolio of Cuban slavery in general and Manzano's text in particular led the 1840 convention to adopt a formal resolution stating that because "the literature of Great Britain exercises so vast an influence over the public opinion of America, British abolitionist periodicals must spread before the American public evidence of the deep indignation of the civilized world against the slaveholding republic."[20] The circulation of Manzano's slave narrative through Cuba, to Great Britain, and finally to the United States points to the complex routes that abolitionist literature traveled and to the intricate transnational influences informing, but too often overlooked in, U.S. slave narrative. Indeed, there are a number of striking similarities between Manzano's 1840 narrative and North American slave narratives like Douglass's 1845 *Narrative of the Life of Frederick Douglass* — similarities that collectively point to the importance of Cuba in shaping the antislavery as well as pro-slavery narratives produced in the United States in the years leading up to the Civil War.[21]

Fifty years later, as the United States undertook control of Cuba in the Spanish-American War, U.S. political commentators would return to the antebellum South's expansionist project in Cuba to deny U.S. imperialist designs on Spanish territory. Murat Halstead's *The Story of Cuba* (1898), for example, asserted that "the ill-fated López expedition . . . was of course in the interest of the formation of more Slave States in the United States" and stated conclusively that the "Cuban filibustering expeditions of a former generation . . . were distinctly to provide for the admission of more Slave States in the American Union."[22] Precisely because they were associated with the South, such imperialist interests had no relation to "the true feelings of the American people and the real state of affairs in the American Union" when war with Spain finally did occur, according to Italo Canini.[23] Because "the general condition of things in the United States is very different from what it had been at the time of the expeditions of López and during the period which immediately followed it," Canini asserted that "the sympathy which the people of the American Union feel for the cause of Cuban liberty is purified from suspicious motives and influences" (109). Indeed, if Cuba had initially been "an object of dread" for the United States because of slavery, "it became at a later period an object of vehement desire" (75), because the United States could no longer "be accused of having gone into this war for want of more territory" (191). "The questions of Annexation, Expansion, and Imperialism," were therefore not part of the U.S. agenda, according to T. G. Steward, as it "launched forces to drive Spain" out of Cuba.[24] Supposedly purified of the self-interested motives that characterized southern efforts to acquire Cuba, the United States was not engaged in "a war of conquest" but merely recognized in Cuba's fight against Spain "the same genius which prompted the thirteen infant colonies to declare themselves free from the mother country."[25] Such declarations of the United States' similarity to Cuba, on the one hand, and its dissimilarity to the antebellum South, on the other, worked to sanitize U.S. imperial designs on Cuba—designs that, as we will see, used racial logic to attempt to make "the lone star of Cuba" "find its place" in "our national emblem" (191).

Cuba Libre

Even as the Confederacy tried to incorporate Cuba as part of its slaveholding territory and the United States tried to distance itself from the southern project to justify its own expansionist designs on Cuba, Cuban revolutionaries sought to create an independent nation founded on antiracism. Between 1776 and 1825, as most of the colonies of North and South America gained independence, Cuba remained loyal to Spain. However, by 1868 Spanish rule had become sufficiently constricting that a handful of prosperous white men struck for independence by freeing their slaves, placing free men of color in local positions of authority, making former slaves soldiers, and calling all black men citizens. Indeed, the three rebellions leading up to circumscribed Cuban independence—the Ten Years' War (1868–78), La Guerra Chiquita (1879–80), and the War of Independence (1895–98)—were all waged by an army that was unique in the history of the Atlantic world because it not only was multiracial but integrated at all ranks. If an integrated army was one cornerstone of the revolution, the other was a powerful rhetoric of antiracism that became more pronounced in the years between the legal end of slavery in 1886 and the outbreak of the third and final war of 1895.

In essays, speeches, newspapers, and memoirs, white as well as nonwhite Cubans consistently claimed that the struggle against Spain had produced a new kind of citizen and a new kind of state. Arguing that war had forever united black and white, they imagined a new nation in which equality was ingrained and thus, as the mulatto general Antonio Maceo wrote, there were "no whites nor blacks, but only Cubans."[26] Leaders such as José Martí, Juan Gualberto Gómez, and Rafael Serra y Montalvo wrote of the union of blacks and whites in anticolonial war and located the symbolic and material birth of the new nation in the alliance between black and white men. Gómez and Maceo were "generals honored and loved" by the insurgents, according to T. G. Steward of the Twenty-fifth U.S. Infantry, because their fully integrated armies "experienced no color difficulties."[27] By declaring that there were no races, integrating their forces, and asserting that racism was an infraction against the nation as a whole, they refuted Spanish assertions that Cuban nationhood was impossible because of the insurgents' racial identity. As General Maceo wrote on May 16, 1876, to Tomás Estrada Palma, president of the rebel republic: "This democratic Republic, which has established as its principle foundation liberty, equality, and fraternity, does not recognize racial hierarchies."[28] Stating that "all inhabitants of the Republic [were] entirely free [and] all citizens of the republic [would be] considered soldiers of the Liberation Army," Article 25 of the 1868 decree on abolition caused slaves to join the Cuban forces by the thousands. As one observer noted, they "marched in companies giving cries of long live Liberty and the whites of Cuba, who only yesterday had governed them with the harshness of the whip and who today treat them as brothers and grant them the title of free men."[29] Rebel propaganda likewise declared that "all men are our brothers, whatever color their skin, whatever their race. . . . Liberty for all men, of all races, of all peoples, in all climates!"[30] A December 1869 rebel periodical similarly proclaimed that "every Cuban (white or black for we are all equal) . . . everyone without distinctions of color . . . can serve . . . their Patria and Liberty." One rebel handbill directed at black manual laborers succinctly summed up the role that race played in founding the Cuban nation as follows: "The blacks are the same as the whites. . . . The Cubans want the blacks to be free. The Spaniards want the blacks to continue being slaves. The Cubans are fighting the Spaniards. The blacks who have any honor should go fight together with the Cubans. . . . Long live liberty!"[31] These claims were substantiated by daily interactions between blacks and whites, as Murat Halstead observed when he described "Negro soldiers on guard" and "black workingmen . . . quickly admitted" into the highest echelons of Cuban rebel leadership.[32] Thus General Weyler's declaration that his policy toward blacks was "just the same as to others" and his decision to constitute his cavalry escort of black men reflected the extent to which he "esteemed them as soldiers" (110).

Yet in the writings of José Martí and black insurgents like Ricardo Batrell Oviedo, we can most clearly see the foundational importance of the ideal of racelessness to Cuban independent nationhood. Professing that race was merely a tool used locally to divide the anticolonial effort and globally by men who invented "textbook races" to justify expansion and empire, Martí concluded that "to dwell on the divisions of race, the differences of race . . . [was] to hamper the public good."[33] For Martí, the Ten Years' War exemplified a Cuban history in which "the Cubans rose up in war, . . . broke the shackles of their slaves; [and] converted, at the cost of their lives, [a] Spanish indignity into a nation of free men." As a result, "blacks and whites became brothers . . . facing death, barefoot all and naked all, blacks and whites became equal: they embraced and have not separated since . . . the souls of whites and blacks [rise] together through the skies."[34] "There will never be a race war in Cuba," according to Martí, because the Cuban Revolution "returned the black race to humanity, and made the dreadful fact [of slavery] disappear"—by giving "life to the black man of Cuba, she was the one that lifted the black man from his ignominy and embraced him—she, the Cuban revolution."[35] This utopian vision of an explicitly antiracist Cuban nationalism had a profound influence on independence efforts because, as Salah Hassan has pointed out, Martí's political rhetoric captured the political and cultural forces driving an increasingly modern Cuban populace in the 1880s.[36] Ricardo Batrell Oviedo's memoir reflected the power of Martí's political vision even as it seemed to bear out Martí's predictions that an antiracist Cuban republic was being born. The black insurgent recalled seeing two soldiers alternately carrying each other across a battlefield as each needed aid. This spectacle of black and white brotherhood, for Oviedo, epitomized "democracy, with all its beautiful attributes . . . there existed 'human reciprocity' — a reciprocity that all civilized peoples, nations, and men struggle to attain." Representing the spirit of "the true 'Cuban people' " where there were "no races," such an idealized image offered a powerful motive not only for Oviedo but for all Cuban revolutionaries to try to realize this model nation for which they fought.[37]

The Color Line

As we have seen, Cuba's rebel leaders denied the existence of race, and a powerful multiracial army waged anticolonial war, but their independence efforts coincided with an international rise in racism and accelerating imperialism. Therefore if W. E. B. Du Bois's declaration that the "problem of the twentieth century [would be] the problem of the color line" finally proved more accurate than Martí's prediction that "this is not the century of struggle of races but rather the century of the affirmation of rights,"[38] it was partially the result of the United States' destruction of a conceptually powerful if unrealized vision of an antiracial and anticolonial Cuban nation. Cuban rebels fought to create a raceless nation in the fifty-year period that began with southern affirmation of racial inequality; but because they encountered European and North American thinking that linked biology to progress and divided the world into superior and inferior races, American involvement in Cuba worked to uphold and extend U.S. racial principles, rather than the idea of racelessness at the center of the Cuban Revolution. Once a movement that was explicitly anticolonial, antislavery, and antiracist came under the influence of a nation then inventing Jim Crow segregation and acquiring a far-flung empire, U.S. soldiers, officers, journalists, and cartoonists propagated images of Cuba as a land of inferior indigenous racial others in order to assert the superiority of whites to rule. As General William Shafter declared in disgust when asked about Cubans' capacity for independent nationhood: "Self-government! Why these people are no more fit for self-government than gunpowder is for hell."[39] Therefore, just as Spanish leaders like provincial governor Camilo Polavieja had tried to make the rebellion imitate their interpretation of it, declaring that "we must remove all white characteristics from the rebellion and reduce it to the colored element, that way it will count on less support and sympathy,"[40] so too did U.S. forces shape Cuban independence efforts to conform with the racial contours of U.S. imperial logic, despite the fact that, as Halstead observed, "the black rebels were among the bravest of the fighters for freedom."[41] Insurgent leaders like General Calixto García unsuccessfully attempted to refute these rewritings of Cuban insurgency by reminding U.S. leaders that "my ragged, hungry soldiers have endured with the resolute sincerity of the American of Saratoga or Yorktown" the hardships of war and therefore deserve to be treated not as "a conquered people" but as "partners in the struggle for independence."[42] However, despite the protestations made by leaders of U.S. occupying forces like Leonard Wood that the United States was "giving the Cubans every chance to show what is in them, in order that they either demonstrate their fitness or their unfitness for self-government," once the United States defeated Spain, American officers "prohibited Cuban soldiers from entering the city that many of them had been born in and at the capitulation the Cubans were not represented, despite the aid they had gratuitously given" to the capture of Santiago.[43]

Although this exclusion, according to one Cuban, made soldiers "feel as the patriots under Washington would have felt had the allied armies captured New York, and the French prohibited the entry of the American and their flag," U.S. commitment to racial inequality shaped rebuilding efforts that drew on the "native white population," as Horace Fisher observed, to establish an "orderly government."[44] Distinguishing "our own American nation," which, according to Italo Canini, was composed of "the positive, practical and daring spirit of the Anglo-Saxon," from Cuba, which combined Spanish blood with "large infusions of the blood of an ignorant and inferior race of the negro," was central to the creation of such a government.[45] Influenced by political commentary that invoked white supremacy to argue for U.S. superiority, Theodore Roosevelt not only read The Superiority of the Anglo-Saxons on his way to Cuba but subsequently described how Edmond Demolins's account of "the reasons why the English-speaking peoples are superior" influenced his attitude toward the Cuban population as a whole.[46] The racial difference between the United States and Cuba proved for Roosevelt and other Anglo-Americans that Cuba could never "attain true liberty and establish sound and lasting republican institutions," because "license and anarchy, not true liberty, is the state of things" in "the countries of Central and South America, which can hardly be called Republics but rather caricatures of a Republic."[47] By relying on the "Spanish race," which exhibited "an individual initiative equal to our own," rather than the Cubans who had helped wrest Cuba from Spain's control, U.S. administrators planned to form a government in Cuba that would subordinate "the mixed and colored races" to the "great races" (50).

"A Policy of Honesty in Cuba"

As we have seen, U.S. involvement in Cuba deployed the same imperial racism that the United States identified solely with the Confederacy, but some advocates of Cuban intervention argued that black U.S. soldiers in Cuba would play a key role in overcoming southern racism at home. Indeed, the writers of *Under Fire with the 10th U.S. Cavalry: A Purely Military History of the Negro* (1899) found in Cuba a powerful refutation of late-century southern racism. Black soldiers being transported to Cuba were the recipients of the benevolent "patriotism displayed by the liberty loving people of this country" until they reached "the South, where cool receptions told the tale of race prejudice even though these brave men were rushing to . . . defend the flag."[48] However, the authors predicted that "the same strong spirit and quickened conscience which took up the cause of Cuba will surely secure justice to the American Negro" (47). In their account of U.S. involvement in Cuba, "white regiments, black regiments, regulars and Rough Riders, representing the young manhood of the North and the South, fought shoulder to shoulder, unmindful of race or color, unmindful of whether commanded by an ex-Confederate or not, and mindful only of their common duty as Americans" (208). Declaring that "there was no North, no South, no black, no white . . . we were at once a compact national force," many soldiers agreed that "both white and colored soldiers had a brotherly affection for each other while on the way to Cuba, in Cuba and on our way back to the U.S.," but some black soldiers wondered "why can't it be so at home?" (49). Yet through their military action in Cuba, according to President McKinley, African Americans were going far toward justifying Lincoln's liberation of the black race for those who remain unconvinced of the black man's patriotism: "If any vindication of that act was needed, it was found when these brave black men ascended the hill of San Juan, Cuba, . . . vindicated their own title to liberty on that field and . . . gave the priceless fight of liberty to another suffering race." The authors agreed that "it was in the memorable siege of Santiago and the never to be forgotten charge up San Juan Hill that [the black soldier] challenged the admiration of the American people and solicited the tumultuous applause of every liberty loving nation throughout the civilized world" (270). A few newspaper men and black activists even argued that "the timeliness and importance of this Afro-American military colonization of Cuba" had the potential to reshape U.S. race relations in the South. "If Cuba becomes a state of the American union," according to the *Springfield Republican* (September 7, 1900), "then no better place could be found in which to assert and establish the principles of free government."[49] "Freedom . . . once being firmly established in Cuba, would then be asserted in South Carolina, Mississippi and Louisiana where liberty now 'lies bleeding' under the heel of a ferocious white minority rule race despotism."[50] Asking readers to "get together and show the imperialists . . . that the liberty ideals of 1776 are still a potential force in the world's affairs," the author of "Immortal Doctrines of Liberty Ably Set Out by a Colored Man" predicted that "Cuba is destined to become the one all embracing liberty issue around which Americans everywhere will have to fight finally for their own freedom rights."[51]

Yet even as some U.S. soldiers believed that their engagement in Cuba would help to reduce domestic racism, the black press remained skeptical about the political possibility of a transnational commerce in racial equality and was quick to identify the hypocrisy involved in fighting a war allegedly to free Cuba when freedom was systematically denied to blacks in the United States. With the quick victory of American arms in Cuba, black newspapers warned that the process of reconstruction on the island would copy that in the American South after the Civil War, with prejudice and Jim Crow substituting for freedom and independence. As the *Richmond Planet*'s 1898 article "The Insurgents and the Government" predicted, "the treatment accorded the colored people soon after the war, the relegating of them to the tender mercies of those against whom they fought in the South is to be repeated in an intensified form upon the soil of the 'Pearl of the Antilles.' " Declaring that "all of the horrors of South Carolina, Mississippi, Louisiana, and Texas will be repeated" in Cuba, the *Planet* asked its readers to "hope that this dark-skinned race may be able to meet the issue more successfully than we have done in a country whose flag is a misnomer, and whose laws are openly defied." Charles Baylor agreed that because "nearly all the leaders and fighters in the Cuban army of liberation are men, who if in South Carolina, Mississippi or Louisiana, would be made to ride in the 'Jim Crow Cars,' " the Cuban leaders who were fighting to achieve "those sublime liberty ideals proclaimed by the British-American colonists of 1776" were destined to be frustrated.[52] Recognizing that "the welfare of the negro race is vitally involved in the impending policy of imperialism" because "the whole trend of imperial aggression is antagonistic to the feebler races," the author of "McKinley's Inconsistencies" declared that the National Afro-American Party, for which he was an advocate, recognized "in the spirit of Imperialism, inaugurated and fostered by the administration of President McKinley, the same violation of HUMAN RIGHTS which is being practiced by the Democratic Party in the recently re-constructed States, to wit: the wholesale disfranchisement of the Negro."[53] The "violation" in McKinley's policy was epitomized by the president's behavior on his 1899 tour of the southern states. The *Washington Bee* addressed the president in an "Open Letter," pointing out that the president "catered to Southern race prejudice [by] . . . receiv[ing] white men at the Capitol in Montgomery, Alabama, and black men afterward in a Negro church, . . . [by] preach[ing] patience, industry, moderation to your long-suffering black fellow-citizens, and patriotism, jingoism and imperialism to your white ones" — in short, by "win[ning] the support of the South" for his "criminal aggression" in Cuba through "shut[ting] his eyes, ears, and lips to the 'criminal aggression' of that section against the Constitution."[54]

No one was more skeptical of U.S. influence on Cuba's struggle to achieve an antiracist nationhood than the African American political activist and father of the black rights movement, W. E. B. Du Bois. Admitting that "the McKinley campaign of '96" was pivotal to the evolution of his political thinking, Du Bois described in detail how McKinley's presidency transformed him from a Harvard student whose "main thought was on my studies" into an active agent in "the midst of political controversy." Du Bois recalled: "By the time McKinley got to work, I began to awaken [and] to realize that I had been wrong in most of my judgments."[55] Du Bois's resulting judgments about U.S. past and present domestic racial policies consistently acknowledged the nation's failure to pursue "a policy of honesty in Cuba."[56] As he declared in an article he wrote in 1908 for the *Horizon*, although "Black men" had "freed Cuba," Anglo-Americans "snatched the victory" away from them and "kicked the 'niggers' back to their places" while "conspiring to perpetuate 'white' rule." Thus "the rape of Cuba" was one of the "blackest things in recent American history — fit to be written down beside the Seminole 'wars' and the looting of Mexico."[57] In the lecture he delivered at the 1891 annual meeting of the American Historical Association, for example, Du Bois highlighted Havana's historical importance to mapping the U.S. slave trade,[58] and in "The Future of the Negro Race in America" (1904) he described "nineteenth-century efforts to civilize the heathen" in places such as Cuba.[59] Contemplating Cuba's renewed importance to advocating for racial equality "through the new imperial policy" of the United States, Du Bois declared that "our protectorate of Cuba" and other geographic locales represented "for the nation the greatest event since the Civil War and demands attention and action on our part."[60] Asking his readers to remember that "the twentieth century will find nearly twenty millions of brown and black people under the protection of the American flag, a third of the nation," Du Bois contended that once "Negro and . . . Cuban . . . stand united," America will "kno[w] no color line in the freedom of its opportunities" (77). Yet once U.S. policy in Cuba was in effect, Du Bois descried "the spectacle of . . . Cuba . . . trying desperately and doggedly to be 'white' in spite of the fact that the majority of the white group is of Negro or Indian descent."[61] Langston Hughes would subsequently agree that while "Cuban law recognizes no differences because of race or color" and "citizens of all colors meet and mingle," "colored people in Cuba" have suffered since "white Americans [gained] control," and those "colored visitors," like himself, "looking anxiously for a country where they can say there is no color line" are destined to be increasingly disappointed.[62] Like Booker T. Washington's commentary on Cuba, these accounts, then, suggest that the "absence of that higher degree of race feeling" in Cuba, which caused "the color line" in Cuba to be drawn only "in a few instances," was of vital conceptual importance to the black rights movement that was gaining momentum in the turn-of-the-century United States.[63]

The Old World Order

As the preceding pages have suggested, throughout the nineteenth century, Cuba served as a powerful site for imagining alternative models of race, nation, and empire, even as Cuba was integral to the creation of an explicitly racialized U.S. imperialism. The long-standing alliances between Cuba and the U.S. South that underpinned turn-of-the-century U.S. empire reemerged yet again in the national imaginary a hundred years after the Confederacy's demise — with the Civil War Centennial commemoration — in order to mitigate the threat that a now Soviet Cuba posed to a United States locked in a Cold War struggle with Russia. A *New York Times* commentator noted that "if the South has lost the Civil War, it is determined to win the centennial," and the veteran black trade unionist Philip Randolph publicly declared that "there is no doubt that the whole Centennial commemoration is a stupendous brain-washing enterprise to make the Civil War leaders of the South heroes and to strike a blow against men of color and human dignity."[64] Yet if the Civil War Centennial seemed to re-energize southerners opposed to Civil Rights by offering them the opportunity to deploy Confederate nostalgia for contemporary racial debates, it coincided with a new intensification of Cold War hostilities that the nation confronted globally. On the same day as the anniversary of Fort Sumter, for example, the Soviet Union put the first man in space; a week later CIA-trained forces landed in Cuba at the Bay of Pigs, and all fifteen hundred invaders were killed or captured in three days, making the operation the greatest defeat for the United States in the Cold War. Castro's Cuban revolution—culminating in the Cuban Missile Crisis—posed the most serious challenge to U.S. regional hegemony in the previous hundred years. Coinciding with this crisis, the Civil War Centennial helped Americans make sense not only of the past but of what one Civil War Centennial commissioner described as "the poison of socialism, internationalism, and communism" that threatened the nation in the present.[65] Seen as a high Cold War era celebration, then, the Civil War Centennial, more than any other public ceremony, according to Richard Fried, mobilized the past and the Confederacy to counterbalance a present in which the nation's global role was threatened by Soviet power. *Look* magazine, for example, published a Civil War Centennial story by the Pulitzer Prize winner McKinley Cantor, entitled "If the South Had Won the Civil War," which predicted that the Confederacy would not have been able to withstand the "somber threat of Communist domination that was spreading like a cold fog across the ocean and chilling the hearts of North Americans."[66] Centennial imaginings of a present-day Confederacy thus helped twentieth-century Americans to rally behind national rather than regional supremacy and to see the outcome of the Cuban Missile Crisis as an unambiguous American victory.[67]

A hundred years after McKinley's administration and fifty years after Kennedy's, Cuba is still the site around which America's dual conceptual commitments to liberty for all and empire converge. Indeed, as Morris Morley has commented, "over the last four decades American Presidents, whether Democrat or Republican, have exhibited a marked reluctance to accommodate themselves to the permanence of Cuba's symbol of resistance to U.S. imperial ambitions."[68] Yet all too often hidden at the center of that convergence is a deep, abiding, unarticulated commitment to a racial state. Projecting racial inequality onto the indigenous communities in which the United States seeks to establish

democracy and protect the principles of social justice, U.S. government officials from McKinley's administration to Bush's have masked the nation's enduring conceptual dependence on white supremacy to naturalize its imperial
agendas. Indeed, this dependence on racial hierarchy has endured Civil Rights
largely through exportation to other geopolitical locations like Cuba. Such a
dependence and the constitutive place of Cuba within it—as the importance of
the recent human rights violations at the U.S. detention center at Guantánamo
Bay, Cuba, and at Abu Ghraib in Iraq suggests—must be acknowledged if we
want to move toward, rather than away from, realizing social justice in a global
era. By shifting the geographic and conceptual coordinates usually defining the
boundaries of the United States to focus on Cuba, "the Pearl of the Antilles"
emerges not so much as an object of U.S. outreach as an agent of U.S. racialized
nationalism. To analyze the nineteenth-century U.S. fascination with Cuba, in
other words, reveals not so much how the subsequently ostracized Cuba threatens U.S. liberal democratic identity, as the Bush administration's recent policies
toward Cuba would have us believe,[69] but rather how Cuba has gradually been
compelled to represent and enable the racial hierarchies that continue to naturalize the United States' imperialist agenda. If "the current Bush administration
is intent on returning us to a . . . geopolitics of empire reminiscent of the eighteenth and nineteenth centuries," as María Josefina Saldaña-Portillo has contended,[70] then excavating the long-standing political significance of "banned"
zones like Cuba reveals how the alliance between race and empire that characterized "the old world order" continues to shape and determine what is too
often identified as the new. We must therefore understand and acknowledge
our own enduring national commitments to racial intolerance—we must consider the possibility that race constitutes and upholds the very process of nation building, as Thomas Holt contends[71]—if we want to keep our "bizarre
obsession" with race from becoming an ever more "dangerous diversion from
reality."

Notes

1   Christopher Marquis, "Bush Proposes a Plan to Aid Opponents of Castro in Cuba,"
    New York Times, May 6, 2004.
2   For commentary on the importance of race to national formation in Latin America,
    see Nancy Appelbaum, Anne Macpherson, and Karin Rosemblatt, eds., *Race and
    Nation in Modern Latin America* (Chapel Hill: University of North Carolina Press,
    2003).

3   For commentary on the interplay between foreign and domestic, see Amy Kaplan, *Anarchy of Empire in the Making of U.S. Culture* (Cambridge: Harvard University Press, 2002).

4   For commentary on the enduring importance of the Cold War to American culture, see Walter Michaels, *The Shape of the Signifier: 1967 to the End of History* (Princeton: Princeton University Press, 2004).

5   For commentary on Cuba and U.S. cultural interaction, see, for example, Rodrigo Lazo, *Writing to Cuba: Filibustering and Cuban Exiles in the United States* (Chapel Hill: University of North Carolina Press, 2005); Louis A. Pérez Jr., *On Becoming Cuban: Identity, Nationality and Culture* (Chapel Hill: University of North Carolina Press, 1999); and Damián Fernández and Madeline Cámara Betancourt, eds., *Cuba, the Elusive Nation: Interpretations of National Identity* (Gainesville: University Press of Florida, 2000).

6   Martin Delany, "Annexation of Cuba," *North Star*, April 27, 1849, 2. Reprinted in *Martin Delany: A Documentary Reader*, ed. Robert S. Levine (Chapel Hill: University of North Carolina Press, 2003), 160.

7   Frederick Douglass, "Cuba and the United States," *Frederick Douglass's Paper*, September 4, 1851. Reprinted in *The Life and Writings of Frederick Douglass*, ed. Philip Foner, vol. 2. (New York: International Publishing, 1950), 159.

8   Oliver Morton, *The Southern Empire: With Other Papers* (Boston: Houghton, Mifflin, 1892), 4, 9.

9   Editor of the *Democratic Review* and the *New York Morning News*, O'Sullivan wrote in July 1845 that it was the "manifest destiny" of the United States to overspread the whole of the North American continent. The term was first heard in Congress in January 1846 in connection with debates on Oregon and became the term explaining the annexation of Texas, as well as the acquisition of lands in Mexico and Central America. See Julius Pratt, "The Origin of 'Manifest Destiny,'" *American Historical Review* 32 (1927): 795–98; John Carl Parish, *The Emergence of the Idea of Manifest Destiny* (Berkeley: University of California Press, 1932); and James B. McMillan, "Historical Notes on American Words," *American Speech* 21 (1946): 180–81. See also Albert K. Weinberg, *Manifest Destiny: A Study of Nationalist Expansionism in American History* (Baltimore: Johns Hopkins University Press, 1935).

10 J. E. Cairnes, *The Slave Power: Its Character, Career, and Probable Designs* (1862).

11 John Stuart Mill, *The Contest in America* (Boston: Little Brown, 1862), 27, 29–30.

12 F. L. Olmsted, *A Journey in the Seaboard Slave States in the Years 1853–1854 with Remarks on Their Economy* (1856; New York: Knickerbocker Press, 1904), 1:201–8, 232–36; 2: 275–77. See also Olmsted, *The Cotton Kingdom* (1861; New York: Modern Library, 1969), xxv–xxvi.

13 Lucy Holcombe Pickens, *The Free Flag of Cuba* (1854; Baton Rouge: Louisiana State University Press, 2002), 68.

14 For commentary on the Confederacy as a separate nation, see, for example, Emory Thomas, *The Confederate Nation, 1861–1865* (New York: Harper and Row, 1979). For commentary on filibustering and the South, as well as William Walker's Janu-

ary 18, 1854, proclamation establishing the independent Republic of Sonora, see Robert E. May, *Manifest Destiny's Underworld: Filibustering in Antebellum America* (Chapel Hill: University of North Carolina Press, 2002), 42.

15 William Gilmore Simms, *Southern Quarterly Review*, January 1852.

16 Samuel R. Walker, "Cuba and the South" (New Orleans, May 20, 1854).

17 Loreta Velazquez, *The Woman in Battle: The Civil War Narrative of Loreta Velazquez, Cuban Woman and Confederate Soldier* (1876; Madison: University of Wisconsin Press, 2003).

18 For an excellent analysis of Velazquez's writing, see Jesse Alemán, "Crossing the Mason-Dixon Line in Drag: The Narrative of Loreta Janeta Velazquez, Cuban Woman and Confederate Soldier," in *Look Away! The U.S. South in New World Studies*, ed. Jon Smith and Deborah Cohn (Durham, N.C.: Duke University Press, 2004), 112–25.

19 David Murray, "Richard Robert Madden: His Career as a Slavery Abolitionist," *Studies* (spring 1972): 41–53, 50.

20 "The Proceedings of the General Anti-Slavery Convention Held in London in 1840," *Eclectic Review*, 1841, 233. For more commentary on the General Anti-slavery Convention and Manzano's slave narrative, see William Luis, *Literary Bondage: Slavery in Cuban Narrative* (Austin: University of Texas Press, 1990), 97.

21 For Manzano's slave narrative, see Juan Francisco Manzano, *The Life and Poems of a Cuban Slave*, ed. Edward Mullen (1840; New York: Archon Books, 1981). For commentary on Richard Robert Madden's involvement with Manzano and Cuban anti-slavery, see Edward Madden, ed., *The Memoirs of Richard Robert Madden, Edited by His Son* (London: Ward and Downey, 1891).

22 Murat Halstead, *The Story of Cuba: Her Struggles for Liberty* (Akron, Ohio: Werner, 1896), 110.

23 Italo Emilio Canini, *Four Centuries of Spanish Rule in Cuba: or Why We Went to War with Spain* (Chicago: Laird and Lee, 1898), 71.

24 Chaplain T. G. Steward, *The Colored Regulars in the United States Army: With a Sketch of the History of the Colored American, and an Account of His Services in the Wars of the Country, from the Period of the Revolutionary War to 1899* (Philadelphia: M. E. Book Concern, 1904), 115.

25 Canini, *Four Centuries of Spanish Rule*, 193.

26 Quoted in Jorge Ibarra, *Ideología Mambisa* (Havana: Instituto Cubano del Libro, 1967), 52.

27 Steward, *Colored Regulars*, 115.

28 Antonio Maceo, *Antonio Maceo: Political Ideology: Letters and Other Documents*, vol. 1, ed. Cuban Society of Historical and International Study (Havana: SCEHI, 1950), 64–65. Cited in Ada Ferrer, *Insurgent Cuba: Race Nation, and Revolution, 1868–1898* (Chapel Hill: University of North Carolina Press, 1999), 27.

29 Carlos de Manuel Céspedes, "Diplomatic Communication," January 3, 1869, in *Letters*, vol. 1, ed. Fernando Portuondo and Hortensia Picardo (Havana: Social Science Editorial, 1982), 142–46. Cited in Ferrer, *Insurgent Cuba*, 38.

30   "October 10," in *La Revolución*, National Historical Archive, Madrid. Cited in Ferrer, *Insurgent Cuba*, 39.

31   Cited in Ferrer, *Insurgent Cuba*, 39.

32   Halstead, *The Story of Cuba*, 110.

33   José Martí, "My Race," in *José Martí: Selected Writings*, ed. and trans. Esther Allen (New York: Penguin Classics, 2002), 318–20.

34   José Martí, "Plato de Lentejas," *Patria*, January 6, 1894; and "My Race," *Patria*, April 16, 1893. Both reprinted in *José Martí: Selected Writings*, 489, 319.

35   "My Race," reprinted in *José Martí: Selected Writings*, 319.

36   Salah D. Hassan, "The Figuration of Martí: Before and after the Revolution," *Radical History Review* 89 (summer 2004): 191–205. See also Susan Rotker, *The American Chronicles of José Martí: Journalism and Modernity in Spanish America*, trans. Jennifer French and Katherine Semler (Hanover: University Press of New England, 2000).

37   Ricardo Batrell Oviedo, *Para la historia* (Havana: Seoane and Alvarez, 1912), 3–4, 166.

38   W. E. B. Du Bois, *The Souls of Black Folk* (New York: Penguin, 1983); and José Martí, "A Vindication of Cuba," in *José Martí: Selected Writings*, 266–67.

39   Quoted in Philip Foner, *Spanish-Cuban-American War and the Birth of American Imperialism, 1895–1902*, vol. 2 (New York: Monthly Review Press, 1972), 394–95.

40   Quoted in Ferrer, *Insurgent Cuba*, 78.

41   Halstead, *The Story of Cuba*, 110.

42   George Clarke Musgrave, *Under Three Flags in Cuba: A Personal Account of the Cuban Insurrection and Spanish-American War* (Boston: Little, Brown, 1899), 358.

43   Leonard Wood to President of the United States, November 27, 1898, in Leonard Wood Papers, Library of Congress, MS box 26; and Musgrave, *Under Three Flags in Cuba*, 355.

44   Quoted in Musgrave, *Under Three Flags*, 365; and Horace Fisher, *Principles of Colonial Government Adopted to the Present Needs of Cuba and Porto Rico and the Philippines* (Boston: L. C. Page, 1899), 28.

45   Canini, *Four Centuries of Spanish Rule*, 189.

46   Theodore Roosevelt, *The Rough Riders* (New York: Scribner's, 1905).

47   Canini, *Four Centuries of Spanish Rule*, 189–90.

48   General Joseph Wheeler, Herschel V. Cashin, Charles Alexander, William T. Anderson, Arthur M. Brown, and Horace W. Bivins, *Under Fire with the 10th U.S. Cavalry: A Purely Military History of the Negro* (New York: F. Tennyson Neely, 1899), 120–21.

49   "Slavery Question in Another Form," *Springfield Republican*, April 16, 1900. Reprinted in *The Anti-imperialist Reader: A Documentary History of Anti-imperialism in the United States*, vol. 1, ed. Philip Foner and Richard Winchester (New York: Homes and Meier, 1984), 168.

50   Chas Baylor, "Hanna, Irelandism and the Color Line in Cuba," *Richmond Planet*, July 30, 1898. Reprinted in Foner and Winchester, *The Anti-imperialist Reader*, 149.

51   "Immortal Doctrines of Liberty Ably Set Out by a Colored Man: The Effect of

Imperialism upon the Negro Race," *Springfield Republican*, September 7, 1900. Reprinted in Foner and Winchester, *The Anti-imperialist Reader*, 177–80.

52 Baylor, "Hanna, Irelandism, and the Color Line in Cuba," 147.

53 "McKinley's Inconsistencies," *Richmond Planet*, July 22, 1899. Reprinted in Foner and Winchester, *The Anti-imperialist Reader*, 163.

54 "Open Letter to President McKinley," *Washington Bee*, October 23, 1899. Reprinted in Foner and Winchester, *The Anti-imperialist Reader*.

55 "From McKinley to Wallace: My Fifty Years as an Independent" (1948), in *W. E. B. Du Bois: A Reader*, ed. David Levering Lewis (New York: Henry Holt, 1995), 483.

56 "New York City, August 3, 1915, to the President of the United States," in *The Correspondence of W. E. B. Du Bois*, vol. 1, *Selections, 1877–1934*, ed. Herbert Aptheker (Boston: University of Massachusetts Press, 1973), 211.

57 W. E. B. Du Bois, "The Negro Voter," *Horizon: A Journal of the Color Line* 4, no. 1 (July 1908): 6.

58 Du Bois, "The Enforcement of the Slave Trade Laws," speech delivered at the American Historical Association annual meeting, December 1891, *AHA Annual Report 1891*. Reprinted in *Writings by W. E. B. Du Bois in Periodicals Edited by Others*, vol. 1, *1891–1909*, ed. Herbert Aptheker (New York: Kraus-Thomson, 1982), 24.

59 Du Bois, "The Future of the Negro Race in America," *The East and the West* (London), January 2, 1904. Reprinted in *Writings by W. E. B. Du Bois in Periodicals Edited by Others*, vol. 1, *1891–1909*, ed. Herbert Aptheker (New York: Kraus-Thomson, 1982), 190.

60 Du Bois, "The Present Outlook for the Dark Races of Mankind," *Church Review* (Philadelphia), October 17, 1900, 95–110. Reprinted in *Writings by W. E. B. Du Bois in Periodicals Edited by Others*, vol. 1, *1891–1909*, ed. Herbert Aptheker (New York: Kraus-Thomson, 1982), 77.

61 *The Correspondence of W. E. B. Du Bois*, vol. 2, *Selections, 1934–1944*, ed. Herbert Aptheker (Boston: University of Massachusetts Press, 1976), 304.

62 Langston Hughes, *I Wonder as I Wander: An Autobiographical Journey* (1956; New York: Farrar, Straus and Giroux, 1984), 11, 14.

63 Booker T. Washington, "Signs of Progress among the Negroes," *Century Magazine* 59 (1900): 472–78.

64 Jon Wiener, "Civil War, Cold War, Civil Rights: The Civil War Centennial in Context, 1960–1965," in *The Memory of the Civil War in American Culture*, ed. Alice Fahs and Joan Waugh (Chapel Hill: University of North Carolina Press, 2004), 237.

65 Richard Fried, *The Russians Are Coming! The Russians Are Coming! Pageantry and Patriotism in Cold-War America* (New York: Oxford University Press, 1998), 127.

66 Cited in Wiener, "Civil War, Cold War," 246.

67 For additional information on the centennial, see William Price, *The Civil War Centennial Handbook* (Virginia: Prince Lithograph, 1961); Maurice Isserman and Michael Kazin, *America Divided: The Civil War of the 1960s* (New York: Oxford University Press, 2000); *The Civil War Centennial: A Report to Congress, U.S. Civil War Centennial Commission* (Washington, 1968); and Robert Cook, "Unfinished

Business: African Americans and the Civil War Centennial," in *Legacy of Disunion: The Enduring Significance of the American Civil War*, ed. Susan-Mary Grant and Peter Parish (Baton Rouge: Louisiana State University Press, 2003), 47–60.

68   Morris Morley, *Unfinished Business: America and Cuba after the Cold War, 1989–2001* (New York: Cambridge University Press, 2002), 1. Morley further asserts that the "Bush and Clinton policy had to do with getting rid of the institutional structures of the Cuban revolution" (5). Thus when George W. Bush became president in 2001, "few issues more starkly revealed the degree to which U.S. policymakers" embraced a foreign policy committed to global imposition of the United States as a single superpower than U.S. policy in Cuba (9).

69   In addition to the plan already mentioned, President Bush has responded to the nearly 500-page report on Cuba he received by placing travel bans on U.S. family members of Cuban citizens.

70   María Josefina Saldaña-Portillo, " 'Wavering on the Horizon of Social Being': The Treaty of Guadalupe-Hidalgo and the Legacy of Its Racial Character in Americo Paredes's *George Washington Gómez*," *Radical History Review* 89 (summer 2004): 136.

71   Thomas Holt, "The First New Nations," in *Race and Nation in Modern Latin America*, ed. Nancy Appelbaum, Anne Macpherson, and Karin Rosemblatt (Chapel Hill: University of North Carolina Press, 2003), xi.

Pleasure and Colonial Resistance

Translating the Politics of Pidgin in Milton Murayama's

All I Asking for Is My Body

Susan Y. Najita

Seven years after José Martí's "Our America," the "formidable neighbor" to his north established itself as an overseas imperial power, claiming, in addition to Cuba and Puerto Rico, Spain's Pacific colonies, the Philippines and Guam.[1] By other means, the United States sealed its naval supremacy over the Pacific through both the Treaty of Berlin (1899), which partitioned Samoa between Germany and the United States, and the Treaty of Annexation (1898), which claimed Hawai'i. Each of these strategic locations became naval outposts, establishing the foundation for what Chalmers Johnson has called an "empire of bases."[2] U.S. control of the Western Hemisphere depended on its Pacific military presence and access to the markets of East Asia. However, as in the cases of Cuba and Puerto Rico, the U.S. imperial design failed to account for its own contradictory impulses, indeed, for the very contradictions that made the annexation of Hawai'i conceivable. If the large presence of African slaves in Cuba and the mixed-race population in Puerto Rico stymied northern notions of racial difference, in Hawai'i the continued survival of Native Hawaiians and the rapidly increasing population of nonwhite plantation laborers formed a multiracial society that "unsettled" the vision of a white settler paradise. The overthrow of Hawai'i's last monarch, Queen Lili'uokalani, by American sugar interests in 1893 (themselves descendants of Protestant missionaries from New England) was aided by U.S. gunboat diplomacy. President Grover Cleveland's denunciation of the overthrow and attempts at annexation detailed in the Blount Report revealed the conflicted nature of U.S. expansion via militarism and the defense of business interests. The contradictions and instabilities of this model have become even more evident in recent years.

There is perhaps no better early example of these contradictions than the post-annexation racialization of Hawaiians and nonwhites. During the territorial period, ranching and plantation interests not only limited native access to land but also instituted a strict 50 percent blood quantum definition, which enacted a kind of legal genocide whereby through intermarriage, Native Hawaiians and their claims to land would cease to exist.[3] Before annexation, the same business interests had also imported large numbers of indentured servants and immigrant labor from a variety of overseas locations, including Portugal, Spain, Germany, and China. In the late 1800s and early 1900s, they contracted workers from Japan, Korea, and the United States' newly acquired colonies, the Philippines and Puerto Rico. In this way, the complex multiracial labor force—the result of transregional and transnational crossings—brought workers from regions across the globe, from Asia, Europe, and even the Americas,[4] to another region, the Pacific. In some cases, U.S. empire itself facilitated internal mobility, as Filipinos and Puerto Ricans migrated across the margins of empire to work and live in another colonial outpost. The complex racial hierarchy of white planters, indigenous Hawaiians, and various immigrant groups was negotiated through the language Hawaii Creole English (HCE), colloquially termed "pidgin" in the islands. While the sheer numbers of nonwhite laborers—including some Hawaiians who worked on the plantations—produced the wealth, prosperity, and political influence enjoyed by the planter elite, this group also unsettled white privilege and security through strikes, work stoppages, and sabotage.[5] As a language that evolves out of the U.S. overthrow of the sovereign Kingdom of Hawai'i, pidgin also indexes transnational conflict. The outlawing of the Native Hawaiian language—'ōlelo Hawai'i—adds another layer to the situation of radical inequity that instigates the culture of resistance that pidgin facilitates. This mode of theorizing the "Americas" allows us to see language not so much as a point of comparison but as a site of interaction and collective resistance among unequal parties. For not only is pidgin a response to the banning of the indigenous language; it also negotiates between the radically different processes of racialization that both indigenous and immigrant groups underwent. Alliance across these different experiences is articulated in the emergence of "local" identity in the post-annexation period, the first major historical emergence of which is the Massie case in the 1930s. More recently, local identity was articulated in the 1960s and 1970s social movements against development that led to the rise of the movement for Kānaka Māoli (Native Hawaiian) sovereignty.[6] The politics of pidgin facilitate the emergence of local identity through a critical alliance, one that recognizes and challenges the way the homeland's cultural values are translated and resignified in the colonial context.

The contradiction between commercial and military interests became undeniable at midcentury, when the largest laboring ethnic group, the Japanese, became a steady source of labor on the plantations. Owing to immigration laws such as the Gentlemen's Agreement that allowed for the immigration of wives, the Japanese by midcentury had established families on the plantations and were second- and third-generation laborers. Planters began to deceptively term them "settled labor," seeking to keep them on the plantations as a captive skilled workforce.[7] The large number of Japanese laborers became a problem for the United States precisely because of its own will to power in the Pacific and Asia, as it competed in the first half of the century with another aspiring imperial power, Japan. The Japanese population—which now included *nisei* who were American citizens by birth—became a perceived military liability, an internal threat to the security of U.S empire. After Japan's bombing of Pearl Harbor, martial law was declared, and Buddhist temples and Japanese language schools were closed. Leaders of the Japanese community were rounded up and interrogated, and some were deported to internment camps on the mainland. Though no Japanese person was ever found to have conspired with the enemy, persons of Japanese ancestry and even those who by physical appearance were suspected of being Japanese were treated with suspicion as a perceived threat.[8]

Milton Murayama's *All I Asking for Is My Body* reveals a fundamental contradiction in U.S. imperial hegemony: the inherently unstable collusion between, on the one hand, commercial interest—and its need for a constant, varied source of cheap, nonwhite labor—and, on the other, U.S. military supremacy through its competition with other emerging empires.[9] In the ethnically segregated plantation camps, Japanese cultural valuation of the family, hard work and suffering (*gaman*), and racial chauvinism (*yamato damashi*) were recontextualized and resignified. The politics of pidgin in Murayama's novel work to critique both Japanese culture—and its imperial resonances—as well as the institution of the plantation. The novel demonstrates a kind of oppositional politics of survival within these systems, a politics whose genealogy can be traced both linguistically and culturally to Native Hawaiian modes of resistance. The protagonist Kiyo's attempt to escape from the plantation system through military service during World War II reveals other contradictions between the oppositional culture of pidgin and U.S. imperial expansion.

Soon after self-publishing his landmark novel in 1975, Murayama discussed his choice to write in dialect and multiple languages. Intending not only to capture the "staccato and refreshingly direct and clear-cut" qualities of pidgin,[10] he also sought to make the reader aware of distinctions in the text between Standard English, pidgin English, Japanese, and pidgin Japanese:

> What posed more of a problem than pidgin was writing in two languages. I wanted the reader to realize when Japanese was being spoken and when pidgin. When Tosh says to his mother, "All I'm asking for is my body," he's speaking Japanese. His limited Japanese makes him translate the pidgin into "Me wa karada dake tanomu" or "Me, I beg only for my body." Not as strong as the pidgin original, but it's awkwardly grammatical. Both brothers think in English and pidgin, and their Japanese is limited and awkward. I've been criticized for stylistic awkwardness in translating what was colloquial Japanese into English. Much of it was intentional. Japanese is a status-conscious language. Colloquial Japanese can exist only among peers and between men and women where the women automatically assume the inferior role.[11]

From the first pages of the novel, Murayama accustoms our ears to these four languages. The novel opens with a family discussion forbidding Kiyo's friendship with an older boy, Makot Sasaki. Kiyo enumerates the four languages parenthetically: "(we spoke four languages: good English in school, pidgin English among ourselves, good or pidgin Japanese to our parents and the other old folks)" (5). This opening scene says much about what can be said, to whom, and in which language. Formal Japanese is the language of the parental world, where Kiyo is told to avoid Makot because the Oyama family, being poor, will be unable to reciprocate; disobeying one's parents is unfilial; and he will "catch a sickness" (3). As Murayama indicates, Japanese is, indeed, a "status-conscious language," one in which Japanese values such as filial piety (*on*) and obligation (*giri*) become means to persuade Kiyo to show concern for the family's reputation. Pidgin Japanese, in contrast, articulates a cultural and generational difference between the Japanese-speaking parents and their English- and pidgin-speaking children. For example, Kiyo's pursuit of a more convincing explanation for why he may not befriend Makot is met with a threat in pidgin Japanese from his father, "If you keep asking 'Why? Why?' I'll crack your head kotsun!" (4). But it is in pidgin English, the language of the children, that Tosh reveals the true reason: "[Makot's] father no work and his mother do all the work, thass why!" (4). In this instance, pidgin is a language of consciousness of colonial oppression that also critiques the Japanese notion of yamato damashi and its complicity with the plantation. Kiyo defines yamato damashi as a "special spirit" that signifies that the Japanese "had more patience, perseverance, reserve, sense of duty, frugality, filial piety, and industry than any other race" (65). The notion of racial purity central to yamato damashi renders the Japanese family complicit with planter colonialism's divide-and-conquer strategy, as Stephen Sumida has argued.[12] By "complicit," I mean that by virtue of occurring within the plantation system in Hawai'i, these values are transformed and in some sense "translated" into complicity with the plantation. It's an unlooked-for connection, coincidental.

If Tosh and Kiyo cannot fully access the Japanese language, they are also denied complete entrance into English and its promises of the ideals of freedom and democracy. The speaking of Standard English at the plantation school occurs in one direction only, from the teacher Snooky to the pidgin-speaking students. In Snooky's lesson on the dangling modifier, Standard English signifies assimilation, outward or not, to U.S. ideals, whether they are represented by the white plantation boss Mr. Nelson or Snooky's Marxist critique. In defending freedom as a primary virtue, Snooky unknowingly reveals the fundamental contradiction of American democracy, "Freedom means not being part of a pecking order. Freedom means being your own boss" (34). Kiyo shows how Snooky's view is contradictory: "Freedom," Kiyo jokes, "means being a plantation boss" (34). Kiyo's immensely understated critique implies the truth about the plantation system that Snooky fails to see: plantation bosses were invariably male and white. The plantation system functioned through racial hierarchies, which Kiyo vividly compares to the camp's sewage system, which runs from the flush toilets of the plantation boss and Portuguese, Spanish, and nisei *lunas* (overseers) to the open ditches of the Japanese and Filipino camps (96). While Snooky's seductive talk of freedom leads Kiyo to eventually yearn for life outside both the plantation system and the Japanese family, his desire for "free-dom from other people's shit"—"to have no part of any shit or any group"—leads him, ironically, on the very next page to place his life in the hands of another racially segregated group fighting for their honor and their lives, the 442nd Regimental Combat Team. As Gary Pak points out, Kiyo's freedom is ironic and ambivalent because "he is fighting for a hungry, emerging American imperialist power, a political power that was responsible for the hegemonic capitalist/colonial order in Hawai'i."[13] Through this exquisite irony, Murayama suggests the racial contradictions inherent in American notions of democracy. All Kiyo and Tosh can ask for are their bodies, not their sense of who they are or the freedom to determine their futures. Identity and freedom are luxuries. Kiyo's body is literally threatened by his existence not only in the camp but also in the war. In fact, the nisei "go for broke" attitude toward the war, as Gary Okihiro has argued, was not an expression of patriotic zeal but a "profound recognition of coercion [on the plantation and in the war], with little choice and even less to lose."[14] The notion of "living on borrowed time" expresses the two forms of almost certain death on the plantation and on the battlefields of Europe. This is the nature of the terrible gamble Kiyo takes to gain his promised freedom: the GI "bill of rights" (didn't he already have one before?) in exchange for risking his life. If he doesn't make it out of the war, he will not only have no freedom to contemplate, he'll be dead. The possibility of freedom becomes, then, a moot question.

Pariahs

Parts I and II of the novel cleverly reveal how Japanese values are reinforced through the othering of pariahs: Obaban, Makot, and his mother, Mrs. Sasaki. Obaban's family disowns her when she violates the Buddhist mourning period. Tosh explains: "Her father been die and she been elope . . . before the forty-nine day mourning period was over. Here you not supposed to even drink sake [rice wine] for forty-nine days, and she been run off and marry Anshan's father" (17). Obaban also refuses a typically Japanese feminine role, the submissive, loyal wife. Her lack of restraint (*enryo*) when it comes to sex—her having "hot pants" (18)—is evident when she divorces this husband to marry a second. Obaban is herself the result of her own father's lack of restraint, since she is the product of an affair between her father and his maid, Masa.[15] She is considered excessive and extravagant in giving Kiyo's mother, upon her marriage, a gold ring made of a $10 gold coin.[16] But perhaps the community's suspicion of Obaban's "prostitution" has more to do with the fact that she does not rely directly on the plantation for her livelihood. Due to her training as a midwife, she is able to "pay[] her own way."[17]

Mrs. Sasaki is also like Obaban: she operates outside the direct control of the plantation and is a sexually immodest woman. Her relatively easy mode of acquiring cash through the sex trade violates gaman. In addition, the family's car signifies the Sasaki's race betrayal, their aspiring to be white (10). But Mrs. Sasaki's promiscuity doubly violates the notion of yamato damashi, the Japanese sense of racial purity and superiority: her involvement with Filipino men blurs racial boundaries, and her questionable livelihood brings shame on her racial group.

This livelihood positions Makot as pariah as well. The truth about Makot is encoded in his name, which simultaneously refers to the Japanese "Makoto" (literally, "truth") and the Filipino name "Markod." His mother's profession and the resulting unconfirmability of Makot's father and racial status threaten the purity of yamato damashi. Furthermore, Makot's lavish generosity toward Kiyo, his ready supply of cash and store-bought food, are signs of expenditure, not frugality. Kiyo's parents read Makot's generosity as an imposition of expected obligations that they could never reciprocate. But Makot's pariah status is also signaled by gender. While the Japanese camp community's work ethic and enactment of yamato damashi are rendered as masculine and Japanese, Makot's ready cash supply and his white-aspiring parents are viewed as effeminate and un-Japanese. Both are othered from the camp community precisely because their transgression of Japanese values produces financial success. Ironically, of course, the Sasakis' sex trade contributes to the smooth functioning of the plantation by helping to make the life of bachelor Filipino men more bearable in a situation of serious imbalance of the sexes.

The question of Makot's homosexual tendencies, however, is an interesting one.[18] The novel suggests that Makot's relation to Kiyo is similar to that of Mr. Sasaki to his wife. Makot asks Kiyo why they can't be friends: "Because I doan treat you right? I treat you okay?" (11). Like Mrs. Sasaki, Kiyo needs to be "treated right." But implicit in this relation is the notion of homosexual pleasure as illicit precisely because it is not productive—specifically, not reproductive—just as Makot's adventures with the boys are always about enjoyment. The scheme to purchase a rifle with the money from selling stolen coconuts evades the economy of production through work; through illicit means, the boys are able to acquire a rather large sum of money for a lavish recreational item. Makot operates according to a logic of pleasure, an evasion of the system of work and production, which also registers as the nonreproductive practices of homosexuality. Regardless of how one reads Makot's sexual politics, the exclusion of the Sasaki family has everything to do with the way Japanese culture unintentionally supports the *haole* camp hegemony, for the othering of Makot's family by the Japanese camp community also maintains a separation between Japanese and Filipinos. And this further supports the plantation's strategy of divide and conquer, prevents the creation of an interethnic alliance between the laboring groups, and helps perpetuate untenable conditions in both camps. Thus parts I and II of the novel lovingly present, as well as slyly critique, the Japanese values and beliefs in Kiyo's family. These Japanese values, in this particular context, willy-nilly support plantation colonialism, its hierarchical structures, and its system of captive labor.[19]

Claiming Murayama for Asian American Literature: Resistance to Assimilation or Colonial Critique?

Critics of Asian American literature have often claimed Murayama's novel for its exploration of immigrant identity and assimilation. For example, Elaine Kim argues that Kiyo becomes an American by abandoning the constricted space of Japanese culture in favor of individual freedom.[20] Stephen Sumida, the first to situate Murayama in the context of U.S. empire, has argued that Japanese values are distorted by the colonial institution of the plantation.[21] My goal here is to put into play an alternative reading that places local ethnic identities in a larger transnational and transregional framework by looking at how pidgin facilitates modes of opposition to both U.S. empire and Japanese imperial values precisely through its deep historical roots in the banning of ʻōlelo Hawaiʻi and its genesis in the loss of native sovereignty. Not only does pidgin represent a radical rejection of both U.S. and Japanese identity, but it makes possible survival within these systems.

To do this, I examine three phrases and their translation or transliteration. The first sentence is "All I'm asking for is my body," which Murayama notes is used to translate from Tosh's awkward pidgin Japanese "Me wa karada dake tanomu," or literally "Me, I beg only for my body."[22] In explaining the awkwardness of the colloquial Japanese, Murayama states that he wanted to show how "Japanese is a status-conscious language."[23] It is also true that the Japanese phrase translated into English appears to be indistinguishable from its Standard English form: "All I'm asking for is my body." Murayama's impartial critique of both systems is borne out even in the language of the novel itself. To Tosh and Kiyo, the two systems appear identical: both systems work, albeit for different reasons, to keep them from escaping the life of the plantation. As Murayama himself stated, "When you're dealing with two conflicting cultures, you face a problem. Are you going to be pro-one, pro-the-other, or impartial? If impartial, how? What I worked out was simple: I will use the same yardstick of honesty on both."[24] It is precisely through translation that Murayama makes his impartial critique. Translation here suggests a kind of equivalence between Japanese and Standard English that mirrors the way Japanese values are put into the service of furthering American imperial power. In other words, translation makes apparent the transnational competition that places local Japanese in such a precarious position at midcentury. While Japanese and pidgin Japanese are presented in translated form, the only language not translated is pidgin English (HCE). What does Murayama's insistence on the nontranslatability of pidgin suggest? If translation signals imperial consciousness produced out of transnational engagements, might pidgin's refusal of translation ground identity in the noncommutability of place and the experience of empire's coercions?

This is borne out in the novel's pidgin title, which prevented its mainstream publication and led Murayama to self-publish the book in 1975. He wrote: "Self-publishing was an act of rebellion like Tosh's refusing to play by the rules and language of 'inherited conventions.' Timidity or conformity to their rule of shame would have made me mute, arthritic, and bitter-bitter-bitter."[25] Here Murayama compares Tosh's refusal of his father's Japanese filial expectations and his mother's superstitions (the "inherited conventions") to Murayama's own refusal to present the novel's title in Standard English. Even as he simultaneously rejects both Japanese and English, he fiercely claims pidgin, a language that signifies in the dominant U.S. culture — and the Japanese culture as well — illiteracy and lack of intelligence. Pidgin becomes the mode in which "local" literature and identity assert themselves as something separate and apart from "American" culture, Japaneseness, and mainland Japanese Americans (*katonks*). When Tosh says to Kiyo, "Shit, all I asking for is my body. I doan wanna die on the plantation like these other dumb dodos. Sometimes I get so mad I wanna kill them [his parents], you know what I mean?" (48), he is referring to the values of on and giri of the Japanese family system, which work in parallel with the plantation system to keep nisei enslaved on the plantations.

In the novel, however, Tosh remains faithful both to his duty as *chonan* (number one son) and to his status as truck driver's helper and champion boxer of the Pioneer Mill's athletic club. However, the subsequent novel *Plantation Boy* details Tosh's struggle to become a draftsman and architect in Honolulu amid the continuing parental demands placed on him as eldest son.[26] Kiyo, as we will see, takes a much more radical position than does Tosh, undermining Japanese values, the family structure, and the plantation system.

But Kiyo's consciousness as a "local," however it may change in the course of the novel, is initially fostered by Tosh and his use of pidgin. Kiyo tells us that Tosh was like a "second father" to him because, unlike his parents, Tosh spoke English (49). It is Tosh's strident use of pidgin that indicates its status as a language of resistance. Tosh's use of pidgin is mirrored in his boxing. Kiyo says: "[Tosh] was getting as fast with his hands as with his mouth" (46). Later Kiyo tells us that Tosh is "blossom[ing] into a picture fighter," a perfect "counterpuncher": "He could dance rings around the guys, throw ten punches and get none in return, but he was a counterpuncher and he looked good only if the other guy was the aggressor" (49). This extends to his relationship with his father, as Tosh explains: "I look like the aggressor, . . . but I not. I fighting for my life. The old man no need be a bully, the system the bully. He can afford to act the nice guy and pretend I doing him wrong. He can afford to be easygoing when he sitting on me and sucking me dry" (56). Tosh reveals the connection between boxing and resistance to both the Japanese family and the plantation system: "You doan know how much he been beat me up when I was a kid. He always called me a crybaby. I was no samurai. I had no *gaman* (patience), no *enryo* (holding back). . . . If I start holding back, I play right into his hands. Hard work, patience, holding back, waiting your turn, all that crap, they all fit together to keep you down" (46). Tosh's discussions with his mother are compared to verbal sparring, the two combatants circling each other in the ring, "going round and round, neither side giving an inch" (65). This defensive structure to Tosh's language and boxing style explains why he keeps returning home to argue with his mother even after the attack on Pearl Harbor has inverted the familial hierarchy and placed him on top (92). For Tosh there is no other available mode except to spar defensively from within the two social structures that oppress him. While boxing allows him a measure of defense against his father and the Japanese codes of manliness he requires, it also extends the false promise of escape from the plantation.

Pidgin is directly compared to boxing when Kiyo watches Tosh's matches: "But I went to see him every time he fought on this side of the island. . . . I'd move and duck and bob and weave and jerk my body right and left with his punches, trying to *give him English*" (51; italics mine). The term "English" here refers to the twist or spin given to a ball, for example, in billiards or baseball. Murayama suggests that Kiyo conveys not English itself but a "twist" on English, an Englishing of English, if you will. Pidgin, then, is a particularly sly and biting critique of U.S. imperialism. But Tosh—though he struggles valiantly to remain true to his ethnic identity—is a fairly limited character. His defensive politics are unable to transform social relations.

The difference between Tosh and Kiyo might be understood in terms of the difference between opposition and resistance. As Ross Chambers explains, resistance implies overt and open challenges to the legitimacy of authority, often in the form of revolution or protest. In contrast, opposition works from within systems of power and thus takes a more covert, disguised, and insidious form. Unlike resistance, which announces its rivalry with authority, opposition evades identification and discipline. It is a mode useful to the system's prisoners, since it refuses incorporation into coercive systems of power. While resistance seeks to reverse power relations—and thereby reinscribes systems of power— opposition allows for survival within the system through the maintenance of dignity and personhood.[27] Tosh can be viewed as an oppositional figure in some ways, since he maintains a defensive posture toward both the plantation and the Japanese family. However, his notions of masculinity and his overt challenges to authority require the continued maintenance of the work ethic and Japanese values, the interests of the plantation and the family. Tosh does not challenge the racial and gendered colonial hierarchies that maintain these structures. Rather, it is the pariah figures who are perhaps more quintessentially oppositional because they transform racial, gender, and sexual hierarchies by transforming desire. In other words, *All I Asking for Is My Body* functions oppositionally as a narrative that has the potential to radically and nonviolently change readers from the inside by producing shifts in identification and desire. In oppositional narrative, the storyteller seduces the reader or listener into perceiving from an oppositional perspective, transforming the reader into a witness to the inhumane conditions of the system, conditions that have been disavowed by the official culture that controls representation (16). The truly oppositional figure is Kiyo, whose innocent child's perspective in "I'll Crack Your Head Kotsun" and "The Substitute" disarms the reader into perhaps seeing pariahs such as Makot and Obaban in transformative ways. Makot's and Obaban's gender and sexual politics begin to signify as oppositional mechanisms for surviving within a system predicated on the cycle of debt and death.

So while Tosh is oppositional only insofar as he survives by maintaining a defensive posture, it is Kiyo who, precisely because of his status as second son, can attempt to escape from the system itself. The ultimate irony of the novel, of course, is the fact that, in enlisting in the military, he is completely aware that he is fighting on behalf of the U.S. system that produced, condoned, and profited from the plantation system, that whatever "freedom" he will be able to obtain after the war is predicated on risking his own life. To examine how the novel sets out this critique, we must look at the origin of the novel's last lines: "I manufactured some of the luck, but I think the Oyama luck has finally turned around. *Take care the body.* See you after the War" (103; italics mine). The phrase "Take care the body" is first uttered by a fellow worker, perhaps the most oppositional figure in the novel, Awai, in chapter 4 of part III.

Chapter 4 is starkly different from the rest of the novel in both narration and content. Unlike the rest of the novel's past tense and autobiographical first-person singular ("I") voice, chapter 4 deploys a peculiar present-tense, first-person plural ("we") voice. It opens and continues throughout in the immediacy of the present tense and briefly switches from third-person plural ("we") to the second-person point of view ("you"), suggesting that the boundaries of the text are broken briefly to include the reader himself or herself as a laborer or actor in the scene's collectivity. Focusing on dialogue and quick description of action and gesture, this chapter resembles a play. We are never actually introduced to the multiracial cast that appears only in this section:

> Lino comes to the next furrow. He steps on his shovel. "Jesus Maria!" he says and flings down the shovel and grabs the pick. "Weee-ha!" Three-Quarter Dalmatio several furrows away shrieks and chants in falsetto, "*Ichiricchi ali bam bam, salagitto a sala bu bam, ama ba yet talan tan tan . . .*" He shovels faster and faster chanting louder. Everybody stops and laughs, "Weeee-ha!" somebody says. "Weee-ha!" another yells louder. Dalmatio chants gasping and flails shovel and red dust into the still air. He's fifty-five, wizened, always working bareback. He works like a madman, in fits of chants, almost jumping up and down, then he lays off the next day. (39)

In this drama, Awai, a twenty-five-year-old Native Hawaiian laborer, playfully confronts his coworker Philemon, a six-foot Filipino who sets the pace for the work gang.[28] This primarily Filipino gang is composed of fourteen Filipinos, one Hawaiian (Awai), and two Japanese (Kiyo and Mr. Nosawa). Murayama's one-act play set within the novel provides the only glimpse into what "local" identity might mean, that is, an identity based on an interethnic alliance among plantation workers, a shared experience of oppression under the plantation system that fueled the strong interethnic labor unions in Hawai'i. The main subject of chapter 4 is Awai's attempt to educate Philemon: " 'Eassy, eassy, all right,' Awai watches Philemon, 'take care the body. You work too hard, bye 'n' bye, the plantation cut down the price. Use your cabeza. . . . You loco, you watch tomorrow, they cut down the price' " (40). Interestingly enough, Awai chooses to use the term "loco," or crazy, but in pidgin, "loco" might also signify as "local," as in "locomoco." Awai uses a gender reversal to educate Philemon, wrestling his opponent and "pump[ing] his hips like Philemon was a woman" (40). Here stereotypical gender roles are inverted. Instead of hard work being associated with manliness, in Awai's logic of survival, hard work is transformed into a feminine sign, someone who is "screwed over" by the plantation. Awai's mode of survival opposes the planter's demand for competitive production through the stimulation of interethnic rivalry. Historically, planters sought to induce Native Hawaiians to be more disciplined workers by importing the Chinese. Pleased to discover that "coolies" worked harder than the natives, planters condescendingly called them *wahine* or "women." [29] Awai's mode of survival reverses this effeminization of the lazy worker, so that the worker who complies with the system of production based on outdoing his fellow workers is feminized. Masculinity, then, is oppositional survival through loafing, pleasure, and concern for the body.

But Murayama's discussion of local identity goes much deeper. The advice "Take care the body" that Awai (and later Kiyo) offers is a pidgin saying whose roots lie much deeper, namely, in the Hawaiian saying "E mālama 'oe i kou kino" (literally, "take care your body"). In *Henehene kou 'aka*," a well-known Hawaiian song from the 1930s (contemporaneous with the time in which Murayama's novel is set), a boy regales his girlfriend with the fun they will have on their next date on a streetcar. The following are the lyrics of the song as sung by Israel Kamakawiwoʻole on his album *Facing Future*. [30]

Henehene kou ʻaka

Henehene kou ʻaka	Your laughter is so contagious
Kou leʻaleʻa paha	It's fun to be with you
He mea maʻa mau ia	Always a good time
For you and I	For you and I

Ka‘a uila mākēneki	The streetcar wheels turn
Hō‘onioni kou kino	Vibrating your body
He mea ma‘a mau ia	Always a good time
For you and I	For you and I

I Waikīkī mākou	To Waikiki we go
‘Au ana i ke kai	Swimming in the sea
He mea ma‘a mau ia	Always a good time
For you and I	For you and I

I Kapahulu mākou	To Kapahulu we go
‘Ai ana i ka līpo‘a	Eating seaweed
He mea ma‘a mau ia	Always a good time
For you and I	For you and I

I Kaka‘ako mākou	To Kaka‘ako we go
‘Ai ana i ka pipi stew	Eating beef stew
He mea ma‘a mau ia	Always a good time
For you and I	For you and I

Our eyes have met	Our eyes have met
Our lips not yet	Our lips not yet
Mālama pono i kou kino	Take care the body
I'm gonna get you yet	I'm gonna get you yet.

Ha‘ina mai ka puana	Tell the refrain
Kou le‘ale‘a paha	It's fun to be with you
He mea ma‘a mau ia	Always a good time
For you and I	For you and I

I'm gonna get you yet.
How much you wanna bet?

The translation here, based on one by Ka‘i‘ini Garza-Maguire, is an extremely "safe" translation, one that disguises some of the "naughty" aspects of this playful *mele*. The first line of the song, "Henehene kou ‘aka," literally means "your laughter teases." The second line, "kou le‘ale‘a paha," is somewhat of an invitation to "le‘ale‘a," which refers to a kind of abandonment to pleasures, sexual, culinary, and otherwise. *Le‘ale‘a*—associated with ritual celebrations in honor of the god Lono, the fertility of the land, and the chief's sexual fertility—was also historically a form of anticolonial resistance.[31] A more vernacular translation of "kou leʻaleʻa paha" might be an invitation to "party!" The mele parallels Kiyo's and Makot's queer friendship of going around town together, eating, and going swimming. Makot's and Kiyo's pleasure through consumption signifies as resistance to colonial structures of production that require frugality, conservation, and work, values that actually produce only debt and death. Notice that Iz's rendition alters the saying to include the word *pono* ("Mālama pono i kou kino"), which signifies the notion of "making right" or achieving a state of "righteousness," particularly in relation to sovereignty. Thus, taking care of the body signals a refusal to work, which calls for a righting of the historical wrong of overthrow and annexation, a call for decolonization that promises to make right the relations between individuals, groups, and their livelihoods.

At the heart of Awai's advice to "take care the body," then, is the implication of indulgent pleasure and ease. As Awai says, "Yep, take care the body. Eassy, eassy. . . . The guy who invented work oughta be shot" (40). But this chapter is not one in which Murayama perpetuates the stereotype of the lazy Hawaiian. As Teresia Teaiwa has theorized, the laziness of the native must be seen as an insistence on pleasure as a means for self-preservation.[32] Rather, Awai's cautionary statement is truly oppositional in the sense that it advises the workers how to survive within a system of oppression, and his advice critiques both the Protestant work ethic and the Japanese sense of gaman, which argue that hard work and sacrifice will guarantee success in the long run. Awai points out that it is precisely these very ideals that lead one to both debt (through lower wages for piecework) and death (the overworked body). In pidgin, both of these terms are indistinguishable aurally as "det." Awai's reminder to loaf places him in the category of pariah along with the Sasakis, Obaban, and one other character, our narrator, Kiyo.

Kiyo takes Awai's advice to heart when he saves the family precisely by undermining the values of gaman, enryo, and *bachi*. Unlike Tosh, who trains for his boxing matches in a diligent and disciplined manner, Kiyo is a quick study. Discovering his "natural left hook" and refusing to train as hard as Tosh, Kiyo fancies that he has "upstaged [Tosh] in one short year" (69). The idea of being a "natural" goes against bachi and the vilification of that which is gotten without struggle. Despite his easy success, Kiyo begins to realize that though boxing is his only way out of the camp, it is too difficult and uncertain a route:

> But I pushed myself and ran and ran, and even as I ran, I kept thinking there had to be an easier way. Boxing wasn't the way. All this work meant

maybe I was going to beat Soga, who got beat easy in Honolulu. But for a Japanese there were no jobs except the plantation, unless you went into business for yourself. Even if you went to college, all you could be was a grammar school teacher, and if lucky, a high school teacher. Unless your family had enough money to send you to dental or medical college, and then you came back and practiced in your old hometown. There was no way out but boxing. (71)

Even Kiyo's stint as a craps shooter is met with quick study and success. Despite never having gambled before, he is able to make $300 his first day with only five practice shots. On his final pass of the dice, he trusts the most effortless of all means to success, luck: "If my luck was so bad I couldn't throw one pass on the up-and-up, then I deserved to lose, it was my proper *bachi*" (102). Interestingly, Kiyo invokes bachi precisely at this moment. One wonders, "Bachi for what?" Kiyo's Japanese upbringing has caused him to anticipate feeling shame and guilt about gaining something valuable without the self-sacrifice and suffering that gaman entails. As he walks away from the craps game with his pockets full of money, he confesses, "I felt bad" (103). He compares the ease of his success to his "left hook": "I'd sleep and wake up and find out it was a dream. It'd been too easy. Like my left hook was so good I got to be another Henry Armstrong without all that roadwork" (103).

Kiyo's quick success in gambling is echoed in the narrative trajectory of the novel that ends with his anticipated and optimistic "See you after the War" (103). His success is borne out by the novel itself, its very existence being reassurance that perhaps Kiyo has survived. But like the craps game, Kiyo's soldiering in the war as a member of the 442nd Regimental Combat Team is also a gamble, one in which he must risk his life to possibly receive long-sought-for citizenship on a par with white Americans. But the GI "bill of rights" only guarantees him a shot at economic freedom — an education and possibly a job off the plantation — if he survives. Like the craps game, which relies on cunning and luck, keeping his body intact in battle and finding a life off the plantation also require a measure of luck. Kiyo's struggle to truly possess his own body in the plantation system is deferred even further on the field of battle, where ironically he is fighting to protect the interests of the very country that benefited from and supported the plantation system. Without Kiyo's transgression of the values of gaman and bachi, he and his family would have remained on the plantation.

Not only do his winnings place Kiyo outside the Japanese family and its values; they also position him as outlaw to the plantation system. Sally Merry points out that gambling was one of the many everyday practices criminalized under the planter oligarchy and its laws. One of the most targeted populations for the criminalization of gambling was the Japanese population.[33] It is not difficult to see how gamblers, tramps, and loafers threatened the smooth working of the plantation, since all three flout the expectation that hard manual work leads to a happy and stable livelihood. Gambling, in particular, offered a means of gaining quick release from financial obligation to the plantation. So Kiyo's easy financial success through gambling also links him again to the loafing Awai, the Sasaki family, and Obaban.

The Politics of Pidgin: Inscription on the Body

John E. Reinecke, in his important study *Language and Dialect in Hawaii: A Sociolinguistic History to 1935*, defined "pidgin" in two ways: as the popular usage for the technical term "Hawaii Creole English" and as a "makeshift language" arising out of trade.[34] In contrast to pidgins, creole languages such as HCE (what I have been terming "pidgin") arise out of conditions of servitude, the subjection to European masters of an imported "servile class" on "tropical or semitropical plantations" (17). The creole as lingua franca negotiates the range of cultural and linguistic differences between laborers and masters and between laborers themselves (17–18). Because the ruling class rarely submits to the speech of the lower class, this lingua franca takes the form of the master's language, becoming a "language of command" (18). The multilingual nature of the servile class also makes the adoption of a single language impossible. Since the master assumes that the lower classes are incapable of speaking his language correctly, a "pulverized" or corrupted version, a creole, comes into usage (18). Over time, HCE signified as illiteracy and a "linguistic handicap" that justified the barring of locals from socioeconomic opportunities.[35] The reality was, however, that little connection existed between the command of Standard English and advancement, as plantations furnished neither opportunity nor incentive (102–3).

More recent work on pidgins and creoles defines these terms somewhat differently from Reinecke's early definition. Greater emphasis has been placed on the unequal nature of social relations in the development of pidgins and the continuity between pidgins and creoles. Hirokuni Masuda argues that pidgin evolves out of unequal power relations when two or more mutually unintelligible languages together meet a higher-status lexical source language.[36] Out of the contact between these languages, the mixed linguistic code of pidgin is created to afford a means of minimum communication. When this language is nativized by children of the second generation or stabilizes over several decades, the pidgin becomes a creole. In the case of HCE and its predecessor, Hawaii Pidgin English (HPE), contact languages included Chinese, Portuguese, and Japanese, for example, which were subordinated to the higher status of either English or Hawaiian, depending on the particular historical moment.[37] D. Bickerton and W. H. Wilson (1987) argue that HPE's successor, HCE, emerges out of annexation, the transition from Hawaiian to English as the official language. This subversion of the Hawaiian language "relexified" Pidgin Hawaiian into Hawaii Pidgin English and then to Hawaii Creole English. However, the relexification of HPE was never entirely completed. Thus HCE contains a large component of Hawaiian words and expressions.[38]

Before annexation almost all Hawaiians and part-Hawaiians learned the Hawaiian language. Missionary schools and seminaries such as Lahainaluna Seminary on Maui published the first religious texts in Hawaiian, including the first translation of the Bible in 1839. The language of law and royalty remained Hawaiian until the 1840s. But increasingly after the Land Division Act of 1848, the Māhele, government business — laws and land titles — was conducted in English. The first English school for children of royalty was established in 1840, and Punahou School, which dispensed an elite English education for the children of missionaries, was established three years later. By 1874 one-fourth of all pupils were studying English.[39] During the years of Kalākaua's reign (1874 to 1891), common schools that taught in the Hawaiian language all but disappeared. By 1888 the government English schools were opened to the public at no cost. English immediately replaced Hawaiian as the official language in 1896, three years after the overthrow. (Not until 1986 was this ban lifted and Hawaiian declared an official language of the State of Hawai'i.) The Hawaiian language was prohibited from being spoken in the schools, and children were beaten for speaking it. According to Bickerton and Wilson, the last generation (until the late-twentieth-century Hawaiian language revival) of Hawaiians and part-Hawaiians outside Ni'ihau who maintained some facility in the language were born between 1905 and 1920. Bickerton and Wilson point out that these individuals were often caught between family who scolded them for using English and teachers (often Hawaiian themselves) who punished the children for using Hawaiian.[40]

Before annexation, Pidgin Hawaiian connected communities who spoke primarily Hawaiian, English, and other immigrant languages. It was at the moment of annexation that Pidgin Hawaiian became relexified as Hawaii Pidgin English — though both languages probably coexisted for some time. Had Hawai'i remained an independent monarchy, immigrants would gradually have been absorbed into the Hawaiian community, but with the increased pressure to learn English and become "good Americans," most Hawaiians and children of immigrants abandoned Hawaiian as a target language.[41] The emergence of HCE began between 1890 and 1910 with the birth of the first generation of native creole speakers.[42] HCE, then, is a fairly "young" language — only about a hundred years old. It emerged out of the loss of lands under the Māhele, the enforced decline of monarchical sovereignty during Kalākaua's reign, the overthrow of Queen Lili'uokalani, and the illegitimate incorporation of Hawai'i as a U.S. territory.[43] Like the Hawaiian language, HCE was also the subject of colonial discipline and eradication through the English Standard schools that came into existence in 1920, not long after the emergence of HCE — and ended just after World War II in 1947. English Standard schools attempted to preserve the English (American) language from the "corrupting influence" of pidgin.[44]

Recent work on lexification fails to note the important grammatical connection between pidgin English and Hawaiian, for pidgin English has probably fewer similarities to English than it has to the grammatical and phonetic structure of 'ōlelo Hawai'i. Indeed, HCE's grammar, inflections, and intonations might be seen as "preserving" some aspects of the outlawed language, Hawaiian. Because HCE was a wholly oral language, completely unstandardized, without an orthography, and not taught formally in schools, it more easily evaded attempts to police or eliminate it from everyday use. In Murayama's *Plantation Boy*, it is precisely the unstandardized nature of pidgin that allows letters from nisei soldiers to slip past government censors.[45] The banning of Hawaiian might be seen as a means of legitimation, a means through which the illegitimate Republic of Hawai'i attempted to naturalize Hawai'i's colonial status and to thereby disavow U.S. involvement in the takeover of a sovereign kingdom. Similarly, the attempt to eradicate pidgin was aimed at assimilating nonwhite immigrant laborers and their descendants to erase the signs of Hawai'i's former sovereign status. English Standard schools were an attempt to Americanize and linguistically whiten people perceived to be unassimilable. These attempts to eradicate pidgin also denied a cultural refuge for speakers of Hawaiian. The persistence of pidgin might also be seen as a mode through which the Hawaiian language, its lexicon, and many of its speech patterns, inflections, and grammatical structures were preserved over the much more extensive years in which the language was banned. Thus we may consider the persistence of pidgin as allowing for an ambivalent existence in the everyday life, both a public and an "underground" mode of maintaining significant aspects of a banned language. As Murayama's character Awai makes obvious, the roots of the "local," in terms of both language and interethnic identification, are firmly rooted in both the Hawaiian language and the history of native and immigrant resistance to colonialism.

   Before suggesting how this might be the case, I'd like to return to Reinecke's discussion of Hawaii Creole English to think about what HCE tells us about the "local" as a response to the unequal social relations under plantation colonialism. According to Reinecke, creoles function as an "interlanguage" or "lingua franca" in three primary ways: (1) as a "language of command"; (2) as a medium of communication between non-English-speaking groups; and (3) as a means of communication between parents (or others of the immigrant generation) and their children who do not speak the parental language fluently.[46] Murayama's novel elaborates how pidgin functions within these three sets of relations. For example, we have seen how pidgin is the language of interethnic solidarity on the plantation, how it is the means by which groups who speak different languages negotiate a mutual, shared politics of oppositionality. We have seen also how Kiyo's and Tosh's use of pidgin signals both displacement from the parents' Japanese culture as well as a placement within the culture of the local. As Reinecke points out, a creole language persists precisely because its speakers have lost their native tongue. Only the master class has the option of reverting to its pure European language should creole speech lose its currency. In the case of Tosh and Kiyo, the United States' entrance into World War II dispels any illusions of returning to Japan. Their experiences on the plantation and in the family have already positioned them as occupying the critical space of the local, in ambivalent relation to both the Japanese culture and American political, economic, social structures. The persistence of HCE in Hawai'i, then, signals the way in which local identity is formed not only out of displacement from homelands but out of a relinquishing of diasporic cultural identifications that this displacement sets in motion. Tosh's local identity takes a peculiarly defensive posture in this new "em-place-ment," a positioning that is critical of both the culture of the homeland and of the colonial structures that have resignified the culture of the homeland.

Perhaps the most important aspect of Reinecke's discussion is the notion that HCE is a "language of command"—a statement whose implications go undeveloped in his study. Reinecke implies both violence and discipline as structures internal to creole language acquisition and usage. The notion of pidgin as a "language of command" suggests not only class hierarchies but also the violence and threat of punishment that those hierarchies require for their maintenance. Interpellation as a laborer on the plantation required learning pidgin in a climate shot through with the threat of violence, physical and psychological. For the children of these first-generation laborers, the acquisition of their native language, HCE, occurred in the context of coerced labor. As is well known, the threat of punishment, beating, whipping, lynching, and perpetual servitude through pay docking were commonplace on the plantation. One planter observed in 1866, "The bare knowledge on [the laborers'] part, of the fact that their master was at liberty to give them a sound flogging, say a dozen lashes well laid on would . . . exert a more healthy influence toward good discipline than all the laws our state affords at present."[47] The black snake whip carried by the luna, or overseer, was a symbol of plantation authority. The Korean laborer Kim Hyung-soon recalled that Korean workers were treated like cows or horses: "Every worker was called by number, never by name. During working hours, nobody was allowed to talk, smoke, or even stretch his back. A foreman kept his eyes on his workers at all times. When he found anyone violating working regulations, he whipped the violator without mercy."[48] Other lunas consistently resorted to kicking, slapping, or physically punishing recalcitrant workers. Masaji Watanabe, a captured deserter, was whipped with a leather lash by the plantation manager. After a time, Watanabe crawled from the plantation office, his shirt and denim pants torn to ribbons, his back covered in blood. Incidents such as these caused the U.S. Labor Commission to conclude in 1910 that lunas on Hawai'i's plantations were "brutal and overbearing" and readily used "physical violence."[49]

Reinecke's discussion suggests the rather haphazard trial-and-error means by which laborers acquired HCE. The laborer's English was

> learned partly off the job, in contacts with shopkeepers, peddlers, and neighbors of other nationalities, but even more on the job, from foremen and fellow employees. It was learned in the functional fashion in which all unformalized, oral speech is learned, as an infant learns his native tongue, by a process of trial and error. The immigrant arrived at last at expressions

that secured results when used with his English-speaking lunas and fellow
workmen. (101)

Because HCE is an oral language with no written orthography or standardization, there is also no systematic means of learning it. Reinecke neglects to
emphasize that the process by which the laborer moves from his "infantile"
attempts at creole to being able to speak to the luna could be a long and painful journey. Documenting this undocumented history of language acquisition,
then, begins with the body and the marks that instantiate and memorialize the
learning of pidgin. Tosh's desire for boxing and Kiyo's desire to leave the plantation is about owning their own bodies, writing their own texts. Owning one's
body and freedom to write one's own story are intimately connected because
of the way in which pidgin is acquired through violence written on the body in
an essentially "foreign" language. The learning of pidgin, then, is simultaneous
with colonial discipline on the plantation precisely because pidgin, according
to Reinecke, is the master's "language of command."[50]

Sally Engle Merry argues that during the 1900s the "criminalization of everyday life" functioned to produce a "free" labor force disconnected from land.
Practices that should have been seen as resistance to forced labor are typically
framed in the discourse of "disorder and immorality." New immigrant laborers
were also singled out as particular threats to public safety and health. The law
and the plantation system it served functioned to forcefully socialize and as-
similate new immigrant workers into the expectations of the planter class. This
does not mean that prohibited behaviors ceased altogether. Rather, these behaviors were slowly folded into existing social structures and hidden as they
assumed a place in the racial hierarchy.[51]

New groups, then, were interpellated as workers on the plantation through
the language of pidgin, which always carried with it the threat or actuality
of physical forms of punishment on the plantation and the criminalization of
everyday life in the court system. Failure to understand the "language of command," then, most definitely entailed discipline of some sort, the stigma of
being a disobedient worker or a criminal. However, unlike the hierarchical,
even patriarchal, languages of Standard English (plantation boss) and Japanese
(Tosh's father), HCE in Murayama's novel assumes a more lateral or horizontal
form where pidgin itself is the language of both authority and resistance, acquired both under the threat of violence and in the informal fraternal structure
of the work gang. Pidgin's dual function, as the ground for negotiating interethnic alliances representative of the local and as the language of command,

signals the ways in which subversion and resistance are inherent to the colonial structure. Internal to, and constitutive of, the colonial hierarchy is the master-slave relation, which requires the production of a creole language, a language that disrupts and corrupts the purity of the master's European language. Pidgin, then, does not function along a single axis; rather, it is simultaneously the language of the plantation, the site for preserving the Hawaiian language, and the site of critical anticolonial consciousness. Pidgin's vibrancy and strength as a language reside in its flexibility, its evasion of standardization, its ability not only to function within a wide array of colonial situations but to provide the basis for survival and modes of resistance.

Today, in the celebration of pidgin and pidgin literature in Hawai'i, pidgin's nonstandardized corruption of English is a central aspect of colonial resistance. Murayama's novel was the first important work to demonstrate the ways in which the language of command used to control workers was appropriated in the production of local literature as an oppositional deployment, a mode through which the plantation and other social institutions that collude with it knowingly or otherwise are critiqued from within. For while the plantation days are in some ways part of the past, there are other structures that remain—U.S. cultural and political hegemony—and others that have taken their place, among them, multinational corporate tourism and the significance of the military in Hawai'i's economy and land use policies.

This rootedness of pidgin within the hierarchical relations of Hawai'i's colonial relation to the United States is precisely why pidgin and pleasure are insufficient modes of resistance in the end for Kiyo. In *Plantation Boy*, the sequel to *All I Asking for Is My Body*, Murayama describes a Kiyo who chooses to leave Hawai'i for a life in San Francisco. One of the reasons for his exile is the perceived limitations of local identity. After his return from serving as an MIS agent in the war, Kiyo describes his ambivalent experiences of interrogating Japanese prisoners of war in the Philippines. He is disillusioned by the ways in which his country has positioned him—a person of Japanese descent able to speak Japanese—as someone who must betray in a very concrete way his sense of being Japanese to prove his Americanness. He is further disappointed by the inability or unwillingness of his local friends to understand his critical perspective on the United States. The postwar Hawai'i he returns to is radically different from the one he left in 1942. In this way, *Plantation Boy* articulates an uneasy space for Kiyo both outside and inside U.S. empire. It is a space that ultimately inhabits a critical relation even to local identity and pidgin, gesturing toward a space beyond pidgin that can only be brought into being through a transformation of the political and economic relation between the United States and Hawai'i, indeed, between the United States and the world.

Notes

1   José Martí, "Our America," in *Our America: Writings on Latin America and the Struggle for Cuban Independence*, ed. Philip S. Foner, trans. Elinor Randall et al. (New York: Monthly Review Press, 1977), 84–94.

2   Chalmers Johnson, *The Sorrows of Empire: Militarism, Secrecy, and the End of the Republic* (New York: Henry Holt, 2004).

3   See J. Kehaulani Kauanui, "'For Get' Hawaiian Entitlement: Configurations of Land, 'Blood' and Americanization in the Hawaiian Homes Commission Act of 1920," *Social Text* 59, no. 17 (1999): 123–44; and Susan Y. Najita, *Decolonizing Cultures in the Pacific: Reading History and Trauma in Contemporary Fiction* (London: Routledge, forthcoming).

4   *Vaqueros* from the Americas established the Hawaiian cowboy tradition, the *paniolo*.

5   See Gary Y. Okihiro, *Cane Fires: The Anti-Japanese Movement in Hawaii, 1865–1945* (Philadelphia: Temple University Press, 1991); Edward D. Beechert, *Working in Hawaii: A Labor History* (Honolulu: University of Hawaii Press, 1985); and Ronald Takaki, *Pau Hana: Plantation Life and Labor in Hawaii, 1835–1930* (Honolulu: University of Hawaii Press, 1983).

6   See Eric Yamamoto, "The Significance of Local," *Social Process in Hawai'i* 27 (1979): 101–15; Jonathan Y. Okamura, "Why There Are No Asian Americans in Hawai'i: The Continuing Significance of Local Identity," *Social Process* 35 (1994): 161–78; and Candace Fujikane, ed., "Whose Vision? Asian Settler Colonialism in Hawai'i" (special issue), *Amerasia* 26, no. 2 (2000): 158–94. For more on the meaning of "Kānaka Māoli," see Richard Kekuni Blaisdell, "Native Hawaiian 1992," in *To Steal a Kingdom*, ed. Michael Dougherty (Honolulu: Island Style Press, 2000), 182–84.

7   See Eileen H. Tamura, *Americanization, Acculturation, and Ethnic Identity: The Nisei Generation in Hawaii* (Urbana: University of Illinois Press, 1994).

8   Lili M. Kim, "When Your Body Becomes the Mark of the Enemy: Pearl Harbor and Korean Americans in Wartime Hawai'i," paper delivered at American Studies Association Annual Meeting, Hartford, Connecticut, 2003.

9   Milton Murayama, *All I Asking for Is My Body* (Honolulu: University of Hawaii Press, 1975). Hereafter cited in the text.

10   Although pidgin English is categorized as a creole language, "Hawaii Creole English," in this chapter I employ the term "pidgin" as the term used in everyday popular speech in Hawaii. See also my discussion of Reinecke later in the chapter.

11   Milton Murayama, "Problems of Writing in Dialect and Mixed Languages," *Bamboo Ridge* 5 (1979–80): 9.

12   Stephen H. Sumida, *And the View from the Shore: Literary Traditions of Hawai'i* (Seattle: University of Washington Press, 1991).

13   Gary Yong Ki Pak, "'E Ala Mai Kākou E Nā Kini Nā Mamo' [We, the Multitudes of Descendants Are Waking Up]: 19th-Century Hawaiian Historiography and the Historical Novel in Hawai'I" (Ph.D. diss., University of Hawai'i-Mānoa, 1997), 190.

14   Okihiro, *Cane Fires*, 255.

15   Milton Murayama, *Five Years on a Rock* (Honolulu: University of Hawai'i Press, 1994), 28.

16   Ibid., 38.

17   Ibid., 53.

18   For early assertions of Makot's homosexuality, see Rob Wilson, "Review: *All I Asking for Is My Body*," *Bamboo Ridge* 5 (1979–80): 2–5. Murayama concurs in "Letter to Darrell Lum," *Bamboo Ridge* 5 (1979–80): 6–7.

19   This is not to support the recent argument that local Japanese are "Asian settler colonialists." Rather, this chapter suggests that the system of plantation colonialism operated and maintained by haole (white American) interests produces this signification of Japanese values. In other words, it is impossible to be culturally Japanese and not support the colonial structure. This assertion is different from arguing that Japanese were settlers who sought to colonize Hawai'i. They lived in plantation housing at the will of the employer, so not in any way could they have been said to have owned or claimed the small plots of land on which they lived in the plantation camps. Further, Murayama's book suggests that due to the barriers to leaving the plantation, "settlement" beyond its boundaries was also often not possible or encouraged. See also Dana Y. Takagi, "Faith, Race, and Nationalism," *Journal of Asian American Studies* 7, no. 3 (October 2004): 271–88.

20   Elaine H. Kim, *Asian American Literature: An Introduction to the Writings and Their Social Context* (Philadelphia: Temple University Press, 1982).

21   Sumida, *And the View*, 1991.

22   Murayama, "Problems," 9.

23   Ibid.

24   Ibid., 10.

25   Murayama, "Letter to Darrell Lum," 7.

26   Milton Murayama, *Plantation Boy* (Honolulu: University of Hawai'i Press, 1998).

27   Ross Chambers, *Room for Maneuver: Reading (the) Oppositional (in) Narrative* (Chicago: University of Chicago Press, 1991), 1–7.

28   For more on Murayama's use of drama, see his "As Close as Possible to Experience," *Hawaii Herald*, December 5, 1980, 1.14, 5.

29   Ronald Takaki, *Strangers from a Different Shore: A History of Asian Americans* (Boston: Little, Brown, 1989), 68.

30   Israel Kamakawiwo'ole, "*Henehene kou 'aka*," *Facing Future* (Bigboy Record Company, 1993).

31   For a discussion of the rites of le'ale'a as a form of resistance, see Lilikalā Kame'elei-

hiwa, *Native Land and Foreign Desires: Pehea lā e Pono ai?* (Honolulu: Bishop Museum Press, 1992).

32   Teresia Teaiwa, "Scholarship from a Lazy Native," *Moana* 2 (spring 1999): 12–14.

33   Sally Engle Merry, *Colonizing Hawai'i: The Cultural Power of Law* (Princeton: Princeton University Press, 2000), 153; see also Takaki, *Pau Hana*, 68–72.

34   John E. Reinecke, *Language and Dialect in Hawaii: A Sociolinguistic History to 1935* (Honolulu: University of Hawaii Press, 1969). Hereafter cited parenthetically in the text.

35   For a discussion of pidgin (HCE) and the erroneous notion that it represents a "linguistic handicap," see Lisa Kanae, *Sister Tongue* (Honolulu: Tinfish, 2001).

36   Hirokuni Masuda, *The Genesis of Discourse Grammar: Universals and Substrata in Guyanese, Hawaii Creole, and Japanese* (New York: Peter Lang, 2000), 17.

37   Kent Sakoda and Jeff Siegel point out that Hawaiian, along with Cantonese and Portuguese, contributed to the structure of Pidgin Hawaiian and Pidgin English. The Japanese language had little effect on the grammatical structure of HCE because of the rather late arrival of the Japanese. By the start of Japanese immigration in 1888, Hawaiian, Chinese, and Portuguese had already "fixed" the form of Pidgin English spoken on the plantations. See Sakoda and Siegel, *Pidgin Grammar: An Introduction to the Creole Language of Hawai'i* (Honolulu: Bess Press, 2003), 11–13. Other linguistic "genealogies" for HCE include the argument that HCE developed out of Hawaii Pidgin English, which itself emerged out of Pacific Pidgin, spoken by traders, seamen, Hawaiians, and Pacific islanders in the late eighteenth century through the mid-nineteenth. See M. F. Goodman, "Review of Bickerton (1981)," *International Journal of American Linguistics* 51, no. 1 (1985): 109–37; J. Holm, *Pidgins and Creoles*, vol. 1, *Theory and Structure* (New York: Cambridge University Press, 1988); and J. H. McWhorter, "The Heart of the Issue: Input Deprivation," *Journal of Pidgin and Creole Languages* 13, no. 1 (1998): 208–10.

38   D. Bickerton and W. H. Wilson, "Pidgin Hawaiian," in *Pidgin and Creole Languages: Essays in Memory of John E. Reinecke* (Honolulu: University of Hawai'i Press, 1987).

39   William C. Smith, "Pidgin English in Hawaii," *American Speech* 8 (February 1933): 15–19.

40   Bickerton and Wilson, "Pidgin Hawaiian," 74, 11.

41   Ibid., 72. J. M. Roberts also suggests that the period from 1880 to 1900 was significant in expanding the prevalence of English, which led to a shift from Hawaiian to English as the principal lexifier language. Roberts, "Pidgin Hawaiian: A Sociohistorical Study," *Journal of Pidgin and Creole Languages* 10, no. 1 (1995): 1.

42   Masuda, *Genesis of Discourse Grammar*, 14.

43   To complicate the discussion of HCE emergence, Sarah Julianne Roberts has recently refuted Bickerton's theory by arguing that Pidgin Hawaiian was not a significant predecessor to HCE but that Pidgin English emerged out of peer relations outside both the English classroom and the home. She argues that among the children of immigrant parents, multilingualism was prevalent during the pre-annexation

period. This description is much more in keeping with Murayama's novel, though it fails to explain the linguistic significance of the Hawaiian language that Bickerton and Wilson's theory provides.

44   Okihiro, *Cane Fires*, 139. Morris Young also discusses Murayama's novel in terms of how literacy is a form of discipline, exclusion, and racialization of Asian Americans within the U.S. nation-state. See Young, *Minor Re/visions: Asian American Literacy Narratives as a Rhetoric of Citizenship* (Carbondale: Southern Illinois University Press, 2004).

45   Murayama, *Plantation Boy*, 20, 50.

46   Reinecke, *Language and Dialect in Hawaii*, 104–7.

47   Quoted in Takaki, *Pau Hana*, 73–74.

48   Quoted in Takaki, *Pau Hana*, 74.

49   Takaki, *Pau Hana*, 75.

50   Extrapolating from Reinecke's claims, whether or not the language of command is Hawaiian Pidgin (HP), HPE, or HCE depends on which historical period one is referring to. However, even though there is a shift in the usage from Hawaiian-based HP to the English-based HCE, the plantation master represents the same class of white Euro-Americans. HP, HPE, and HCE in the context of the plantation would function as languages of command.

51   Merry, *Colonizing Hawai'i*, 189, 205.

Experimental Dreams, Ethical Nightmares

Leprosy, Isolation, and Human Experimentation

in Nineteenth-Century Hawaii

Nicholas Turse

In August 1886, the *Medical News* reported that George L. Fitch, a physician "in charge of lepers in the Sandwich Islands," had been conducting experiments "to inoculate the [leprosy] virus into healthy persons."[1] Fitch's research, even in the context of lax controls on human experimentation during the nineteenth century, was particularly egregious. Apparently without anything resembling informed consent, and perhaps under the guise of providing treatment, Fitch also infected children with the deadly disease of syphilis, in addition to carrying out other heinous human experiments. Yet in the context of the Hawaiian experience, Fitch's research wasn't beyond the pale. Even more astonishing is the possibility that, perhaps, Fitch was the *best* of Hawaii's experimentalist physicians.

In recent years, many scholars have called attention to the widespread medical research performed on human populations during the nineteenth and twentieth centuries.[2] Rising out of the dual traditions of the French clinic and the German hospital, human experimentation exploded with the bacteriological and parasitological revolutions of late-nineteenth-century medicine, bringing to the fore ethical and biomedical concerns that are still as relevant today as when they first entered the arena of debate.[3] Yet while we have come to recognize the experimentalist mind-set of modern biomedicine, certain aspects of its history have largely been neglected—notably, experimentation in colonial and neocolonial contexts.[4]

This chapter investigates one underanalyzed neocolonial experience—public health and medical interventions against leprosy in Hawaii during the late nineteenth century. Although a number of authors have examined facets of this subject, none have adequately addressed the experimental ethos that permeated the world of Hawaiian leprosy during this period.[5] While one author noted that Hawaii became "a laboratory of the world," he based this assertion on the belief that Hawaii had provided a single "human guinea pig on whom to experiment" and a later research facility that was unsuccessful in attracting volunteers. As a result, he noted, "The idea of the island as laboratory had failed."[6]

In reality, human experimentation in Hawaii was much more widespread. I contend that Hawaii became an extraordinary arena for experimental leprosy research undertaken on human populations. Appreciating that many colonies (and contexts) served such a purpose during the late nineteenth century, I argue that Hawaii differed not in the kind but in the degree of experimentation in specific reference to leprosy.

While not truly a colony in a technical sense, the Hawaiian islands were certainly engaged in a colonial relationship with the United States during the latter half of the nineteenth century.[7] During this period, most notably the 1880s, native Hawaiians were subject to what we might term grossly imperialistic experimental medicine. I argue that this experimental ethos resulted from the archipelago's unique status as a neocolony of the United States,[8] in which a minority native population of dark-skinned racial Others were dominated by white foreign capitalist interests set on forging close ties with the United States. This led to the creation of a public health system and biomedical ethos that valued the economic interests of white foreigners over the welfare of native Hawaiians.

While it is true, as Megan Vaughan notes, that aside from their affliction, Hawaiian lepers, as dark-skinned racial Others, already carried the stigmas (such as being considered primitive, savage, sexually promiscuous, and ignorant, among other negative stereotypes) common to various "Others" in all manner of contexts, the doubly stigmatized Hawaiian leper provided something more than what the British colonial experience in Africa yielded: the African as an object of knowledge.[9] The Hawaiian leper was additionally a target of white hopes to eradicate the infectious and unclean Other.

Moreover, the Hawaiian leper was not simply a diseased entity to be dumped in an out-of-the-way place to create a dichotomy between sick/Other/island and well/Western/mainland zones, as Ron Edmond suggests, but *foreign* research material to be experimented on in an attempt to cure the "diseased island" and make the *dangerous* tropics safe, and profitable, for white mainlanders. Thus, while leprosy was endemic to Europe and known to have been brought to the islands by outsiders, the malady came to be seen as a thoroughly native Hawaiian disease requiring intervention by white authorities. Edmond has rightly observed, however, that "among the white Protestant establishment in Honolulu leprosy came to be seen not only as a native disease but also as a just punishment for a diseased culture."[10] As such, the disease was targeted for heroic medical eradication by the white Protestant establishment, not coincidentally at a time when the native Hawaiian population itself was increasingly being socially, politically, and economically marginalized and, through immigration policies, numerically minimized in proportion to the total population of the archipelago.

Disease and the Colonial Experience in Hawaii

When Captain James Cook first visited Hawaii in 1778, the native population was, apparently, remarkably healthy. After the once geographically isolated islands became increasingly involved in the global trade economy, and as the nineteenth century progressed and mercantilism gave way to capitalism, Hawaii underwent a great change. In a short time, what began as a small enclave of *haole* (white foreigners and mainlanders and, later, also Hawaiian-born whites) missionaries and merchants and an economy based on whale oil and sandalwood gave way to an influx of white businessmen and their plantation agriculture and industrialized sugar mills.[11]

With foreign visitors came the exotic diseases of the European world, such as influenza, measles, tuberculosis, and syphilis, which led to the type of depopulation that decimated aboriginal and Amerindian populations elsewhere in the New World. The indigenous Hawaiian population numbered perhaps as many as one million in the late eighteenth century.[12] By 1896, only 24,000 native islanders remained.[13] Clearly, foreign incursions exacted a terrible toll on the Hawaiian people.

While the Kingdom of Hawaii (unified by King Kamehameha in 1795) was originally dominated by British interests, American influence in the islands grew steadily throughout the 1800s. Not coincidentally, over time, a near-constant ebbing of native Hawaiian political, economic, and social power took place. Until 1848, no private property existed in Hawaii. By 1886, after haole business interests had pressured the kingdom to recognize Western notions of property rights, foreigners owned two-thirds of the islands' lands.

By 1896, Hawaiians were a distinct minority in the archipelago, with Asians (from Japan and China) comprising 40 percent of the population and haoles 20 percent.[14] The great Asian influx to the islands, which took place primarily during the 1870s and 1880s, was brought about by the demands of haole agribusiness for more plantation workers. At the same time, the leaders of the five largest sugar companies in the islands ("the Big Five") and assorted haole allies used a private militia known as the Hawaiian Rifles to force the Hawaiian king David Kalakaua to sign the "bayonet constitution." This 1887 document allowed for much greater governmental participation on the part of haoles.

By 1893, however, haoles demanded even more power and, with the aid of the U.S. Navy, overthrew Queen Lili'uokalani. The Republic of Hawaii was then founded, with the haole Sanford Dole as its president, and promptly set about politically marginalizing native Hawaiians through a new constitution that reduced indigenous islanders to only 20 percent of the voting population. The conquest of Hawaii finally ended in the aftermath of the United States' great foray into imperialism, the Spanish-American War. Through a joint congressional resolution passed in 1898, Hawaii was annexed and by 1900 became a full-fledged U.S. territory.[15]

As haole interests began to dominate the Hawaiian islands, all things native became increasingly vilified. Just as climatological theories of the nineteenth century branded Hawaii as a dangerous environment of tropical miasma, racial theories rooted in social Darwinism branded Hawaiians as "heathen" and "semi-savage" primitives.[16] Thus developed a lay view of the Hawaiian as a polluted reservoir of disease, a view that meshed well with existing medical doctrine and became especially manifest in public health policies during the period of the haole consolidation of power (1887–97).[17]

Leprosy in Hawaii

One of the more spectacular and dreaded imported maladies to afflict the Hawaiian population, in terms of stigma rather than gross loss of life, was the ancient disease of leprosy. Long shrouded in shame and mystery, today leprosy is known as Hansen's disease (named after the discoverer of the causal bacteria) and is understood as a chronic infectious disease, caused by the *Mycobacterium leprae*, that affects the skin and peripheral nerves, causing victims to experience muscle weakness, paralysis, and in some cases sores, inflamed lesions, and deformities of the limbs, eyes, and face.[18]

As leprosy, known as Mai Pake (Chinese sickness),[19] spread throughout the islands, the haole establishment, dominated by business interests in the fruit and sugar industries, was loath to acknowledge the disease's presence for fear of economic repercussions.[20] Accordingly, the Hawaiian Board of Health did not even mention the presence of leprosy in its inaugural handout of 1850.[21] However, by the 1860s the disease was causing such "great alarm [in] the community" that even the Hawaiian Board of Health physician Dr. W. Hilldebrand was forced to admit that leprosy was endemic among the Hawaiian population. This avowal of the presence of disease set in motion a series of official debates that culminated in the enactment of the 1865 Act to Prevent the Spread of Leprosy.[22]

Enacted during the reign of the "puppet Hawaiian king" Kamehameha V, at the urging of "haole eminences" on the Board of Health as a public health measure designed to thwart the proliferation of the disease, the 1865 act authorized government lands to be set aside for the isolation and seclusion of people deemed by the Board of Health to be stricken with, or capable of spreading, leprosy. Further, the act empowered law enforcement officials to arrest and deliver to the Board of Health "any person alleged to be a leper" for mandatory medical inspection.[23] It also set into motion the creation of an entire network of facilities for the containment and isolation of lepers.[24] One of these, the Kalawao Leper Settlement, which was established in 1866 on the east side of the Kalaupapa Peninsula on the island of Molokai, became famous for its large size and for the Catholic missionary priest Father Damien de Veuster, who ministered to the settlement's lepers from 1873 until his death from leprosy (which attracted worldwide attention) in 1889.[25]

The decision to employ isolation was made easier because the disease was largely extinct in Europe (although it was endemic in Norway) and was relatively rare in the United States. As such, only small populations of Westerners were subject to lazarettos and leper settlements. By contrast, most leper colonies existed in colonial contexts.[26] And since poor, dark-skinned, racial Others of India, Africa, Asia, and the Pacific islands made up the majority of the world's cases, white Western authorities had little impetus to shift from this paradigm. Thus the disease increasingly took on a "tropical" and, although it was known to have been imported to the islands, a *native* etiology in Hawaii.[27] This understanding of leprosy as a *foreign* disease of racial Others follows Michael Worboys's argument that the concept of "tropical" disease was rooted in issues of imperialist social, economic, and political control.[28]

In the year following the 1865 Act to Prevent the Spread of Leprosy, 141 persons were sent to the newly created Kalawao Leper Settlement on the island of Molokai to be isolated from the rest of island society. Of them, only two (both Chinese immigrants) were not native Hawaiians.[29] Pennie Moblo states that although "from the time Hawaii initiated a policy of segregation the rate was stable[,] averaging about 135 new cases [of leprosy] per year," there was a haole perception that the disease was on the increase throughout the islands and that drastic measures were needed to halt the spread of a burgeoning epidemic. While the steady rate of new cases points to flaws in the effectiveness of compulsory isolation of lepers, an examination of incarceration rates demonstrates that during the ten years of greatest haole oppression (1887–97, the decade of the so-called reform government and the Hawaiian Republic), lepers were confined in numbers far exceeding the rate of the spread of the disease.[30]

Hawaiian leprosy also began to take on increasing significance as ties between the archipelago and the United States became stronger (e.g., when the Treaties of Reciprocity in 1876 and 1886 removed trade barriers) and American annexation of the islands became a greater possibility.[31] Dr. Prince A. Morrow, a physician from the United States who traveled to Hawaii to chronicle possible public health concerns that might impede U.S. annexation, wrote: "When it is considered that more than ten per cent. of the Hawaiian race are affected with leprosy it becomes a serious question as to what will be the affect [*sic*] of the absorption of this tainted population upon the health interests of this country."[32]

While Morrow reported that there were only approximately 1,200 lepers at the Molokai settlement, his figures also included the "probably two or three times as many" lepers that he concluded lived among Hawaii's 35,000 (according to his estimates) natives.[33] Similarly, another American commentator, Dr. Burnside A. Foster, made reference to a fellow physician's statistics (presumably Morrow's) that held that nearly 10 percent of Hawaiians were lepers. However, Foster's own statistics, which were published less than a year after Morrow's 1897 account, dramatically increased the estimated number of afflicted Hawaiians from Morrow's approximation of between 2,400 and 3,600 to a staggering 6,000, or 17 percent of the native population.[34]

While only sixteen whites were sent to the Molokai settlement between 1866 and 1885, some 2,997 native Hawaiians were banished there. By 1900, while only 1 in 1,847 haoles were afflicted with leprosy, 1 in 39 Hawaiians were said to have the stigmatized malady.[35] It should be noted that in addition to factors of social causation, such as poverty, poor nutrition, Western medical interventions (such as arm-to-arm smallpox vaccination), and cultural practices (such as communal poi eating) that contributed to the prevalence of the disease in the native population, the ratio of native Hawaiian to white Western lepers was inflated by the fact that foreign sufferers were, for many years, allowed to leave the islands and were offered repatriation to their homelands if suspected of having the illness.[36] Although even white Western commentators such as Morrow recognized that the percentage of Hawaiians was inflated by the non-Hawaiians' ability to leave the islands, above all, haoles held that it was "because [the Hawaiian] fails to realize the danger that menaces him, apart from the extreme receptivity of his system to the bacillus of leprosy, a condition lacking in other races domiciled in Hawaii . . . [that] he (the Hawaiian) is the weak link in our chain of national health defense."[37]

Not only were Hawaiians cast as physically inferior and thus exceptionally susceptible to leprosy, but they also failed to fear the disease, which Megan Vaughan has noted was generally considered to be a sign of being uncivilized.[38] Thus haole and Western authorities embraced the practice of isolating lepers. The Harvard leprologist James C. White captured the haole public health sentiment when he wrote: "If Draconian laws regarding marriage and intercourse could stamp out consumption and syphilis, as some day they will, who would feel that he had the right to oppose them? Lepers belong to the dangerous classes of the community which require perpetual confinement, and the sooner this remedy is applied the less seeming cruelty will attach to it."[39]

This sentiment found a receptive audience among whites eager to marginalize the dark-skinned Others that stood between them and total control of the archipelago. Yet what is most telling is that this overwhelmingly pro-segregation sentiment among haoles intensified at the same time that prevailing medical opinion had begun to turn decidedly against the mandatory isolation of lepers. As the etiology of the disease came to be better understood by nineteenth-century scientific standards, many medical researchers began to espouse the belief that while the malady was communicable, it was certainly no more, and probably less, contagious than tuberculosis or syphilis.

By 1862, the Leprosy Committee of the Royal College of Physicians, London, could report that the "all but unanimous conviction of the most experienced observers in different parts of the world is quite opposed to the belief that leprosy is contagious or communicable by proximity or contact with the disease."[40] In 1865, the same year that the haole-led Hawaiian Board of Health enacted sweeping pro isolation legislation, anticontagion sentiment was strengthened when the Leprosy Committee stated unequivocally that leprosy was never communicable and was a hereditary, constitutional disorder. Even over twenty years later (1889), when British authorities published the results of another scientific inquiry in which eminent medical authorities such as Patrick Manson and James Cantlie, along with one thousand physicians across the globe, came to the same conclusions, Hawaiian haoles (and, increasingly, American commentators)[41] remained adamant that isolation was the necessary means to effectively prevent the spread of the illness.[42]

Experimentation on Hawaii's Lepers

While some medical authorities never wavered from their belief in leprosy's communicability and after the 1897 World Leprosy Conference in Berlin, the disease's infectious nature was rarely questioned, the actions of the Hawaiian Board of Health from 1865 onward show that their beliefs were certainly rooted in something other than the prevailing biomedical and scientific thinking of the era.[43] While leprosy was later found to be contagious, the established medical and scientific canon of the mid- to late-nineteenth century held otherwise. As Pennie Moblo argues, haole authorities were more concerned with establishing and displaying their power over the *sick* native through repressive public health policies than medically addressing the illness.[44]

Related to Hawaii's insistence on a policy of strict isolation was its preferred biomedical protocol. Moblo contends that the palliative treatments (medicated baths and herbal salves) that lepers were fond of were shunned by haole authorities, who were more interested in spending available funds on the "extermination of the pathogen with harsh experimental drugs."[45] This parallels the late-nineteenth-century shift in Western public health practice brought about by the bacteriological revolution, in which older sanitarian notions of eliminating filth were replaced by targeted public health interventions designed to identify and eradicate disease-causing microorganisms.[46]

I would further argue that severe treatment protocols were indicative of an experimental ethos fostered by haole public health and medical authorities who sought to eradicate leprosy for the sake of white Western interests. As such, to counter growing Western perceptions of rampant leprosy in the archipelago that could damage haole business, ties to the United States, and hopes for annexation, the Hawaiian Board of Health created a medico-cultural environment that promoted unbridled experimentation and encouraged practitioners to use all means at their disposal to eradicate the disease.[47] Writing just after the United States had annexed the islands, Dr. D. A. Carmichael, a physician with the United States Marine Hospital Service (which later became the U.S. Public Health Service) dispatched to the islands on the approval of President McKinley, applauded this ethos, what Dr. Carmichael termed the Hawaiian government's "liberality" in allowing physicians to undertake relatively unfettered medical experimentation and employ all manner of treatments.[48]

No one person exemplified the experimental ethos surrounding leprosy in Hawaii as much as Dr. George L. Fitch. An 1870 graduate of Bellevue Hospital Medical College in New York, Fitch arrived in Hawaii on December 13, 1880. First appointed as the government physician to the northern district of the island of Kauai, he then became the surgeon in charge of the government dispensary in Honolulu and also medical superintendent of the Kakaako Branch Leper Hospital. In 1882 Fitch was also selected as the medical superintendent of the Kalawao Leper Settlement by the Hawaiian Board of Health, a position in which he served while retaining his other two government appointments.[49]

Fitch became well known in Hawaii for his views on the relation between the two stigmatizing diseases of leprosy and syphilis. Ignoring the prevailing medical opinion that held the two diseases to be unrelated, Fitch espoused the belief that leprosy was in fact "a fourth stage of syphilis" and therefore generally noncontagious and noncommunicable — except by hereditary transmission. Fitch theorized that the disease especially ravaged Hawaiians because this fourth stage only occurred endemically in races previously untouched by syphilis, as well as in those individuals whose bodies had "reverted" to a more primitive state.[50]

Fitch's hereditarian views are indicative of common prebacteriological medical opinions of the nineteenth century that held that diseases, and sometimes immunities, were in some way transmissible to offspring.[51] While novel in Hawaii (although leprosy was in some ways tacitly thought of as a punishment for native sexual promiscuity),[52] Fitch's leprosy-syphilis connection was hardly new, but it had been abandoned by the large majority of the Western biomedical establishment.[53]

Fitch, however, continued to adhere to a leprosy-syphilis relationship, which provoked anger from the haole medical fraternity, and then the greater haole public, in Hawaii. Undaunted, he continued to publicize his opinion that the two diseases were related by lecturing and publishing articles on the subject.[54] One such article appeared in the September 1892, (New York) *Medical Record*.[55] Titled "The Etiology of Leprosy," the piece advanced Fitch's leprosy-syphilis hypothesis and reviewed leprosy literature and case histories supporting his theory. The article also included a number of reminiscences and personal anecdotes from Fitch's days in Hawaii, which he used to bolster his medical theories. In the middle of this otherwise innocuous article, however, the doctor made a startling disclosure — an admission that Fitch openly broadcast — that exemplifies the experimental ethos surrounding Hawaiian leprosy.

In 1900, the antivivisectionist American Humane Association looked back in horror at Fitch's "utterly loathsome and abominable experiments" as they reprinted a portion of the haole physician's 1892 article (while stating that it was impossible to publish the full details of the ghastly research). The experiments that they recounted, which began on November 14, 1883, centered around Fitch's supposition that leprosy and syphilis were the same disease. In an effort to prove this, Fitch scraped the scab off a mucous patch on the lip of a syphilis-infected Hawaiian woman and, using ivory vaccine points, proceeded to inoculate six syphilis-free "leper girls under twelve years of age." Not content with one lone trial, a month later, Fitch took "the virus from a hard chancre on the penis of a Portuguese" and transferred it to the arms of the same children.[56]

In the eyes of the American Humane Association, experimenting on children by inoculating them with a loathsome and lethal disease such as syphilis was abhorrent. The fact that the girls were already suffering from an incurable disease made subjecting them to infection with a more lethal disorder even more horrifying.[57] For Fitch, however, this was a valid experiment designed to prove his theory. Soon after the second inoculation, Fitch found a new cohort of fourteen lepers and proceeded to inoculate them with syphilis as well. Similarly, Fitch also found some thirty Hawaiian men and women who were infected with syphilis, and presumably free of leprosy, and inoculated them "with blood and serum obtained from scarified leprous nodules." According to the American Humane Association, the individuals were experimented on "with[out] their consent or . . . any comprehension of intent" by a physician who hid his experimental intentions behind the "guise of administering a remedy for their complaints!"[58]

Shocked and appalled by Fitch's unabashed admission, the American Humane Association lamented the fact that while the Cruelty to Animals Act of 1867 had greatly curtailed animal experimentation in Great Britain and that in America support for antivivisection campaigns was increasing, Fitch was openly performing "human vivisections" in Hawaii.[59] Moreover, the American Humane Association was not alone in its condemnation. The antivaccination leprologist William Tebb wrote with specific reference to Fitch's inoculations, "Is it not time to put a stop to the torture to which incurable sick lepers are subjected by drug and inoculation, and let these miserable creatures be made as comfortable as tender nursing, varied occupations, and amusements will allow, and permit them to die in peace?"[60]

These sentiments, published a year after Fitch's *Medical Record* article, articulate a therapeutic sensibility that was apparently foreign to Fitch and, as we shall see, to other Hawaiian leprologists. In reference to Fitch's experimentation, Tebb also wrote, "One thing is certain, the unfortunate patients dread the experimental treatment to which they are subjected by lepra experts, often escaping from lazarettos and secreting themselves in the gullies and fastnesses of the hilly regions and in the jungle to avoid the terrible ordeal to which they would probably be subjected."[61] But was this truly the case? Were lepers fleeing from Fitch's experimental "treatments"?

By 1883, after years of Fitch's experimentation, the Hawaiian Board of Health had had enough of him and began to agitate for his removal from office. A libel suit, initiated by Fitch against the Hawaiian *Saturday Press*, who had criticized the physician's medical acumen and pronounced his actions as superintendent of the leper settlement to be "criminal," soon turned into an indictment of Fitch. Hawaii's physicians, pharmacists, politicians, and businessmen weighed in on Fitch, his peculiar medical theories, and his treatment of leprosy. The doctor soon found himself castigated in court by the judge and insulted by numerous haole witnesses, while his suit against the newspaper was dismissed.[62]

Attacks by the haole community proved too great for Fitch to bear, and in December 1884 he resigned his government positions and took up private practice. Shortly thereafter, he was on the losing end of a street fight with the secretary of the Hawaiian Board of Health, F. H. Hayselden, and not long after this incident the embattled experimenter left Hawaii. Yet far from rejoicing at the news of Fitch's coerced resignations, many Hawaiians wrote to the board in protest. In fact, native islanders circulated a "petition signed by many subjects of the Kingdom," asking that Fitch be reinstated to his posts. The Board of Health unanimously rejected the idea.[63]

Fitch, it appears, was very different from other physicians serving the Hawaiian leper communities—his leprosy-syphilis views aside. While other haole officials, such as those on the Hawaiian Board of Health, were reportedly "not too well loved by the Hawaiian people," Fitch, who openly condemned the practice of enforced isolation (he spoke openly of its "really brutal severity") of Hawaiian lepers and used his noncontagion beliefs to speak out against the practice, was embraced.[64] Fitch also endeared himself to the native population by engaging in acts of charity, such as providing free medical care to the poor every day. Further, his belief in the social origins of the disease (he wrote of inadequate "food supply and manner of living" as causative agents) and the hands-on character of his care (as he interacted with lepers with no fear of contagion), which other haoles described as "reckless and careless," appear to have endeared him to his Hawaiian patients.[65]

From the Hawaiian King Kalakaua and Queen Kapiolani and their royal court to the lepers whom he treated at his three medical posts, Fitch was, apparently, universally praised by native Hawaiians. Arthur Mouritz, Fitch's successor as medical superintendent of the Kalawao Leper Settlement, related that Fitch had "gained the inner confidence of the Hawaiian people more than any other foreign physician" and remembered that even many years after Fitch had left Hawaii, "lepers were always calling for Kauka Pika's (Hawaiian for Dr. Fitch) medicines." Wrote one patient, "[Dr. Fitch] has tried to do us some good—not stood off at a distance and [poked] us with a stick. The other doctors came for the salary and not to benefit the lepers."[66] Thus the Hawaiian Board of Health had *saved* the islands' lepers from their most beloved physician and further had not even done so in the paternalistic best interests of the patients under their care. Rather, they forced Fitch out of Hawaii for the very reasons the lepers wanted Kauka Pika to stay.[67]

Fitch's notion of leprosy as syphilis was troubling to the haole establishment not because it was *bad* science (although authorities often paid lip service to this reason) or led him to undertake dangerous experiments, but because it undermined the Board of Health's efforts to isolate lepers and eradicate leprosy. Because Fitch believed leprosy was a noncontagious stage of syphilis, he discharged between forty and fifty patients from the Kakaako Branch Leper Hospital in just one year, drawing the ire of haole authorities. Similarly, in the three years (1882–84) that Fitch was head of the Kalawao Leper Settlement, more patients were discharged or unaccounted for than had been released in the previous seven years combined.[68]

The Hawaiian authorities accused Fitch of "criminal mismanagement of leprosy" for none of the reasons the American Humane Association would have
made the same complaint. While antivivisectionists abroad castigated Fitch
for his outrageous medical experiments on human populations, haole interests
found only Fitch's proclivity "to experiment with his theories" that leprosy was
syphilis, and hence noncontagious, to be "an outrage."[69]

Experimentation after Fitch

While Fitch was driven from Hawaii, experimentalism was most certainly not.
In fact, the experimental ethos had long been institutionalized by Hawaiian
haoles. In 1874 the Hawaiian legislature had appropriated six thousand dollars
to two foreign physicians, C. T. Akana and a Dr. Powell, so that six leprosy
"patients were experimented upon with various drugs."[70] While drug treatment differs markedly from the horrific trials carried out by Fitch and was used
by leprologists throughout the world, it is instructive to note that government
funds were earmarked for experimentation as early as the mid-1870s.[71] Further,
it is also important to know that drug trials promising the hope of a cure for
the disease were considered worthwhile undertakings, whereas palliative treatments were generally devalued and suppressed.

One method of leprosy experimentation that did receive wholehearted haole
support took place in 1884, when the Hawaiian Board of Health petitioned
King Kalakaua's Privy Council to commute the death sentence of a Hawaiian
named Keanu to life imprisonment. Far from acting out of sheer benevolence,
the board sought to use the convicted murderer in a human leprosy experiment
"for the advancement of science" and asked that Keanu "submit to inoculation
with leprosy" to ascertain the contagiousness of the disease.[72] The Privy Council
granted the request, and Keanu signed a written consent allowing Dr. Edward
Arning (who had been an adversary of George Fitch) to inoculate him with the
disease.[73] A leprous nodule excised from the cheek of a young leper was im-
planted in Keanu's right arm. Twenty-five months later, in October 1886, Keanu
began exhibiting signs of leprosy; by the next year, he was a confirmed leper,
and his case became world renowned.[74] In 1888, after four years of confinement
in Oahu jail, Keanu's leprous appearance caused him to be labeled "a men-
ace." He was then moved to the Molokai Leper Settlement, where he died on
November 18, 1892.[75]

To a number of foreign medical observers, such as the British leprosy expert William Tebb, Keanu's death sentence by way of leprosy was a brutal punishment that, even for a capital crime, was "utterly unjustifiable." Similarly, Dr. William Jelly, in an 1887 piece in the *British Medical Journal*, wrote: "I daresay the poor Kanaka convict [Keanu], had he known what leprosy is, would, without hesitation have preferred the guillotine, the garrote, or the hangman's rope." The cruelty of the case even prompted Dr. F. B. Sutliff, a haole physician who had spent years studying leprosy in Hawaii, to "suppose no other man will ever be purposely inoculated with leprosy."[76]

Just two months before Keanu began exhibiting signs of leprosy, on July 1, 1886, Edward Arning, like George Fitch before him, left Hawaii. Despite the criticisms of Arning's experimentation from abroad, it was not ethical concerns that caused the Hawaiian Board of Health to terminate his services. In actuality, the board felt that Arning was too cautious and overly scholarly in his work, and although he advocated strict segregation policies, his experiments were not perceived as sufficiently virulent in attacking the leprosy pathogen.[77]

Another prominent experimentalist haole physician of the era was Dr. Arthur A. Mouritz, who arrived in Hawaii in 1883, was appointed to a number of medical posts, and also became involved in haole business interests. A practicing physician until his death in 1943, Mouritz also conducted his "own experiments, extending over many years," on human subjects. For example, he engaged in experimental trials in which he allowed fleas, "bedbugs," and mosquitoes to feed on lepers so that he might ascertain if an insect vector was involved in the transmission of leprosy.[78]

A more ethically disturbing line of research in Mouritz's vast array of experimental work was his use of completely healthy subjects as clinical research material. Over a period of three years, beginning in December 1884, Mouritz carried out experiments at the Kalawao Leper Settlement in which he attempted to infect leprosy-free persons with the dreaded disease. Using "abundant supplies of leprous serum" obtained from the blisters of patients in the leper settlement, the haole physician (like Fitch and Arning) undertook inoculation experimentation to settle the long-held point of contention as to the contagiousness of the disease.[79]

For his first subject, Mouritz selected a thirty-one-year-old male Hawaiian whom he referred to as "A." The Hawaiian had come to the physician claiming to suffer from Mai Pake, an assertion that Mouritz, after examining the patient, did not believe. Stridently declaring his leper status, "A" continued attempting to convince Mouritz of his supposed affliction. Sensing an opportunity, the haole physician "informed 'A' that [he] would use certain measures to decide his case." According to Mouritz, the would-be leper responded that, barring "hypodermic treatment," he would "submit to any other medicines that [Mouritz] might see fit to use" to ascertain if he was a leper. Mouritz seized the opportunity to perform his leprosy investigation; the method—inoculate "A" with leprosy.[80] Over the next three years, Mouritz used similar techniques to inoculate other nonleprous research subjects (males "B" through "J" and females "O" through "S") with leper blister serum, blood, saliva, and leprous vesicle fluid.

While the story of the experimentation undertaken on the thirty-one-year-old "A" appears to be an extremely sinister case of medical imperialism in which a patient was unequivocally denied informed consent and was, under the guise of testing and treatment, used as a research subject, Mouritz wrote of this trial, decades later, with no qualms. The haole doctor remembered, "The Leper Settlement on Molokai maintained [an] abundance of healthy kokuas [nonleprous attendants], all willing to be experimented on by inoculation, serums and any other means likely to develop leprosy; the artificially made lepers hoping to obtain board and lodging, for the remainder of their lives; being listed as lepers—livelihood, and existence without working being provided by the Board of Health."[81]

Mouritz recounted being "pestered and annoyed daily with requests to examine purposely caused lesions . . . generally consisting of incised, contused, or lacerated wounds." Along with the physical mutilation of their bodies, Mouritz also wrote of feigned pains, paralyses, and anesthesia exhibited by Hawaiians. For the haole doctor, only malingering and the indolence of the Hawaiian Other could be the rationale for such behavior: "What other country of the world save in Hawaii, would people be found willing to take chances of acquiring a loathsome and incurable disease? the sole object to be gained for the loss of health and shortened lives, *being maintained at public expense.*"[82]

Yet if one examines the recorded accounts of Mouritz's inoculation experiments from 1884 to 1887, an alternative reasoning emerges that both offers a countertheory to the haole assumption of native slothfulness and explains why, in fact, a Hawaiian might cause self-inflicted wounds and volunteer for medical experimentation. While recounting the research undertaken on test subject "B," who lived at the settlement to take care of his leper mother, Mouritz stated that the Hawaiian admitted a desire to become afflicted with leprosy in order to prevent himself from being evicted from the settlement after the death of his mother. Like "B," Mouritz claimed that all his other test subjects desired to be classified as lepers, and, it is worth noting, all were firmly rooted in the culture of the leper settlement at Molokai. For example, male test subjects A, C, E, F, and I, as well as female test subjects O, P, Q, R, and S, were married to leper spouses, while males D and G cared for their leprous siblings.[83]

Perhaps the most telling of the narratives, however, is that of "Q," a thirty-five-year-old woman who had lived at the Kalawao Leper Settlement. "Q," who had seen leprosy claim her four husbands and three children, was declared to be free of the disease herself. Like "Typhoid Mary" Mallon, the New York City woman who once bemoaned being "banished like a leper" by the city's Department of Health, "Q" was stigmatized for somehow acting as a healthy carrier of leprosy, infecting her previously unleprous husbands and children with a disease she did not herself possess. Depicted almost as a leprous black widow, with a "comely and graceful" appearance and a plethora of suitors, "Q" was the object of much "comment and gossip" for "the speedy way in which all of [her] husbands . . . became lepers."

After the death of her fourth husband, the Hawaiian woman decided she would never marry again and refused the advances of all would-be suitors. "Q" took up hat making, clothes washing, and sewing at the leper settlement but feared she might be expelled, as she did not have leprosy, nor did she have any family members left at the settlement.[84] According to Mouritz, "This woman 'Q' had fears that she would be deported from Kalawao. During her fourteen years of residence all her friends and relations outside had died, and she regarded herself as a homeless outcast, if she had to remove from the Settlement."[85]

Despite recounting her reasoning, Mouritz still insisted that the woman's willingness to acquire leprosy was simply a means to achieve "life-long residence, food and lodging." For Mouritz it seemed inconceivable that anyone should want to acquire leprosy or the label of leper, although he understood that, generally, Hawaiians did not fear the disease or shrink from what he termed "careless contact with leprosy."[86] It was not even within Mouritz's realm of comprehension that being devoid of a community and kinship structure was in some way worse than having leprosy.

Yet while Mouritz was critical of what he regarded to be abnormal Hawaiian attitudes to leprosy, his experimental protocols would have been seen as equally unusual by many of his counterparts practicing medicine elsewhere. When in 1891 the French physician Victor Cornil merely described, in a journal article, the homotransplantation of cancerous material into an anesthetized woman without her consent, performed by a nameless foreign surgeon, he was soundly criticized by both French and American medical professionals.[87]

Even in other colonial contexts, guidelines for biomedical ethics were very different from those in Hawaii. Like Mouritz, Fitch, and Arning, S. P. Impey, chief and medical superintendent of the Robben Island Leper and Lunatic Asylum in Cape Colony, South Africa, wished to engage in human experimentation, but unlike his Hawaiian counterparts, he was unwilling to do so. Impey believed that attacks of the dermal infection erysipelas would "destroy the bacilli" and the dreaded "disease [of leprosy] could be cured." Yet, he wrote, "I have not felt myself justified in putting my opinion on this matter to a practical test in the leper wards of Robben Island Asylum, though many patients expressed their willingness to undergo the ordeal."[88]

Similarly, Dr. Beaven Rake of the Trinidad Leper Asylum, who wished that the British government might sanction the inoculation of "two or three condemned criminals" for leprosy research, did not undertake experiments similar to the biomedically dangerous, large-scale trials carried out by Fitch and Mouritz.[89] Other human leprosy experiments did take place outside the Hawaiian context, such as Daniel Danielssen's 1844 experiment in which he (in keeping with early notions of self-experiment as an ethical necessity) "inoculated himself, two assistants and one nurse, attendants [*sic*], at the Bergen [Norway] Hospital, with leprous blood, serum and blood from leprous tubercules."[90] Similarly, a Dr. Profeta apparently inoculated ten persons, including himself, with leprous matter.[91] In other trials, experimentalist physicians Campana, in 1882, and Havelbug, in 1891, infected two and at least five lepers, respectively, with erysipelas in order to affect the progress of their disease. In both instances, the treatments were found to be worthless, if not detrimental, and were discontinued.[92] Dr. R. H. L. Bibb admitted that he had inoculated a leper with erysipelas in 1891 but in 1894 emphatically declared that such lines of experimentation should never be undertaken, as "such crude inoculations are too dangerous for applications even on lepers."[93]

Likewise, the historian Diana Obregon recounts that in Colombia, in 1893, Dr. Daniel Vega conducted a series of experiments similar to Fitch's, in which Vega inoculated fourteen healthy children (supposedly volunteers) with leprous serum and blood. However, unlike Fitch's experiments, which the physician himself publicized in journal articles, Vega's were kept secret from the public.[94] Thus, while deleterious human leprosy experiments were undertaken elsewhere, they were not as numerous or as publicly avowed and accepted as those conducted in Hawaii. Clearly, the biomedical methods employed by other colonial leprologists varied greatly from those employed in Hawaii in both purpose and number.

Perhaps the most telling evidence of the existence of an atypical nature of the experimental ethos surrounding leprosy in Hawaii is the history of George Fitch's career as a medical researcher. While Hawaii had afforded Fitch limitless opportunities to engage in all manner of human experiments, his career as a physician in California (where he settled after being driven from Hawaii) was very different in terms of the ease of conducting human biomedical research. Eager to prove his leprosy-as-syphilis hypothesis and continue the inoculation trials he had begun in Hawaii, Fitch searched California for subjects on whom he could carry out his experiments. However, he found it quite difficult and in 1892 lamented, "Since coming to San Francisco [in 1886] I have tried, on several occasions, to get the opportunity [to inoculate a leper with syphilis], but so far without success." Thus, where Fitch had free rein while practicing medicine in Hawaii and experimented on untold numbers of lepers (at least fifty, but possibly more), after six years in San Francisco, he was still searching for his first mainland research subject.[95]

By the late nineteenth century, the leprologist William Tebb had written that the "rage for experimental research has long since passed the bounds of decent humanity, and many who have investigated the facts are of the opinion that legislation ought to be specially invoked in the interest of these, the most hapless members of the human family," and physicians such as Bibb and Sutliff, among others, had become vocal opponents of using lepers as test subjects.[96] Further, the stigma and fear that leprosy produced no longer gave physicians carte blanche in their quest for cures. Evidencing this fact, leprology's most eminent figure, Gerhard A. Hansen, the Norwegian leprologist who discovered the leprae bacillus and for whom the disease is now named, was stripped of his medical license in 1880 for inoculating a female patient with leprosy.[97]

The fact that Hansen's patient already suffered from another variant of leprosy (tuberculoid), that Hansen felt the trial would cause her little harm, that his patient hadn't "actively opposed the experiment," that he could and would remove the leprous nodule if the transference were successful, and that the new leprosy failed to take hold in her body made no difference to the Bergen, Norway, law courts, which found their national medical hero guilty of malpractice. Hansen was stripped of his medical license and dismissed from his position as a resident physician in the Bergen Medical Hospital; his case clearly articulates the medical ethics and standards of leprosy research outside the Hawaiian context.[98]

Hawaii's haole leprologists, however, operated with a different set of values. In the case of Arthur Mouritz's inoculation of healthy persons with leprosy, the haole doctor saw no ethical and moral obstacles but instead found, like his fellow haole experimenters, a "splendid field for experimental work was at hand, and stretching all questions of professional ethics . . . did not hesitate to avail [him]self of the opportunities afforded . . . for testing the inoculability of leprosy."[99]

Hawaiian Leprosy: Resistance and Rebellion

While one might assume that the rampant, reckless, and unchecked experimentation performed by Fitch, Mouritz, and other haole physicians might have provoked outrage and protest among Hawaii's native lepers, this was not the case. In fact, it was not until the haole consolidation of power (1887–97), and the increasingly repressive isolation policies that accompanied it, that Hawaiian lepers began to actively resist haole public health and medical initiatives.[100] It was not grossly unethical medical experimentation that led to increased leper resistance, but instead, wrote Jonathan Kay Kamakawiwo'ole Osorio, "a steadily growing divergence between the economic and social fortunes of haole and kanaka [Hawaiian]" and "animosity . . . due to racist portrayals of kanaka in the haole press and Natives' disgust with the foreigners' arrogance."[101]

In September 1890, under the police powers granted by the 1865 Act to Prevent the Spread of Leprosy, a deputy sheriff and two police officers were dispatched to arrest Kealoha, a Hawaiian leper who had refused to submit to compulsory isolation. The police approached Kealoha's home and ordered him to surrender. Soon afterward, one of the law officers lay dead while the remaining two (one of them shot through the arm) ran from Kealoha's home.[102] This was far from being an isolated incident; in numerous instances, leprosy victims, according to Arthur Mouritz, "resist[ed] deportation to [the leper colony on the island of] Molokai by use of fire arms."[103]

Another such act of resistance, the so-called Leper War on the island of Kauai, exemplified the spirit of anger and defiance of the leper community in the decade of haole consolidation. In the late 1880s, leprosy sufferers, led by the native leper Judge J. Kauai, fled from the Hawaiian Board of Health and its chief law enforcer, Marshal of the Kingdom E. G. Hitchcock (known by the sobriquet "the Holy Terror"), to live in the isolated Kalalau Valley on the island of Kauai. Around 1890, the lepers were joined by a similarly afflicted Hawaiian cowboy and marksman named Koolau. For the next several years, the group was able to live in peaceful seclusion. After the haole ouster of Queen Liliʻuokalani in 1893, however, the newly independent Republic of Hawaii decided that in the interest of preserving the islands' economic well-being, leprosy needed to be more strictly controlled.[104] In July 1893, deputy sheriff Louis H. Stolz decided to carry out the wishes of the Board of Health and "tackle the leper problem in Kalalau alone." Having been told that the lepers in the valley were prepared to resist capture, Stolz took with him a .45-70 Winchester magazine rifle. This proved to be insufficient. Stolz tracked down Koolau and told him he would be deported, without his wife and child, to Molokai. Koolau then shot and killed Stolz.[105]

The news of Stolz's killing spread quickly and prompted the new Hawaiian government, under the direction of president Sanford Dole, to declare martial law and dispatch a gunboat, a howitzer, and troops to deal with the leper insurrection.[106] Although he had stood up to the president of the United States, Grover Cleveland (who had called for the restoration of Queen Liliʻuokalani), Dole found it impossible to contend with Koolau's rebellion.[107] Taking a defensive position on a ledge of the valley wall, with his wife and son in tow, Koolau sent two haole soldiers to their graves—while a third accidentally killed himself. With three soldiers dead and little prospect of assaulting Koolau's well-camouflaged valley redoubt, the army of the Hawaiian Republic fired nineteen howitzer rounds in the leper marksman's direction (all of them missing Koolau and his family) and retreated to Honolulu. Victorious in his battle with government forces, Koolau, his wife, and their son lived in the valley until 1896, when the leper cowboy succumbed to his disease.[108]

Not all lepers took up armed resistance, but many still exhibited a hostile reaction to the haole consolidation of power. Increasingly, Hawaiians became angered at haole claims of Western biomedicine's superiority to irregular palliative treatments, such as herbal baths. Yet, as Pennie Moblo rightly observes, even as lepers became disillusioned, "It was not [Western] remedies [that Hawaiian lepers] objected to; the patients continued to try every promising treatment that came along and experimented with their own as well."[109] Lepers did, however, become quickly dissatisfied when vaunted Western methods failed, and by 1899, the American leprologist Prince A. Morrow reported that a resident physician of Molokai had told him that "the scientific treatment of leprosy cannot be carried out because not more than ten per cent. of the patients will continue it for six months."[110]

While some insiders may have begun to sense a shift in Hawaiian attitudes, U.S. public health officials apparently saw only the long-standing experimentalist ethos and the possibilities it afforded the public health and biomedical establishments. In September 1898, just two months after the U.S. annexation of the archipelago, the American physician and leprosy commentator Burnside Foster articulated a mission for the United States' medical and public health communities—"freeing Hawaii from the curse of leprosy." For Foster, leprosy represented an opportunity for American medicine and public health, not to aid a suffering population, but to produce a luminary in the tradition of Pasteur, Jenner, Lister, and Robert Koch.[111] In fact, after the annexation of the archipelago, Koch—who discovered the bacterium that causes tuberculosis—visited Molokai and himself advocated the same approach, suggesting that resources be allocated not to the "care of the highly developed cases" but to leprosy research. To this end, a large sum of money was diverted from funding a leprosarium on Molokai to pay for experimental work on the disease.[112]

In this same spirit, in 1909 the U.S. Public Health Service opened a $300,000 research unit, the United States Leprosy Investigation Station (with the inauspicious acronym USLIS), near the existing Molokai settlement.[113] Yet while an experimental ethos had long typified Western medical and public health interventions in regard to leprosy in Hawaii, indigenous lepers' willingness to participate in human experiments had all but disappeared. Resentment over long-standing haole and foreign racism and arrogance, anger stemming from the haole consolidation of power, the emergence of a resistance movement within the greater Hawaiian society to haole domination,[114] the truly imperial status of U.S. Health Service physicians (as opposed to previously local haole doctors), and the long history of ineffective Western "curative" efforts, among other factors, apparently caused Hawaiian lepers to balk at serving as human guinea pigs for U.S. government physicians.

Additionally, according to J. D. Soviero, Dr. Walter R. Brinckerhoff, an assistant pathologist at Harvard Medical School and director of the USLIS, "had problems . . . with the native Hawaiians . . . and with his attitude toward [leprosy] which he regarded as a hated wartime enemy to be attacked and vanquished."[115] Brinckerhoff later complained that a "contradictory and irrational certainty [was] expressed by some patients that they were being 'rounded up' by USLIS scientists not for treatment but for use as 'experimental animals.'"[116]

The Hawaiian historian A. O. Bushnell wrote that soon lepers' "outrage grew into scorn for [USLIS] and hatred for the very people who professed to come to help them."[117] This popular discontent made it impossible, writes Sheldon Watts, for USLIS personnel to "persuade Molokai's lepers to volunteer for live experiments."[118] As a result, only nine of the nine hundred Molokai lepers consented to experimentation, and those few who did "had little liking for it[,] proved uncooperative . . . [and] rebelled against the rigor of the treatment and confinement of living within the grounds," before eventually abandoning the medical regimen for the "unlimited freedom offered at the settlement." By 1911, the American investigators realized the futility of continuing their research and were ordered by the U.S. Public Health Service to close the Molokai leprosy station.[119]

It was not until 1969 that Hawaii's leprosy isolation laws were finally abolished. Today the dwindling number of former Hansen's disease patients who still live on the site of the former leper settlement do so of their own volition.[120] On December 22, 1980, U.S. president Jimmy Carter signed Public Law 96-565 establishing the 10,700 acre Kalaupapa National Historical Park on the island of Molokai. The infamous settlement, "once a community in isolation, now serves as a place for education and contemplation," says the promotional language on the park's website.[121]

Conclusion

Like so many other colonial contexts of the era, late-nineteenth-century Hawaii saw Westerners subject the indigenous population to racist policies that resulted in social, political, and economic marginalization. As with other such zones, biomedical and public health imperialism was another product of the colonial project. The Hawaiian experience was, however, in an effort to foster the interests of agribusiness and annexation, marked by particularly harsh public health protocols and an environment that encouraged unrestrained human experimentation by the medical establishment. Suffering under oppressive economic and social conditions and emigration policies that ensured that they made up the overwhelming majority of leprosy cases, Hawaiian lepers came to be viewed as a reservoir of disease and a resource for Western biomedicine's eradication efforts. As a result, the archipelago came to serve as a testing ground where native Hawaiians were used as experimental material in ways that were, however ironically, anathema to most of the Western medical establishment.

With the haole consolidation of power (1887–97), continued racism toward native Hawaiians, and increasingly repressive isolation policies, the public health and biomedical interventions involving leprosy underwent a fundamental change. Just as native Hawaiians took up arms in rebellion against the haole government,[122] so their leper brethren exhibited increasing resistance to compulsory isolation — some going so far as to take up arms themselves. After the annexation of the archipelago by the United States, leper resistance manifested itself in increasing skepticism toward Western biomedical and public health interventions. While the U.S. government attempted to build on the experimental ethos surrounding Hawaiian leprosy and continue the tradition of using Hawaiian lepers as research material, they soon found that 1900s Hawaii was very different from the Fitch-Arning-Mouritz era of the 1880s. No longer would Hawaiians be willing participants in experimentation that had brought none of the cures long promised by Western biomedicine.

On an archipelago — as far from the mainland as haole therapeutic sensibilities were from the Western mainstream — Hawaiians suffering from leprosy were subjected to grossly imperialistic public health and biomedical protocols that encouraged harsh public health isolation and deleterious experimentation policies. Even the lepers' most favored Western physician, George Fitch, was perhaps their worst biomedical threat. In the end, however, resistance by a vulnerable subpopulation of an already stigmatized and marginalized minority was able to triumph over the experimentalist designs of an imperial colonizer and force the closure of the U.S. government's expensive laboratory for human experimentation. In doing so, the indigenous lepers, now living in the U.S. territory of Hawaii, joined the ranks of others across the Americas who were able to resist measures imposed from without by white Westerners and defend themselves against imperial designs.

Notes

I would like to thank the faculty and students in the Program in the History and Ethics of Public Health and Medicine, Department of Sociomedical Sciences, Mailman School of Public Health, Columbia University. Special thanks go to two anonymous reviewers from the *Radical History Review*, Sandhya Shukla, Heidi Tinsman, Amy Fairchild, David Rosner, and especially Nancy Stepan.

1   "News Items," *Medical News*, August 14, 1886, 194.

2   See Susan Lederer, *Subjected to Science: Human Experimentation in America before the Second World War* (Baltimore: Johns Hopkins University Press, 1995); David

Rothman, *Strangers at the Bedside: A History of How Law and Bioethics Transformed Medical Decision Making* (New York: Basic Books, 1991); Allen M. Hornblum, *Acres of Skin: Human Experiments at Holmesburg Prison* (New York: Routledge, 1998); James H. Jones, *Bad Blood: The Tuskegee Syphilis Experiment* (New York: Free Press, 1993); Jay Katz, *Experimentation with Human Beings: The Authority of the Investigator, Subject, Professions, and State in the Human Experimentation Process* (New York: Russell Sage Foundation, 1972); Jonathan D. Moreno, *Undue Risks: Secret State Experiments on Humans* (New York: W. H. Freeman, 1999); and Allen M. Hornblum, "They Were Cheap and Available: Prisoners as Research Subjects in Twentieth Century America," *British Medical Journal* 315, no. 7120 (November 29, 1997): 1437–41.

3 Lederer, *Subjected to Science*, 7–8.

4 This is certainly not to suggest that others have not dealt with certain aspects of colonial experimentation. See Eli Chernin, "Richard Pearson Strong and the Iatrogenic Plague Disaster in Billibid Prison, Manila, 1906," *Reviews of Infectious Diseases* 11, no. 6 (November–December 1989): 996–1004; Chernin, "Ross Defends Haffkine: The Aftermath of the Vaccine-Associated Mulkowal Disaster of 1902," *Journal of the History of Medicine and Allied Sciences* 46, no. 2 (1991): 201–18; Ilana Löwy, "From Guinea Pigs to Man: The Development of Haffkine's Anticholera Vaccine," *Journal of the History of Medicine and Allied Sciences* 47, no. 3 (1992): 270–309; and Megan Vaughan, *Curing Their Ills: Colonial Power and African Illness* (Stanford: Stanford University Press, 1991), 29–53, 78–84; and Sheldon J. Watts, *Epidemics and History: Disease, Power, and Imperialism* (New Haven: Yale University Press, 1997), among others.

5 See Pennie Moblo, "Defamation by Disease: Leprosy, Myth and Ideology in Nineteenth Century Hawaii" (Ph.D. diss., University of Hawaii, Manoa, 1996); Moblo, "Institutionalizing the Leper: Partisan Politics and the Evolution of Stigma in Post-monarchy Hawai'i," *Journal of the Polynesian Society* (New Zealand) 107, no. 3 (1997): 229–61; Moblo, "Leprosy, Politics and the Rise of Hawaii's Reform Party," *Journal of Pacific History* 34, no. 1 (1999): 75–89; O. A. Bushnell, "The United States Leprosy Investigation Station at Kalawao," *Hawaiian Journal of History* 2 (1968): 76–94; Rod Edmond, "Abject Bodies/Abject Sites: Leper Islands in the High Imperial Era," in *Islands in History and Representation*, ed. Rod Edmond and Vanessa Smith (New York: Routledge, 2003), 133–45; Sheldon J. Watts, *Epidemics and History: Disease, Power, and Imperialism* (New Haven: Yale University Press, 1997), 64–68; and Zachary Gussow, *Leprosy, Racism, and Public Health Policy: Social Policy in Chronic Disease Control* (San Francisco: Westview Press, 1989).

6 Edmond, "Abject Bodies," 136–37.

7 For more on Hawaii as a colony, see Sally Engle Merry, *Colonizing Hawai'i: The Cultural Power of Law* (Princeton: Princeton University Press, 2000).

8 Vaughan, *Curing Their Ills*, 10. Rod Edmond and Vanessa Smith, introduction to *Islands in History and Representation*, ed. Rod Edmond and Vanessa Smith (New York: Routledge, 2003).

9   Vaughan, *Curing Their Ills*, 8.

10   Edmond, "Abject Bodies," 136.

11   Merry, *Colonizing Hawai'i*, 22.

12   Alfred W. Crosby, "Hawaiian Depopulation as a Model for the Amerindian Experience," in *Epidemics and Ideas: Essays on the Historical Perception of Pestilence*, ed. Terence Ranger and Paul Slack (Cambridge: Cambridge University Press, 1992), 188–89, 176. See also A. O. Bushnell, *The Gifts of Civilization: Germs and Genocide in Hawai'i* (Honolulu: University of Hawaii Press, 1993), 266; and Moblo, "Defamation by Disease," 39.

13   Michael Haas, *Institutional Racism: The Case of Hawaii* (Westport, Conn.: Praeger, 1992), 5.

14   Ibid., 5, table 1.1.

15   Ibid., 9–11.

16   "The Lepers of Molokai," *Overland Monthly and Out West Magazine* 11, no. 1 (July 1873): 89.

17   Pennie Moblo terms this era the decade of the reform government and the Hawaiian Republic. Moblo, "Defamation by Disease," 52.

18   T. C. Neylan et al., "Illness Beliefs of Leprosy Patients: Use of Medical Anthropology in Clinical Practice," *International Journal of Leprosy* 56 (1988): 231–37, quoted in M. J. de Mallac, *A Fresh Look at Hansen's Disease* (New York: Vantage Press, 1992), 2; "Leprosy," *Morbidity and Mortality Weekly Report* 48 (December 31, 1999): 174–76.

19   Arthur Albert St. M. Mouritz, *The Path of the Destroyer: A History of Leprosy in the Hawaiian Islands and Thirty Years Research into the Means by Which It Has Been Spread* (Honolulu: Honolulu Star-Bulletin, 1916), 28; Watts, *Epidemics and History*, 65–66.

20   William Tebb, *The Recrudescence of Leprosy and Its Causation: A Popular Treatise* (London: Sonnenschein, 1893), 10, 162; Watts, *Epidemics and History*, 65–66.

21   "Hawaiian and Norwegian Leprosy," *Boston Medical and Surgical Journal* 108, no. 15 (April 12, 1883): 45.

22   Mouritz, *Path of the Destroyer*, 29–33.

23   Tebb, *Recrudescence of Leprosy*, 312; Mouritz, *Path of the Destroyer*, 33–34.

24   Watts, *Epidemics and History*, 41–43; "Frequently Asked Questions about Kalaupapa," Kalaupapa National Historical Park website, http://www.nps.gov/kala/docs/faq.htm; Edwin K. Chung-Hoon, "Leprosy in Hawaii," *Hawaii Medical Journal* 1, no. 1 (September 1941): 39–40.

25   Edmond, "Abject Bodies," 135.

26   For a listing of leprosy settlements in "tropical" countries, see Leonard Rogers and Ernest Muir, *Leprosy*, 3rd ed. (Baltimore: Williams and Wilkins, 1946), 108–18.

27   Watts, *Epidemics and History*, 65–66; Board of Health of the Territory of Hawaii, *The Molokai Settlement, Territory of Hawaii, Villages of Kalaupapa and Kalawao* (Hawaiian Gazette, 1907), 7; Mouritz, *Path of the Destroyer*, 28; John D. Hillis, *Leprosy in British Guiana: An Account of West Indian Leprosy* (London: J & A Chur-

chill, 1881), 147–48; Moblo, "Defamation by Disease," 69, table 3; Diana Obregon, "Building National Medicine: Leprosy and Power in Colombia, 1870–1910," *Social History of Medicine* 15, no. 1 (April 2002): 96.

28   For more, see Michael Worboys, "The Emergence of Tropical Medicine: A Study in the Establishment of a Scientific Specialty," in *Perspectives on the Emergence of Scientific Disciplines*, ed. Gerard Lemaine et al. (Chicago: Aldine, 1976). See also W. M. Gibson, *Report of the President of the Board of Health to the Legislative Assembly on Leprosy* (Honolulu, 1886).

29   Moblo, "Defamation by Disease," 69, table 3; Obregon, "Building National Medicine," 96.

30   Moblo, "Defamation by Disease," 53.

31   Haas, *Institutional Racism*, 9.

32   Prince Morrow, "Leprosy and Hawaiian Annexation," *North American Review* 165 (November 1897): 588, 590.

33   Morrow's figures exceed by 10,000 other estimates of the number of Hawaiians in the archipelago in 1896. Hass, *Institutional Racism*, 5.

34   Morrow's report put the "actual" figure of Molokai lepers at "1,200 or more." Morrow, "Leprosy and Hawaiian Annexation," 588; Burnside Foster, "Leprosy and the Hawaiian Annexation," *North American Review*, September 1898, 300, 304.

35   Moblo, "Defamation by Disease," 69, table 3; Mouritz, *Path of the Destroyer*, 21.

36   Rogers and Muir, *Leprosy*, 52; Moblo, "Institutionalizing the Leper," 242.

37   Mouritz, *Path of the Destroyer*, 10.

38   Vaughan, *Curing Their Ills*, 80.

39   James C. White, "The Question of Contagion in Leprosy," *American Journal of the Medical Sciences* 84, no. 168 (October 1882): 454.

40   Hillis, *Leprosy in British Guiana*, 176.

41   For examples, see J. R. Tryon, "Leprosy in the Hawaiian Islands," *American Journal of the Medical Sciences* 170 (April 1883): 443; and James C. White, "The Question of Contagion in Leprosy," *American Journal of the Medical Sciences* 84, no. 168 (October 1882): 434–54.

42   "Leprosy Not Contagious," *Sanitarian* 37 (1896): 471; "Hawaiian and Norwegian Leprosy," *Boston Medical and Surgical Journal* 108, no. 15 (April 12, 1883): 45; Rogers and Muir, *Leprosy*, 52.

43   Rogers and Muir, *Leprosy*, 64.

44   Moblo, "Institutionalizing the Leper," 229; Gussow, *Leprosy, Racism, and Public Health Policy*, 95; Rogers and Muir, *Leprosy*, 52, 113.

45   For more on the haole aversion to the palliative therapies favored by lepers, themselves, see Moblo, "Institutionalizing the Leper," 244–47. For more on the harsh medications used in leprosy treatment during the nineteenth century and the early twentieth, see Hillis, *Leprosy in British Guiana*, 209; Prince A. Morrow, *Leprosy* (New York: William Wood, 1899), 575, 586; and Rogers and Muir, *Leprosy*, 237–39.

46   Judith W. Leavitt, *Typhoid Mary: Captive to the Public's Health* (Boston: Beacon Press, 1996), 23–24.

47   For more, see Pennie Moblo, "Blessed Damien of Molokaʻi: The Critical Analysis of Contemporary Myth," *Ethnohistory* 44, no. 4 (autumn 1997): 698–99.

48   D. A. Carmichael, "Leprosy in the Hawaiian Islands," *Medical News*, January 21, 1899, 95; J. D. Soviero, "The Nationalization of a Disease: A Paradigm?" *Public Health Reports* 101 (July–August 1986): 399–404.

49   "George L. Fitch," in *In Memoriam—Doctors of Hawaii* (Hawaii Medical Library, Mamiya Medical Heritage Center), http://hml.org/mmhc/mdindex/mdindex .html; George L. Fitch, "The Etiology of Leprosy," *Medical Record: A Weekly Journal of Medicine and Surgery* (New York) 42, no. 11 (September 10, 1892): 293–303.

50   Fitch, "Etiology of Leprosy," 293.

51   Watts, *Epidemics and History*, 150–51. For more on hereditary predisposition in leprosy, see Rogers and Muir, *Leprosy*, 59–60; Fitch, "Etiology of Leprosy," 293; and *Leprosy and Libel: The Suit of George L. Fitch against the Saturday Press* (Honolulu: Saturday Press Print, 1883), 12.

52   Edmond, "Abject Bodies," 136.

53   Gavan Daws, *Shoal of Time: A History of the Hawaiian Islands* (New York: Macmillan, 1968), 209; Hillis, *Leprosy in British Guiana*, 210; *Leprosy and Libel*, 10–11; Mouritz, *Path of the Destroyer*, 160, 138.

54   In 1885 Fitch published the same article in both the *Pacific Medical and Surgical Journal* and the *Western Lancet*. Fitch, "Etiology of Leprosy," 295; "George L. Fitch," http://hml.org/mmhc/mdindex/mdindex.html.

55   Fitch, "Etiology of Leprosy."

56   *Human Vivisection: A Statement and an Inquiry*, 3rd ed. (American Humane Association, 1900), 7–8; Fitch, "Etiology of Leprosy," 297.

57   *Human Vivisection*, 8.

58   Ibid.

59   Ibid.

60   Tebb, *Recrudescence of Leprosy*, 349.

61   Ibid., 348.

62   "Leprosy in the Hawaiian Islands," *Boston Medical and Surgical Journal* 110, no. 20 (May 15, 1885): 474–75. The trial proceedings were eventually published as a pamphlet. For more on the Fitch trial, see *Leprosy and Libel*.

63   George L. Fitch, "Transcript of Adv.," [*Pacific Commercial Advertiser*, now the *Honolulu Advertiser*], July 11, 1887, George Fitch Files, http://hml.org/mmhc/ mdindex/mdindex.html; Fitch, "Etiology of Leprosy," 297; Mouritz, *Path of the Destroyer*, 55, 100; "Arthur Alfred St. Maur Mouritz," in *In Memoriam—Doctors of Hawaii* (Hawaii Medical Library, Mamiya Medical Heritage Center), http://hml .org/mmhc/mdindex/mdindex.html.

64   Fitch, "Etiology of Leprosy," 301; Mouritz, *Path of the Destroyer*, 55, 70; "Leprosy in the Hawaiian Islands," 475.

65   There are alternative interpretations of Fitch's true feelings toward his patients: Moblo, "Defamation by Disease," 302; Jacob Adler and Robert M. Kamins, *The Fantastic Life of Walter Murray Gibson: Hawaii's Minister of Everything* (Hono-

lulu: University of Hawaii Press, 1986), 162; Fitch, "Etiology of Leprosy," 301; Fitch, "Transcript of Adv.," June 18, 1881, George Fitch Files; Mouritz, *Path of the Destroyer*, 55; "A Veritable Valley of Death," *Current Literature* 1, no. 2 (August 1888): 156.

66   Mouritz, *Path of the Destroyer*, 54; Fitch, "Transcript of the Adv. Daily," [*Pacific Commercial Advertiser*, now the *Honolulu Advertiser*], January 22, 1883, George Fitch Files, Mamiya Medical Heritage Center, Archives and Medical Museum at Hawaii Medical Library, Honolulu, Hawaii.

67   "George L. Fitch," http://hml.org/mmhc/mdindex/mdindex.html; "Leprosy in the Hawaiian Islands," 475; Mouritz, *Path of the Destroyer*, 54.

68   Moblo, "Defamation by Disease," 194; "Leprosy in the Hawaiian Islands," 474.

69   "Leprosy in the Hawaiian Islands," 474.

70   Tebb, *Recrudescence of Leprosy*, 315; "C. T. Akana," in *In Memoriam—Doctors of Hawaii* (Hawaii Medical Library, Mamiya Medical Heritage Center), http://hml .org/mmhc/mdindex/mdindex.html.

71   For examples of various leprosy drug therapies in the late nineteenth century, see Hillis, *Leprosy in British Guiana*, 209–34.

72   Mouritz, *Path of the Destroyer*, 152–53.

73   Ibid., 154.

74   Ibid.

75   Later it was allegedly found that many members of Keanu's family were afflicted with leprosy, calling into question the findings of the study. Tebb, *Recrudescence of Leprosy*, 123; Mouritz, *Path of the Destroyer*, 154; Carmichael, "Leprosy in the Hawaiian Islands," 94; R. H. L. Bibb, "The Nature and Treatment of Leprosy," *American Journal of the Medical Sciences* 108, no. 6 (November 1894): 550.

76   Tebb, *Recrudescence of Leprosy*, 125; William Jelly, "Leprosy," *British Medical Journal*, (September 24, 1887); Tebb, *Recrudescence of Leprosy*, 127.

77   "Edward Arning," in *In Memoriam—Doctors of Hawaii* (Hawaii Medical Library, Mamiya Medical Heritage Center), http://hml.org/mmhc/mdindex/arning.html.

78   While repulsive to modern sensibilities, trials such as these were common for the era. Carmichael, "Leprosy in the Hawaiian Islands," 95; Mouritz, *Path of the Destroyer*, 98, 138, 101; Nancy Stepan, "The Interplay between Socio-economic Factors and Medical Science: Yellow Fever Research, Cuba and the United States," *Social Studies of Science* 8 (1978): 401.

79   It is worth noting that November or December 1884 was about the time when George Fitch was forced out of Molokai by the Hawaiian Board of Health. Mouritz, *Path of the Destroyer*, 140–41.

80   Ibid., 141.

81   Ibid., 140.

82   For more on the Western fixation with supposed Hawaiian indolence, see R. D. K. Herman, "The Coin of the Realm: The Political Economy of 'Indolence' in the Hawaiian Islands," *History and Anthropology* 11, nos. 2–3 (1999): 387–416; and Mouritz, *Path of the Destroyer*, 140.

83   Mouritz, *Path of the Destroyer*, 142, 144–46.

84   Leavitt, *Typhoid Mary*, 180.

85   Mouritz, *Path of the Destroyer*, 149.

86   Ibid., 149, 58, 140.

87   Lederer, *Subjected to Science*, 10–11.

88   Beaven Rake, *Report on Leprosy in Trinidad for 1890*, quoted in Tebb, *Recrudescence of Leprosy*, 323; Samuel P. Impey, *A Handbook on Leprosy* (Philadelphia: Blakiston, 1896), 100–101; Morrow, *Leprosy*, 586–87.

89   Tebb, *Recrudescence of Leprosy*, 322–23. See also Frances A. Doughty, "Altruism and the Leprosy," *The Chautauquan: A Weekly Newsmagazine*, July 1890, 446.

90   Lederer, *Subjected to Science*, 18; Mouritz, *Path of the Destroyer*, 138–39.

91   Henri C. Leloir, *Traité pratique et théorique de la lèpre* (Paris: Aux Bureaux du Progrès Médical, 1886), 237–38, quoted in Tebb, *Recrudescence of Leprosy*; Albert Abrams, "Leprosy," *Medical News*, October 7, 1893, 403; Mouritz, *Path of the Destroyer*, 398; Fitch, "Etiology of Leprosy," 297; Rogers and Muir, *Leprosy*, 89.

92   Rake, *Report on Leprosy in Trinidad for 1890*, quoted in Tebb, *Recrudescence of Leprosy*, 323; Morrow, *Leprosy*, 586–87.

93   Bibb, "Nature and Treatment of Leprosy," 562.

94   Obregon, "Building National Medicine," 101.

95   "George L. Fitch," http://hml.org/mmhc/mdindex/mdindex.html; "Transcript of Adv.," July 11, 1887, George Fitch Files; Mouritz, *Path of the Destroyer*, 55; Fitch, "Etiology of Leprosy," 297; "Arthur Alfred St. Maur Mouritz," http://hml.org/mmhc/mdindex/mdindex.html.

96   Tebb, *Recrudescence of Leprosy*, 346–47; Bibb, "Nature and Treatment of Leprosy," 562.

97   It is important to note that leprosy experimentation was often undertaken on human, rather than animal, subjects because scientists were long unable to find an animal receptive to Hansen's bacillus. Obregon, "Building National Medicine," 101; Lederer, *Subjected to Science*, 12.

98   G. A. Hansen, *The Memories and Reflections of Dr. G. Armauer Hansen* (Wurzburg, Federal Republic of Germany: German Leprosy Relief Association, 1976), 19–21.

99   Mouritz, *Path of the Destroyer*, 141.

100   For more, see Moblo, "Defamation by Disease," 63–103.

101   Jonathan Kay Kamakawiwoʻole Osorio, *Dismembering Lahui: A History of the Hawaiian Nation to 1887* (Honolulu: University of Hawaii Press, 2002), 191.

102   Mouritz, *Path of the Destroyer*, 71.

103   Ibid.

104   "George L. Fitch," http://hml.org/mmhc/mdindex/mdindex.html; Mouritz, *Path of the Destroyer*, 70; Walter Lefeber, *The American Age: United States Foreign Policy at Home and Abroad, 1750–Present* (New York: W. W. Norton, 1994), 179; Watts, *Epidemics and History*, 66–67.

105   Moblo, "Institutionalizing the Leper," 234; Mouritz, *Path of the Destroyer*, 73–74.

106   For more, see "The Hawaiian Lepers: Fifteen Taken to Honolulu—the Others Resist Capture," *New York Times*, July 16, 1893, 14.

107   "Sanford Dole," in *The Columbia Encyclopedia*, 6th ed. (New York: Columbia University Press, 2000); Lefeber, *The American Age*, 179.

108   For more on Koolau (also known as Koʻolau or Kaluaikoʻolau) the leper, see John Sheldon, "The True Story of Kaluaiko'olau or Ko'olau the Leper," trans. Frances N. Frazier, *Hawaiian Journal of History* 21 (1987): 1–41; and Frances N. Frazier, "The 'Battle of Kalahau,' as Reported in the Newspaper Kuokoa," *Hawaiian Journal of History* 23 (1989): 108–118. Mouritz, *Path of the Destroyer*, 74–75; Watts, *Epidemics and History*, 67.

109   Moblo, "Leprosy, Politics and the Rise of Hawaii's Reform Party," 79.

110   Fitch, "Etiology of Leprosy," 301; Morrow, *Leprosy*, 593.

111   Foster, "Leprosy and the Hawaiian Annexation," 300, 305.

112   H. Brett Melendy, *Hawaii: America's Sugar Territory, 1898–1959* (Lewiston, N.Y.: Edwin Mellen Press, 1999), 164.

113   Bushnell, "The United States Leprosy Investigation," 85; Watts, *Epidemics and History*, 67.

114   "Revolt in Hawaii: Robert Wilcox Leads an Armed Uprising of the Natives," *Washington Post*, January 19, 1895, 1.

115   J. D. Soviero, "The Nationalization of a Disease: A Paradigm?" *Public Health Reports* 101 (July–August 1986): 399–404.

116   Bushnell, "The United States Leprosy Investigation," 85.

117   Ibid., 86.

118   Watts, *Epidemics and History*, 67.

119   Bushnell, "The United States Leprosy Investigation," 86, 88. Moblo gives the date of the station's closing as 1913. Moblo, "Defamation by Disease," 291.

120   As of October 2003, there were twenty-seven patients residing at Kalaupapa Settlement. Tom Workman (superintendent of Kalaupapa NHP), electronic mail message to Nick Turse, October 21, 2003.

121   Zachary Gussow places the change in Hawaiian public health policy regarding leprosy even later, stating that it took place in 1974. Gussow, *Leprosy, Racism, and Public Health Policy*, 107; "Frequently Asked Questions about Kalaupapa," Kalaupapa National Historical Park website, http://www.nps.gov/kala/docs/faq.htm; Mona R. Bomgaars, "Hansen's Disease, the Year 2000, and Hawaii," Communicable Disease Report, Hawai'i Department of Health, Communicable Disease Division, January–February 1999, 1.

122   "Blood Spilled in Hawaii," *Boston Daily*, January 19, 1895, 1; "Rebellion in Hawaii," *Los Angeles Times*, January 19, 1895, 6.

Tracking the "China Peril" along the U.S. Pacific Rim

Carpetbaggers, Yacht People, 1.2 Billion Cyborg Consumers,

and the Bamboo Gang, Coming Soon to a Neighborhood Near You!

Rob Wilson

The yellow peril! It is not racial, it is spiritual [otherness]. It does not involve inferior values; it involves a radical strangeness, a stranger to the weight of its past, from where there does not filter [to the Euro-based self] any familiar voice or inflection, a lunar or Martian past.

— Emmanuel Levinas,
"The Russo-Chinese Debate and the Dialectic"[1]

Given the aggravated flows of globalization we experience on the home front, as well as the siren call of a postcolonial hybridity that often elides discrepant histories, semiotic mobility, market fusion, and cross-regional mixture help turn the framework of national belonging into a more riddled ethnoscape of transnational becoming. Capitalist flight and informational imbalance, not to mention cybernetic hypertechnologies of interconnection and techno-unity, aggravate a world in flux and geopolitical becoming. Despite the uncanny return to Cold War forms of national security and paranoid belonging used in the Bush II regime, the Americas as "homeland" are becoming a maze of globalizing and localizing forces that disturb frameworks of nation-state modernity, prior assumptions of area studies, and bounded national canons of self-representation and regional containment. Regions from the Asia-Pacific to Latin America are being recoded and reshaped to fit the transnational imperatives of the global economy, but not without protest forces of globalization-from-below mobilizing an array of forces to oppose the sublimated reshaping via APEC (Asia-Pacific Economic Cooperation) and NAFTA. What we do need, following the critical lead of José Martí's North-South reformulations in "Our Americas," are

more multisituated paradigms of regional interaction "focusing on shared histories of connection and interaction between peoples across, beyond, or underneath national boundaries and borders."[2] Bill Maurer gestures toward such a
transregional paradigm in a recent "Worldings" special issue of *Comparative
American Studies* when he observes that global-local marketizing sites in the
Caribbean (like St. Lucia) are recentering "and redefin[ing] the boundaries of
its 'region,' making it a node for Chinese capital and simultaneously a part of
China through the financial center of Hong Kong."[3] Our modes of hemispheric
unity are no longer adequate to such flows that trouble North-South or East-
West segregations or regional containments via land or nation-state site.

This essay offers kaleidoscopic moments of a reinvigorated yellow-peril discourse, a racial-cultural formation newly instantiated in the contradictory
global circumstances of our time. Whatever the peril and promise of the Pacific
posed as a region of transnational interface and transcultural possibility, we
need to delve into the ever-shifting discourse of U.S. Orientalism as a neo-
racialized process of geopolitical othering and what Gayatri Spivak warily calls
the "crisis management" of transnational circuits and planetary emergence.[4]
We need to track the recurring projection of Levinas's "radical strangeness"
along the transnationalizing Pacific Rim, even as it persists down into the
post–September 11 U.S. security-state apparatus. This phobic othering persists at the same time that the Asia-Pacific region of APEC is morphing into
a porous, user-friendly, ever-globalizing space of post–Cold War, postbinary,
"post-Orientalist" interaction and communal hybridity—*the* neoliberal capitalist space, as it were, of global-transnational flows.[5] Tropes of *traveling* and
figurations of cultural-political *displacement* have emerged, increasingly, to
pack these ambivalent ingredients and historical discrepancies into the uneven makings of some "imagined transnational community," as Martí's own
career trajectories had allowed him, with critical force, to link New York City
to Havana, or the ruses of Ariel to the laments and counter-energies of Caliban.[6] Migrants of labor class and professional management expertise; tourists of
exotic otherness; pilgrimages to and from former sites of the sacred; nomads of
stateless becoming; borderlanders of transcultural shuttling; diasporas of ambivalent belonging; exiles of coerced or principled distancing—all these and
more call out to be historicized as constituencies of refigured regional identity within the global-local antidiscipline of "transnational cultural studies."
Areas are being recoded and reframed by transnational forces and cosmopolitical movements in ways we have yet to realize or fully critique.

As we move toward the contradictory formation of the Asia-Pacific as a horizon of possibility, we need to look back and challenge "Asia," for example, or that even more Eurocentric holdover, East Asia, as categories of area formation. "It had been one of the enduring ironies of the study of Asia that Asia itself, as an object," Harry Harootunian has warned in the nativist-deconstructing speculations of *History's Disquiet*, "simply doesn't exist."[7] Harootunian is speaking from a post–Cold War position of U.S. global hegemony in which the quasistable "field-imaginaries" of area-studies-based frames like "Asia" or "East Asia" or "the Pacific"—or "Japan," "Korea," or "China," for that matter—no longer exist in the same bounded, monolingual, or homogeneous way. This is due not only to the collapse of Cold War binaries but also to the transnational flux of global capitalism. At a knowledge/power level of university and research institutions, the crisis-management eruption of transdisciplinary forms like "postnational," "planetarity," or "cosmopolitical" have sprung up like a thousand post-Maoist flowers in Chicago, New York, Washington, and Honolulu, often funded by Ford Foundation and Rockefeller grants to help reshape and recode region, nation, and the world beyond area studies frameworks that their earlier funding by these same players had helped to bring into institutional realization.[8]

Given these global-local transformations of prior area-based or nation-centered frames, the utopian appeal of the Pacific Rim as a globalizing site of transnational co-prosperity and capitalism's transcendental future (embodying some "megacity" Pearl River sprawl effect and a kind of commodity-driven cyborg subject formation) no longer beckons with the same gleaming promise.[9] For a metonymy of this effect, consider the graying, flat skylines of high-rise Tokyo and the romantic dead-end entropy set in loser bars and bad whiskey ads in Sophia Coppola's *Lost in Translation* (2003), not to mention the emperor-worshiping genuflections of Tom Cruise in *The Last Samurai* (2003), who postures a nostalgic form of Meiji Japan so post-Orientalist and Asia-Pacific history-denying in its longings that it stands for a higher and more sublimated mode of U.S. neo-Orientalism altogether.[10] But any version of the U.S. Pacific Rim discourse can no longer just factor in Japan as the sublime dynamo of transpacific transnational *promise* (as model minority in the global sphere) and *peril* (as threat to U.S.-run geopolitical stability and economic supremacy in the region): China, with its huge rural-urban shifts to global capitalist restructuring and huge port-city nexus on the transpacific front, and India, with its booming offshore service resources and data connectivity via transnationalized megacities of silicon skills, are overflowing the nation-state confines of Asia regional containment.[11]

This U.S. ambivalence toward Asian power in the region (meaning the "promise" as mimic model and "peril" as rising threat) is not a function of deep-national psychic structures but an effect of history and geopolitical entanglement in the Pacific, nation, place, and world. Nonetheless, the trans binary Pacific Rim effect of imagined transnational community still functions as a key U.S. neoliberal capitalist space, as it were, of global-transnational flows. Whatever the stasis and dead-end effect of global capitalism as portrayed in the burned-out careers and lost romances metonymized in the entropic Tokyo urbanscape of *Lost in Translation*, the Pacific Rim remains a key locus of global capitalist dynamism in all its hyperspeculative risk as well as more phobic labor-class modes of transnational othering and transnational and transcultural becoming. We see such interaction of money, custom, and power in Pam Chun's memoirlike novel *The Money Dragon*, which records the alignment of the Chinese middle-class diaspora with the Hawaiian nation and its opposition to the American commercial forces that would oppose Hawaiian sovereignty. The routes of transpacific money quite early accommodate to rooted Hawaiian power, though the gender and class imbalances disturb the Chinese patriarch known as "the money dragon," who attempts to maintain financial power and familial succession with uneven success.[12] A more critical and impious look at the postmodern transpacific region is established by the Korean installation artist Cho Duck-Hyun, who uses faux archaeology to establish (through faked canine statuary buried at the Asian Art Museum in San Francisco in 2003) the "primordial" ties of Korea to the American West Coast, as if to predate the waves of Chinese and Japanese settlers in the region and to disturb the frontier ideology of white Anglo settlement on the Pacific coast from yet another "borderlands" angle of vision, in-mixture, and transcultural interaction.[13]

This contemporary Pacific Rim nexus is surely a swirling and uneven mess, full of huge rural-urban imbalances and labor-capital injustices and IMF ruses, all the more aggravated by the contradictions of peril and promise after 9/11. Allow me to juxtapose some uneven instances. King Sihanouk of Cambodia, influenced by the struggle for queer marriage rights and legal legitimacy in the left-coast city of San Francisco, suddenly decreed in a handwritten message on his website that Cambodia would allow "marriage between man and man . . . or between woman and woman."[14] Gap Inc., a San Francisco–based garment nexus that makes post-hip clothes for yuppies trying to look like Jack Kerouac on weekends, includes Old Navy and Banana Republic shops under its corporate domain, with some 3,009 factories scattered across fifty countries in its global *contado*. Its annual revenues are close to U.S. $16 billion even in a bad year. China, with 241 factories, was accused of seventy-three plant violations in a recent public-relations attempt by Gap to improve its U.S.-global image by surveying and monitoring work conditions in its Technicolor-garment "sweatshops."[15] Geo-strategically centered around an offshore conglomeration of nuclear submarines, aircraft carriers, and cruise missiles based at Pearl Harbor and linked to the DMZ and Iraq theaters of war, RIMPAC 2004 went on holding its biennial multinational Pacific exercise in Hawaiian waters off Kauai by blasting decommissioned navy destroyers that had served in the Cuban blockade, the war in Vietnam, and surveillance of the Soviet Union into suboceanic oblivion and decay.[16] Full of market boom-and-bust vitality, Japan, Korea, Taiwan, China, and Singapore went on serving that global cheerleader for *New York Times* neoliberalism, Thomas L. Friedman, as global "model minorities" figuring economic growth and entrepreneurial creativity to show backward countries "cursed with oil" like Iraq and other Middle Eastern polities tied to "pathologies of the Arab world" how they might survive the new global order of transnational capitalism cum U.S.-hegemonic mimicry.[17]

Resisting Bollywood coverups in pelvic love and cultic folk dance, Arundhati Roy went on decrying real-virtual discrepancies and "the most violent increase in rural-urban income inequalities since independence" in techno-rife India.[18] At the blockbuster level of spectacular capitalism, *Kill Bill* and anime-based films escalated the inter-Asian and global cultural cachet of "cool Japan" and Hong Kong martial arts film genres and action techniques in a transcultural outburst of sexuality, violence, digital Zen, cyberspace flight, and Asia-pop idolatry.[19] Meanwhile, back in the hypermediated states of Hollywood distraction, a *haole* politician and missionary offspring named Ed Case in multicult Hawaii courted Asia-Pacific ethnic votes by urging viewers of the mass-music TV show *American Idol*, "If you want to show your support for Asian-Pacific Americans tonight, you know what number to call on what TV show right now, Jasmine [Trias, a local Filipina seventeen-year-old who can barely sing] just finished singing."[20] A million plus cell phone calls from Hawaii kept the scrappy Jasmine in the *Idol* running. Clearly, whatever the global plight, the transpacific fuses and confuses transnational peril and promise, pulling race, class, nation, technology, and gender into odd and uneven juxtapositions from the king of Cambodia and Gap Inc. to the postcolonial longings for ethnic recognition at Maryknoll High in Honolulu.[21]

At the "Race, Class, Citizenship, and Extraterritoriality" conference held in San Francisco on November 14–15, 1997, on the reactionary return of yellow-

peril discourse around the Wen Ho Lee travesty, Colleen Lye had warned me
that the title for my talk "Tracking the 'Chinese Peril' along the U.S. Pacific Rim:
Carpetbaggers, Yacht People, 1.2 Billion Cyborg Consumers, and the Bamboo
Gang, Coming Soon to a Neighborhood Near You!" was "just a bit over the top,
Rob." That hyperbole of a subtitle aimed to evoke the contradictory working-
class threat of (1) a transnationalized "Chinese" mass labor force and (2) phobias of offshore financial capital, lurking fears of multicultural otherness inside
the nation, and the return to a "Cold War demonology" that still haunts the
U.S. political imaginary of Asia, if not the global empire itself.[22]

These white-nativist fears of, as well as global longings for, the vast markets
of consumers and producers in mainland China went back at least to the transnational U.S. configurations of the railroad barons and vast global wheat markets that Frank Norris memorably portrayed in the reconfigured Californian
geography and closed-frontier mythology of his 1901 novel *The Octopus*, with
its global capitalist mandate to agribusiness forces, "We must march with the
course of Empire, and not against it," and open the Asian markets of China for
any crisis of overproduction or impending trade imbalances that might threaten
the calculus of U.S. market advantage in Chicago, New York, and San Francisco.[23] The transnational did suggest the forging of "contact zones" of postcolonial entanglement in Pacific port cites like Shanghai and San Francisco, but
it also suggests the colonial dynamics of global capitalism and uneven Euro-
American treaties and racial policies in which national mythologies like those
of Frank Norris in hyper-Californian vastness were forged.[24]

To invoke Slavoj Žižek's paradoxical terms that would provoke defamiliarization of the nation by mingling dialectical antagonisms of Hegel with the
ideological irreducibility of the Lacanian Real that is the core fantasy of any "nation thing," a postsocialist China rising into global power and force of transnational dynamism in the region threatens to dispossess Americans of their once-
vaunted national stability, potency, and border closure that they already (as an
ever-transnationalizing economy and market-driven Empire) *lack*. "The basic
paradox [of the nation as ideological fantasy structuring social antagonisms
and the traumas of excess that is global capitalism] is that our [nation] Thing
is conceived as something inaccessible to the other and at the same threatened
by him." China, as a would-be global superpower, is no less caught up in the
sublime mazes of this self-other binary of wounded and neocolonized nationhood.[25]

As Bruce Cumings put the case for the neoparanoid return to the global security-state apparatus under post-9/11 U.S. hegemony in the Asia region with its vast transnationalizing economies and rogue-state nuclear, biological, and terrorist threats, "Clearly, though [as in the phobic case of the Taiwanese American physicist Wen Ho Lee], a place called *China* still provides a convenient Rorschach inkblot for every conceivable American projection [of regional threat], no matter how wild or foolish."[26] No "parallax" vision of double seeing or evocations of a warily deconstructive trans/national entanglement in hybridity or commodity glut can undo the threatened *bad-narcissism* of these two huge injured or endangered global superpowers (U.S. and China) as they seek to project and maintain their civilizational dominion and diminishing national sovereignty over the dynamism of the ever-transnationalizing Pacific. I am not here suggesting any co-prosperity or the evenness of global power or North-South or rural-urban justice; more so, I am demanding the need to envision what Harootunian calls (after Johannes Fabian's anticolonial and worlded anthropology) the "coevalness" of global modernity and theorizing the conjunctive forms of life under everyday capitalism.[27]

American citizens under the neonativist Bush II regime face a moment of massive global *decentering* in which the U.S. geopolitical imaginary, transformed at both the global-transnational and local-subnational levels of social structure, now and again threatens to turn hugely phobic, reactive, reterritorial, and unilateralist. If this is a superpower and neoempire of multiple centers and liberal modes, as Michael Hardt and Antonio Negri have claimed in *Empire* (2000), it is a confused one caught between the residual ideology of constitutional republicanism and the futurist techno-apparatus of military domination and antipopulist manipulation dependent on will, deception, market supremacy, and force.[28] "The world is facing many issues that might be called the dark side of globalization," Japanese prime minister Yoshiro Mori had shrewdly warned the sixteen-member South Pacific Forum meeting held in Tokyo in April 2000, promising amplified financial support to the smaller players in the interior Pacific, after disruptive protests at the World Trade Organization meeting in Seattle and the World Bank in Washington had brought this "dark side of globalization" to the forefront of the global mass media and its U.S. mass-media news center, CNN.[29]

While at the forefront of the transnationalization of markets, the U.S. polity threatens (as in its recurring anti-immigrant acts of state policy and superpower "embargo" policies) to police and close the geopolitical borders of its immigrant-enriched states of California, Florida, and Texas (via ad hoc "propositions" of impurity and illegality targeted against Mexico and subaltern parts of Asia and the Middle East) as mongrel dilutions of the Anglo-Saxon core culture.[30] Related to this security-state strategy would be the move (at the macro-level) to isolate and scapegoat "Asian" transnational capitalists (by some neo-Orientalist ruse of collapsed categories, "Asian American" citizens) as diasporic and quasi-authoritarian operators of some vast, devious, and sublime "Greater China." I do want to make it clear that by castigating state and cultural-political forms of U.S. imperialism (and its tactics and discourses of neo-Orientalism) in our transnational and postcolonial moment, I am by no means absolving mainland China of its own will to imperial overextension and cultural-political hegemony (via forms of internal colonialism) over heteroglossic spaces of local-national difference in the region from Taiwan, Mongolia, Hong Kong, or Tibet and inter-Asia as forms of emergent collectivity.

Whatever the lines of flight and conjunctions of transcultural hybridity that do seem more possible in the region, "Orientalism" as such refuses to go away in our so-called post–Cold War moment of transnationalization and global expansion and neoliberalism across the Asia-Pacific. Thus the paradoxical rise of *neo-Orientalism* (as tracked here in various U.S. genres, from journalistic social science to novels and movies, not to mention newer genres of corporate cyberpunk) demands interrogation and critical resistance on the part of American cultural studies. Doing transpacific cultural studies, as it were, demands tracking domination and emergence inside the transnational market dynamics of APEC and the WTO, as I have elsewhere claimed.[31]

Tracking U.S. Genres of Transnational Otherness

The "Chinese Peril" threat often seems to be working overtime these days, imaged forth like some kind of neo-transnational Jew or "indefinable sublime X" figure (see Slavoj Žižek, *Enjoy Your Symptom!*),[32] now and again called on (as free-floating sign of late-capitalist excess) to suture the U.S. national borders of some segregated nativist selfhood by evoking sublime specters of white-collar criminality and huge "underground empires" of high-capitalist liquidity (on the one hand) and more clannish, even premodern, forms of post-Fordist slavery into noncontract cyborg labor (on the other, *Blade Runner* end of the class spectrum) now seen as spreading across what Bill Gates (in *The Road Ahead*) so charmingly calls our brave new transnational world of "Friction-Free Capitalism."[33] Deformed works of essentializing social science cum neo-Orientalism like Joel Kotkin's *Tribes* and Murray Weidenbaum's *The Bamboo Network* are emerging in which "the Global Chinese" are not emerging as "model minorities" of the Pacific transnational sphere but are figured essentially (in tones of resentful admiration) as diasporic tribal-ethnic "Jews" whose transpacific banking and neo-Confucian familial nexus can now provide them with a vast transnational infrastructure and labor hinterlands for their belated will to (covert) world domination.[34]

My subtitle packs into itself these contradictory images of the "Chinese Peril" and seems to be a fair plot summary of the thematics and image patterns of a work of journalistic social science like Sterling Seagrave's *Lords of the Rim* (1996), not to mention the neo–Cold War sublimity of post-Soviet Hollywood movies like Richard Gere's kangaroo-court chiller *Red Corner* (1997), which is not so much about the framing of one well-off liberal U.S. lawyer by a Kafkaesque court system (recalling the brutality cum Middle Eastern Orientalism of Oliver Stone's *Midnight Express* [1978]) as it is about circulating the large-scale framing of "China" as the despotic space of brutal indifference to human rights and the indictment, finally, of one slick Chinese transnational businessman for his murderous version of Yellow Cowboy Capitalism on the Beijing frontier.

Or here we might consider, as well, Michael Crichton's deviously articulated best-selling novel *Airframe* (1996), which cannot resist — in its hysterical exposé of Pac Rim aeronautic industry power dynamics and mass-media corruption (via the linked multi-billion-dollar "airframe" deals between Norton Aircraft and the People's Republic of China that impact U.S. labor contracts via offshore contracting and covert technology transfer) — to indict, finally, a Hong Kong–Chinese jet pilot of Trans-Pacific Air (Captain John Chang), who clannishly lets his smirking engineer son (Tommy Chang) pilot a flight in which fifty-six people are injured and four die because of air turbulence caused by (what else?) Chinese pilot error.[35] As the killer-capitalist TV producer named Dick Shenk screams at his L.A. reporter working up ("framing") the story out of its historical context for maximal U.S. mass-media impact, "Jesus fucking Christ, I got a hole in the show the size of Afghanistan and you're telling me you've got a *bad parts* story? Featuring Yellow Peril Pilots? Is that what you're telling me?" (342).

Belatedly enough, this is exactly what the Japan-bashing author of *Rising Sun* (1992) is telling us via his phobic plot of transnational Chinese capitalism and binary-driven thematics of East-West subjectification. Crichton has yet another story of yellow peril rising to tell us about how transnational capitalism really works on the Rim, and this time the new bad agents crisscrossing the phobic "transpacific" are not the *Japanese Rising* but those *Greater Chinese* labor hordes of financial globalization and cultural opacity who are coming en masse to ruin your neighborhood labor unions, tamper with your homey ethics of compassion and politics of human rights, and even corrupt the safety of your midnight air flights (airframes) from Beijing and Singapore to Hong Kong, Honolulu, Vancouver, and Los Angeles. (All these coastal sites figure in the novel's "Asia-Pacific" as if some devious trade zone of inscrutable customs and irrational codes that defy Euro-American liberal free-market transparency.)[36] Crichton, like the ever-earnest liberal muckraker Richard Gere, will set the region straight and laugh all the way to the movies, bookracks, and bank, doing so in his liberal goodwill and American common sense of enforcing global justice, human rights, feminism, and free markets on the world.[37]

From the model-minority tropes of Yao Ming, to the yellow-peril discourse of SARS in the perilous seasons of war and bioterrorism of 2003, the one-party market state of post-Maoist Chinese might very well get caught up in the binary structures of U.S. Orientalist discourse and its search for a perilous form of civilizational otherness the superpower-state seems to have settled on, at least for now, in oil-rife Iraq and the Persian Gulf states. Working in another genre of mass-mediated common sense, Howard Stern, on trash-talking radio from New York City, described the earlier version of (transnational) flu from Asia in phobic terms expressive of the U.S.-style white male "falling down" into lethal hatred and threats of preemptive world war: "Those damn Chinese. You know everything bad comes from China. It never fails. We should just nuke 'em. There are too many of them anyway."[38]

The earlier specter of "Asia Gate" in 1997 as a reawakening of yellow-peril discourse (not in Hollywood this time, but in Washington) should remind us of the North-South *unevenness* of class formations and uneven media dynamics in the Asia-Pacific region, the power of spin control via phobic U.S. ideology returning into our global news stories, films, and novels, as well as the uneasy fit of "Asia" as a quasi-Orientalist category collapsing diverse immigrant trajectories (from subaltern workers of subminimal wages to transnational political operators of right-wing cosmopolitanism) into itself as a unifying trope for racialized otherness in our transnational era of cross-border flows. The Pacific Rim can be figured less as a utopia for U.S. market forms and outlets and more as a footloose and deracinated capital of ethnic nepotism, slave labor in sweatshop factories, dynastic banking and criminal networks, and inscrutable cultural and legal codes. The "Greater Chinese" are being credited with this nowadays, even the ability to buy and glad-hand the former U.S. president Bill Clinton and various Pac Rim mayors and senators into the immense new pockets of transnational "guanxi."³⁹

Whatever the political accountability of U.S. Democratic Party funding deals cut on Hong Kong yachts or in Taiwanese temples and so on, the *extraterritorial* outreach of U.S. Orientalism keeps on overextending itself into the far reaches of our hypermediated social reality as across the space-time of nation-state borders. Thus the global technologies of the Hollywood blockbuster genre can all too easily sublate the local-national terrain into its own codes and "transnational imaginary," not, of course, without tactics of resistance and cultural-political challenge on the receiving end.⁴⁰ Class imbalances are once again entwined in the racialized figures of transnational otherness, and these binary projections demand some trenchant unpacking, if only to interrupt the flow of neo-Orientalism into our national-popular genres of Hollywood common sense.

Still, in mapping the political dynamics of "transcultural flows" across the compressed space-time of the Asia-Pacific, we need not follow a liberal apologist like John Naisbett down the transnational superhighway to high-capitalist euphoria, in his puffery of "Asia megatrends," to deduce that some "global paradox" of large meeting small can, at times, intensify the power and potential of the local, subnational, ethnic, or tribal to alter the seamless workings of global domination and transnational forms. At this point, we do need to account for the *uncanny* (outside-the-home) return (seemingly arising from inside the U.S. political unconscious in its residually imperial overextension) of discursive and material-symbolic formations like "the yellow peril," which historians of war like John Dower have traced as operating from the social Darwinist era of Jack London, Frank Norris, and Teddy Roosevelt, et al., down into the racial terrors and struggle for global hegemony across the region that culminated in World War II.

The contagion of the extraterritorial at times seems like a figuration of the extraterrestrial returning from the outer-space discourse of the Cold War to terrorize the cheery affluence of the Clintonesque home front. For no matter how much we try to "post" or render hypertextual and playfully hybrid the discursive frameworks of John Dower or Edward Said, "Orientalism" refuses to be *posted* or deconstructed from inside the U.S. national imaginary even during this hyperinteractive moment of transnational-transcultural flow.⁴¹

To evoke another example of U.S. cultural spin control in which the Chinese diasporic populations are evoked as some kind of transnational peril, in Alexander Besher's "novel of virtual reality" and cyberpunk business-as-usual called *Rim* (1994), we see that the social Darwinism of the transnational free market, with all its lurid games of macho competition and corporate killing, has gone inward into virtual reality and a financialized cyberspace. The Asia-Pacific has all but been materialized—and internalized—into the space-time compression and fake humanity of techno-euphoric cyberspace, that flip upside of America's transnational Rim phobia. The novel's setting is 2027, and Sartori Corporation (owner of a virtual reality entertainment empire based in a virtual Neo-Tokyo inside of Tokyo) is embroiled in cutthroat corporate warfare to preserve its market share. The Asia-Pacific becomes the space of the Keiretsu wars, with both white-collar crime and Tibetan mystical quests for the digitalization of consciousness and the discovery of a "new Matrix" frontier being the order of the day. The character Frank Gobi is the American transnational-romance-quest hero (perhaps Besher's idealized self-image of himself as a "consulting futurist on Pacific Rim Affairs for Global Business Network"?) trying to save the Japanese corporations from mutual destruction and "data muggings" and to free cyberspace for open libidinal usage.[42]

This cyber-novel remains prophetic in its figurations of Pacific Rim peril and promise, tracking the geo-material shifts of transnational racism and post-socialist paranoia. The geo-scenery of Besher's neocapitalist *Rim* is at once phobic and techno-Orientalist Pac Rim (elsewhere in cyberspace, Tokyo, and Berkeley, Gobi trades in Orientalist sexuality with several Japanese corporate princesses): "Rowdy groups of wealthy Greater Chinese businessmen milled about in front of glitzy Hong Kong–style hotels with atrium lobbies, preparing to head down to the Grant Avenue restaurants in New Chinatown" (65). Hong Kong and San Francisco, Los Angeles and Tokyo: the Pacific Rim has merged into one border-fusing culture of cybernetic capitalism. As Besher's narrator notes an array of "Rim carpetbaggers and keiretsu types," the scenery gets more ominous, suggesting the reign of gangsterism and warfare in the region, as connected to the yellow peril of China: "There were a couple of Greater China arms dealers, noticeable in their sharkskin suits of gray shantung silk. Flaunting jade rings the size of Kowloon and Seiko-Rolexes loaded with the latest Hsinchu Park circuitry on their pudgy wrists, the GCs looked more like rich uncles on holiday than they did merchants of death. . . . One of the North Koreans on board, a traveling salesman from Pyongyang, judging from his Kim Jong Il memorial bouffant hairdo—was already drunk and getting red in the face" (131–

32). Okay, by now you get the picture: a kind of neo-Orientalism here directed not against Japan but against the Greater Chinese and Third World peoples of Northeast Asia, while global Japanese and American corporate forces try to outwit each other for ultimate control of Asia-Pacific cyberspace, now imagined as a vast market of entertainment, libidinous foreplay, and catapulting profits.[43]

In works of cybernetic science fiction and global mapping like *Rim* or William Gibson's techno-euphoric transnational romance of "virtual media" fame and capitalist rapacity as high finance and fashion, *Idoru* (1996),[44] the Asia-Pacific geography has—all too predictably—turned lurid, techno-Orientalist, racially phobic, and politically regressive: in Besher's mapping, the United States and Japan align themselves for domination of the Internet frontier and try to exclude that "invisible empire" of the Overseas Chinese who would practice their own clannish forms of gangsterism and subterranean capitalism as they belatedly seek to become, as one British journalist of social science puts it, "Lords of the Rim." It is as if *Scarface* meets *Godfather III* in some cyberspace Chinatown, and the Americans, Tibetans, and Japanese get to play TNC Boy Scouts to keep the town safe for profit, libidinal pleasure, and new video games.

Analyzing Global-Local Dialectics and Transpacific Flows: Somebody Is Still Singing the APEC Blues

Inside the globalizing economy, global-local encounters intensify and "lines of flight" would fight against the stability and power of territory and state identity; for by some David-meets-Goliath-and-wins paradox, *the local can count even more as the global ground of creation and invention.*[45] In a strong or dialectical sense, *globalization* implies that the ongoing decentering of Euro-American cultural schemata, master narratives, and media has to be taken into account, and those modernist nation-state binaries of center-periphery mapping must be seen again in situated ways related to shifting (decentering) forces of class, place, race, and gender.[46] At times it seems as if the "world-system" model itself is dissolving in the Asia-Pacific, as in other sites of global-local interchange from Honolulu to Taipei, as the continental trajectory of Manifest Destiny dissolves into the dirty, magical waters of the Pacific.

"I describe China more as Europe," remarked John Farrell, president of Coca-Cola's China division in Hong Kong, to *Newsweek* in 1995, lured as such transnationals are by the massive, late-capitalist sublimity of 1.2 billion consumers on the post-Communist mainland all chiming in, "Let's Coke" or "Let's buy a motor scooter today!" Farrell's "Go-China" mandate to these transnational companies sounds like he has been studying postcolonial cultural studies readers in Melbourne and Birmingham or Taipei, as he calls for *heightened localization*, a process of getting your transnational feet on the ground and thus connecting with networks of transmission and step-by-step exchange (gathering so-called Chinese "mothers-in-law"): "Every region has distinct groups. You need local knowledge to get by," as the man selling soda in Hong Kong said.[47] *Globalize or die, globalize or your locality will fade into political-economic oblivion*, would be one way of putting the transnational mandate in the Asia-Pacific, as it continues to be reshaped by the APEC forces of today.[48] Whatever the view from the "road ahead" of Pac Rim instant-billionaire Bill Gates, the cultural and economic news is not all that upbeat and uncritical. As John Dower reminds us in *War without Mercy*, the postwar Asia-Pacific is haunted by the "race hates" and "race wars" that deformed the prior vision of inter-Asia as a region of mutual co-prosperity and coexistence just half a century ago; so we need to guard against the emergence of "provocative racial and martial idioms" done over in a new, transnational key.[49]

I can only begin to suggest the genealogy of the "Chinese Peril" as a cultural-ideological signifier as this has been constructed from inside an *American* trajectory, unlocking its power-laden connotations as the U.S. Pacific emerges from out of "Orientalist" images of vast Asian markets down through the phobic sublimity of Melville's white whale and Jack London's social Darwinist slime, down into the neofrontier of cyberspace mapped by Besher and Gibson, et al., where tousle-headed Bill Gates of Microsoft would welcome the global village, with U.S.-innocent arms, to what he enthuses is the "friction-free capitalism" or "cowboy capitalism" taking place (recalling the Gold Rush that built up California and opened "the Wild West" in 1849) inside Silicon Valley, if not all along "the Internet Goldrush."[50]

The United States is furiously transnationalizing and postcolonizing as it heads into what many would now lobby for as the "Pacific Century." But only by some massive feat of symbolic *displacement* and disavowal can the U.S. geopolitical imaginary go on blaming and scapegoating Pacific Rim nations like Japan, India, and China (those rising yellow-peril powers) for a process of capitalist dismantling and offshore restructuring that the United States has itself initiated and aggravated (as a multinational superpower) all along since the decolonization crisis of the 1960s and the oil crisis of the 1970s.[51] The global-local moment of threatened national sovereignty is, to be sure, a phobic moment of cultural-political *decentering*, representing a crisis that is at once (to invoke the Chinese ideogram) a moment of great political "danger" and "opportunity."

To invoke Gilles Deleuze and Félix Guattari on neocapitalism as a mode of loosening desiring-production and outer-national becoming, the line of flight of capitalist deterritorialization and geopolitical becoming is not just *from west to east* but *from north to south* as well, in all the imbalance and disruption that this world-system model of "developed underdevelopment" implies. "Dirty money" flows into clean money, and hard money into soft, and it does not do simply to project (from Washington and Hollywood domains) this process onto transnational others ruining the globalization game and corrupting the (unfree and unevenly regulated) free market. To put it bluntly, China and the United States too often confront each other through the gaze of two gigantic narcissisms and social-symbolic convictions of large-scale exceptionality and spatio-temporal difference, even more so as these superpowers become entangled in the Asia-Pacific with interconnected economies and a militarized nuclear infrastructure held in regional reserve.

U.S. citizens live in an era of liberal obliviousness and media spectacles when, as the distinguished Cuban literary critic Roberto Retamar reminds us of North-South imbalances, "it is said that imperialism has ceased to exist, or when its reality is hidden behind terms such as globalization or New World Order" or masqueraded in metropolitan discourses and what he calls (with the skepticism of a Caribbean-based Caliban toward North Atlanticist Prospero's ever-white magic of techno-speak cultural domination) the "semantic carnival" of hypertextual postcoloniality.[52]

One can only ask, as the ground of this U.S. national self-identity and the North American political economy goes irrevocably *offshore*, who will now get to play the forces of "yellow peril" threat to these denationalized and trans-nationalized visions of euphoric killer capitalism, white mythology, and tropes of superpower sublimation?[53] The answer in 1997 (as in the imperial crisis of 1898), not to mention the neo-Orientalism in the Arab-demonizing wake of 9/11, was becoming clear and all too repetitive to those who would remain vigilant about the workings of U.S. national culture, in its cheery-pluralist outreach as Empire across the transnationalizing-localizing Asia-Pacific borders.

Connected to the Americas as a site of transregional interaction and source of multisited critique, the Pacific Rim remains a locus where tactics of cultural nationalism, user-friendly postcolonialism, and an uncritical brand of global capitalism are no longer enough. We do need to imagine a mode of U.S.-China geopolitics that is not a future brand of civilizational superiority and national supremacy. The regions we live in demand more from us, living as we do on the transpacific transcultural front of future possibility and newness: if "America is the country of the two M's — John Milton and Milton Friedman," as one culture critic recently quipped, we need not let our gnostic brand of Puritanical evangelism cum market fundamentalism turn the world of the Americas into a huge Las Vegas.[54]

Notes

1   Emmanuel Levinas, "The Russo-Chinese Debate and the Dialectic," in *Les imprevus de l'histoire* (Saint Clément: Fata Morgana, 1989), 172. Challenging Levinas's claim to a "respect for alterity [which] is unconditional" except when it actually encounters the real geopolitics and enduring Orientalism of actual self-other and East-West encounters (as here between China and Russia or Palestine and Israel), Slavoj Žižek urges that "respect for alterity *means nothing*" outside these struggles for ideological hegemony and the antagonisms and gaps of social fantasy. See his *Organs without Bodies: On Deleuze and Consequences* (London: Routledge, 2004), 106.

2   Sandhya Shukla and Heidi Tinsman, editors' introduction to "Our Americas: Political and Cultural Imaginings," special issue, *Radical History Review* 89 (2004): 2.

3   Bill Maurer, "Ungrounding Knowledges Offshore: Caribbean Studies, Disciplinarity, and Critique," *Comparative American Studies* 2 (2004): 336.

4   For a translational version of "transnational literacy" and "crisis management" in U.S. area studies, ethnic studies, and comparative literature, see Gayatri Chakravorty Spivak, *Death of a Discipline* (New York: Columbia University Press, 2003), especially chapter 3, "Planetarity," as a challenge to U.S. globalism from the internationalist Left that cannot be merely "antiglobal" as a reaction to neoliberal domination.

5   On U.S. Orientalism, see Edward W. Said's defamiliarization of postwar liberal humanities and social science in *Orientalism* (New York: Vintage, 1979), 284–328, which tracks the discourse of State Department–driven "American Orientalism" as a formation of area studies in the 1950s. See also Brian T. Edwards, *Morocco Bound: Casablanca to the Marrakech Express* (Durham: Duke University Press, 2005), on the geopolitical, institutional, and cultural shaping of American Orientalism as a racial reconfiguration, 1942–73; as well as the superb study of U.S.-Asian foreign policy and discursive interconnection by Colleen Lye, *America's Asia: Racial Form and American Literature, 1893–1945* (Princeton: Princeton University Press, 2005); and Christina Klein, *Cold War Orientalism: Asia in the Middlebrow Imagination, 1945–1961* (Berkeley: University of California Press, 2003).

6   See Paul Giles, "The Parallel Worlds of Jose Marti," *Radical History Review* 89 (2004): 185–90, on the scalar and locational shifts in Martí's vision of the Americas as region.

7   Harry Harootunian, *History's Disquiet: Modernity, Cultural Practice, and the Question of Everyday Life* (New York: Columbia University Press, 2000), 25.

8   See the trans-area geopolitical speculations in Masao Miyoshi and Harry Harootunian, eds., *Learning Places: The Afterlives of Area Studies* (Durham: Duke University Press, 2002); David Leiwei Li, ed., *Globalization and the Humanities* (Hong Kong: Hong Kong University Press, 2004); and Bruce Robbins and Pheng Cheah, eds., *Cosmopolitics: Thinking and Feeling beyond the Nation* (Minneapolis: University of Minnesota Press, 1998). In each of these multidisciplinary collections, I have an essay theorizing transformations of the Asia-Pacific as a site of transnational as well as transdisciplinary contradiction and global-local struggles of emergence and hegemony.

9   The promise of capitalism's creative-destructive ethos still drives the market-geared urban forms and shopping-mall cities of China, as outlined in the Harvard Design School Project on the city, *Great Leap Forward*, ed. Rem Koolhaus et al. (Cambridge: Harvard Design School, 2001).

10 For earlier versions of this "post-Orientalist" discourse, see Christopher Leigh Connery, "Pacific Rim Discourse: The U.S. Global Imaginary in the Late Cold War Years," in *Asia/Pacific as Space of Cultural Production*, ed. Rob Wilson and Arif Dirlik (Durham: Duke University Press, 1995), 30–56.

11 On rural-urban imbalances in globalizing India, see Gayatri Spivak, "Megacity," lecture delivered at the University of California, Santa Cruz, May 13, 2004; on rural-urban boom and bust in China, see "The Second Industrial Revolution [in China]," *BBC News*, May 12, 2004. See also the globalization tactics and national crisis management of postsocialist Chinese knowledge/power as mapped in Wang Hui, *China's New Order: Society, Politics, and Economy in Transition* (Cambridge: Harvard University Press, 2003), particularly section 3, "Alternative Globalization and the Question of the Modern."

12 Pam Chun, *The Money Dragon* (Naperville, Ill.: Sourcebooks, 2002). "Al Leong spun his web, as all successful Chinese businessmen do, tied by affiliation and camaraderie, knotted by marriage and business deals" (73). Such deals include the local Chinese support of the Hawaiian monarchy as naturalized citizens (42).

13 See Cho Duck-Hyun, "The Dogs in the Pit," as portrayed in *Leaning Forward, Looking Backward: Eight Contemporary Artists from Korea* (Seoul: National Museum of Contemporary Art, 2003); and installation handouts from the Asian Art Museum in San Francisco, October 18, 2003–January 11, 2004.

14 "Cambodia King Backs Gay Marriage," *BBC News Online*, February 20, 2004.

15 Michael Liedtke, "Gap Inc. Details Working Conditions in Global Garment Factories," *San Francisco Chronicle*, May 13, 2004, business section.

16 Timothy Hurley, "Navy Destroyer to Go Out in Blaze of RIMPAC Glory," *Honolulu Advertiser*, May 4, 2004.

17 Thomas L. Friedman, "Cursed with Oil," *New York Times*, May 9, 2004, Op-ed page.

18 Arundhati Roy, "Let Us Hope the Darkness Has Passed: India's Real and Virtual Worlds Have Collided in a Humiliation of [BJP] Power," *Guardian*, May 14, 2004.

19 See Susan Peques, "*Samurai, Lost in Translation* boost Japan's Cinematic Potential," *Japan Today*, January 16, 2004.

20 Wayne Harada and Zenaida Serrano, "Jasmine Weeps as *Idol* Judges Pan Performance," *Honolulu Advertiser*, May 12, 2004.

21 On Jasmine Trias as a figure for Hawaiian Asia-Pacific localism, see Michael Tsai, "Hawaii Sees Itself in Sweet, Tough Jasmine," *Honolulu Advertiser*, May 16, 2004. For this story, I thank Pam Kido, who is working on a dissertation on the contradictions and alliances between Hawaiian indigenous and local identity formations.

22 On the Cold War demonizing of the island nation of Cuba as a space of Stalinized unfreedom and the implementation of U.S. "embargo" policies that go back to extensions of the Monroe Doctrine in Latin America and the Pacific, see Roberto Fernández Retamar, "The Enormity of Cuba," *Boundary 2* 23 (1996): 165–90, which was written partly as a response to "Asia/Pacific as Space of Cultural Production," a special issue of *Boundary 2* 21 (1994), and thus attempts to think (critically in a counterliberal way) our transnational moment of "borderlessness" in the Pacific and Asia versus real blockades in the NAFTA and APEC region.

23 Frank Norris, *The Octopus* (New York: Penguin, 1987), 306–7.

24 On the dialectics of transnationalism in coastal cities like Shanghai and the more utopian "contact zone" formulations of California-based scholars like Mary Louise Pratt or authors like Gloria Anzaldúa, see Arif Dirlik's historical overview, "Transnationalism, the Press, and the National Imaginary in Twentieth Century China," *China Review* 4 (2004): 11–25.

25 Slavoj Žižek, *Tarrying with the Negative: Kant, Hegel, and the Critique of Ideology* (Durham: Duke University Press, 1993), 203.

26 Bruce Cumings, preface to *Parallax Visions: Making Sense of American–East Asian Relations*, 2nd ed. (Durham: Duke University Press, 2003), viii.

27 This is one of Harootunian's methodological claims in *History's Disquiet*: to push toward trans-area linkage.

28 Bruce Cumings and Paul Bové outlined the antipopulist workings and right-wing institutions of this post-9/11 U.S. apparatus at the "Imminent Questions" conference, New York University, April 29–May 1, 2004. Critiques of Hardt and Negri's U.S.-romanticized "Empire" thesis and claims for the "multitudes" of the transnational peripheries seem pathetically belated at this point, but see Paul Bové's "Afterword: Can We Judge the Humanities by Their Future as a Course of Study," in *Globalization and the Humanities*, ed. David Leiwei Li (Hong Kong: Hong Kong University Press, 2004), 274–78.

29 "Japan Promises Aid to South Pacific," *Honolulu Advertiser*, April 23, 2000, A2.

30 For an influential version of this Anglo-Saxon-based neonativism, see Louis Menand, "Samuel B. Huntington's New Nativism," *New Yorker*, May 17, 2004, 92–

98; and Samuel P. Huntington, *Who Are We? The Challenges to America's National Identity* (New York: Simon and Schuster, 2004).

31   Rob Wilson, "Reframing Displacements in the U.S. Pacific and Asia/Pacific Field-Imaginary," *Journal of Asian American Studies* 6 (2003): 199–205.

32   Slavoj Žižek, *Enjoy Your Symptom! Jacques Lacan in Hollywood and Out* (New York: Routledge, 1992), 170. On tactics of social-symbolic "suturing" of capitalist excess by tactics of national-popular hegemony ("the nation-thing"), also see Žižek, "Formal Democracy and Its Discontents," chapter 9 of *Looking Away: An Introduction to Jacques Lacan through Popular Culture* (Cambridge: MIT Press, 1992).

33   Bill Gates, "Friction-Free Capitalism," chapter 8 of *The Road Ahead* (New York: Penguin, 1996). On class divisions between "uptown" versus "downtown" Chinese within aggravated transnational flows of capital and labor, see Peter Kwong, *The New Chinatown* (New York: Hill and Wang, 1996); and Kwong, *Forbidden Workers: Illegal Chinese Immigrants and American Labor* (New York: Hill and Wang, 1997).

34   Joel Kotkin, *Tribes* (New York: Random House, 1994); Murray Weidenbaum, *The Bamboo Network* (New York: Martin Kessler Books, 1996). I thank David Palumbo-Liu for these two references, as well as for his ongoing studies of the threat to U.S. "national sovereignty" represented by such figurations of the transnational Chinese.

35   Michael Crichton, *Airframe* (New York: Knopf, 1996), 340–41.

36   Crichton's narrator admits this early in the novel through the American passenger, Emily Jansen, in musings such as the following: "The fact that the crew was Chinese didn't trouble her. After a year in China, she admired the efficiency and attention to detail of the Chinese. But somehow the whole flight [a Trans-Pacific charter from Hong Kong] just made her nervous" (3). Her phobia will be enacted by events in *Airframe* as her attempt to counter her Waspish Orientalism proves mistaken and the *Chinese are finally to blame* for the plane's faulty and less-than-modern performance.

37   Christopher Connery has reminded me, in a response to this paper, that "Japan bashing" (as described and resisted by cultural-political critics like Masao Miyoshi and Harry Harootunian, et al.) is a longer-lasting discourse, relating to the racial phobias and mutual atrocities of World War II (only sixty years back), but also because U.S. politics and policies toward mainland China have historically had an "extraterritorial" dimension to them. There has been, more recently, some distance and attempt at mutuality, to achieve some double-coded space(s) of negotiable *difference* between these superpowers allowed for that was not just "colonial" or "imperial." For a rich discussion of this and related problems of "theorizing [modern] China" in the "postcolonial" (and counter-Maoist) work of Rey Chow, et al., see Chris Connery, "The China Difference," *Postmodern Culture* 2 (1992): 1–12. On the complicated relationship of bondage and breakage between imperial Japan and China, see Stefan Tanaka, "*Shina*: The Separation of Japan from China," chapter 3 of *Japan's Orient: Rendering Pasts into History* (Berkeley: University of California Press, 1993).

38 I thank Jon Michael Varese for this example of yellow-peril discourse and "U.S. cultural commentary" heard by him on a car radio in Santa Cruz, California, December 9, 1997, as he pondered work for my graduate seminar in "De-Orientalizing the American Pacific."

39 See Aihwa Ong and Donald Nonini's cautionary collection *Ungrounded Empires: The Cultural Politics of Modern Chinese Transnationalism* (New York: Routledge, 1997); as well as the locally situated and transnational essays by Leo Ching and Fred Chiu in *Asia/Pacific as Space of Cultural Production*, ed. Rob Wilson and Arif Dirlik (Durham: Duke University Press, 1995), for example, on "Pacific" dynamics emerging within the Chinese-nationalist hegemony of Taiwan as against seeing Taiwan as postmodern space dominated by Japanese and U.S. consumer flows.

40 On the problematics of global-local interactions that are not just reducible to neocolonial or Orientalist ones, see Rob Wilson and Wimal Dissanayake, eds., *Global/Local: Cultural Production and the Transnational Imaginary* (Durham: Duke University Press, 1996).

41 Recall Edward Said's grim insight in *Orientalism* when he situates the "myths and lies" of such discourse within the geopolitics of its prestructured affiliations: "One ought never to assume that the structure of Orientalism is nothing more than a structure of lies and myths which, were the truth about them to be told, would simply blow away" (6). The hold of "myths" on nations, as Žižek variously shows, is not that easy to demystify, as they help structure modes of daily living and social reality.

42 Besher, *Rim: A Novel of Virtual Reality* (London: Orbit, 1994), 57.

43 In Samuel P. Huntington's mapping of U.S. "national interests" in this era of post–Cold War risk and multicultural particularism cum civilizational standoffs, China looms as a threat to U.S. interests as "regional hegemon" in East Asia: "Conceivably China could become a new enemy. Certainly, important groups in China think of the United States as *their* enemy. A China threat sufficient to generate a new sense of national identity and purpose in the United States is not imminent, and how serious that threat is judged to be will depend on the extent to which the Americans view Chinese hegemony in East Asia as damaging to American interests" in the transnational era. Huntington, "The Erosion of American National Interests," *Foreign Affairs* 76 (1997): 48. While even *Time* magazine now worries, "Has America Become a Global Bully?" in Europe and Asia (August 4, 1997), Huntington fears that the liberal-market regime has lost its national resolve and will to international intervention; indeed, for him the United States has lost its will to be a global hegemon and to shape international politics to its own Western-democratic ends. John Updike's Rabbit Angstrom is his hero: "Without the cold war," Huntington invokes Rabbit, "what's the point of being an American?" (29). Huntington grows nostalgic for such Cold War resolve and maps the world accordingly to its binary phobias and disseminates them into Euro-Asia for good measure. Empire nowadays is not so much criticism as a superlative frame.

44 William Gibson, *Idoru* (New York: Berkeley Books, 1996).

45   John Naisbett, in *Global Paradox*: *The Bigger the World Economy, the More Powerful Its Smallest Players* (New York: Avon, 1994) and *Asia Megatrends* (1995), argues for a transnational embrace of a "thinking globally, acting locally" paradox he sees driving economies of "the Asia-Pacific," which, through an expanded "Global China" region, will lead the world into what he boasts is the triumphant "Pacific Century." These pro-market books of Pacific Futurism are widely translated and popular in Asia-Pacific markets, as are the more divisive works of political economy by Samuel Huntington warning of recurring "civilizational" standoffs between "East" and "West"; see Kuan-Hsing Chen, "Watch Out for Civilizationalism: Huntington and Nandy," in *History and Theory of Cultural Studies*, ed. Lee Yu-cheng (Taipei: Institute of Academia Sinica, 1997).

46   See the "transnational feminist" essays gathered in Inderpal Grewal and Caren Kaplan, eds., *Scattered Hegemonies: Postmodernity and Transnational Feminist Practices* (Minneapolis: University of Minnesota Press, 1994).

47   *Newsweek*, February 20, 1995, 12.

48   The dominant framework for the current use of "Asia-Pacific," APEC refers to the Asia-Pacific Economic Cooperation. Increasingly endorsed as a liberalizing market mechanism by the Clinton administration and a bubble-burst Japan following the U.S. model of segmented "deregulation," APEC was formed in 1989 (without U.S. support) to help ease trade barriers and to liberalize and integrate markets in the region. ASEAN struggles to maintain some measure of regional autonomy within APEC's "Asia-Pacific" as against Europe and NATO forms.

49   See John Dower, *War without Mercy: Race and Power in the Pacific War* (New York: Pantheon Books, 1986), 314. As Andrew Mack and John Ravenhill remind us, "For four decades following the end of World War II, the politically divided Asia-Pacific was the principal battleground on which global Cold War rivalries were fought. Wars first in China, then Korea, Vietnam, and Cambodia pitted the United States and its allies against nationalist movements that, assisted by the two great communist powers, fought under the banner of revolutionary socialism." Mack and Ravenhill, "Economic and Security Regimes in the Asia-Pacific Region," in *Pacific Cooperation: Building Economic and Security Regimes in the Asia-Pacific Region* (Boulder, Colo.: Westview, 1995), 22.

50   Silicon Valley — a massive synergy of Stanford University, Hewlett Packard, high-tech wizardry, teamwork, and flexible new forms of venture capitalism — seems to be the key global model for a "new cybernetic frontier" of transnational capitalism (one that has been adopted, for example, by the Research and Science Industrial Park of Hsinchu, Taiwan, ROC, with its close ties to neighboring National Chiao-Tung and National Tsing-Hua University). In the U.S.-based vision (sublimating capitalist rapacity into harmony) of John Doerr, financial mega-agent in "Silicon Valley, the brutally competitive cluster of technology companies from Intel to Apple," "The conventional wisdom about Silicon Valley is that it's filled with wild-eyed and woolly entrepreneurs who are totally independent, who absolutely insist on succeeding or failing on their own merits — you know, cowboy capitalism and

the Wild West. That may have been true in the past. It's definitely not true today."
Doerr was interviewed by William C. Taylor and Alan A. Weber, former editors of
the global-local journal the *Harvard Business Review,* for their book *Going Global:
Four Entrepreneurs Map the New World Marketplace* (New York: Penguin, 1997).

51 "Multinational" was refigured by the United Nations planners into "transnational"
when the former term came under third-world critique in the 1960s: see John L.
Daniels and N. Caroline Daniels, *Global Vision: Building New Models for the Corporation of the Future* (New York: McGraw-Hill International Editions, 1994).

52 Retamar, "The Enormity of Cuba," 179–82. I should say that *island nations* whose
political fates are entangled in the history of U.S. imperialism in the inter-Americas
and Asia-Pacific nexus, like Cuba and Hawai'i (and, to some extent, Taiwan, in its
own way seeking semiautonomous status off the coast of the PRC) remain *wary* of
this North American discourse of "the postcolonial" as a way of mapping the global
political-economy and nationalist struggles of Third World and Fourth World cultural studies. On this see Kuan-Hsing Chen, "Not Yet the Postcolonial Era: The
(Super) Nation-State and Trans*nationalism* of Cultural Studies: Response to Ang
and Stratton," *Cultural Studies* 10 (1996): 37–70.

53 On "denationalizing" citizenship and social struggles for justice in our era of transnationalization, as this affects Asian Americans and Asian American studies, see
Sau-Ling C. Wong, "Denationalization Reconsidered: Asian American Cultural
Criticism at a Theoretical Crossroads," *Amerasia Journal* 21 (1995): 1–27; and Arif
Dirlik, "Asia on the Rim: Transnational Capital and Local Community in the Making of Contemporary Asian America," *Amerasia Journal* 22 (1996): 1–24, where he
warns against ruses of diasporic opportunism in coding transnational capitalism
into multicultural liberalism and eliding the social struggles of the revolutionary
1960s. On these new configurations and linkages between Asian area studies and
Asian American and ethnic studies, see also Shirley Geok-lin Lim, John Blair Gam-
ber, Stephen Hong Sohn, and Gina Valentino, eds., *Transnational Asian American Literature: Sites and Transits* (Philadelphia: Temple University Press, 2006);
and Natascha Gentz and Stefan Kramer, eds., *Globalization, Cultural Identities, and
Media Representations* (Albany: SUNY Press, 2006).

54 On the American brand of gnostic religion making and market pragmatism, see
Harold Bloom's *American Religion: The Emergence of a Post-Christian Nation* (New
York: Touchstone, 1993), a prophetic cultural critique of Bush-era fundamentalism.

Uprooted Bodies

Indigenous Subjects and Colonial Discourses

in Atlantic American Studies

Michelle Stephens

In 1991 Maxine Hong Kingston described Leslie Marmon Silko's epic novel *Almanac of the Dead* as an invocation of "the voices of the ancestors and spirits, telling us where we came from, who we are, and where we must go."[1] Kingston's language reminds one of Gloria Anzaldúa's much earlier description of the *mestiza*, the mixed-race Mexican–Native American woman who seeks "a piece of ground to stand on . . . a homeground where she can plumb the rich ancestral roots into her own ample *mestiza* heart."[2] In much of her framing of *Borderlands/La Frontera*, Anzaldúa focused on the spirits that inhabit the geographical borders between one place and another — "the actual physical borderland . . . [of] the Texas-U.S Southwest/Mexican border."[3] Though Silko's novel is partly set in the same physical location, here the terrain is history, not just the borders between past and present and future, but also the borders that trace, map, and separate the different peoples and histories that occupy and constitute the world of the colonial Americas. Silko's novel provides us with one singularly coherent instance in which both new subjects and old cultures emerge from a transatlantic history of the Americas, told both through an interdisciplinary lens and against the backdrop of multiple and heterogeneous movements throughout Atlantic space.

By invoking the image of "uprooted bodies," this essay seeks to complicate our conceptions of the rootedness of the "indigenous" in Atlantic and American history. Through a reexamination of certain approaches to colonial history and discourse, I suggest that we may profit from seeing the indigenous as some of the most mobile populations, and tropes, in transatlantic space, subject to myriad forced migrations and settlements across colonial space, but also multiply subjected and interpellated by those movements and forms of colonial authority. As such, the indigenous become the image not so much of the rooted as of the ones who have lost through force—and therefore are most actively seeking to reclaim—earth, land, and homes. As Anzaldúa described her own Chicana sense of the history of the people of the Southwest: "We were jerked out by the roots, truncated, disemboweled, dispossessed, and separated from our identity and our history."[4]

An image of the indigenous as mobile and "uprooted" would also require us to think further about the nature of the forces that put various indigenous populations and other Atlantic subjects into motion across the Atlantic and, historically and imaginatively, about their response to those forces. Vijay Prashad has said: "The romance of the 'indigenous' treats them as if they are trapped in the local while the rest of the world (us) is seen as footloose in the global."[5] His language is appropriate here, for trapped in the local also often means trapped to and on the land, but as Prashad continues, "Oppressed peoples who live off land that is increasingly being swept up in the onrush of agrobusiness and extractive industries face a multifaceted challenge, not one that can be grasped within the one-dimensional idea of the indigenous." As will be the case here, to shift our understanding of the indigenous in the present, Prashad finds himself returning to and retelling their stories from the past.[6]

Different and more mobile paradigms for thinking about the indigenous also reveal the many and multiracial populations moving constantly throughout transatlantic history, traveling together on the same ships, working together in the same islands and on the same plantations, populations interacting in ways that are fully unable to be captured by the simple dualisms that have so structured our theorizing of intersubjective relations in the colonial world, the dualism of Self and Other. Rather, Atlantic histories reveal the various triangulations and quadrilateral human relations made possible, by force and by necessity, in colonial space.

The *Oxford English Dictionary* defines the "indigenous" as those "born or produced naturally in a land or region; native or belonging naturally to," and cites one of the word's first usages in 1646 in the literature of exploration and discovery, when one Sir T. Browne made the following observation: "Although . . . there bee . . . swarmes of Negroes serving under the Spaniard, yet were they all transported from Africa . . . and are not indigenous or proper natives of America."[7] Here we see a clear opposition between the "transplanted" African and the native Indian, an opposition integral to any instinctive understanding of the term "indigenous." However, what the *OED* definition does not explicitly state is that the transplanted were also themselves once indigenous to somewhere else, an elsewhere intimately connected to the new places they were transplanted to in a colonial political economy. So what separates the transplanted from the indigenous is not so much a dichotomous relationship to land and native attachments but the degree to which one has been uprooted or forced into exile from home. And what unites the black African and the Native American is precisely their shared, vindicationist urge to reclaim both land and history from their European expropriators.

Silko's novel fully recognizes and explores this connection, taking a precolonial and premodern desire for economic justice and historical vindication and turning it into a postmodern alliance between indigenous South Americans and urban African Americans, all border-crossing between past and present together as they imagine and construct their alliances with each other. In this reading of the novel, one primary figure of interest is the African American character Clinton, both a kind of modern-day African American Caliban, intent on vindicating and reclaiming his history, and an elaboration of the more contemporary trope for the urban, black, and male colonial subject, the "native son" of Richard Wright's Bigger Thomas and also Ralph Ellison's invisible man. Through Clinton, Silko is able to articulate a very different view of colonial history in the Americas, as the African American character becomes the vehicle or trope through which Silko can imagine a world beyond the simple dualism of colonizer and colonized. Scholarly interpretations of the trope of Caliban, the classic figure for the colonized subject from Shakespeare's 1611 play *The Tempest*, have provided different paradigms for thinking about the colonial encounter and different ways of constructing the racial bodies encountering and being encountered in colonial spaces. Multiple meanings have been captured by what we may call the "sign of Caliban," the earliest use of Caliban as a trope being by none other than Shakespeare himself. As scholars of the period have pointed out, the figure in the play and the space of the island more broadly capture Renaissance constructions of indigenous Native Americans as noble savages, and the New World as a new utopia, a place for uprooted Europeans to start over and to construct new and ideal societies.[8]

In the Anglophone Afro-Caribbean context of the twentieth century, a nationalist and postcolonial world, Caliban became the figural meeting ground for the confrontation between colonized and colonizer. As George Lamming put it, "Caliban himself like the island he inherited is at once a landscape and a human situation."[9] For Lamming, Caliban is decidedly black, a vision also captured in Aimé Césaire's Francophone retelling of the drama in his 1969 play *A Tempest*, where Césaire rewrites Caliban as the postcolonial revolutionary hero, informed by the language of negritude.[10]

But in the Latin American context there developed a slightly different shift in emphasis, with Roberto Fernández Retamar's construction of Caliban as the very site of *mestizaje*—the mixing of bodies to create a mixed body, the mulatto, the blending of black, native, and white to create a New World self.[11] As Retamar proclaimed in 1971:

> Our symbol then . . . is Caliban. This is something that we, the mestizo inhabitants of these same isles where Caliban lived, see with particular clarity. I know no other metaphor more expressive of our cultural situation, of our reality. . . . What is our history, what is our culture, if not the history and culture of Caliban?[12]

In *The Dialectics of America*, José David Saldívar identified what he called a "school of Caliban" in the Americas, in which "different (imagined) national communities and symbologies are linked by their derivation from a common and explosive reading of . . . *The Tempest*."[13] Each of these constructions of Caliban dramatizes a way of representing the colonial encounter, a way of capturing in a trope the oppositional relationship between colonized and colonizer, and the ontological relationship between Self and Other. However, as tropes for different constructions of national identity across varied geographic spaces in the United States, Latin America, and the Caribbean, these various Calibans also all exist in separate epistemological universes. Within the terms of each construction of the trope, Caliban can exemplify only one kind of relationship between a singular colonizer and a singular colonized. In other words, for the thrust of the metaphor to work, Caliban cannot simultaneously represent black, native, mestizaje, and white populations and bodies. Vijay Prashad cautions against this—difference becoming grafted onto one metaphoric and symbolic body—in his discussion of a "polycultural" approach to the history of the Americas.[14]

Prashad borrows his notion of "polyculturalism" from Robin D. G. Kelley, whom he quotes further, saying: "All of us, and I mean ALL of us . . . are the inheritors of European, African, Native American, and even Asian pasts, even if we can't exactly trace our blood lines to all of these continents. . . . We were multi-ethnic and polycultural from the get go."[15] Yet, "in search of our mulatto history," Prashad also warns, "to transform difference into the body is an act of bad faith, a denial of our shared nakedness."[16] Prashad's final call is, in essence, to uproot difference from the body itself, thereby uprooting different bodies from rigid, racist notions of their culture-bound histories and identities.

As these multiple Calibans emerge in literary discourse across the Americas, we should realize that it is not so much the presence of the Other but the presence of *multiple* Others that is at issue in the various meanings circulating around this paradigmatic trope for colonial subjectivity. It is that very multiplicity, even chaos, that gets organized by the use of tropes such as the figure of Caliban to represent the multiracial colonial subject as a singular body and being.

Using Silko's text as a starting point, this essay will sketch new directions for the study of colonial discourse and history in the Americas by deploying notions of the "uprooted" and the "indigenous" to further read this "polycultural" body in Silko's "invocation of the ancestors" in her epic of the Americas. I close by returning briefly to a reading of the trope of Caliban that leads in similar directions as Silko's text. Ultimately the goal is to suggest how new kinds of readings can help us reimagine a figure such as Caliban as a hybrid trope for American indigeneities, bringing discussions of indigeneity and race together and bringing Native American studies into a more active dialogue with contemporary "American" fields such as Latin American, African American, Asian American, and American studies. This dialogue would begin by recovering the colonial world as multiracial and focusing on the impact of race in shaping a differentially racialized colonial "America."

Indigenous Movements

Much work remains to be done in comparing Marx's American and European writings, and in thinking about how his observations about the historical development of capital were shaped by his European context. Caribbean, Latin

American, and African American intellectuals have been among the few who have tried to link Marx's analysis of history to the racial history of slavery and colonialism, probably the most common and controversial area in which this question has been raised.[17] The Caribbean radical C. L. R. James was distinctive for being one of the first to recognize that some of those connections could be made directly from and in some of Marx's own writings. In an article written in the early 1940s, James quoted from a letter that Marx wrote to Engels in which Marx commented on historical events in the United States, saying, "In my opinion the biggest things that are happening in the world today are, on the one hand, the movement of the slaves in America . . . and, on the other, the movement of the serfs in Russia."[18] Marx's comment not only connected the histories of the European serf and the African American slave but also saw as their key joining force their movements across their respective continental landscapes.

The historians Peter Linebaugh and Marcus Rediker have provided a concrete historical justification for linking European and American populations in time through a history of their shared movements in space. In their magisterial study of the Atlantic, the authors point out that, during the early years of the seventeenth century, acts of "expropriation," the removal of various subject populations from their lands, ensured the successful transfer of imperial power from "Mediterranean kingdoms and city-states [such as] Spain [and] Portugal" to "the Atlantic maritime states of northwest Europe [such as] (France, the Netherlands, and England)."[19] Expropriation, as a historical phenomenon broadly conceived, tragically connected Old World and New World histories and subjects during this period. In Linebaugh and Rediker's account, changes central to the development of early modern capitalism, such as "the shift in agriculture from arable subsistence to commercial pasturage; the increase of wage labour; . . . the growth of world trade; the institutionalization of markets; and the establishment of a colonial system," were all made possible by "a profound and far-reaching cause: the enclosure of land and the removal of thousands of people from the commons."

> Expropriation was the source of the original accumulation of capital, and the force that transformed land and labor into commodities. . . . As landlords dispossessed European workers . . . European merchants dispossessed native peoples in the Americas. . . . The dispossession and relocation of peoples [were] a worldwide process [that] helped to organize the middle passage between Old World expropriation and New World exploitation.[20]

Silko's *Almanac of the Dead* is a novel explicitly set within, and referencing, this complex set of expropriations and movements across both New and Old World transatlantic spaces, and involving both New and Old World populations. In the more contemporary 1970s, Anzaldúa movingly described one moment in this history, retelling the story of the development and settlement of the southwestern United States from the perspective of the dispossessed and, in this case, landless Chicanos and Chicanas:

> In the 1930s, after Anglo agribusiness corporations cheated the small Chicano landowners of their land, the corporations hired gangs of *mexicanos* to pull out the brush, chaparral and cactus and to irrigate the desert. The land they toiled over had once belonged to many of them, or had been used communally by them. Later the Anglos brought in huge machines and root plows and had the Mexicans scrape the land clean of natural vegetation. . . . In the 1950s I saw the land, cut up into thousands of neat rectangles and squares, constantly being irrigated. . . . More big land corporations came in and bought up the remaining land.[21]

But Anzaldúa also described a centuries-long response on the part of her people and their ancestors to their continuous history of uprooting:

> We have a tradition of migration, a tradition of long walks. Today we are witnessing *la migración de los pueblos mexicanos*, the return odyssey. . . . This time, the traffic is from south to north.
>
> *El retorno* to the promised land first began with the Indians from the interior of Mexico and the *mestizos* that came with the *conquistadores* in the 1500s. Immigration continued in the next three centuries, and, in this century, it continued with the *braceros*. . . . Today thousands of Mexicans are crossing the border legally and illegally.

Here Anzaldúa ascribes to different kinds of historical movements a shared purpose, an uprooted people's response to the economic forces destroying their ways of life and cultures. Over time that response shares similar features, subjection by the same forces of capitalist expropriation in contemporary forms, and the same response of a continuous movement north over both territory and history.

What was implicit in Anzaldúa in 1987 is developed and made more explicit in Silko's *Almanac of the Dead*, where an inchoate historical response becomes a politically self-aware and vindicationist urge to reclaim the land and history lost. The power of a vindicationist reading of history, one that provides a lens into the polyculturalism of history by revealing different peoples' shared dispossession by hegemonic material economic forces, drives a second important character in Silko's novel, Angelita La Escapía, a "colonel in the Army of Justice and Redistribution," an indigenous group of freedom fighters in Mexico.[22] First raised by nuns and missionaries, and then trained by Cuban revolutionaries, La Escapía could be described as the daughter of Anzaldúa's "Malinali Tenepat, or Malintzin," the "Indian woman in us" who has become the betrayer, "la Chingada—the fucked one."[23] But Silko's Angelita La Escapía is no victim; she is victim turned vengeful destroyer. Animated by her own vindicationst urge to both redeem her people's history and literally reclaim their land, La Escapía takes on as her central interlocutor none other than the author of the story of capitalist historical development himself, Marx.

La Escapía's political training by Cuban revolutionaries first begins to make sense when she is introduced to Marx's writings. In Marx La Escapía finds a recognizable way of understanding history: history telling as the unearthing of the palimpsestic record of stories from the now dead labor that has gone into the making of modern capitalism. As the narrator describes:

> Marx was the first white man La Escapía had ever heard call his own people vampires and monsters. . . . Tribal people had had all the experience they would ever need to judge whether Marx's stories told the truth. The Indians had seen generations of themselves ground into bloody pulp under the steel wheels of ore cars in crumbling tunnels of gold mines.[24]

Marx's writings, and specifically his identification of the same forces of history that have expropriated her own people's modes of production and being, serve as the catalyst for La Escapía's desire for vindication: "From that point on the words of Marx had only gotten better. The stories Marx related, the great force of his words, the bitterness and fury—they had caught hold of La Escapía's imagination then." She reads in his writings direct connections between the capitalist histories of an industrializing Europe and the polycultural histories of the indigenous on both the African and American continents:

> Angelita had read the words of Marx for herself. Marx had never forgotten the indigenous people of the Americas, or of Africa. Marx had recited the crimes of slaughter and slavery committed by the European colonials who had been sent by their capitalist slave-masters to secure the raw materials of capitalism—human flesh and blood. With the wealth of the New World,

the European slave-masters and monarchs had been able to buy weapons
and armies to keep down the uprisings of the landless people all across
Europe. (315)

Here La Escapía constructs both a coeval and a causal relationship between the
exploitation of expropriated and transplanted peoples in the colonial worlds
from the fifteenth century onward and the actions of the developing metropolitan states against their own domestic and expropriated populations.

But for La Escapía, precisely what Marx had also missed was the living reality
of the colonial world being destroyed by these forces, and the forms of its survival in the interface or border between capitalist colonial expansion and the
precolonial worlds of indigenous Americans and Africans. In the emerging
present lay the active residues of the conquered past. It is here, in the power of
stories to reanimate historical memory as a political force in the present, that
the vindicationist spirit is born:

> The stories of the people or their "history" had always been sacred, the
> source of their entire existence. If the people had not retold the stories,
> or if the stories had somehow been lost, then the people were lost; the
> ancestors' spirits were summoned by the stories. This man Marx had
> understood that the stories or "histories" are sacred; that within "his-
> tory" reside relentless forces, powerful spirits, vengeful, relentlessly seek-
> ing justice. (316)

In La Escapía's analysis, Marx had only been able to see and record the specters
of the past surrounding him in Europe. What was incomprehensible to him
were the very different historical forces and memories taking shape in both Old
and New World colonial spaces and traveling across the Atlantic:

> Marx had been inspired by reading about certain Native American com-
> munal societies, though naturally as a European he had misunderstood a
> great deal. . . . Marx understood what tribal people had always known:
> the maker of a thing pressed part of herself or himself into each object
> made. Some spark of life or energy went from the maker into even the
> most ordinary objects. . . . Generation after generation, individuals were
> born, then after eighty years, disappeared into dust, but in the stories, the
> people lived on in the imaginations and hearts of their descendants. Wher-
> ever their stories were told, the spirits of the ancestors were present and
> their power was alive. (520)

In indigenous histories, then, lay the true meaning of polycultural forces that even Marx had been too bound in his own culture to understand and interpret. "When [revolutionaries] denied indigenous history, they betrayed the true meaning of Marx. [But] not even Marx had fully understood the meaning of the spiritual and tribal communes of the Americas" (314).

Silko's critique of Marx, articulated through Angelita La Escapía, depends on her return to, and deformation of, the idealism that Marx's materialism was meant to challenge. In Silko's novel the Hegelian language of the spirit of history is both invoked and powerfully reversed, a reversal meant to reveal and vindicate the premodern histories and colonial peoples excluded from the Hegelian dialectic of world history that Marx inherited: "He had sensed the great power these stories had—power to move millions of people. Poor Marx did not understand the power of the stories belonged to the spirits of the dead" (521). It is these vindicationist spirits, the memories and histories of colonial indigenous peoples, that mobilize the migration North that ultimately ends the novel (424–28). *Almanac of the Dead* closes with a revolutionary and angry vision of polycultural solidarity, as a "People's Army" of "landless Indians," together with homeless African Americans and Vietnam War veterans, move across the United States in a south–north, rather than east–west, direction, "all [their] energy [channeled] into one desire: to retake the land" (523). This shift in geographic direction is itself symbolic of a reversal of history, as south moves north, indigenous Mexican and African American, to reclaim land and history from Euro-America.

For Silko, the past, the dead labor of all those peoples living in the polycultural colonial worlds that Marx's story of history could not encompass, is striking back:

> For hundreds of years white men had been telling the people of the Americas to forget the past; but now the white man Marx came along and he was telling people to remember. The old-time people had believed the same thing: they must reckon with the past because within it lay seeds of the present and future. (311)

Marx is both Angelita's connection to her own desire for vindication and the historian whose story of capitalism must be uprooted by the colonial subject to reveal the indigenous histories that lie buried underneath. It is in Angelita La Escapía's connections to a second character, Clinton, that the polyculturalism of American colonial history achieves its own vindication in the novel.

Angelita's connection to Clinton is enacted through a similar relationship to Marx, for as Clinton also says elsewhere in the novel: "Clinton swears he is no Marxist. African and other tribal people had shared food and wealth in common for thousands of years before the white man Marx came along and stole their ideas for his 'communes' and collective farms. 'White man didn't even invent communism on his own,' Clinton said" (408). Dispensing with Marx and a history of the Americas told purely from the perspective of the history of capitalism and imperial expansion, Silko can recount instead a history of the forces, peoples, and histories uprooted by capitalism, a polycultural history of both the uprooted native and the transplanted indigenous in the Americas, united in their belief in the sacred power of their alternative historical memories. In so doing, Silko fundamentally reimagines what is shared among, and what is different between, the New World black, European, and Native American populations that inhabit, move across, and map the geography of the novel.

The character Clinton is introduced early on as a descendant of both black and Native American peoples:

> Clinton had been told by the old women talking when he was still a kid; they had been discussing all the branches of the family. The original subject had been marriages with whites, but one whole branch in Tennessee had been married to Indians, "American Indians." "Native Americans." . . . Clinton had not got over the shock and wonder of it. He and the rest of his family had been direct descendants of wealthy, slave-owning Cherokee Indians. (415)

Prashad's "strange," "mulatto" histories in the Americas appear here, but mulatto understood as relations not between white and black but between native and black, mestizo; a history that places a racially complex and layered Native American tradition, represented in Silko's novel, in dialogue with the motley and diasporic African American tradition represented in equally layered "epic" texts such as the African American Martin R. Delany's *Blake, or The Huts of America*.[25] Clinton's revolutionary impulses take the form of his desire to do radio broadcasts across the Americas, and "his first broadcast in the reborn United States was going to be dedicated to the children born to escaped African slaves who married Carib Indian survivors. The first broadcast would be dedicated to them—the first African-Native Americans."[26]

These blendings of black and Indian are Clinton's deepest interest, and tracking down these "mulatto" histories forces him to trace a racial geography, and a personal genealogy, that extends beyond the United States into the black islands of the West Indies—from the state of Tennessee in the United States to Haiti and the Americas more broadly:

> Clinton remembered those old granny women sitting with their pipes or chew, talking in low, steady voices about in-laws and all the branches of the family. The branch of the family that was Indian always bragged they were the *first* black Indians. . . . The black Indians of the family had stories about the very first black Indians.
>
> The first black Indians had lived in high mountain strongholds where they launched raids on the plantations and settlements below. Some said the first black Indian medicine man had been a Jamaican who wandered Haiti, calling himself Boukman. (418)

Through Clinton's family tree, Silko takes us on a journey that begins in Tennessee and ends with the maroons of the Caribbean, and one specific figure, Boukman, the folk hero who stands in black Atlantic history as the catalyst for the first black slave revolution on the island of Haiti.

Clinton is important to the novel precisely because he has a lot more to say about the generative, as opposed to the destructive, powers of vindicationist histories of the Americas. First and foremost, in Silko's American history the colonizing self is Other, and it is the colonizer who has himself been uprooted from his land, his history, and therefore crucial aspects of his human identity. As one Native American elder in the novel reminisces:

> from their flimsy attachments to one another and their children to their abandonment of the land where they had been born . . . [he] thought about what the ancestors had called Europeans: their God had created them but soon was furious with them, throwing them out of their birthplace, driving them away. The ancestors had called Europeans "the orphan people" and had noted that as with orphans taken in by selfish or coldhearted clanspeople, few Europeans had remained whole. (258)

Here it is European consciousness that is split by the transatlantic uprooting, and in her mention of the Christian deity, Silko signals that she is also interested in presenting an alternative cosmogony. As the elder's storytelling continues, we realize that he is engaged in the act of deforming European histories of colonization and destabilizing the colonizer as the subject of those histories.

This is the specific project that the African American character Clinton articulates most fully elsewhere in the novel. Clinton describes his "problem with history" as his despair with narratives of the fatefulness of the colonial encounter. As he says, "Even Black Studies classes got boring . . . once European conquerors showed up in Africa. . . . Clinton had always got a sick feeling in his stomach as the days in class passed and the terrible, fateful day approached; the day was when the first European slave-traders had appeared at African slave markets and not at the slave markets in France and England" (419–20). For Clinton, it is the supposed stability of the European subject in this narrative, surrounded by the displaced, decentered, and enslaved colonial populations circulating around him, that produces the character's vertiginous sense of despair.

Silko destabilizes the colonizer's clearly defined narrative of inevitable conquest precisely to create a space for adjacent narratives: "The old man talked about other times and other worlds that existed before this present one" (259). The gods, spirits, and ancestors in *Almanac of the Dead* all represent an awareness of colonial Atlantic history as a dynamic palimpsest, constituted by the residues of multiple world-historical stories, not just competing histories but also competing cosmologies. The spirits and gods in Silko's tale, the "dead" who also perform in Joseph Roach's circumatlantic cities, do not just reside in the past, or just in the Old World.[27] They too crossed the oceans with colonizers, workers, and slaves, and like the moving, multiracial human populations around them, they too were changed by the journey. In Silko's novel, the spiritual and "otherworldly" register is also a fundamentally earthly and historical one, very much attached to, and a part of, the species-being of the humans whom the gods travel alongside. As Clinton further describes:

> Clinton wanted black people to know all their history; he wanted them
> to know all that had gone on before in Africa; [but also] how great and
> powerful gods had traveled from Africa with the people. . . . There had
> been an older and deeper connection between Africa and the Americas,
> in the realm of the spirits.[28]

In Clinton's recounting, though at first "it must have seemed to the Africans who had survived ocean crossings, that their gods had indeed forsaken them," the African transplants soon discover their precolonial histories embedded in the New World landscape around them, embodied, but also now mutated, in still living, but enraged, spirits:

From the beginning, Africans had escaped and hid in the mountains where they met up with survivors of indigenous tribes hiding in remote strongholds. In the mountains the Africans had discovered a wonderful thing: certain of the African gods had located themselves in the Americas as well as Africa. . . . Right then the magic had happened: great American and great African tribal cultures had come together to create a powerful consciousness within all people. (416)

"Slavery joined forever the histories of the tribal people of the Americas with the histories of the tribal people of Africa," Clinton asserts, creating "Creole Wild West Indians," Silko's beautifully and multiply layered term that powerfully conjoins black American and Afro-Caribbean histories and identities, the "Creole" and "West Indian," with Native and Anglo-American histories of the "Indian" and the "Wild West" (419).

These merged New World ancestral spirits are not identical with the ones that had been left behind. As Clinton also describes, "The Americas were full of furious, bitter spirits; five hundred years of slaughter had left the continents swarming with millions of spirits that never rested and would never stop until justice had been done." What has been added—the deforming force, one might say—is a vindicationist desire to avenge their shared losses, what Walter Mignolo has also called the return of the "barbarian" Other.[29] Anzaldúa represented this uprooted Other as a "mulatto" body and story that could not be pinned down, as she described her own narrative of "the new mestiza" in 1987:

I see a mosaic pattern (Aztec-like) emerging, a weaving pattern, thin here, thick there. I see a preoccupation with the deep structure, the underlying structure, . . . the scaffolding. If I can get the bone structure right, then putting flesh on it proceeds without too many hitches. The problem is that the bones often do not exist prior to the flesh. . . . I see a hybridization of metaphor, different species of ideas popping up here, popping up there, full of variations and seeming contradictions, though I believe in an ordered, structured universe where all phenomena are interrelated and imbued with spirit.[30]

The "marriage" of African and American tribal spirits in *Almanac of the Dead* evokes the process both cultural anthropologists and linguists have described as "creolization," the term signifying for anthropologists the activity of cultural mixing, for linguists a particular form of language. In the study of languages, as the linguist Thomas Hylland Eriksen has described, "The term Creole has a relatively fixed meaning. According to the recent *Penguin Dictionary of Language*, for example, a creole is 'a pidgin language which has become the mother tongue of a speech community. The process of expanding the structural and stylistic range of the pidgin is [what is called] creolization.' "[31]

Both cultural and linguistic definitions of the "Creole" rest on an understanding of the term as precisely the form of colonial identity that is the antithesis of the indigenous. As Eriksen also describes, "Creoles are uprooted, they belong to the New World, are the products of some form of mixing, and are contrasted with that which is old, deep and rooted." What Silko is capturing here in fiction, in this "marriage" of "the spirits of Africa and the Caribbean Islands," is a sense of the more active role of indigenous histories, even when far away from the places and times in which they originated. This much more mobile and syncretic vision of the merging of native African and American premodern cultures and indigenous tribal bodies of tradition provides us with a much more mobile vision of "indigenous" subjects and cultural forms, uprooting them from meaning simply "that which is old, deep and rooted."

Silko's merging of African and American pre-European cultures also enacts at an imaginative level an insight that still, surprisingly, feels new to both linguistics and cultural anthropology, as well as the study of American and European literatures. This is the notion that almost any cultural history and language, once you move back in time beyond the moment of colonial encounter, is impure. The Cambridge historian Richard Drayton uses the term "synchronic palimpsests" to capture the notion that both history and language consist of multiple mergings, blendings, and hybridizations beyond the archetypal instance of "mixing" represented by the encounter between colonized and colonizer.[32]

Drayton also argues that we see these multiple traces of the indigenous — the rooted, the ancestral, the African — as still active in our present-day American languages, literatures, and cultural forms. In other words, they function not simply as "cultural retentions" but rather in a much more active sense, as potential cultural "reversals," residual forms and structures of feeling that reappear precisely when dominant linguistic and cultural forms go into crisis. With this insight, Drayton has attempted to rethink the degrees of incommensurability that may exist between different cultures and languages, not simply as questions of identity and difference, but rather as active historical processes still present and shaping languages and forms of potential communication that are always in the making.

The Caribbean poet and literary critic Edward Kamau Brathwaite has also described similar processes of creolization and reversal in the local context of the English-speaking Caribbean. As Brathwaite stated in his 1979 essay "History of the Voice":

> We in the Caribbean have a similar kind of plurality: we have English, which is the imposed language on much of the archipelago. . . . [But we also] have the remnants of ancestral languages still persisting in the Caribbean. There is Amerindian. . . . We have Hindi . . . and there are also varieties of Chinese. And, miraculously, there are survivals of African languages. . . . What these languages had to do . . . was to submerge themselves—but they reappear in popular forms such as calypso.[33]

For both Brathwaite and Drayton, these ancestral languages that have been submerged do not simply ossify to become the dead traces of lost indigenous and tribal cultures. Rather, as with Silko's angry spirits, they reemerge precisely when the dominant language and culture go into crisis, especially a crisis of meaning. For Silko, colonialism itself represents a European crisis of meaning, as Enlightenment thinkers found themselves questioning, and fundamentally rethinking, what it meant to be human upon their encounters with native African, American, and Asian racial Others. The reemergence and vengeful energy of Silko's African and American spirits are fueled precisely by this crisis in Western culture, the fracturing of species-being created by the very forces that Europeans first unleashed to understand and organize the worlds of color they encountered, uprooted, and put into motion across the Atlantic. As Silko's narrator ironically comments, "Now Clinton understood why European philosophers had told their people God was dead: the white man's God had died about the time the Europeans had started sailing around the world."[34]

Silko's novel asks us to recognize the multiplicity of the colonial subject in American and English literary studies, moving away, once and for all, from imagining a fictive Other to engaging with the actual and multiple colonial selves who traveled in Atlantic space. Circumatlantic paradigms indicate the scholarly emergence of residual, resistant meanings, populations, and bodies in colonial history, a space of multiple subjections by history, of both European and indigenous populations being subjected by, and resistant to, history. Atlantic studies requires the creation of New World epics and metanarratives, stories such as Silko's that go back in time and range widely across space. These circumatlantic histories may be the key to overthrowing once and for all the Self-Other divide, rediscovering the complexity of colonial worlds that are much more complicated spaces than the dualistic world inhabited by the European imperial self and the racialized colonial Other. And what better way to rethink this colonial world in a more polycultural and dynamic way than to rethink the very figure for that world that has dominated contemporary literary scholarship — not Anzaldúa's new mestiza, exactly, but Shakespeare's native barbarian, Caliban.

The Creole Wild West Indian

At the beginning of a discussion of "the constitution of the discourse of English colonialism," Peter Hulme offered two definitions of the word "tropics."[35] The first, which he took from the *OED*, designates the tropics as "the torrid zones" of the world; in the second he defined "tropics [as] the process by which all discourse constitutes the objects which it pretends only to describe realistically and to analyze objectively." Using a slightly different definition of the word "trope," one in which the term designates, as "in rhetoric, a word or expression used in a different sense from what it properly signifies," Srinivas Aravamudan, a scholar of the eighteenth century, performs his own tropological activity on the word "tropic" by using it to develop his idea of the "tropicopolitan subject." As he puts it, "I would like to propose the term tropicopolitan as a name for the colonized subject who exists both as fictive construct of colonial tropology and actual resident of tropical space, object of representation and agent of resistance."[36] As a tropical trope, then, the colonial becomes a certain kind of complex subject-object in transatlantic space, and Caliban a figure whose journey through literary discourse reveals both the "hybridization of metaphor" that Anzaldúa saw in her story of the mestiza, and the limits of that very construction of the uprooted colonial body.

Whose is the racial body represented in the image of the (European) Self, given the multiple types of European bodies circulating in transatlantic space — the working class, elites, Spanish, Portuguese, French, English, Dutch? And whose is the racial body represented in the image of the Other, the colonized — native African, Native American, Asian indentured servant, New World slave, woman?

The distinctiveness of one recent approach to the trope of Caliban, Peter Linebaugh and Marcus Rediker's opening historical discussion of the seventeenth-century Atlantic context for Shakespeare's play in *The Many-Headed*

Hydra, is precisely the authors' ability to overcome dualistic limits in how we construct colonial encounters in the Americas. We see merely one instance of this in their use of the trope of Caliban. In a narrative that places multiple racial bodies in Atlantic spaces, especially aboard ships, the wreck of one particular ship, the *Sea-Venture*, in 1609 stands as the paradigmatic account that starts the book. This story reveals a group of European colonists who, though they crossed the ocean intending to join other colonists and settlers in Virginia, once shipwrecked, attempt to rebel from the colonizing mission by refusing to leave the island of Bermuda, much to the "chagrin of the officers of the Virginia Company."[37] Linebaugh and Rediker argue that we should read the mutiny of this "motley crew," which included "sailors, laborers, craftsmen, and commoners of several sorts, including two Native Americans," as a choice to resist the interpellations of the colonial authorities.[38] Historically fascinating, this episode is also literarily significant, for this was the incident from which Shakespeare drew in writing *The Tempest*.

By embedding the Shakespearean drama back within this polycultural Atlantic history, a history that includes both cooperative and confrontational relations between members of several different racial communities, Linebaugh and Rediker are able to broaden their interpretation of Caliban as a trope. Rather than seeing him as a singular racial figure, the image of the colonial, or even "mixed" Other, they recast him as part of a tripartite relationship with Trinculo and Stephano, the two working-class European characters in the play. To use their description:

> Cooperation [on the island] bound together many different kinds of people [and] . . . such cooperative resistance shaped Shakespeare's conception of the conspiracy waged in *The Tempest* by Caliban the slave, Trinculo the jester, and Stephano the sailor. . . . Caliban himself embodies African, Native American, Irish, and English cultural elements, while Trinculo and Stephano represent two of the main types of the dispossessed in . . . England. . . . Their cooperation eventually evolves into conspiracy and rebellion of the kind promoted on the island of Bermuda by the commoners of the *Sea-Venture*.[39]

Here are the figures of dead labor from both the New World and the Old, reanimated and connected in a new memory and story of their history. In Linebaugh and Rediker's historicized reading of the play, the Caliban of nationalist revolt becomes instead the figure for a different form of resistance, the cooperative and subversive linking of both Europeans and members of indigenous populations in an alliance attempting to create alternative notions of community and subjectivity within colonial space.

Whose are the multiple bodies coming into "contact" in Atlantic space? What are the various forms of contact occurring throughout that space, in all their historical contingency? How, historically, did colonial subjects form allegiances and construct differences in their efforts to make themselves at home in a multiply racial, heterogeneous, hybrid world? These are the questions that animate my own conception of an Atlantic America and the transatlantic study of New World cultures. By interpreting Shakespeare's play simply as one staging ground for delineating a genealogy of meanings for, and ways of thinking about, the multiple subjectivities circulating in transatlantic space, one would hope to see both the colonial Self (traditionally conceived as the English and European colonizer) and the colonial Other (traditionally conceived as the native and enslaved subject) as much more complex figures, involved in much more complex relationships, over five centuries of colonization and settlement in the New World.

In her essay "Why Did the Europeans Cross the Ocean? A Seventeenth Century Riddle," in the seminal 1993 collection *Cultures of United States Imperialism*, Myra Jehlen uses the space of the transatlantic to stage and subsequently explore crucial questions concerning the legacies of difference generated by and in the colonial encounter.[40] Jehlen rehearses a debate between Tzvetan Todorov and Abdul JanMohamed in the mid-1980s, a debate concerning the nature of power as it shaped and governed intersubjective relations in colonial America.[41] As Jehlen describes, Todorov's goal was to critique the process of "othering," a critique he extended to an essay by JanMohamed entitled "The Economy of Manichean Allegory: The Function of Racial Difference in Colonialist Literature."[42] JanMohamed's argument that "genuine and thorough comprehension of Otherness is possible only if the self can somehow negate or at least severely bracket the values, assumptions, and ideology of his culture"[43] prompted Todorov to object "that we should be careful not to exaggerate differences." As he also stated:

> Human beings are not trees, and they can be uprooted without provoking such dramatic consequences. . . . We are not only separated by cultural differences; we are also united by a common human identity, and it is this which renders possible communication, dialogue, and, in the final analysis, the comprehension of Otherness.[44]

Paul Gilroy's recent turn "against race" also attempted to make such a move against difference, fifteen years after the Todorov-JanMohamed debate. Gilroy's work provides evidence that we have not yet discovered how to extricate ourselves from this ontological and epistemological divide between Self and Other, at least not within the theoretical rubrics offered by postcolonial theory and Continental philosophy.

Gilroy lays a path through such a dilemma when he posits the notion of diaspora as offering an experience of "uprooting" that does not emphasize difference so much as it reveals the commonalities humans shared in certain movements. Working with similar organic metaphors, Gilroy asserts:

> The word [diaspora] comes closely associated with the idea of sowing seed. . . . Imagine a scenario in which similar — though not precisely identical — seeds take root in different places. Plants of the same species are seldom absolutely indistinguishable.[45]

What is suggestive in Gilroy's formulation of diaspora is the idea that the very problem with the Self-Other divide is an inability to imagine species consciousness, human identity, as inherently multiple. The debate between JanMohamed and Todorov concerning the legacy of difference is still shaped by a deeply embedded assumption in contemporary scholarly discourse, itself a legacy of Enlightenment thought and European Continental philosophy. This is the idea that both the European self and the colonial Other, literally and figuratively, inhabit singular consciousnesses; that we, as individual human beings, construct and inhabit inherently singular notions of human subjectivity. In other words, it is as if human identity, the self, can only, in a given instance, be one thing, a thing that then necessarily has to be negated to comprehend its dualistic Other.

What would a different understanding of subject formation in the Americas look like, one that attempted to move beyond this epistemological divide between mutually antagonistic histories of the European Self in the Americas and (his) ever persistent Other, the colonial, "native," subject? Todorov and Gilroy both argue in slightly different ways that the challenge we face in comprehending Otherness is to construct a language of the universal that will allow us to communicate with each other as human beings. But the medium here also bears a contradictory message, for no form better expresses the complexity of the colonial universe than the creolized languages of the Americas. We might do better to follow the lead of scholars such as Prashad in his attempts to recount a very different understanding of human being and history. As Prashad also argues: "A close engagement with the concept of . . . the polycultural . . . not only encourages the inherent complexity of cultures, but . . . also stakes its claim to political, and delimited, claims rather than the pretense of universal, and nonembodied, values." Prashad continues, "Polyculturalism does not posit an undifferentiated 'human' who is inherently equal as the ground for its critique of the world, one that says something like 'we are all human after all.' Instead it concentrates on the project of creating our humanity. 'Human' is an 'unfinished product.' "[46] One might imagine a tree that, transplanted by histories of colonialism and diaspora, creolized in its branches, has yet to fully flower and grow. Prashad asserts, "A polycultural humanism" is precisely that which "sets in motion the processes that might in time produce a humanity that is indeed in some way equal."[47] The universal, then, resides at the end of our collective human species-history, the utopia we are working toward making, not the origin we have already left behind.[48]

In closing, then, the notion of "uprooted bodies" is meant to resonate here methodologically, as novels such as Silko's, with which this essay began, benefit well from a diachronic interpretive approach that links colonial and precolonial histories of both the New and Old Worlds with contemporary nationalist and postcolonial geopolitical and cultural formations in the Americas. Such a reading can serve as a metaphor for how we approach a field such as the Atlantic Americas. Coverage of such a broad span of time and over such complexly differentiated spaces requires collaboration among, and dialogue between, scholars located across a number of different fields and time periods. It is precisely these interdisciplinary openings and conversations, an uprooting of multiple forms of knowledge about the Americas from their traditional disciplinary moorings, that can be liberating in an Atlantic studies framework. As scholars move and dialogue across different time periods in circumatlantic conversations that remain, nevertheless, locally grounded, they have the potential to introduce the ideals of interdisciplinarity within the traditional fields of the disciplines themselves. The challenge for contemporary literary theory and historical scholarship on the Americas will be our ability to develop the capacity to speak in multiple tongues, both literally and disciplinarily, as we recognize the multiplicity of the colonial subject in American and English literary and historical discourse.

Notes

1 Leslie Marmon Silko, *Almanac of the Dead* (New York: Penguin Books, 1992). Maxine Hong Kingston's comment is prominently displayed on the front cover of this paperback edition of the novel.

2 Gloria Anzaldúa, *Borderlands/La Frontera* (San Francisco: Aunt Lute Books, 1987), 23.

3 Ibid., vii.

4 Ibid., 8.

5 Vijay Prashad, *Everybody Was Kung Fu Fighting: Afro-Asian Connections and the Myth of Cultural Purity* (Boston: Beacon Press, 2001), 48.

6 See Prashad's elaboration of an Afrocentric-Dalitcentric worldview similar to the conjoining of African and Native American histories that will be described here in Silko's narrative (ibid., 46–56).

7 http://dictionary.oed.com.

8 See, for example, Stephen Orgel, introduction to *The Tempest* (New York: Oxford University Press, 1987), 30–36. Also see Peter Linebaugh and Marcus Rediker, *The Many-Headed Hydra: Sailors, Slaves, Commoners, and the Hidden History of the Revolutionary Atlantic* (Boston: Beacon Press, 2000), 8–35.

9 George Lamming, *The Pleasures of Exile* (Ann Arbor: University of Michigan Press, 1992), 118.

10 Aimé Césaire, *A Tempest*, trans. Richard Miller (New York: Ubu Repertory Theater Publications, 1986).

11 Roberto Fernández Retamar, *Caliban and Other Essays* (Minneapolis: University of Minnesota Press, 1989). The postcolonial writer Salman Rushdie evokes a similar meaning of the trope in his infamous novel *The Satanic Verses* (New York: Viking, 1989).

12 Retamar, *Caliban and Other Essays*, 14.

13 José David Saldívar, *The Dialectics of Our America: Genealogy, Cultural Critique, and Literary History* (Durham: Duke University Press, 1991), 123.

14 Vijay Prashad, "Bruce Lee and the Anti-imperialism of Kung Fu: A Polycultural Adventure," *Positions: East Asia Cultures Critique* 11, no. 1 (spring 2003): 52.

15 Ibid., 53.

16 Ibid., 36.

17 For more of a broad survey of this discussion, see most famously Eric Williams, *Capitalism and Slavery* (Chapel Hill: University of North Carolina Press, 1944); but also William A. Darity, "The Williams Abolition Thesis before Williams," *Slavery and Abolition* (London) 9 (May 1988): 29–41.

18 Letter from Marx to Engels, quoted in C. L. R. James, "Negroes in the Civil War: Their Role in the Second American Revolution" (1943), reprinted in *C. L. R. James on the "Negro Question,"* ed. Scott McLemee (Jackson: University Press of Mississippi, 1996), 107.

19 Linebaugh and Rediker, *The Many-Headed Hydra*, 15–16.

20   Ibid., 16–17.

21   Anzaldúa, *Borderlands/La Frontera*, 9.

22   Silko, *Almanac of the Dead*, 309.

23   Anzaldúa, *Borderlands/La Frontera*, 22.

24   Silko, *Almanac of the Dead*, 312.

25   Martin R. Delany, *Blake, or The Huts of America* (1861–62; Boston: Beacon Press, 1970). See in particular chapter 20, "Advent among the Indians," in which the African American–West Indian protagonist Henricus Blake, a fugitive slave attempting to organize resistance among slaves in the South, joins forces briefly with the Native American peoples of "the United Nation of Chickasaw and Choctaw Indians" (88).

26   Silko, *Almanac of the Dead*, 410.

27   Joseph Roach, *Cities of the Dead: Circum-Atlantic Performance* (New York: Columbia University Press, 1996).

28   Silko, *Almanac of the Dead*, 416.

29   Walter Mignolo, "Globalization, Civilization Processes, and the Relocation of Languages and Cultures," in *The Cultures of Globalization* (Durham: Duke University Press, 1998), 32–53. To quote more fully from Mignolo: "Thus, the organic intellectuals of the Amerindian social movements (as well as Latino, African American, and women's) are precisely the main agents of the moment in which 'barbarism' appropriates the theoretical practices and elaborated projects, engulfing and superseding the discourse of the civilizing mission and its theoretical foundations. The 'frontier of civilization' in the late nineteenth century has become the 'borderland' of the end of the twentieth century" (45).

30   Anzaldúa, *Borderlands/La Frontera*, 66.

31   Thomas Hylland Eriksen, "Tu dimunn pu vini kreol: The Mauritian Creole and the Concept of Creolization," lecture presented at the University of Oxford in 1999 under the auspices of the "Transnational Connections" program.

32   I am indebted to Professor Richard Drayton for kindly sharing his work and current research, both in conversation and in a talk at Mount Holyoke College entitled "What Happens When Two Ways of Knowing Meet?" (March 27, 2003).

33   Edward Kamau Brathwaite, "History of the Voice," in *Roots* (Ann Arbor: University of Michigan Press, 1993), 259–61.

34   Silko, *Almanac of the Dead*, 417.

35   Peter Hulme, "Hurricanes in the Caribbees: The Constitution of the Discourse of English Colonialism," in *1642: Literature and Power in the Seventeenth Century: Proceedings of the Essex Conference in the Sociology of Literature*, ed. Francis Barker et al. (Colchester: University of Essex, 1981).

36   Srinivas Aravamudan, *Tropicopolitans: Colonialism and Agency, 1688–1804* (Durham: Duke University Press, 1999), 4.

37   Linebaugh and Rediker, *The Many-Headed Hydra*, 10.

38   Ibid., 27.

39   Ibid.

40   Myra Jehlen, "Why Did the Europeans Cross the Ocean? A Seventeenth Century

Riddle," in *Cultures of United States Imperialism*, ed. Amy Kaplan and Donald Pease (Durham: Duke University Press, 1993), 41–58.

41   Ibid., 49.

42   Abdul R. JanMohamed, "The Economy of Manichean Allegory: The Function of Racial Difference in Colonialist Literature," in *"Race," Writing, and Difference*, ed. Henry Louis Gates Jr. (Chicago: University of Chicago Press, 1986), 78–106. This essay originally appeared in a special issue of *Critical Inquiry* 12, no. 1 (autumn 1985): 59–87.

43   Ibid., 84.

44   Quoted in Jehlen, "Why Did the Europeans Cross the Ocean?" 50.

45   Paul Gilroy, *The Black Atlantic: Modernity and Double Consciousness* (Cambridge: Harvard University Press, 1992), 125–26.

46   Prashad, *Everybody Was Kung Fu Fighting*, 40.

47   Ibid., 69.

48   Walter Mignolo has called this replacing the quest for the universal with the "pluriversal" and "diversal." "Critical Cosmopolitanism Revisited," paper presented at "Beyond the Boundaries of the Old Geographies: Natives, Citizens, Exiles, and Cosmopolitans," Hampshire College, Amherst, Mass., October 27, 2001.

Blackness Goes South

Race and Mestizaje in Our America

Rachel Adams

On the circuitous inter-American route linking the black Atlantic to the border-lands, there may be no better guide than José Martí. He is not an unbiased observer, and twenty-first-century travelers must inevitably grapple with the contradictions underlying his understandings of race. On the one hand, Martí articulates a diverse and inclusive racial politics. His U.S. journalism reflects concern about the injustices committed against African, Asian, and indigenous Americans. His "Nuestra América" calls on native intellectuals "to rescue the Indian, to make a place for the competent Negro, to fit liberty to the body of those who rebelled and conquered for it." On the other, Martí seeks to tran-scend racial distinctions altogether by replacing them with national or Pan-American identifications. Writing in favor of Cuban independence, he famously claimed that "a Cuban is more than mulatto, black, or white." And an equally famous phrase in "Nuestra América" reads, "There can be no racial animosity, because there are no races."[1] Martí's vision of a transcendent *mestizaje* in which racial differences are erased by shared political commitments thus rests un-comfortably against his recognition that racism is a persistent reality of his time. And although he is sometimes aware of the broad panoply of American races, his conceptualization of mestizaje, like that of many other Latin American thinkers, privileges the fusion of European and indigenous roots at the expense of other racial groups, particularly blacks.[2] As Susan Gillman puts it, "A fundamental contradiction . . . emerges between race and *mestizaje* in its nineteenth-century formulations: the call for a new race of mixed beings is also a call for racelessness, for citizens defined by national rather than racial membership."[3] While Gillman locates this contradiction in Martí's nineteenth-century moment, it endures in many Latin American countries where official ideologies of mestizaje effectively erase the more hybrid composition of actual populations.

This essay takes the contradictory views of race in Martí's "Nuestra América" as a point of entry into a discussion of the conflicted place of blackness in the history of U.S.-Mexico relations. Mexico, to a greater extent than countries with more visible black populations such as Cuba, Brazil, or Colombia, vividly instantiates the tensions characteristic of Martí's thought. There a celebratory discourse of mestizaje is employed as a tool of national unification while the African heritage is suppressed, despite the fact that it is so pervasive among the Mexican populace that it has been described as a "third root."[4] For Mexicans, the acknowledgment of blackness is blocked by a version of mestizaje that recognizes only European and indigenous ancestry. When the Mexican politician José Vasconcelos famously labeled mestizos *la raza cósmica* in 1925, he codified the mixture of black, Indian, and Spaniard into the nation's official ideology. But since then, thanks in part to the infiltration of U.S.-style racial politics, blackness has virtually been erased from collective understandings of Mexican heritage. This explains why Mexicans — unlike Canadians, who have made much of their nation's role in harboring fugitive slaves — have largely ignored the fact that the abolition of slavery played a central role in the War for Independence; that the Mexican Constitution (unlike that of the United States) explicitly guaranteed equality for all citizens regardless of race; and that Mexicans consistently thwarted U.S. slavery by helping fugitives to escape and refusing to include them in any extradition treaty signed with the United States. The history of Afro-Mexicans has been no more visible from the U.S. side of the border, despite a heightened diasporic consciousness among African Americans. To acknowledge blackness south of the border would require unsettling racial narratives that put African Americans at the center of the history of slavery and its aftermath. In the United States, the story of African American struggles and victories has overshadowed that of blacks in other parts of the Americas.

Recently, the growing interest in black diaspora has prompted efforts by a small group of scholars, authors, and artists who seek to reclaim the history of Afro-Mexicans and to bring the tensions between race and mestizaje into the public eye.[5] Such work has great promise for Americanists because of its potential to build a bridge between two strands of transnational scholarship that have become central to the field: Paul Gilroy's concept of the black Atlantic, which knits together Africa, Europe, the Caribbean, and North America as participants in the transatlantic slave trade and progenitors of a diasporic black culture, and Chicano studies' focus on the borderlands, the contact zone that links the United States to Latin America.[6] This essay connects the borderlands to the black Atlantic by arguing for the unacknowledged importance of Mexico in the history of U.S. slavery. In doing so, it seeks to expand the terrain of border studies by offering an alternative genealogy of cultural crossing and to revise the collective imagined geographies of the Americas by questioning the cultural associations surrounding "North" and "South."

I begin by examining how these directional biases undergird the historical study of slavery in North America. Mexico's role as a harbor for fugitive slaves has been overlooked in favor of narratives that locate freedom exclusively in the North. The dominance of these narratives is tied to a nationalist blind spot in the historiography of U.S. slavery, which tends to view "the South" as being confined within U.S. borders. The cultural significance of North and South looks quite different when the South is conceived as the region encompassing Mexico and the rest of Latin America. Contemporary representations in literature and the visual arts have played a vital role in the creation of revisionist geographies of the Americas. More than a hundred years after the abolition of slavery in North America, authors and artists such as the novelists Gayl Jones and Guillermo Sánchez de Anda, the filmmaker John Sayles, and the photographer Tony Gleaton are beginning to probe the historical amnesia that has erased the presence of blackness south of the border. Their work is the subject of the second part of my essay. Employing a range of inventive formal strategies, these artists take on the difficult task of excavating an Africanist presence in Mexico and the U.S. Southwest, regions that have long been dominated by other racial narratives but still contain the submerged traces of alternative histories of blackness in the Americas.

Alternative Fugitive Cartographies

In the history of North American slavery, Canada has been enshrined as the terminus of the Underground Railroad, a bastion of freedom that welcomed fugitives at the end of a long and arduous journey. Although significant numbers of slaves escaped by running south to Mexico or elsewhere in the Americas, "the South" is persistently held up as the epicenter of unfreedom in contrast to the northern states and Canada. This directional bias has much to do with the authority granted to slave narratives as a form of historical evidence. Produced under the auspices of white abolitionists in Canada and the northern United States, the slave narrative is the most formulaic of genres. One of its primary conventions is the story of harrowing passage from south to north. As Francis Smith Foster characterizes the slave narrative's structure, from the first page "the identification of the slave's birthplace fixed the South-to-North axis of the narration and introduced the theme of the journey to the promised land. The South was described much like a wilderness of untamed land, ineffective religion, and savage brutality, while the North became the location of enlightened Christianity, harmony, and brotherhood."[7] In the slave narrative's imagined geography, north and south are far more than regional locations or points on a compass; they are the very distinction between freedom and bondage itself. Often this literary convention is taken as a form of historical data about the actual routes of fugitive slaves, while paths less fully recorded in print have been occluded from the historical record.

Slave narratives reflect a more pervasive cultural bias toward the North that is manifest in nineteenth-century U.S. religious discourse, popular culture, and foreign policy. To the north were the British, who had come to an uneasy coexistence with the United States following the War of 1812, which concluded with a mutual recognition of military strength. To the south, the Spanish empire was in decline. The United States took advantage of the vulnerable border region with frequent attempts to seize land, often in the interest of expanding slave territory. In his autobiography, the Reverend J. W. Loguen, a former slave, insightfully summarizes this directional bias. Describing a failed annexation of Canadian land, he concludes that "the filibusters were thus promptly taught that incursions for the conquest of northern Territory were less adapted to the national taste, than like forays for the conquest of Texas, Mexico, Cuba, and the Isthmus. The instant and decided check given to this northern move, effectually curbed unlawful enterprises in that direction; and the only vent for national passions in this regard has been found to lay in the South."[8] According to national policy as well as popular consciousness, the southern borderlands were chaotic and shifting, the South itself a place of decadence and excess. Populated by a mixture of indigenous tribes and Spanish, French, and British colonists, the region was often treated as if it were up for grabs. It was hotly contested by both pro- and antislavery factions, who recognized land as the key to victory for their cause. The closer that slaves were to the United States' southern border, the better they must have understood the connection between their bondage and the fate of the nation's shifting boundaries.

Revising many of the conventions of slave narratives written under the sponsorship of white patrons, Martin Delany's *Blake* (1859–62) provides a more hemispheric view of fugitive geography that takes into account the racial dynamics and political stability of different regions of the Americas. Delany's unfinished novel of revolution recognizes Canada as a place of refuge but ultimately rejects it in favor of Latin America as the ideal location for black resettlement. The first part of *Blake* echoes the structure of a slave narrative as its protagonist leads a group of fugitive slaves to Canada, which he calls "a free country."[9] However, once his friends are safely settled there, Henry criticizes Canadians for their failure to uphold the egalitarian principles set forth by British law, then departs for the south. In Cuba he initiates his radical plan for revolution. Henry's geographical trajectory corresponds to sentiments expressed in Delany's 1854 pamphlet entitled "Political Destiny of the Colored Race on the American Continent," which lists Canada as one of several "places of temporary relief, especially to the fleeing fugitive—which, like a palliative, soothes for the time being the misery," only to reject it as a "permanent [place] upon which to fix our destiny; and that of our children, who shall come after us."[10] In addition to the accusations of racism he makes in *Blake*, Delany has other reasons for opposing long-term colonization in Canada. One is that he predicts its imminent annexation by the United States. Another is that it does not fit his criteria for a new homeland dominated by blacks. As Gregg Crane has argued, Delany's revolutionary vision relies on a majority black population, since he cannot imagine a society in which the dominant group can be trusted to protect the rights of minorities.[11] Thus Henry must leave Canada for Cuba, whose racial demographics make it a more appropriate place to plot his unrealized rebellion. Half a century before Martí, Delany saw revolutionary potential in Cuba. However, in contrast to Martí, who called for the subordination of racial differences to national purpose, Delany articulates an early version of diasporic consciousness in which blacks identify across national boundaries to the exclusion of other groups.

Whereas Cuba is the locus of Delany's radicalism in *Blake*, his pamphlet "Political Destiny" suggests other possible sites of relocation, most strongly advocating emigration south of the U.S. border. Although at other points in his career Delany would support black recolonization of Africa, "Political Destiny" is important to my argument because it assesses the potential of Mexico and Central America as homelands for freed slaves. Delany asserts that black people have a divine right to remain on the American continent because it was "designed by Providence as a reserved asylum for the various oppressed people of the earth, of all races."[12] He claims not only that black people belong in America by virtue of their oppression, but that they in fact "discovered" it long before the Europeans, having arrived as a part of the ancient "Carthaginian expedition." According to Delany's revisionist history, black people are a long-standing presence in the New World, rather than being the unwelcome newcomers they are often mistaken for. Thus, he insists, "Upon the American continent . . . we are determined to remain, despite every opposition that may be urged against us."[13] The task Delany lays out is a matter of geographic reeducation to teach slaves the benefits of flight to the south: "They already find their way in large companies to the Canadas, and they have only to be made sensible that there is as much freedom for them South, as there is North; as much protection in Mexico as in Canada; and the fugitive slave will find it a much pleasanter journey and more easy of access, to wend his way from Louisiana and Arkansas to Mexico, than the thousands of miles through the slave-holders of the South and slave-catchers of the North, to Canada. Once in Mexico, and his farther exit to Central and South America and the West Indies, would be certain."[14] Although his revolutionary vision of black resettlement was interrupted by the Civil War, Delany significantly revised the geographic imaginary of the slave narrative by representing Mexico and Central America as alternatives to Canada.

Other opponents of slavery would attempt to put the alternatives envisioned by Delany into practice. When the Philadelphia abolitionist Samuel Webb inquired about the relocation of former slaves, the Mexican government expressed its willingness to accept new immigrants. Vice president Valentín Gómez Farías responded to Webb's letter: "If they [the former slaves] would like to come, we will offer them land for cultivation, plots for houses where they can establish towns, and tools for work, under the obligation [that they will] obey the laws of the country and the authorities already established by the Supreme Government of the Federation."[15] Responding to a similar invitation, the Black Seminoles—former slaves of the Seminole tribe—traveled to Mexico in 1849. Initially the arrangement promised to be mutually advantageous. In crossing the border, the Black Seminoles hoped to evade the slave owners who threatened their freedom in Florida. For its part, the Mexican government sought to populate the sparsely inhabited border region with settlers who might help to fight off hostile Indian tribes and invaders from the United States.[16] Although the relocation ended in disappointment on both sides, the Black Seminoles remained in Mexico until after the Civil War.

The most ambitious plan for relocation was devised by Benjamin Lundy, a Quaker and publisher of the first abolitionist periodical, the *Genius of Universal Emancipation*. Like Delany, Lundy thought comparatively about Canada and Texas (then a part of Mexico) as potential homes for a black colony and concluded in favor of Texas.[17] At considerable cost to his health and finances, Lundy traveled to Mexico in search of available land and permission to establish a colony. His journals document encounters with a number of black people who expressed enthusiasm about joining the new settlement, as well as others who were already settled comfortably in Mexico, several in mixed marriages to Anglos or Mexicans. Interrupted by the Texas uprising, Lundy's project remained unrealized. Other migrants, including a free black named Luis N. Fouché, and a group of former slaves who traveled from New Orleans to Veracruz, successfully petitioned for land to establish colonies in Mexico.[18]

Black resettlement south of the border was an attractive prospect for more ambivalent opponents of slavery who worried about the presence of a free black population in the United States.[19] They saw an opportunity in the annexation of Texas, which could serve as a safety valve to siphon off unwanted elements from the continent. In 1844 Senator Robert J. Walker of Mississippi argued that as slave labor used up land in the South, planters and slaves would migrate into Texas. Masters who found the land beyond the Texas border inadequate for new plantations would be forced to free their slaves, who would continue to move south, where "the sparse population occupying the land would welcome the Negroes and treat them as equals."[20] A similar case was made in the late 1850s when one Frank P. Blair Jr. of Missouri proposed a "drainage system" whereby the U.S. government would buy large blocks of land south of the border for the resettlement of freed blacks. He argued that as they vacated more desirable regions, the former slaves "would be succeeded by the most useful of all the tillers of the earth, small freeholders and an independent tenantry. The influx of immigrants from Europe and the North, with moderate capital, already running into Maryland and Virginia, would, as these States sloughed the black skin, fill up the rich region round the Chesapeake Bay."[21]

In arguing for population drift to the south, Walker claimed that, unlike the white population of the United States, who would never treat freed blacks as equals, Latin Americans "cherish no race prejudice against Negroes."[22] While this was not entirely true, Mexico refused to sign any treaty requiring the extradition of fugitive slaves to the United States, and Mexicans were known regularly to help slaves to escape.[23] Even before Mexican independence, the Spanish — who were slave owners themselves — had a history of encouraging British and American slaves to escape by promising freedom in exchange for military service and conversion to Catholicism.[24] With independence from Spain, Mexico turned the strategic objection to slavery into official policy. According to Rosalie Schwartz, "The Federal Act of July 13, 1824 . . . specifically prohibited the commerce and traffic in slaves from any country, and declared that slaves introduced contrary to the tenor of the act would be free simply by the condition of their being in Mexican territory."[25] To a certain extent, Mexicans assisted fugitives and refused to return escaped slaves out of a genuine abhorrence of slavery.[26] Mexico inherited New Spain's legacy of liberalism on matters of race, an attitude that grew from the relatively contained and fluid relations of slavery within colonial Mexico, the high degree of racial mixture, and a Catholic emphasis on the fundamental equality of souls within colonial Mexico.[27] But Mexicans also helped the fugitive slaves out of a desire to discourage Anglo-American settlers along the northwestern border by establishing obstacles to slaveholding in the region.[28] The reasoning was that the more difficult it became to keep slaves in proximity to Mexican territory, the less incentive there would be to introduce this costly form of property into the region.

Evidence of the large number of slaves who did escape into Mexico must be found in the words of outraged slave owners and observers, since the slaves left no written record themselves. Without the culture of abolitionism that flourished in the northern United States and British Canada, there was little incentive for those who fled south to set their stories to paper. There was neither an audience nor a marketplace to make such a product financially viable. Former slaves south of the border confronted the additional challenge of linguistic difference as they encountered populations who spoke Spanish or indigenous languages. Since the communities they entered were often nonliterate, there was little incentive to learn to write or to record their stories in print. These circumstances pose an interesting challenge to the logic of the slave narrative, which assumes that the desire to be literate and to record one's experiences on paper necessarily came with the desire for freedom. The slaves who ran south were no less determined to escape their bondage but lacked the cultural context that would drive them to produce slave narratives. Conditions of illiteracy, linguistic differences, and extreme poverty did not mean that the fugitive slaves didn't tell their stories: in the mid-twentieth century, historians and anthropologists began to collect the remarkable oral narratives generated by slaves who had escaped to freedom and passed their stories down over several generations.[29] Absent the strict generic formulas of slave narrative, these stories are often partial, fragmented, and varied in form and content.

Some fugitives who fled south, particularly from Georgia, Alabama, Louisiana, and other states in the vicinity, joined the Florida Seminoles. Settled in Spanish territory, the Seminoles were slaveholders themselves but were known to be far more lenient than white masters. Their twentieth-century descendants claimed that the Seminole slaves' "everyday life was idyllic compared to that of plantation slaves."[30] According to the historian Kenneth W. Porter, many slaves in the region were motivated to escape from their Anglo owners by the promise of a better life under the Seminoles. Often the Seminoles and their slaves were enlisted to help the Spanish in military conflict against the United States. During the siege of St. Augustine in 1812, Colonel Thomas A. Smith wrote that the Seminoles had "several hundred fugitive slaves from the Carolinas & Georgia at present in their Towns & unless they are checked soon they will be so strengthened by [more] desertions from Georgia & Florida . . . it will be found troublesome to reduce them."[31] His words provide evidence of the large numbers of fugitives in the region, and their willingness to fight against the power that had enslaved them. The military prowess of the Black Seminoles is a legend that survives into the present.

Texas was an even greater source of conflict between slaveholders and their opponents. When slavery was abolished in Mexico in 1829, a large and influential population of slaveholding colonists from the United States ensured that Texas would be exempt from the new legislation. Mexico saw this arrangement as a means of keeping peace in the region while deterring further Anglo colonization by simultaneously recognizing existing slavery and prohibiting the introduction of new slaves. Nevertheless, proximity to free territory enticed many slaves in Texas to escape south to freedom, often with the help of local

Mexicans.[32] In planning his assault on the Alamo, General Antonio López de Santa Anna, president of Mexico and commander of the Mexican army, promised to free the Texas slaves.[33] This is an especially interesting detail, given that he was widely characterized in the United States as a ruthless and unforgiving tyrant. During the Texas War of Independence, many slaves either joined the Mexican forces or took advantage of the confusion to flee across the border. Following the annexation of Texas by the United States, the chaos increased as more slave owners arrived and their chattel attempted flight across the border in large numbers. According to the historians John Hope Franklin and Loren Schweninger, "During the 1840s and 1850s, southern Texas became a thoroughfare for slaves crossing the border to freedom in Mexico."[34] In a complaint made before the General Assembly in Austin, a delegation of slave owners stated, "You are well aware of the insecurity of Slave Property in this County . . . and will at once perceive the necessity of enacting an appropriate remedy."[35] A resident of San Antonio wrote in 1855 of the difficulty of keeping slaves in border regions: "The number of negroes in the city and indeed in all this part of the state is comparatively small. . . . They cannot be kept here without great risk to their running away. . . . [There are] always Mexicans who are ready and willing to help the slaves off."[36]

The vigor of Texan demands for help with the return of fugitive slaves attests to the significance of the problem. Although there are no print autobiographies about escape from Texas, oral histories of former slaves corroborate the accounts of slaveholders. One Walter Rimm recalled a runaway he had encountered in the woods and speculated that "maybe he got clear to Mexico, where a lot of slaves ran to."[37] Another named Felix Haywood compared the prospects of escape, north and south:

> Sometimes someone would come along and try to get us to run up North and be free. We used to laugh at that. There was no reason to *run* up North. All we had to do was to walk, but walk *south*, and we'd be free as soon as we crossed the Rio Grande. In Mexico you could be free. They didn't care what color you were, black, white, yellow, or blue. Hundreds of slaves did go to Mexico and got on all right. We would hear about them and how they were going to be Mexicans. They brought up their children to speak only Mexican.[38]

From the standpoint of a slave in Texas, it is easy to see why flight to the south seemed like a much better proposition than flight to the north. That Haywood, who claimed to like his life as a slave and never attempted to escape, was well acquainted with the adventures of those who had fled illustrates the ubiquity of such stories.

The most detailed contemporary description of slavery in Texas comes from Frederick Law Olmsted, who published an account of his travels there in 1860. *Journey through Texas* confirms the frequency with which slaves fled to Mexico and the Mexican abhorrence of slavery, concluding, "No country could be selected better adapted to a fugitive and clandestine life, and no people among whom it would be more difficult to enforce the regulations vital to slavery."[39] While journeying through Mexico, Olmsted encounters a number of former slaves who have relocated south of the border, such as a man living in Piedras Negras who informs him that "runaways were constantly arriving here; two had got over, as I had previously been informed, the night before. He could not guess how many came in a year, but he could count forty, that he had known of, in the last three months. At other points, further down the river, a great many more came than here" (324). He claims that "the Mexican Government was very just to them, they could always have their rights as fully protected as if they were Mexican born." Olmsted validates his informant's account by noting that it was corroborated by other stories he had heard: "I believe these statements to have been pretty nearly true; he had no object, that I could discover, to exaggerate the facts either way. . . . They were confirmed, also, in all essential particulars, by every foreigner I saw, who had lived or traveled in this part of Mexico, as well as by Mexicans themselves, with whom I was able to converse on the subject" (325). Of the fugitives' fates, Olmsted observes that those living closer to the border suffer far more than those who move deeper into Mexican territory. "The runaways are generally reported to be very poor and miserable, which, it is natural to suppose, they must be," he writes. "Yet there is something a little strange about this. It is those that remain near the frontier that suffer most; they who have got far into the interior are said to be almost invariably doing passing well" (326). Since life was harder for blacks in northernmost Mexico, many returned to the United States following the Civil War. This was the case with the Black Seminoles, some of whom went on to become Indian fighters for the U.S. Army. But those who made it to a better life in regions more distant from the U.S. border were absorbed into the Mexican population. Because they typically settled in rural, nonliterate communities, their stories remain unrecorded, and the reconstruction of their history must necessarily be partial and fragmentary. The problem is compounded by the erasure of black ancestry in Mexico's official ideology, which effectively denies the existence of these populations.

In truth, the U.S. slaves who escaped into Mexico were but a small part of an already significant black presence south of the border. In the sixteenth century and the early seventeenth, Mexico was an important location for the Spanish slave trade. The dwindling of the native population as a result of disease and overwork required the Spanish to introduce African slaves into colonial industries such as mining, sugar culture, and urban textiles.[40] At least 200,000 Africans were brought to Mexico as slaves, so that by 1810 they made up more than 10 percent of the population, at times outnumbering the indigenous inhabitants.[41] During the War of Independence, Mexicans promised the abolition of slavery and equality for all citizens, which, as we have seen, provided a strong incentive for U.S. slaves to cross the border. In contrast to the United States, where miscegenation was discouraged, African slaves and their descendants were absorbed into the Mexican population, so that instead of distinct groupings of black and white, a large percentage of the Mexican people contained at least some African heritage. Demographers estimate that much of this process had taken place by 1900.[42] By the time the slaves fleeing the United States entered Mexico, there would have been very few Mexicans of purely African descent, but many with one or more black ancestors. Significant numbers of Afro-Mexicans lived in the north and thus would have been among the first Mexicans encountered by fugitives from U.S. slavery.[43]

However, Mexico's resistance to acknowledging its "third root," combined with the hegemony of U.S.-centered racial narratives, has effectively obscured the black presence south of the border. In the United States, an emphasis on the North as the direction of freedom erases the important role played by Mexicans in the history of North American slavery and abolition, while in Mexico, the official postrevolutionary rhetoric of mestizaje occludes the presence of blackness in national history and culture. These erasures are the context for the revisionist work of twentieth-century authors and artists who use a combination of historical excavation and imagination to fill gaps in the historical record.

South to Mexico

Narratives about flight from slavery and the southern U.S. border conjure up a history that — at least from the perspective of the victims — existed *only* through oral transmission until the mid-twentieth century. Thus contemporary representations of that history seek to represent many events that were never recorded at all, surviving only through oral transmission and more inchoate forms of cultural memory. This silence presents both challenges and opportunities for imaginative work. The artists considered here draw on a range of formal devices to tackle the dynamics of memory and storytelling in the absence of recorded history. Taken together, their work represents a marked surge of interest in the submerged histories of blacks in the U.S. Southwest and Mexico, as each artist seeks to unmask, and then to work through, the tensions between race and mestizaje. Each takes a particular approach to the uneven and limited historical evidence at his or her disposal. I have labeled these approaches the "borderlands," the "national," and the "diasporic," each category corresponding to a distinctive regional geography and spatial understanding. Gayl Jones and John Sayles are most representative of the borderlands perspective, a transnational paradigm that seeks overlaps between U.S. and Mexican histories. By comparison, Guillermo Sánchez de Anda is nationalistic in focus, attempting to reclaim the Afro-Mexicans for the purposes of a progressive, multiracial Mexican politics. Tony Gleaton's work, like certain aspects of Jones's, falls into the diasporic category, a perspective that emphasizes transnational connections among people of African descent. Although these divisions are intended to clarify the distinctive perspective of each author, they often overlap within a single work.

The suppressed history of flight across the southern border is a recurring theme in Gayl Jones's massive, sprawling novel *Mosquito* (1999). This is an ideal topic for Jones, who has frequently written about slavery from an inter-American perspective in her fiction, poetry, and criticism. Her first novel, *Corregidora*, is named for a brutal Brazilian slave owner who "fucked his own whores and fathered his own breed," a line of scarred, mixed-race female descendants.[44] As one of the characters tells Ursa, the novel's protagonist, "You seem like you got a little bit of everything in you."[45] In *Corregidora*, containing "a little bit of everything" means carrying the weight of the collective oppression experienced by people of the New World. A blues singer, Ursa seeks an appropriate expression for the burden of ancestral possession: "I wanted a song that would touch me, touch my life *and* theirs. A Portuguese song, but not a Portuguese song. A new world song. A song branded with the new world. I thought of the girl who had to sleep with her master and mistress. Her father, the master. Her daughter's father. The father of her daughter's daughter. How many generations?"[46] Ursa's "new world song" would connect singer and listener with the violence of a brand, but also with the communicability of a trait passed from one generation of women to the next.

Although New World slavery is a similarly vivid presence in *Mosquito*, its protagonist is less brutalized by her connection to it. The idiosyncratic Sojourner Nadine Jane Johnson (aka Mosquito) is a truck driver who lives and works in the U.S. Southwest. Stridently independent, she refuses alliances with any group or collectivity, including the truckers' union. When she finds a Mexican dissident named Maria hidden in the back of her truck, she is introduced to the covert world of Sanctuary, a movement to assist political refugees. Initiated by U.S. religious communities in the 1980s, Sanctuary sought to shelter the victims of political oppression who tried to cross the Mexican border as they fled from El Salvador, Honduras, and Guatemala, where oppressive military regimes had risen to power with covert aid from the U.S. government. In *Mosquito*, Sanctuary is described as a present-day Underground Railroad, a term that forms a bridge between past and present but, even more interestingly, links the paths of escape across the United States' northern and southern borders. Spanning the geography of North America, *Mosquito* reflects on the ruptures and continuities in the history of flight from injustice, uncovering the repressed legacy of blacks in Mexico and Central America by way of comparison with their African American and African Canadian counterparts.

Nadine is primed to connect the histories of northern and southern flight by a family history that is genuinely continental in scope. Like many black Americans, the Johnsons locate U.S. slavery at the root of their family tree, attributing their surname to a "John" who fought for the Union during the Civil War. Although "somebody told me that Johnson were my slave name," Nadine insists, "we changed us name after Emancipation to the name of John, so's it wasn't a slave name, it were a Emancipation name."[47] The distinction is significant. Unlike Ursa Corregidora, who is damaged by the knowledge that she bears the name of a cruel slave owner, the Johnsons are proud of a genealogy rooted in freedom. They trace another early North American relative to the black regiment that fought for the English "up in Canada" during the Revolutionary War (351). Yet a third set of Johnson roots extends to the south, giving Nadine a familial link to the region where she lives and works. She explains: "Us family history say that some of us Johnsons originated in Mexico, that we was originally Mexican Africans, then if that is true history then maybe that's why I's never had the typical American attitude towards Mexicans. I know I don't look like no Mexican, but family history say there's a little Mexican in me" (317). These

Latin American origins, which she recalls numerous times during the course of the novel, are central to the recovery of a history even more submerged than that of the Underground Railroad: the blacks in Mexico.

Nadine attributes her affinity for the Southwest and its inhabitants to traces of Mexican blood in her own ancestry. In contrast to her easy association with the Chicanos and Mexicans she meets during her travels, she notices that her Chicana friend Delgadina is decidedly reticent on the subject of black Mexican history. Delgadina is representative of a collective resistance among Mexicans and Mexican Americans to acknowledging black ancestry. As Nadine puts it, "Ain't never heard nobody talk about African Mexicans, though" (189). Given this silence, it is particularly important for her own circuitous narrative detours to call up a black presence in Mexico that remains little known and shrouded in shame. At one point, Nadine is gratified to learn that Amanda Wordlaw, a renowned author of romance novels featuring African American characters, is writing a book called *A Natural History of Afro-Mexico*, "which deals with the African presence in Mexico, from the slaves who jumped slave ships to seek refuge in Mexico to others who traveled south to Mexico rather than north to Canada" (362). The fictional character Amanda Wordlaw joins a small but growing number of authors working to recover a black Mexican history that extends back even further than the fugitive slaves from the United States to the Africans imported by the Spanish beginning in the 1590s.

By designating Sanctuary an Underground Railroad, the novel invites comparisons between north and south. Indeed, the Sanctuary movement encompasses the entire continent and beyond, often identifying Canada as a potential place of refuge for Latin American dissidents threatened with deportation from the United States. Recalling Delany, the work of Sanctuary in the present is informed by the long history of North American places of refuge. Having driven transcontinental routes into Canada as well as Mexico, Nadine has considerable experience with the very different personalities of the two regions. She describes the border between the United States and Canada as "the free border" in comparison with its heavily policed Mexican counterpart (131, 239). The characters in *Mosquito* are well aware of the state's power to control the movement of people and goods at its borders. As a truck driver, Nadine regularly experiences the impact of restrictive state power when she is stopped, searched, or interrogated by border patrols. She remarks of the INS: "I guess a lot of them immigration agents acting on what they believe. But then they got what you call the state behind them. The state be saying, I got your back, so it pretty easy for them to act on what they believe, I mean, when they believe the same thing the state believe" (313). In contrast to the immigration agents, members of the Sanctuary movement describe themselves as working *against* the interests of nation-states, in favor of a higher international or human law. From their perspective, states are responsible for the injustice of national borders, which are open to commerce and the right kinds of travelers (Nadine remarks, "The rich don't have borders" [297]), and closed to those most in need of passage.

As *Mosquito* vividly illustrates, the conditions of any one border are best understood comparatively and with a deep view of history. The comprehensive view required to combat the injustices of U.S. immigration policy is available only by considering circumstances at both land borders, by recognizing North America as a unit rather than as three discrete nations. Nadine's rambling monologues do this and more, weaving connections among blacks on the North American continent, as well as in the Caribbean, South America, and Africa. The narratives she summons forth brilliantly rewrite the map of fugitive cartography by emphasizing the importance of the U.S.-Mexico borderlands to black history and culture in the Americas. Unfortunately, as the protagonist's nickname suggests, they are delivered in a voice that many have found so relentless and annoyingly circuitous as to be virtually unreadable.[48] Unlike her invention the best-selling author Amanda Wordlaw, or Ursa Corregidora, whose singing has the searing impact of a brand, Jones may not perform the work to which her protagonist aspires, the work of making Afro-Mexican history a part of collective North American consciousness.

John Sayles's 1996 film *Lone Star* shares *Mosquito*'s South Texas setting and its concern with the impact of the U.S.-Mexico border on those who live in the region, especially those overlooked by dominant historical narratives. Like Jones's novel, the film draws comparisons across time and space and, at the same time, is, as Sayles describes it, "very much about the specifics of a particular place and history — the Texas-Mexican border with its baggage of wars and racial politics."[49] Sayles's South Texas is made up of a familiar mix of Anglos, Mexicans, and Chicanos, as well as an African American family with deep roots in the region. What interests Sayles about this region is its diverse population and multiple and contradictory histories. In Frontera, a fictional town where high-school teachers and parents argue about the meaning of the Alamo and illegal immigrants run through homeowners' backyards, history is a matter of considerable urgency. Each of the film's central characters is drawn into a quest for knowledge about his or her personal history, which becomes entwined with the collective histories of the region. Sayles uses a repeated visual device to illustrate the enduring impact of the past on the present. When someone begins to remember the past, a point-of-view shot pans slowly across space, but also through time. When the camera comes to rest, we have entered the space of memory. This visual motif illustrates the power of memory to resurrect important past events as vividly as if they were occurring in the present. It also emphasizes how particular spaces become so laden with history that they function as portals into the past.

African Americans in *Lone Star* have a particularly conflicted relationship to local history in Frontera. Flashbacks depict the more vibrant black community of a generation ago. Now it is largely associated with the local army base, which is scheduled to close in two years. The popular hangout Big O's Roadhouse seems to be patronized primarily by the black servicemen and women who will soon be relocated. As its owner, Otis Payne, describes their dwindling numbers, "There's not enough of us to run anything in this town." A small minority overlooked by the town's political disputes, African Americans find their primary occupation in the army, a national, rather than a local, institution. The film is ambivalent in its depiction of the military, which is the source of pride and professional success for African American men like Otis's son, Colonel Del Payne, but is also the agent of a culture that does not belong to them. As one private explains her enlistment, "It's their country. This is one of the best deals they offer." Her comment underscores the uneasy position occupied by black people in *Lone Star*. Their fraught relationship to both local and national culture crystallizes in their identification with the migratory, multiracial figures of the Black Seminoles.

Given the importance of the military in *Lone Star*, it is fitting that the Black Seminoles—whose best fighters joined the U.S. Army when they returned from Mexico after the Civil War—are central to a series of encounters among three generations of Paynes, the film's African American family. Colonel Del Payne returns to his hometown when he is sent there to oversee the closure of the military base. An incident of violence involving an enlisted man requires Del to visit his father's bar (Big O's) to investigate. There he finds a sign posted outside that reads: "BLACK SEMINOLE EXHIBIT—REAR ENTRANCE." Del, who has long been estranged from his father, shows no interest in the collection of artifacts and documents that make up the exhibit, which Otis describes as his "hobby." However, it will resurface later when Del visits Otis's home and discovers that on the wall next to Otis's Black Seminole collection hang news clippings and photographs chronicling Del's military career. Having failed to be a good father, Otis compensates by creating an archive devoted to the success Del has achieved on his own. In this, Otis resembles many other characters in *Lone Star*, who shrink from difficult interpersonal situations by retreating into stories about the past. There is far less at stake in claiming the Black Seminoles as his blood relatives than in attempting to come to terms with his estranged son. However, the possibility of retreat is more an impression than a reality, since the film insistently points to the links between past and present. The question that each character faces once the past erupts is how he or she will use it to act in the present. At the same time that Otis announces his connection to the Black Seminoles, he concludes that "blood only means what you let it," a statement that has as much significance for his relationship to Del as it does to his more distant ancestors.

Another scene of encounter mediated through the Black Seminoles occurs when Del's son Chet, who has never met his grandfather, visits Big O's. Although he recognizes Chet immediately, Otis does not acknowledge it. Instead, his first words to his grandson are "That's John Horse." In place of an awkward introduction, Otis begins to relay the history of the Black Seminoles, prompted by questions from Chet. Chet's genuine surprise and curiosity about the unknown history stands in marked contrast to his father's lack of interest. Otis tells him of the Black Seminoles' return from Mexico after the Civil War, when some of the bravest warriors were organized into a celebrated regiment of the U.S. Army called the Seminole Negro Indian Scouts. When Chet asks incredulously if Indians fought against Indians, Otis answers, "They were in the Army. Like your father." This is the first time Otis intimates that he knows Chet's identity. The distant history of the Black Seminoles serves to mediate the more difficult problem of Otis's strained relationship to Del. Having made his connection with Chet, Otis explains that he is interested in the Black Seminoles because "these are our people," a veiled suggestion of belated interest in his own family. Through their meeting, Chet gains a connection with his grandfather, as well as with a heroic and little-known strand of North American history.

By embedding the story of the Black Seminoles within a contemporary story about the struggles of Mexican Americans, the film suggests a parallel between the two groups, both of which traversed the U.S.-Mexico border (albeit in different directions) in search of better lives. It shows Mexicans employing desperate measures to cross the border, only to find that the United States is hardly the Promised Land they had imagined. The new immigrants face prejudice, corruption, and difficult working conditions, as well as the constant threat of repatriation. The haunting presence of the Black Seminoles is a reminder of the historical injustice of slavery that stains U.S. history. Their work as Indian fighters with the U.S. Army further recalls how often minority groups have been thrown into combat against one another in the service of national interests. Arguments about the Alamo recall Texas's own conflicted past. Although only Anglos and Chicanos participate in the debate over the high-school curriculum, the presence of African Americans in the region recalls that slavery was a crucial motivating factor in the annexation of Texas. As framed by *Lone Star*, the southwestern border is a contested zone for black as well as Mexican American history.

Mosquito and *Lone Star* recover the suppressed histories of African Americans in the U.S. Southwest and northern Mexico. Both connect the history of slave resistance with the current struggles of Mexican *indocumentados*. They represent the borderlands as a space where the legacy of the black Atlantic meets up with that of other minority groups. The revisionist energies of both works emphasize the northern side of the border by demonstrating how the recovery of suppressed histories and the drawing of unfamiliar historical parallels challenge dominant narratives about race and nation in the United States. They leave open the question of those fugitive slaves who chose not to return and instead put down roots in Mexico. Theirs may be the most submerged history of all, one that remains relatively untouched by artists and historians alike. While there is now a growing body of work on blacks in Mexico, few scholars recognize the African American connections described here. Nor are they acknowledged by black Mexicans themselves, who typically do not understand race in diasporic terms that would allow it to serve as a point of identification across national categories.[50] Afro-Mexicans are believed to descend from the Spanish slave trade (and hence, the narrative goes, to have been almost entirely assimilated—read *invisible*—by 1900) or to be migrants from the Caribbean.[51] The novelist Guillermo Sánchez de Anda and the photographer Tony Gleaton are both intent on making blackness visible within Mexican contexts.

Guillermo Sánchez de Anda's *Yanga* (1998) is one of the few works of Mexican fiction to address what the historian Ben Vinson calls Mexico's "racial amnesia."[52] Self-consciously foregrounding the difficult work of historical recovery, the novel frames the history of Yanga, a Nigerian slave who led a successful thirty-eight-year revolt against the Mexican Crown ending in 1609, within the fictional narrative of Silverio, a contemporary journalist who becomes obsessed with unearthing Yanga's past. Silverio comes upon his story accidentally while on assignment to cover a government assault on a group of neo-Zapatistas holed up in the town of Yanga, which is located in Veracruz, home to one of the largest Afro-Mexican communities in the nation. A monument dedicated to the revolutionary leader who is the town's namesake sparks Silverio's curiosity. Like *Lone Star*, *Yanga* invests particularly charged places with the power to instigate the excavation of buried history. For Silverio, who begins to recognize parallels between the Zapatistas' current struggle for justice and Yanga's seventeenth-century rebellion, the town becomes a crucible of revolutionary energies destined to erupt during moments of particular historical crisis.

However, Yanga's revolt differs from other revolutionary moments in Mexico's past in that it is linked to the unacknowledged history of the Afro-Mexicans. To understand it, Silverio must first "reconocer la importancia de la 'negritud' en la historia de Mexico" (recognize the importance of "negritude" in the history of Mexico).[53] The importance and difficulty of this task are underscored by his local informant, Don Tiburcio, who tells him: "Tienes la gran oportunidad de escudriñar en un episodio trascendente de nuestra historia patria y de América, muy poco conocido, tal vez ignorado, quizá repudiado" (You have the great opportunity to examine a transcendent episode in our nation's history and that of America, one that is very little known, perhaps ignored, perhaps repudiated) (39). As he pursues the story of Yanga's victorious struggle against the Mexican military, Silverio undertakes the larger project of uncovering Mexico's forgotten black roots.

Silverio understands Yanga's radical legacy as a corrective to the current state of corruption and indifference plaguing "el México de hoy con sus carencias y limitaciones, con el abuso de autoridades y caciques y la inconciencia e indolencia de sus habitantes, los cuales no están dispuestos a realizar sacrifico alguno en aras del bienestar colectivo" (contemporary Mexico, with its deficiencies and limitations, with the abuses of authorities and political bosses and the thoughtlessness and indolence of its inhabitants, who aren't disposed to make the slightest sacrifice on the altar of the collective good) (126). Ultimately Sánchez de Anda relates the history of Yanga in the hope that it might redeem Mexico from its current political malaise. Unlike Jones or Sayles, he is uninterested in building bridges between the United States and other parts of the Americas; rather, he sees Afro-Mexican history as a strike in the war against Yankee hegemony. Although he claims that Yanga's revolt represents a "transcendent episode" in American history, Sánchez de Anda shares Martí's skepticism about the role of the United States in the Americas. This is evident when Silverio orders a Coke during his meeting with Don Tiburcio and is told, "Es mejor que tome un café, pues sólo los negros americanos abreban de las aguas negras del imperialismo yanqui" (Better to drink a coffee, since only the colored Americans imbibe the black waters of Yankee imperialism) (36). Later Silverio warns that if Mexico fails to recognize its own constitutional principles of universal equality, "dentro de unos años nos invadirán los gringos aduciendo que los mexicanos somos el pueblo 'de mañana' " (within a few years the gringos will invade us, predicting that the Mexicans are the people of the future) (63). While criticizing the state for its authoritarianism and neglect of its own people, Sánchez de Anda frames his protest against the threat of U.S. imperialism in national rather than diasporic terms. His goal is to reclaim the history of Afro-Mexicans for Mexico, to awaken the nation's slumbering revolutionary energies.

In many ways an ideal visual counterpart to Sánchez de Anda, the photographer Tony Gleaton also aspires to make the black component of Mexican ancestry visible. However, his purpose is to uncover the inter-American connections by excavating the Africanist genealogies in Mexico. Of mixed African and European heritage, Gleaton sees his project as both a cultural study and a more personal investigation of his own roots. A period of extensive travel in Mexico gave him an opportunity to photograph black populations concentrated on the Gulf Coast of central Veracruz and along the Pacific in Costa Chica, where poverty and geographic remoteness have kept them isolated from the national community. His series *Tengo casi 500 años* also includes images of blacks in El Salvador, Belize, Guatemala, Colombia, and other parts of Latin America.[54] Gleaton describes these photographs as part of a concerted effort to restore to public consciousness a people who have been nearly lost to history, in a region where the discourse of mestizaje has erased the presence of blackness and black citizens endure abiding prejudices and inequality. By combining images shot in Mexico and in other Latin American countries, *Tengo casi 500 años* suggests the continuity of black roots throughout the hemisphere.

The most striking feature of Gleaton's photographs is their beauty and formal virtuosity. His subjects are often children, sometimes posed in tender, intimate contact with adult companions. At first glance, these images may appear to be documentary because the subjects are framed in the context of daily life. However, Gleaton works in the tradition of classic portraiture, posing his subjects and positioning the camera to maximum aesthetic effect. As one catalog de-

1 Tony Gleaton, no. 332, "Pero no hay negros en El Salvador" (But there are no blacks in El Salvador), Santa Rosa de Lima, El Salvador. Copyright 1992, *Africa's Legacy in Mexico*. All rights reserved.

scribes the alignment of Gleaton's aesthetic and political objectives, "Eschewing the faux objectivity of the documentary photographer, Gleaton's photographs indicate both a subtle presence and a pronounced artistry. Subjects are indeed directed, often self-consciously posed within arranged scenes, to realize the artist's visual narration of the legacy of colonialism — an evolving African-derived black culture. Images possess a 'look' of effortlessness, candidly observed shots, yet are often later further manipulated to perfect the Gleaton effect. And it is this mélange of actuality and artifice that widens our comprehension of the Presence Africane in the Americas."[55]

2   Tony Gleaton, no. 149, "Jardín del paradiso" (Garden of Paradise),
Corallero, Oaxaca, Mexico. Copyright 1991, *Africa's Legacy in Mexico.*
All rights reserved.

Gleaton speaks frankly about posing his subjects to stand in as participants
in a larger narrative about the Africanist legacy in Latin America: "There is no
question about my repositioning subjects to create an effect, or having fathers
embrace sons at my suggestion rather than theirs. The photographs that I create are as much an effort to define my own life, with its heritage encompassing Africa and Europe, as an endeavor to throw open the discourse on the
broader aspects of 'mestizaje,' the 'assimilation' of Asians, Africans, and Europeans with indigenous Americans."[56] This statement clarifies Gleaton's conviction that the subjects of his photographs are simultaneously individuals and

3 Tony Gleaton, no. 129, "Abuelita y nieta" (Grandmother and Granddaughter), Cuajinicuilapa, Guerrero, Mexico. Copyright 1986, *Africa's Legacy in Mexico*. All rights reserved.

metaphors for his personal quest to uncover his heritage in the Americas. Yet at the same time that he understands his subjects as aspects of his own past, Gleaton somewhat contradictorily claims to "give a narrative voice by visual means to people deemed invisible by the greater part of society. . . . I deliberately craft an 'alternative iconography' of what beauty and family and love and goodness might stand for—one that is inclusive, not exclusive."[57] Like Jones and Sayles, Gleaton's goal is to resurrect suppressed histories and to give voice to those who have been left out of official narratives. Whether he achieves that goal is another question. Without Gleaton's print text, these gorgeous images

4   Tony Gleaton, no. 135, "La pollería" (The Chicken Seller), Cuajinicuilapa, Guerrero, Mexico. Copyright 1987, *Africa's Legacy in Mexico*. All rights reserved.

are more mute and static artifacts than participants in a narrative of their own self-expression.

Sometimes Gleaton's political message is explicit, as in a photograph titled "Pero no hay negros en El Salvador" (El Salvador, figure 1). Two boys turn to the camera with looks of skepticism and anxiety. Read in context, it is clear that their physical appearance — tightly curled hair, dark skin, and broad features — is meant to undermine the title's statement of protest. More often, Gleaton's photos are untitled or captioned to evoke pastoral or familial connotations. The posed, motionless quality of his subjects is compounded by their rural sur-

5   Tony Gleaton, no. 111, "Pescador con red" (Fisherman with Net),
Corallero, Oaxaca, Mexico. Copyright 1987, *Africa's Legacy in Mexico*.
All rights reserved.

roundings, which suggest a people barely touched by modernity. For example,
in "Jardín del paradiso" (Mexico, figure 2), a naked boy peers out from behind
a tree, his lower body concealed by foliage. Shot in deep focus, the image reveals
an expanse of field, trees, and grazing animals stretching to the horizon. There
are many images of parents and children posed to suggest the unbroken continuity of generations (Mexico, figure 3). Others provide more context, showing
people working at humble occupations such as chicken vendor, fisherman, or
barber (Mexico, figures 4–6). Or they are arrested in moments of leisure: men
playing dominos (Colombia), drinking beer (Panama), or reclining together

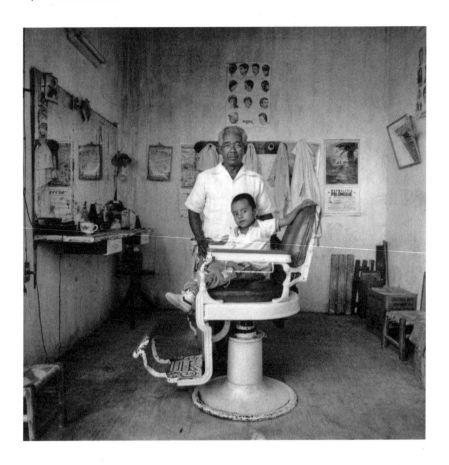

6   Tony Gleaton, no. 113, "Peluquería" (Barbershop), Pinotepa Nacional, Oaxaca, Mexico. Copyright 1990, *Africa's Legacy in Mexico*. All rights reserved.

(figures 7–8). Unlike the texts discussed earlier, in which the artist retraces the tracks of previous generations, Gleaton's work suggests that he is the first to cover this ground. His path leads him to discover people untouched by time or modernity. These photographs lack the deep historical consciousness that animates the work of Sayles, Jones, or Sánchez de Anda. Their stasis — which likens them to the objectifying, primitivist impulses of earlier ethnographic photography — threatens to undermine Gleaton's revisionist impulse.

When modernity does intrude into these images, the feeling is jarring and anachronistic. For example, a photograph called "Las muñecas" (Mexico, fig-

7   Tony Gleaton, no. 417, "Sin título" (Untitled), Barlovento, Venezuela.
Copyright 1994, *Africa's Legacy in Mexico*. All rights reserved.

ure 9) pictures a group of dark-skinned, curly-haired girls holding two battered
white dolls. The dolls' blonde hair and Western clothes bespeak another world,
governed by different standards of beauty and femininity. In an untitled photo,
three boys stand in the open window of a house (Honduras, figure 10). The boy
in the middle has turned his back to the photographer to display the Adidas
symbol cut into the back of his short, nappy hair. The logo and worn, Western-
ized T-shirts seem out of place in the series of more timeless pastoral images. In
both photographs, it is clear that these well-worn artifacts and icons of Western
consumer culture are deeply meaningful to their owners, who are not frozen in
time but instead living in a moment where globalization has reached the most

8   Tony Gleaton, no. 361, "Sin título" (Untitled), Darien, Panama.
Copyright 1992, *Africa's Legacy in Mexico*. All rights reserved.

remote corners of the planet. It is Gleaton's youngest subjects who confront
seismic changes that have the potential to teach them difficult lessons about
prejudice and inequality, but also help them to recognize connections with
blacks in other parts of the world. Although this is not necessarily Gleaton's
understanding of his own photographs, they have been adapted by others as
illustrations of the as yet unrecognized extent of the black diaspora.

   Despite the contradictions in Gleaton's message, his project makes an important and virtually unique statement about the recovery of cultural memory.
Like Sayles and Jones, he seeks to unearth buried Afro-Mexican and American connections by excavating American spaces that have long resisted such a

9   Tony Gleaton, no. 125, "Las muñecas" (The Dolls, or Four Young Girls, Two Dolls), El Ciruello, Oaxaca, Mexico. Copyright 1987, *Africa's Legacy in Mexico*. All rights reserved.

history. But Gleaton's work is doubly important because he moves south of the U.S. border to some of the poorest and most marginalized areas of Mexico. He thus begins to retrace the presence of blackness among Mexico's mestizo populations, which is a legacy of the Spanish slave trade as well as the little-known history of the fugitive slaves who traveled south and stayed there. Whereas the large African population introduced in the sixteenth and seventeenth centuries is believed to have been completely assimilated, Gleaton photographs black communities in remote regions of Mexico, where they remain isolated from the general population. To make blackness visible south of the border is to con-

10   Tony Gleaton, no. 327, "Sin título" (Untitled), Limón, Honduras.
Copyright 1992, *Africa's Legacy in Mexico*. All rights reserved.

tribute to a largely overlooked chapter in black diasporic consciousness, which
has found African roots more affirmingly acknowledged in other parts of Latin
America, but seldom in Mexico, as well as adding a more nuanced understanding of "the South" to the imagined geographies of U.S. racial history.

Guided by the ambiguous voice of José Martí, this essay has traversed a circuitous path from the nineteenth century to the present, revealing along the way
an often overlooked connection between the American slave trade and the U.S.-
Mexico borderlands. This connection is important to U.S. history because it re-
vises the map of fugitive cartography drawn by slave narratives, which has often
guided nation-centered understandings of slavery. Recovering the stories of the

slaves who fled south makes slavery more central to the notion of "the border-lands" that has inspired much recent work in American studies. Those stories are equally important to Latin American history, which so often subordinates race to mestizaje, losing sight of its more hybrid ancestry and erasing ongoing problems of racial discrimination and injustice. Locating blackness south of the U.S. border opens up new possibilities of diasporic community based on a shared past and common struggles in the present. It is no accident that these connections have been most compellingly expressed in the arts, which recognize the crucial role of the imagination by filling the gaps left by an absence of historical data and solidifying local, national, and diasporic sensibilities. It is important that we listen to the voices contained in these representations, or we risk losing the varied and multidirectional routes of freedom followed by America's subaltern populations.

Notes

1   José Martí, "Our America," in *José Martí Reader: Writings on the Americas*, ed. Deborah Shnookal and Mirta Muñiz (Melbourne: Ocean Press, 1999), 119.

2   Anani Dzidzienyo, "Conclusions," in *No Longer Invisible: Afro-Latin Americans Today* (London: Minority Rights Group, 1995), 345–58; Alan Knight, "Race, Revolution, and *Indigenismo*: Mexico, 1910–1940," in *The Idea of Race in Latin America, 1870–1940*, ed. Richard Graham (Austin: University of Texas Press, 1990), 71–113.

3   Susan Gillman, "*Ramona* in 'Our America,' " in *José Martí's "Our America": From National to Hemispheric Cultural Studies*, ed. Jeffrey Belnap and Raúl Fernández (Durham: Duke University Press, 1998), 96.

4   Luz María Martínez Montiel, "Africa's Legacy in Mexico: Mexico's Third Root," http://www.smithsonianeducation.org/migrations/legacy/almthird.html (accessed October 5, 2006).

5   Despite a lack of official recognition, there is a growing body of scholarship on blacks in Mexico that began with Gonzalo Aguirre Beltrán's *La población negra de Mexico* (Mexico City: Fondo de Cultura Económica, 1946). See also Herman Lee Bennett, *Lovers, Family, Friends: The Formation of Afro-Mexico, 1580–1910* (Durham: Duke University Press, 1993); Colin Palmer, *Slaves of the White God* (Cambridge: Harvard University Press, 1975); Martha Menchaca, *Recovering History, Constructing Race: The Indian, Black, and White Roots of Mexican Americans* (Austin: University of Texas Press, 2001); Ben Vinson, *Bearing Arms for His Majesty: The Free-Colored Militia in Colonial Mexico* (Palo Alto: Stanford University Press, 2001).

6   Paul Gilroy, *The Black Atlantic: Modernity and Double Consciousness* (Cambridge: Harvard University Press, 1993).

7   Frances Smith Foster, *Witnessing Slavery: The Development of Ante-bellum Slave Narratives* (Madison: University of Wisconsin Press, 1979), 76.

8   J. W. Loguen, *The Rev. J. W. Loguen, as a Slave and as a Freeman: A Narrative of Real Life* (New York: Negro Universities Press, 1968), 345.

9   Martin Delany, *Blake, or The Huts of America* (Boston: Beacon Press, 1970), 30.

10   Martin Delany, "Political Destiny of the Colored Race on the American Continent," in *Pamphlets of Protest: An Anthology of Early African-American Protest Literature, 1790–1860*, ed. Richard Newman, Patrick Rael, and Philip Lapsansky (New York: Routledge, 2001), 230.

11   Gregg Crane, "The Lexicon of Rights, Power, and Community in *Blake*: Martin R. Delany's Dissent from *Dred Scott*," *American Literature* 68, no. 3 (September 1996): 527–53.

12   Delany, "Political Destiny," 234.

13   Ibid., 235.

14   Ibid., 238–39.

15   Cited in Quintard Taylor, *In Search of the Racial Frontier: African Americans in the American West, 1528–1990* (New York: Norton, 1998), 38–39.

16   On the Black Seminoles, see Kenneth W. Porter, *The Black Seminoles: History of a Freedom-Seeking People* (Gainesville: University Press of Florida, 1996); Rosalie Schwartz, *Across the Rio to Freedom: U.S. Negroes in Mexico* (El Paso: Texas Western Press, 1975); and Ronnie C. Tyler, "Fugitive Slaves in Mexico," *Journal of Negro History* 57, no. 1 (January 1972): 1–12.

17   Benjamin Lundy, *The Life, Travels and Opinions of Benjamin Lundy* (New York: Augustus M. Kelley, 1971), 96. On Lundy, see also Schwartz, *Across the Rio to Freedom*.

18   Schwartz, *Across the Rio to Freedom*, 40–41.

19   D. W. Meinig, *The Shaping of America: A Geographical Perspective on 500 Years of History*, vol. 2 (New Haven: Yale University Press, 1993), 298; Schwartz, *Across the Rio to Freedom*.

20   Schwartz, *Across the Rio to Freedom*, 29.

21   Cited in Meinig, *The Shaping of America*, 305.

22   Schwartz, *Across the Rio to Freedom*, 29.

23   Josefina Zoraida Vázquez and Lorenzo Meyer, *The United States and Mexico* (Chicago: University of Chicago Press, 1985), 28–29.

24   This greater atmosphere of racial tolerance had its roots in the Old World. Some critics have argued that during the Enlightenment, Spain's Islamic heritage gave rise to a culture that saw slavery as a temporary condition and pluralism as the norm. See Patricia Seed, *American Pentimento: The Invention of Indians and the Pursuit of Riches* (Minneapolis: University of Minnesota Press, 2001); and Jaime Rodriguez, "The Emancipation of America," *American Historical Review* 105, no. 1 (February 2000): 131–52; Rodriguez, "La Antigua Provincia de Guayaquil en la época de la Independencia," in *Revolución, Independencia y la nuevas naciones de América*, ed. Jaime E. Rodriguez (Madrid: Fundación Mapfre-Tavera, 2005), 511–56; and Rodriguez, "Ciudadanos de la Nación Española: Los indígenas y las elec-

ciones constitucionales en el Reino de Quito," in *La mirada esquiva: Reflexiones históricas sobre la interacción del Estado y la ciudadanía en los Andes*, ed. Marta Iroruzqui (Madrid: Consejo Superior de Investigaciones Científicas, 2005).

25 Schwartz, *Across the Rio to Freedom*, 7.

26 Schwartz, *Across the Rio to Freedom*.

27 Vázquez and Meyer, *The United States and Mexico*, 18.

28 Schwartz, *Across the Rio to Freedom*, 37.

29 See Jeff Guin, *Our Land before We Die: The Proud Story of the Seminole Negro* (New York: Putnam, 2002); and Porter, *The Black Seminoles*.

30 Porter, *The Black Seminoles*, 6.

31 Cited in Porter, *The Black Seminoles*, 9.

32 On Mexican help to fugitive slaves, see Neil Foley, *The White Scourge: Mexicans, Blacks, and Poor Whites in Texas Cotton Culture* (Berkeley: University of California Press, 1997); Taylor, *In Search of the Racial Frontier*; Schwartz, *Across the Rio to Freedom*; and Ruthe Winegarten, *Black Texas Women: 150 Years of Trial and Triumph* (Austin: University of Texas Press, 1995).

33 Taylor, *In Search of the Racial Frontier*, 41.

34 John Hope Franklin and Loren Schweninger, *Runaway Slaves: Rebels on the Plantation, 1790–1860* (New York: Oxford, 1999), 115.

35 Ibid.

36 Ibid., 26.

37 Ronnie Tyler and Laurence R. Murphy, *Slave Narratives of Texas* (Austin: Encino Press, 1974), 68.

38 Ibid., 69.

39 Frederick Law Olmsted, *A Journey through Texas* (New York: Burt Franklin, 1969), 454. Hereafter cited in the text.

40 Patrick J. Carroll, "Africa in the Americas: Blacks in Mexico," http://www.humanities-interactive.org.

41 Aguierre Beltrán, *La población negra de Mexico*, 200; Bobby Vaughn, "Blacks in Mexico: A Brief Overview," http://www.mexconnect.com.

42 Carroll, "Africa in the Americas"; Steve Sailer, "Mexico's Missing Blacks," May 8, 2002, http://www.upi.com.

43 Dedra S. McDonald, "To Be Black and Female in the Spanish Southwest: Toward a History of African Women on New Spain's Far Northern Frontier," in *African American Women Confront the West, 1600–2000*, ed. Quintard Taylor and Shirley Ann Wilson Moore (Norman: University of Oklahoma Press, 2003), 32–52.

44 Gayl Jones, *Corregidora* (Boston: Beacon Press, 1975), 9.

45 Ibid., 80.

46 Ibid., 59.

47 Gayl Jones, *Mosquito* (Boston: Beacon Press, 1999), 322. Hereafter cited in the text.

48 The reviewer James A. Miller wrote that the novel "aspires to the condition of 'truth,' of 'experience in all its formlessness and apparent chaos' " ("A Talker, a Tale-Teller, a Sojourner," *Boston Globe*, January 17, 1999, E3), while Tom Leclair

commented more critically that it "reads like 2,000 pages of Gertrude Stein's 'Melanctha,' aggressively digressive, frequently vapid, and stupefyingly repetitive" (review of *Mosquito*, January 21, 1999, http://www.salon.com).

49   John Sayles, introduction to *Men with Guns and Lone Star* (London: Faber and Faber, 1998), viii.

50   Bobby Vaughan, "Afro-Mexico: Blacks, Indígenas, Politics, and the Greater Diaspora," in *Neither Enemies nor Friends: Latinos, Blacks, Afro-Latinos*, ed. Anani Dzidzienyo and Suzanne Oboler (New York: Palgrave Macmillan, 2005), 125–27.

51   The anthropologist Bobby Vaughn is conducting important research on contemporary Afro-Mexicans. His preliminary findings reveal that the Afro-Mexicans of Veracruz trace their origins to Cuba, while those in Costa Chica lack a consciousness of their slave ancestry and often claim to come from the descendants of shipwrecks. Vaughan, "Mexico in the Context of the Transatlantic Slave Trade," *Diálogo* 5 (2001): 1–11; and Vaughan, "Afro-Mexico," 118–36.

52   Vinson, *Bearing Arms for His Majesty*.

53   Guillermo Sánchez de Anda, *Yanga: El Guerrero Negro* (Mexico: Círculo Cuadrado, 1998), 39. Hereafter cited in the text.

54   Tony Gleaton's photographs from the series *Tengo casi 500 años: Africa's Legacy in Mexico, Central and South America*, are part of the Southwest Collection Special Collection Archives, Texas Tech University.

55   Warren Chrichlow, "Tony Gleaton," Wedge Gallery review, April 30, 2001, http://www.wedgegallery.com.

56   Tony Gleaton, "Africa's Legacy in Mexico: Oaxaca Diary," http://www.smithsonianeducation.org/migrations/legacy/almdia.html (accessed October 5, 2006).

57   Tony Gleaton, cited in copy for "Tracing African Roots throughout the Americas," http://www.aarl.denverlibrary.org.

Queer Harvests

Homosexuality, the U.S. New Left, and

the Venceremos Brigades to Cuba

Ian Lekus

Early in 1969, Students for a Democratic Society (SDS), the largest white student organization of the sixties in the United States, stood teetering at the brink of implosion, torn apart by competing factions. Confronted by the potential collapse of SDS, its leaders launched a project that they hoped would rejuvenate the movement. Inspired by Cuba's material advances and resistance to U.S. policy since the 1959 revolution, SDS began mobilizing hundreds of Americans to travel south to cut sugar cane, contributing their labor to the island's export harvest. On these Venceremos Brigades, participants would, in the words of organizers Sandra Levinson and Carol Brightman, "gain direct experience with a Third World socialist revolution and a greater understanding of 'revolution' as something which entails much more than guns in the hills, something which means hard work every day."[1] Brigade organizers in the United States recognized that the daily work of harvesting sugar cane and living together in the new socialist Cuba offered *norteamericanos* the potential of sowing a new revolutionary culture to import back home.

Visions of revolutionizing American culture notwithstanding, the Venceremos Brigade leaders operated under deeply entrenched *yanqui* assumptions of how Cuban culture worked, especially regarding norms of sexuality and gender on the tropical island. In the eyes of these Brigade organizers romanticizing their hosts, the nascent gay liberation movement in the United States represented an unacceptable, imperialist challenge to both Fidel Castro's government and Cuban society at large. The organizing committee of the Brigades eventually implemented what amounted to a "Don't ask, don't tell" policy that demanded lesbians and gay men not discuss their sexual orientation if they wanted to participate in the work trips. The antigay vitriol and even violence of some heterosexual Brigadistas prompted others to recognize and reject the homophobia so common in the New Left. For queer Brigadistas, living, working, and organizing in the arduous intimacy of the Brigade camps, the romance of the Cuban Revolution proved heartbreaking. The official antigay Brigade policy dovetailed with the Cuban revolutionary state's own crackdown on homosexuality. Lesbian and gay male Brigadistas were widely harassed and ultimately formally excluded from the promise of building a more democratic society.

The history of the Venceremos Brigades powerfully illustrates transnational solidarity in the Americas while also vividly underscoring the limits of that solidarity. Seen through the lens of sexuality in particular, the Venceremos Brigades expose the boundaries of revolutionary change on both sides of the Straits of Florida—through the New Left's political and cultural rebellion, as well as through the Cuban Revolution's euphoric first decade of popular mobilization and Pan-Americanism. Both the Cuban state and U.S. Brigadistas generated and enforced deeply oppressive sexual ideologies and regimes that represented the very antithesis of emancipation and freedom. On the Venceremos Brigades, U.S. radicals rehashed long-standing mainstream *norteamericano* stereotypes of Latin *machismo* and in the process reinscribed the sexual hierarchies governing colonial relations in the Americas. As such, transnational solidarity never escaped the long shadow of U.S. imperial designs on Cuba and the greater Caribbean. Even the most passionately anti-imperialist politics remained intractably grounded in hemispheric relations of empire, a dynamic laid bare by the controversies that erupted between the Brigade organizers and the Gay Liberation Front over the Cuban government's incarceration of thousands of gay men and other dissidents.

As part of the 1970 Gay Pride Week festivities in New York, celebrating the first anniversary of the Stonewall riots, the newspaper *Gay Power* scheduled a midnight benefit screening at the Elgin Theater for the night of June 25. But that Thursday evening, as the event's organizers arrived, they discovered that local organizers for the Venceremos Brigades had also reserved the theater to show films on Cuba and Vietnam at the same late hour. The *Village Voice* correspondent Jonathan Black reported that the Brigadistas had learned of *Gay Power*'s prior booking but went ahead with their own fundraiser all the same, with the blessing of the theater's management. When the gay liberation activists arrived, they turned off the projector and asked that since this was Gay Pride Week, would the Brigadistas hold their event some other night? The pro-Cuba organizers refused, first suggesting the same of the gays, then offering to split the evening's take — a moot proposal, given how few people had arrived to see either group's films.

Tensions soon escalated as the gay activists reported that some Brigadistas called them "faggots" and threatened to rape them. Gay Liberation Front (GLF) members proclaimed their solidarity with the achievements of the Cuban Revolution but strongly denounced Castro's government for its hostility toward homosexuals. One GLF activist expressed his outrage that "members of the Brigade have the nerve to show us pictures of concentration camps for homosexuals, camps they never saw, and tell us they were just nice health camps, that they were places where homosexuals were being helped to get their thing together."[2]

As the conflict intensified, the activist Allen Young felt trapped in an untenable position. A year earlier, the Liberation News Service (LNS) editor had been invited to visit Cuba and had toured the island during February and March 1969. What he saw contrasted sharply with the grinding poverty he had observed during earlier travels through Chile and Brazil. At the same time, he kept silent about his own attraction to men while Cuban Communist Party leaders defended the removal of lesbians and gay men from foreign ministry posts and army officers condemned homosexuality more broadly. Young reported how the local men he met cruising Havana's streets (some who defended the revolution and its material accomplishments, as others criticized the government's encroachments on individual freedom) all shared a depression rooted in the incompatibility of their hopes for finding love, sex, and secure work with the ideology and policies of the new Cuba. Disturbed by these discoveries, but still committed to the advances in literacy, housing, health care, and the general welfare made since 1959, Young returned to the United States and took up the post of treasurer for the Venceremos Brigades organizing committee. He even posed for a recruitment poster amid a stand of sugar cane, carrying a machete and decked out in Cuban army fatigues. His Brigadista colleagues had no idea how such antigay prejudices had upset Young, nor did they know of his growing involvement with the GLF chapter in New York.[3]

So when Allen Young attended the fundraiser at the Elgin Theater, he was "frightened and confused" at the unfolding conflict between his two worlds. As he wrote a year later, "I sat on a fence, supporting *Gay Power* at first, but eventually losing patience with the gays' anger and militant struggle. Finally, I shouted something about being part of an 'international communist movement,' hoping that the gay people would shut up so we could watch movies about Vietnam. I am still ashamed of how I behaved that night . . . though mostly I am angry at how the straight movement made me reject my gay sisters and brothers."[4] Thirty years later, Leslie Cagan remembered the confrontation quite differently. Cagan, a New York University antiwar organizer, had traveled to Cuba in late 1969 as one of the 216 North Americans on the first Venceremos Brigade. She recalled that when a fellow pro-Cuba organizer had beckoned to her and Young, saying, "Come on, let's get out of here, let's get away from those people," Young had responded, "I *am* one of those people."

For both Young and Cagan, their memories of this brief exchange represent their far longer quests to integrate their sexuality with their politics, as well as the same struggles of gay men and lesbians in the New Left more generally. While this discussion lasted but a moment, it sets the tone for how both Young and Cagan interpret their lives as members of—or refugees from—a mass movement. For Young, the evening's confrontation encapsulated the anger and pain generated by the ways that the New Left's homophobia made it impossible for him to participate in the movement. But for Cagan, still two years from coming out as a lesbian within the feminist movement, this pronouncement was a "brave" act that began the slow process of integrating her political and sexual identities. Their shared personal and political heritages—the children of pro-Communist parents—made Young's declaration resonate even more intensely for Cagan. Allen Young's coming out stunned many of his old comrades, prompting some of them to reconsider their antigay attitudes. The ensuing discussions between the GLF and local Brigade organizers led a handful of GLF activists to join the third contingent of North Americans who set sail for Cuba in August 1970.[5]

Incidents such as the confrontation at the Elgin Theater, along with other antigay incidents on subsequent Brigade trips to Cuba, shocked many individual heterosexual Brigadistas into recognizing the depths of hatred that gay men and lesbians faced even within the New Left. At the same time, the stance taken by Young and other GLF Brigadistas hardly swept away such prejudice. In fact, the opposite held true. The involvement of the GLFers in the third contingent — or on the Third Wave, as each delegation was enumerated in the argot of the Venceremos Brigades — set in motion a chain of events that in 1972 led the project's National Committee to bar lesbians and gay men from participation unless they kept silent about their sexuality.

The Brigade organizers, like many of their fellow New Left comrades more generally, demonstrated the limits of their ability to incorporate sexual freedom into their visions for political and social transformation — if they did so at all. To those inspired by Marxist theory or by the machismo-tinged aesthetics of Castro and Che Guevara, homosexuality represented either bourgeois decadence, a vestige of capitalism that required eradication, or a joke worthy of derision, dismissal, and harassment.[6] Gay liberation, in their minds, distracted attention from the more serious work of revolution. Akin to those stateside white activists who mimicked the antigay posturing of Eldridge Cleaver and select other black nationalists, some U.S. Brigadistas cited traditional patterns of gender relations in Cuban culture to frame their attitudes as revolutionarily correct.

But even as the Brigade leadership exhibited the dogmatic rigidity so characteristic of SDS's sectarian splinters, the broader experience of going to Cuba, of risking personal safety to carry out difficult political labor far from home for a just cause, hearkened back to 1964's Freedom Summer, when white college students had streamed into Mississippi to register black voters and forged a "beloved community" with African American activists. To be sure, the sectarianism and racial dynamics of radical politics in 1969 seemed a far cry from that earlier moment, but underneath the more militant rhetoric of revolution lay striking similarities. Once more, young Americans — spanning racial divides this time, but united by their shared national identity — traveled to an even deeper South seeking a more just way of living and of organizing society. The norteamericanos looked to learn from Cuba's experiences in forging a New Man, el hombre nuevo, over the past decade. The weeks and months spent by the Brigadistas working in the fields, living and sleeping in the close quarters of tent camps, and touring the former American-occupied territory generated the intimacy for a unique social-movement culture to emerge, one shaped by those immediate conditions within a framework rooted in Cold War geopolitics

and the long history of U.S.-Cuban relations. Now, to be sure, U.S. supporters of the Cuban Revolution positioned themselves politically in opposition to
Western imperialism. Even so, the personal relationships developed between
Cubans and norteamericanos on the Brigades remained inescapably entangled
in the imperial system that tied their respective nations together.[7]

A decade before the first Venceremos Brigade, the Cuban Revolution had
fired the imagination of Americans of all sorts—a reaction that flowed from
what Louis Pérez has called the "pervasive ambivalence" that defines U.S.-
Cuban relations.[8] As Van Gosse has shown, in the immediate aftermath of Ful-
gencio Batista's overthrow, the American media painted Fidel Castro as a "rebel
with a cause." Castro, dubbed the "bearded rebel scholar," appeared on the
cover of *Life*. Even President Eisenhower retroactively proclaimed U.S. support
for the revolution and recognized the new government in Havana. But as Castro
authorized the seizure of American holdings and the executions of hundreds
of army and police officers, mainstream U.S. reactions toward the revolution
grew steadily icier.[9]

But despite the chill, Yankee *fidelistas* continued to organize for better relations between the two nations. The image of Cuba as a land where racism
had supposedly vanished, a powerful national mythology rooted in the thirty
years of war for independence from Spain, inspired Americans battling white
supremacy at home. Moreover, young white men alienated from the clean-cut
middle-class Cold War culture of consensus found in the "bearded rebel" a
role model who fused revolutionary protest and virility. The Fair Play for Cuba
Committee mobilized many students later active in the New Left in support of
better U.S.-Cuban relations after the chill had set in. While Castro embodied the
various hopes of his American supporters, some of these fidelistas denounced
the Cuban elites who fled to Florida after 1959 as *los maricones*. Slurring anti-
communist Cubans as homosexuals not only represented the counterpoint to
Castro's reputed virility but also evoked the sexual economy that had thrived
in Havana under Batista.[10]

During Batista's rule, bankrolled by the Mafia and American corporate interests, "Cuba was," in Gosse's words, "where respectable North Americans went
to gamble without restraint, to see live sex shows of the most inventive character, to indulge without fear of discovery in whoring with partners of either
sex, to eat and drink cheaply, to be waited on hand and foot—all in an environment as close at hand as Miami, and completely geared to servicing their
tastes."[11] Allen Ginsberg, soon to be a hero of the New Left and the counter-

culture, visited Cuba in late 1953, tempted by rumors of Havana's sexually per-
missive culture. Disappointed by not finding any orgies, he traveled onward
to Mexico. In a 1970 issue of *Gay Scene*, Todd Anders fondly reminisced about
the nightly shows of "Superman," a dark-skinned local so nicknamed for his
extraordinary physical endowment. The paying crowd would marvel at Cuban
youths, male and female, who would mount themselves upon Superman; an
extra sum would allow audience members to attempt to replicate this feat themselves.[12]

For years, North Americans as well as wealthier Cubans themselves would
attend such sexual circuses, multiracial playgrounds kept fully staffed by locals
seeking relief from the island's unrelenting poverty. The revolutionary government made eradicating this colonial economy a priority. The new authorities
closed down the shows and drove owners and performers into northern exile.
They also launched programs to retrain female sex workers for new careers in
more respectable fields such as seamstry. Carrying out these campaigns allowed
the regime to reclaim the national honor — as defined in heterosexual masculine terms — of the Cuban people.[13] Policies of sexual reform were central to the
revolutionary government's agenda for social uplift, which also included massive campaigns for improved literacy, health care, and housing. But given the
especially sexualized nature of Cuba's past relationship to the United States,
as relations between Havana and Washington strained to the breaking point,
sexual reform became all the more important to symbolizing the revolution's
rejection of yanqui domination.

By 1969, the revolutionary government had withstood a decade of economic
and political assaults from the government of the United States. These overt
and covert operations included the 1961 CIA-organized invasion at the Playa de
Girón (Bay of Pigs) by Cuban exiles, repeated attempts to assassinate Castro,
paramilitary attacks on various economic targets, and disruptions of the island's
trade with Western Europe. As industrialization faltered, sugar "offered an
obvious and relatively cost-effective method of reversing the mounting balance
of trade deficits by mobilizing efforts around a sector in which Cuba possessed
adequate personnel and sufficient experience," as Louis Pérez explains. Export-
ing sugar to the Soviet bloc firmly tied Havana to Moscow's metropole, and
Castro dedicated Cuba to harvesting ten million tons by 1970. Billboards proclaimed, "¡Los diez milliones van!" (The ten million are going [for export]!),
and grilled readers, "What are you doing towards the ten million?"[14]

When Fidel Castro renewed his call for the great sugar harvest on New Year's

Day in 1969, SDS delegates were in Havana for the occasion. Upon inquiring how they might best support the *zafra* (harvest), the delegates were invited to come into the fields and cut sugar cane themselves. When they returned home to the United States, they borrowed the famous revolutionary cry "¡Patria o Muerte! ¡Venceremos!" (Fatherland or Death! We will triumph!) to begin organizing the first Venceremos Brigade. Recruiters mobilized primarily young Americans to break the official U.S. embargo on travel and trade with Cuba, to cut sugar cane for the zafra, and, for later contingents, to harvest fruit and work in housing construction.[15] The organizers turned to the prisons, gangs, and armed forces of the United States to sign up alienated blacks, Chicanos, Puerto Ricans, and working-class whites. Students, Black Panthers, trade union activists, GI organizers, and military veterans swelled the ranks of the Brigades as well, as did many young people with no specific affiliation. Margot Adler, a future correspondent for National Public Radio, recalled that her fellow travelers on the First Wave included "Quakers committed to total nonviolence as well as at least a dozen Weathermen, who viewed their sojourn in Cuba as part of an effort to recruit members for the coming struggle back home."[16]

In attempting to develop a revolutionary political culture, Brigadistas repeatedly referred back to Cuba's long history of antiracist and anticolonial resistance, as well as to the contemporary Black Power and feminist movements in North America. They constantly emphasized the crucial goal of building solidarity across divides of nationality, race, and gender, based on understanding each other's struggles, cultures, and problems. The recruiters sought to organize "a racially and sexually mixed group which exhibited no racist or chauvinist attitudes."[17] Americans arrived in Cuba to signs proclaiming instead "Como en Vietnam" (Like in Vietnam), the omnipresent reminders of the Southeast Asian liberation struggles and resistance to U.S. foreign policy. Such sweeping appeals to unity had their limits, however, as the lesbians and gay men on the Venceremos Brigades soon discovered. Revolutionary promises were betrayed by news of the Cuban government's widespread persecution of homosexuals, most notably the imprisonment in forced labor camps of gay men along with other dissidents. The everyday antigay attitudes of some of their fellow Brigadistas compounded the disillusionment. However, barely a handful of participants identified openly as lesbian or gay on the first two waves, and few if any early Brigadistas appeared to raise the question of the camps with their Cuban hosts.

The first several Brigades took place during a critical window in the history of the U.S. New Left. By late November 1969, when the First Wave came ashore in Cuba, SDS lay in ruins. The Weathermen and other factions vying for control of SDS instead fatally shattered the organizational structure of the movement. Most activists turned to other antiwar and antiracist groups, local projects such as GI coffeehouses, or even the growing feminist, gay liberation, and ecology movements. The death of SDS notwithstanding, opposition to the Vietnam War and to American foreign policy in general grew steadily. Just before the First Wave sailed into Havana, over a million Americans took part in the October Moratorium and the November Mobilization against the Vietnam War. Within such a climate, support for "the first free territory of the Americas" a mere ninety miles south of Key West became a logical extension of the anti-imperialist movement in the States.

Ultimately, hundreds of American youths responded to Castro's appeals to join the zafra, taking the rare opportunity to "actually practic[e] a form of foreign policy in their own lives," as the *Viet Report* writer and Venceremos Brigades National Committee member Carol Brightman explained.[18] As frustration mounted over the inability to end the war in Southeast Asia, doing hands-on labor in Cuba offered the chance to see immediate results from one's work. For Clint Pyne, an antiwar organizer at the University of North Carolina, going to Cuba offered a way to support "another alternative for development in Third World countries . . . a separate path from what was seen as a racist, imperialist regime in the United States and the Third World regimes it spawned."[19]

Traveling to Cuba also offered a certain masculine romantic thrill. A story on the Brigades in the *Fifth Estate*, the Detroit underground newspaper, proclaimed: "The war against imperialism must be fought with machetes, hoes, and tractors, as well as with rifles and bullets."[20] A subsequent article echoed the call for the strenuous manly labor of revolution, declaring "the Cuban's [*sic*] guns are ours. Our guns will be theirs," and explained that what guns represented had been reversed (though not displaced) from repression and terror to revolution and its defense.[21] The recruitment poster featuring Allen Young in Cuban army fatigues and holding a machete reinforced the image connecting Americans to Third World armed rebellions. Robbie Skeist, a veteran Chicago draft resistance and gay liberation organizer who participated in the Second Wave, reflected on this exotic appeal of the revolutionary tropics for "a bunch of urban, kind of under-traveled, under-exercised kids . . . who go off to a very exciting country," laboring under the warm sun, "getting tan and muscular."

The idealism and commitment of young Cubans, the climate of camaraderie, of being beleaguered in the face of an enemy, all inspired the North Americans on the Venceremos Brigades to give their labor to the revolution, Skeist recalled.[22]

Back at home, the Brigadistas endured harassment for their open defiance of the Cold War blockade. A Detroit contingent setting out in February 1970 to meet the remainder of the Second Wave's 687 Brigadistas halfheartedly posed as a ski group bound for Canada but fooled neither the FBI nor journalists. The press mocked the skiers with questions such as "How much cane do you plan to cut in New Brunswick?" as police photographers captured the whole farce on film. In August 1970, as some of the 405 members of the Third Wave embarked from Saint John, New Brunswick, one Miami radio station warned listeners how the Brigadistas would be trained in guerrilla warfare.[23] Perhaps the most virulent denunciation of the Venceremos Brigades came on the floor of the United States Senate from Mississippi's segregation stalwart James Eastland, who promised "to drive from those shadows the missiles — in human form — which have been fashioned on that Communist island and fired at America."[24] However, Senator Eastland's dire warnings notwithstanding, not even Brigade infiltrators sent by U.S. authorities could testify that they had witnessed any Americans ever receiving military training in Cuba.[25]

The arduous process of getting to Cuba, amplified by these roadblocks and condemnations, reinforced the Brigadistas' sense of besieged adventure. Long, cramped boat rides from Canada and Mexico provided the uncomfortably intimate conditions for gay liberation politics to collide with New Left homophobia. Circumventing the U.S. government ban on direct travel to Cuba, Third Wave passengers sailing from Saint John to Havana in August 1970 set up various caucuses on the boat — a women's caucus, a Chicano caucus, a third world women's caucus, and so on. The GLF activists organized one as well, drawing a stream of queries from their shipmates, ranging in tone from curious to hostile: "What is the material basis of your oppression?" "Do you relate to Third World struggles? Can you?" The GLFers handed out copies of *Come Out!* and Carl Wittman's "A Gay Manifesto" to interested comrades.

Like many of their New Left comrades stateside, some heterosexual men sailing to Cuba bandied about homophobic slurs to denigrate the targets of scorn and derision. When one referred to Richard Nixon as a "faggot," Earl Galvin reminded them that Nixon was in fact heterosexual. Galvin found himself the target of abuse from several black Brigadistas, some of who cited Stalinist anti-gay doctrine, while others made sweeping generalizations about "fags." Clint

Pyne, who was friends with gay liberation activists in Chapel Hill though not yet identifying himself as gay or bisexual, was astonished by the vitriol directed at Galvin and the others. Three decades later, Pyne remembered thinking at the time, "What a colossally stupid waste of energy. I thought this was about revolution and economics . . . not about who cums what way." The reluctance of white heterosexual Brigadistas to challenge the chest-pounding posturing or the ideology of their African American comrades at this point exacerbated what appeared to be a conflict between white gay men and lesbians versus straight-identified African Americans and other third world activists.[26]

These tensions continued to mount after the Third Wave landed in Cuba. On this Brigade, Jesse Fallon, physically threatened on multiple occasions with violence by fellow norteamericanos on his work contingent, was told, "The most revolutionary thing I could do . . . was to confront my homosexuality and change it and become a man"; if he "was really proud of being a faggot [he] should stand up and punch this guy [provoking him] in the mouth."[27] Step May reported how one straight-identified African American man was harassed for attending gay liberation rap sessions. Fallon estimated that on his brigade there were at least six to eight gay and lesbian Brigadistas of color who would not come out publicly, as had the white GLFers, because of rhetoric from other third world movement representatives condemning homosexuality as a "white man's disease." For some men of color, Fallon argued, their antigay attitudes derived from their experiences with homosexuality in prison, where gay men ranked at the bottom of the social order. For others, their scorn for homosexuality was linked to their past hustling for bourgeois white johns; their slurs of Galvin and others as "faggots" spoke to their own marginalization within the colonial sexual economy of North America and the Caribbean.[28]

The Third Wave, which included the gay liberation activists Earl Galvin, Jesse Fallon, Richie Koob, Step May, Nancy Adair, and Clint Pyne (Adair and Pyne publicly identified as gay upon returning from Cuba), was beset with all sorts of conflicts and controversies. Even before this contingent set out for Cuba, and even after the negotiations following the Elgin Theater incident, the Brigade organizers' limited tolerance for gays quickly became apparent. Jim Fouratt, who helped organize GLFers to join the Third Wave, had expected to go to Cuba and help with the harvest himself. Stunned by his rejection, Fouratt was told that it was believed that his agenda in going to Cuba was to organize lesbians and gay men there, which was unacceptable to his revolutionary comrades. Fouratt fought back, pointing out that he did not speak Spanish and adding, with his cutting flair for the dramatic, "that it would be exceedingly difficult to organize Cuban gays on the basis of blow jobs alone." His colleagues were unswayed by his firm grasp on the challenges facing gay organizing in Cuba, however, and Fouratt remained stateside.[29]

The strife surrounding homosexuality mirrored the broader battle lines drawn along racial, ethnic, and gender lines on the Third Wave. Teresa Meade, a student activist from the University of Wisconsin, reported that in the Brigade camps, white gay men were physically attacked in their beds and their mosquito nets were sabotaged, allegedly by men from the Third World movements. These attacks angered the Cuban sponsors, despite their antipathy toward gay liberation. The gay men received support from some of their white heterosexual comrades, thus alienating some of the African Americans and Latinos on the Brigades. Black gay men in the camps, Meade later discovered, came up to the white gay men and told them, "Listen, you know—if we come out on this side for gays, we're dead, so we're not going to." The African American lesbians involved were upset by the attacks, Meade reported, but were rankled as well by what they perceived as a racist response to an already troubled situation. To further complicate issues, as Meade discovered, at least one of the black perpetrators of these attacks turned out to be an undercover FBI agent. J. Edgar Hoover's bureau deftly exploited the white New Left's tendency to romanticize third world peoples, "because nobody could cause problems more than an FBI plant who was a Third World person in that kind of environment," Meade later reflected.[30]

On all the Brigades, the challenging physical labor, the uncomfortable living conditions, and the political infighting all encouraged battles over a broad range of issues. Voyagers sailing to Cuba for the First Wave suffered the tight quarters of a cattle boat converted for human cargo. Margot Adler's work brigade lived in canvas tents with double-decker bunk beds in the hills of Aguacate, enduring temperature swings from the eighties during the daytime to near-freezing cold at night. The political climate proved equally volatile, as ideological tensions became particularly visible along the fault lines of race, ethnicity, and gender. Adler and Cagan both recalled the rebellion of Brigadista women who had been told they couldn't cut sugar cane—a labor best left to men, according to the Cuban men coordinating the zafra. Instead women were scheduled to stack the cut cane for mechanized pickup later. Some Brigadistas (both men and women) did not want to question the ways of their hosts, but others argued that American women and men should divide the tasks of cutting and piling—

suggestions that were slowly implemented, creating an increasingly egalitarian work environment.[31]

In what Carol Brightman described as the "intimate hard-pressed conditions in these tents," sex became a flash point around which many conflicts flared up. For the Brigadista bunking down alone after working in the fields from 5 a.m. to 11 a.m. and 3 p.m. to 7 p.m., the sounds of lovemaking echoing through the canvas tent flaps did little to foster solidarity beyond the couple in question. When Margot Adler and another friend raised this issue, several other women informed them that they "were not being good revolutionaries, that it was 'un-communist' to be possessive of one person, and that [they] should understand the need to 'smash monogamy.'" Adler also noticed how relationships took place between American men and women and between Cuban men and American women, but never involving Cuban women—an observation that recalls the patterns of, and tensions surrounding, interracial relationships in the Mississippi Freedom Summer. When Adler pointed out that Cuban women were not having sex either, she was told that that was because of their "different 'cultural situation.'" She also watched in dismay as Cuban men dismissed politically the American women they found most attractive. "One of the smartest and most educated of the women [who] could easily have posed for a *Playboy* centerfold [and] could outtalk me on Marxist theory any day of the week . . . couldn't get anyone to listen to her," Adler reported.[32]

While many Cubans and Americans wrestled with the place of gender in making revolutionary societies, some Brigadistas from the sectarian Left had all the answers they needed. An early Brigadista dismissed the importance of "anything that does not pertain to production" in his work brigade's meeting. One of his comrades in the same work contingent declared, "I don't consider Women's Lib and black nationalism to be part of a Communist revolution. . . . I did not come here with the intention of talking politics. I came to cut sugar cane." Other Brigadistas preferred to tackle the questions raised by women rather than wait for the revolution to solve sexism automatically. However, one work brigade's attempt to resolve clashes between men and women foundered when the men tried to divide the women into two camps: "Female Lib and real women." Racial solidarity took precedence over disputes between men and women for some blacks, Chicanos, and Puerto Ricans, both male and female, as some people of color argued that sexism was a concern for middle-class whites, but not for them.[33]

By the Third Wave, explosive disputes over ideological differences and mundane matters came as no surprise to either the Cubans or the American Brigade organizers. The third contingent arrived not long after Castro's July 26 speech acknowledging that the 1969 zafra had harvested only 8.5 million tons of sugar—a record yield, but still far below the expectations of a nation where virtually every able-bodied citizen had contributed his or her labor. Notwithstanding the popular slogan "Turn Setback into Victory," the psychological impact was compounded by the devastation of most other sectors of the Cuban economy resulting from the diversion of necessary resources to the sugar harvest.[34] Various factors contributed to doom the ambitious goal of ten million tons, including mechanical difficulties in the processing mills, broken Soviet combines ill-suited to the local terrain, and alternating torrential rains and droughts—the latter perhaps due to CIA-sponsored seeding of Cuban-bound rain clouds in an attempt to undermine the zafra.[35]

Arriving too late in the year to be of much use for the next zafra, the Third Wave Brigadistas were assigned to pick lemons and oranges and to plant and fertilize citrus trees on la Isla de los Pinos (the Isle of Pines), off the southern coast of western Cuba.[36] These fruits, like the sugar harvested by the first two waves, were destined primarily for kitchen tables in the Soviet Union, not Cuba. The Third Wave arrived at the Havana harbor to see locals dancing and singing on the docks; the warm welcome continued with friendly signs all along the road to the next boat that would take the Brigadistas to la Isla de los Pinos. However, any notions of revolutionary harmony evaporated swiftly. The Brigadistas from Denver and Boulder, shocked to discover their planned tropical vacation at the beach actually required demanding labor in the citrus harvest, returned early to Colorado. Teresa Meade's work group included seven African Americans from Minnesota, led by three men who declared the Black Panther leadership "too right wing." The other four black Brigadistas from the Twin Cities—two women and two boys—developed fine relationships working with white Brigadistas, straight and gay. However, out of the three male leaders, one or two were eventually sent home early for breaking into rum stores, pulling a knife on a Cuban man, and attempting to rape a Cuban woman—prompting suspicions among their fellow Brigadistas that they were in fact FBI infiltrators sent to stir up trouble. Evelyn Chatters testified to the U.S. House Committee on Internal Security that the Third Wave also endured "absenteeism from work, fights . . . a lot of petty stealing of underwear, pants, things like that . . . [and] one racial incident."[37]

Some norteamericanos drew strength from their contributions to an international revolution. From Camp "Heroic Viet Nam," near the town of "Free Algeria" where they picked fruit, Clint Pyne and another Tar Heel Brigadista wrote to *Carolina Plain Dealer* readers of spending a week working in the fields alongside Vietnamese and Laotians, and of the excitement surrounding Salvador Allende's election in Chile.[38] But despite the global perspective, local relations among the Americans proved anything but inspiring. Mirroring the New Left's internal battles over identity politics on the mainland, conflicts among Brigadistas multiplied to the point where, as Earl Galvin later wrote in *Come Out!* "it looked for a bit as though we were on the verge of a 6-way war. Blacks vs. Puerto Ricans, Chicanos vs. Whites, men vs. women."[39]

The attacks on GLFers won them sympathy, according to Galvin. He reported that during the first week in camp, the Brigadista in the next bed over would yell each night, "There's a faggot in my bed!" He also walked in on this same comrade telling another Brigadista that he needed some "homosexual repellent." But sometimes the antigay vitriol provoked critical reflection. The same man who called for "repellent" a few days later came over to Galvin, shook his hand, and told him that he was "starting to think about the whole thing." Within the painful intimacy of Venceremos Brigade tent camps, many heterosexual activists learned the intensity and virulence of the homophobia endemic to Western society—in this case, experiencing both the American and Cuban variants—and took their initial steps to incorporate homosexuality into the New Left vision for social transformation. Earl Galvin claimed how as he and his fellow gay liberationists garnered "the support of almost all of the white people (weak though it may be for many), GLF became sort of a 'white' issue," further exacerbating the racially charged movement culture.[40]

While tensions flared over race and gender, over ideology and nationality, and over the logistics of work as well as over homosexuality, *only* lesbians and gay men came to be excluded from the Venceremos Brigades. Cuban officials and American Brigade organizers made allowances for the other conflicts—but not those regarding homosexuality—as part of the challenges facing revolutionaries. Individual Cubans repeatedly expressed their solidarity with the American gay liberation movement: Earl Galvin reported how on the sea voyage to Havana, Cubans asked for GLF buttons that read "out of the closets and into the streets," and one even mimeographed and distributed copies of the letter Huey Newton had just published in the *Black Panther* declaring his support for gay liberation and the women's movement.[41]

Cuban authorities took a more ambiguous public stance toward the norteamericanos from GLF. The powers that be did not initially pass any formal judgment on the American movement, nor for the most part did they interfere directly with the activities of the GLFers working and touring the island. On the Second Wave, at least, Robbie Skeist reported how asking about local gay life did not ruffle Cuban officials, though his questions infuriated Brigade organizers.[42] But such patience withered during the Third Wave, as local authorities' fears of a possible challenge to political and sexual order *in Cuba* mounted. When GLFers organized a workshop for their comrades and their Cuban hosts, similar to those organized on American trade unionism and anti-imperialism by other Brigade caucuses, the local authorities made no attempt to interfere with Americans attending but barred Cubans in the camps from doing so. There was one exception, Clint Pyne later recalled: "Some [Cuban] with enough status to get away with attending," possibly a film director, did ultimately participate.[43]

Given the political capital provided by the Venceremos Brigades (as a U.S. organization openly undermining yanqui imperialism), Cuban authorities appeared generally reluctant to constrain the Brigadistas' activities, even those conducted by gay and lesbian participants. At the same time, the *remote* possibility that the GLF might inspire dissent on the island alarmed Cuban officials and U.S. Brigade organizers. This norteamericano movement, notwithstanding its calls for sexual freedom in the context of fundamental social and economic transformation, placed an inordinate priority on the pleasure of the individual over the welfare of the nation—at least as seen through official Cuban eyes. While socialist theory considered organized democratic activity necessary for bringing revolution to the capitalist world, such independent actions threatened the collective achievements of the new Cuba—at least according to this logic.

The roots of the National Committee of the Venceremos Brigades' decision to officially prohibit openly lesbian or gay participants from taking part lay in North American assumptions about "traditional" Cuban gender relations and their presumed inherent difference from those in the United States. Furthermore, the decision stemmed from Brigade leaders' refusal to criticize revolutionary Cuba's public campaign against homosexuality and their apologist acceptance of the policy as an expression of Cuban national culture and self-determination. But the revolution's 1965 establishment of the UMAP camps (Unidades Militaries para el Aumento de la Producción, or Military Units to Increase Production) to "rehabilitate" effeminate men and other dissidents neither reflected timeless Cuban machismo nor demonstrated a reflexive response to liberation from colonial domination. Though revolutionary policy certainly drew on a range of preexisting Cuban notions about homosexuality, it most immediately signaled the ascendancy of Soviet — namely, Stalinist — definitions of socialist morality that equated homosexuality with capitalist individualism, idleness, and medical pathology. The UMAP camps marked the establishment of *new* state apparatuses that, despite their precedents in medical, criminal, and religious institutions, aspired to new levels of systematic sexual surveillance.

Frequently, the process of consolidating a postrevolutionary social order has included proclamations of a new sexual morality as an integral component of claiming to create a wholly new society. Cuba proved no exception to this, as evidenced by post-1965 campaigns to forge a New Man (el hombre nuevo) — a concept borrowed from the Russian Revolution and reinvigorated by Che Guevara. Cuba's hombre nuevo was to be endowed with a new *conciencia*, or consciousness, free from the vestiges of decadent bourgeois values. Similar to his Soviet predecessor, the Cuban New Man found inspiration in collective welfare and national achievement rather than individual success. Work provided the foundation of new moral consciousness: as Louis Pérez explains, "the development of the *hombre nuevo* [and] economic growth were proclaimed to be one and the same process."[44]

The New Man was also explicitly masculine and virile. Yet whereas Soviet notions of virility had been tied more explicitly to the promotion of procreative revolutionary families, the hombre nuevo's first love was more clearly the Cuban Revolution itself. Though the New Man was necessarily heterosexual, he was not automatically married with children. Indeed, neither Castro nor Guevara was ever primarily celebrated as a revolutionary father or husband; instead they were glorified as permanent soldiers. This glorified the fraternal bonds among men and evinced an eroticism that both fueled revolutionary zeal and posed the danger of queer perversion. Yet according to the long-standing logic within Cuban culture (and more generally throughout Latin America and other parts of the world) that only the *passive* (receiving) member of a male-male sexual encounter was homosexual, the New Man's very *active* position in all public activities reassured his sexual normalcy — regardless of the actual nature of his private life.[45]

Not surprisingly, the formal persecution of homosexuals focused disproportionately on men charged with visible effeminacy; correspondingly, men accused of lacking proper revolutionary commitment were labeled *maricones*, a term that simultaneously meant "faggot" and "coward."[46] As such, it was precisely the New Man's fundamentally *masculine* meaning that overwhelmingly made men rather than women the targets of antihomosexual policy. Despite the revolution's dedication to women's emancipation, women were in fact *not* centrally figured by the concept of the hombre nuevo. This ideology, layered atop the enduring belief (shared by revolutionaries and nonrevolutionaries alike) that female sexuality and virtue more generally derived solely from their relationships to men, made it difficult to conceive of lesbianism as an issue, let alone a counterrevolutionary threat.

Given Cuba's historic subjugation and resistance to U.S. colonialism, the revolutionary embrace of Soviet definitions of gender, sexuality, and labor was important to emphatically rejecting the Batista-era exploitation, when the island was treated as an erotic playground for norteamericanos. Yet at the same time, revolutionary policy actually reinvigorated and hardened notions of "the homosexual" that were themselves the products of capitalism and imperialism, especially the late-nineteenth-century U.S. and European scientific discourses of normative civilization.[47] But Stalinist faith in the state's ability to reshape the individual, plus its puritanical conflation of heterosexual morality and hard work on behalf of revolutionary society, meshed well with both Cuba's dramatic Cold War realignment and the masculine ethos of the Cuban Revolution itself. As Castro declared—in a manner no doubt unintentionally recalling the virile hero of San Juan Hill, Teddy Roosevelt—the new Cuba needed "strong men to fight wars, sportsmen, men who had no psychological weakness."[48]

The revolution's explicit targeting of homosexuals coincided exactly with Cuba's formal adoption of Marxism-Leninism in 1961 and the nation's realignment with Moscow. In the first two years of the revolution, many bars catering to a homosexual clientele remained open. But following the 1961 merger of the Twenty-sixth of July Movement with the Cuban Communist Party, and the overwhelming victory at the Bay of Pigs, the Havana police launched Operation Three P's, targeting "pederasts, prostitutes, and pimps" in the Colón district. Ensuing arrests, dismissals, and repression of artists and independent publications reinforced the equation of political nonconformity with gender and sexual dissent in public. Through the next few years, police sweeps combed the island's beaches for sexual deviants, while the Lacra Social police units patrolled the streets, harassing and arresting the "social blights," including beatniks, marijuana smokers, and other youthful offenders. Prime targets for the Lacra Social included *las locas* (literally, the crazy ones), the queens whose effeminate characteristics and defiant, outlandish style made them easily identifiable as nonconformists; police interpreted wearing hair long, tight pants, or beards as evidence of homosexuality.[49]

While countless Cubans enthusiastically devoted their labor to building a new society in the spirit of what Ian Lumsden terms "revolutionary volunteerism," their efforts were augmented by the toil of thousands incarcerated in the UMAP camps for various crimes of "delinquency."[50] According to José Yglesias, the UMAPs "were begun to take care of young men of military age whose incorporation into the Army for military training was considered unfeasible. Young men known to avoid work and study were candidates; so were known counter-revolutionaries; and also immoralists, a category that included homosexuals."[51] Those consigned to the harsh conditions of the forced labor camps in the province of Camagüey included many thousands of youths with long hair and flashy clothing, overly independent authors, Jehovah's Witnesses and Seventh-Day Adventists, and effeminate gay men.[52] The UMAP camps took as a slogan Lenin's promise: "Work Will Make You Men."[53]

In a 1965 interview with the American journalist Lee Lockwood, Fidel Castro explained that while "that problem [of homosexuality] has not been sufficiently studied," his government considered it its "duty to take at least minimum measures to the effect that those positions in which one might have a direct influence upon children and young people should not be in the hands of homosexuals, above all in educational centers." Like many of his norteamericano neighbors, Castro's distaste for homosexuality reflected the belief that youth—the future and the focus of the revolution—were particularly susceptible prey for gay men. Ultimately he concluded that the leadership "would never come to believe that a homosexual could embody the conditions and requirements of conduct that would enable us to consider him a true Revolutionary, a true Communist militant. A deviation of that nature clashes with the concept we have of what a militant Communist must be." While lesbians remained invisible to Castro, gay men would be rehabilitated when possible, and above all, youth needed protection from influences that would undermine their "spirit of discipline."[54]

In the UMAPs, the homosexual prisoners received disproportionate abuse from hostile guards and, along with thousands of heterosexual fellow prisoners, endured daily political indoctrination seminars, grueling labor under the blazing sun, corporal punishment, and torture. The miserable living conditions and the verbal and physical abuses drove some inmates to suicide and fostered an enduring climate of terror. By 1968 the UMAPs were closed because of pressure from Castro's Mexican and European allies, along with outraged complaints from the Cuban Union of Writers and Artists. Even so, rumors of the existence of similar forced-labor camps for gay men persisted at least through the Third Wave, and the climate of fear remained deeply entrenched for years to come. Charges of homosexuality were used to purge Cuba's universities, the arts, and the writers' unions. Authorities shut down the Teatro Estudio because so many of its members were gay. Painters were purged from the Cubanacán art school solely on account of their homosexuality, and faculty were dismissed and students expelled from the University of Havana for the same reason. Gay writers, perhaps most famously Reinaldo Arenas, were censored, harassed, and imprisoned for their refusal to obey artistic dictates from above; from the vantage point of the state, sexual and political dissidence became inseparable.[55]

These stories quickly became familiar to Allen Young and the GLFers on the Venceremos Brigades. One Cuban lesbian working for the Ministry of the Interior overcame her fear of public disclosure long enough to discuss with Young her private opposition to the crackdown against las locas and her concern for her own situation.[56] A cultural official whom Young picked up, who served his militia duty religiously and donated his extra time and energy to farm work to support the revolution, believed that the state's antigay hostility would recede over time. Young met with numerous veterans of the anti-Batista movement who, although the Party denied them membership on account of their homosexuality, continued to support their government and volunteer with the zafra or the militia.[57]

For Young, a former student of C. Wright Mills, who came to terms with his same-sex desires in Rio de Janeiro and at one point acknowledged that "being back in the tropics made [him] unabashedly horny," these encounters devastated his romantic vision of Latin America.[58] Young had spent the better part of the decade studying Spanish and Portuguese and traveling extensively south of the Rio Grande. "It didn't take long for me to feel a deep love, an emotional as well as intellectual commitment, to the people of Cuba and the rest of Latin America," he wrote, and the inspiring accomplishments of the revolution contrasted starkly with the widespread misery he found elsewhere in the region.[59]

Over the course of his 1969 and 1971 trips to Cuba, Young related years later, "I discovered (not in a well-lit moment, but gradually, with thought) that the revolution I loved so dearly was built on lies, repression and tyranny." Young grew deeply skeptical of the revolution's proclaimed accomplishments in literacy and its uneven distribution of resources and came to loathe its ever-intrusive neighborhood watchdogs, the Committees for the Defense of the Revolution. The journalist found the lack of an independent press further evidence of the limits of freedom in Cuba.[60] The regime's unwillingness to concede that challenges posed by feminists and black nationalists in North America might apply to the Cuban context—indeed, its insistence that it had solved or was solving all problems related to racism and sexism—also frustrated Young.[61] In the end, he recalled in an interview, "I had reached the conclusion that Castro was a tyrant who persecuted gay men and lesbians, and who was essentially no different than Stalin or Mao or Ceausescu."[62] For someone so emotionally invested in Cuban politics, Young's realizations amounted to nothing less than a mortal blow to his search for beloved community. Like many heterosexual New Leftists who romanticized parts south, reality could not hope to match fantasy, and his passionate affair with Latin America grew steadily stormier.

Young's break with Cuba came slowly. In the spring of 1970, he took part in a forum with returned Second Wave Brigadistas at a GLF meeting in New York. Other participants included three recently returned Brigadistas who tried to sell the GLF on the accomplishments of the Cuban Revolution. "One [speaker] said he was gay; the others hid behind the label 'bisexual,'" snapped Martha Shelley in her denunciation of their position and Cuba's antigay policies published in the *Liberated Guardian* and distributed by Liberation News Service. Shelley's closing salvo took aim at the Cuban government and heterosexual New Leftists unwilling to condemn homophobia: "You are all the same to us, black, white, communist, capitalist, radical, liberal—you who are convinced that you are intrinsically healthier or better than gays. 'Marxist,' schmarxist— get off our backs!"[63] Responses ran in gay newspapers across the country debating the merits of Shelley's argument and how gay liberation should position itself toward Cuba. Meanwhile Allen Young, long ago swaddled in red diapers, chafed at Shelley's closing line at first but eventually came to agree.[64]

From that contentious spring onward, the battle lines between gay progressives and Cuba's defenders hardened steadily, as reports of the Gay Pride Week incident, the traumas experienced by the Third Wave GLF Brigadistas, and the Cuban policies appeared regularly in North American underground and gay newspapers. Contingents of Brigadistas continued to set sail for Cuba, and in April 1971, halfway through the Fourth Wave's two-month visit, the First National Congress on Education and Culture reiterated, to great fanfare, the unequivocal position of the state. The congress passed a declaration that left no doubt of the primacy placed by the Communist Party on the collective welfare over individual sexual freedom. It affirmed "the social pathological character of homosexual deviations [and] resolved that all manifestations of homosexual deviations are to be firmly rejected and prevented from spreading." Individuals attempting to "corrupt the morals of minors, depraved repeat offenders and irredeemable anti-social elements" faced severe penalties for their transgressions. The Congress rebuked "false intellectuals" who claimed "homosexuality and other social aberrations [as] expressions of revolutionary spirit and art, isolated from the masses and the spirit of the Revolution." Extensive sex education, purged of any homosexual instructors, would ensure the welfare of Cuban youth.[65]

The policies of the Cuban government notwithstanding, to date no conclusive evidence has surfaced that the decision to exclude lesbians and gay men from any of the Brigades originated in Havana. In fact, the Cuban liaisons to the Brigades had asked Robbie Skeist to help organize the Fourth Wave, despite the *American* organizers' distaste for Skeist's refusal to follow "the party line." Meanwhile, one regional committee rejected his friend Joel Hall, who at first seemed an ideal candidate for the Brigades—an African American from the ghettos of Chicago experienced with the Black Panthers and antiwar organizing. But the regional committee told Hall—a GLF Chicago leader and cofounder of Third World Gay Revolution—that "he wasn't political enough." Skeist argued, "The American group that was doing it was extremely antigay, and their own antigay attitudes were reinforced in the official Cuban policy."[66]

While tales of the harassment endured by GLFers while cutting cane and harvesting fruit surely led many New Leftists to question their support for Cuba, the gay liberation activists committed their most grievous offense, in the eyes of the National Committee of the Venceremos Brigade, by drawing attention to the limits of the revolution. Their accounts made explicit the Cuban government's distaste for dissent, from fashion and gender behavior to control over the media. After Liberation News Service distributed articles sympathetic to gay liberation and critical of Cuba and the Brigade organizers, it was barred from taking part in a Havana conference on radical journalism in January 1972.[67]

In the process of meeting Cuban lesbians and gay men, reporting how Castro's government institutionalized homophobia, and demonstrating that there was no place for Cuban lesbians and gay men in the socialist society, the GLF Brigadistas practiced their own form of foreign policy akin to that conducted by all Brigadistas traveling to Cuba. Allen Ginsberg, in a September 1972 interview with Allen Young for *Gay Sunshine*, remarked that this was "one of the most useful things that gay lib did on an international scale."[68] Indeed, such GLF actions challenged what remained of the New Left with the conviction that individual sexual freedom and personal dignity could not be sacrificed on the altar of material progress on either side of the Straits of Florida.

In what amounted to a rejection of gay liberation in both Cuba and the United States, the National Committee of the Venceremos Brigade issued its new recruitment policy barring participation by self-avowed lesbians and gay men in January 1972. The explanatory statement denied any "material basis for the oppression of homosexuals" and disavowed the existence of work camps. The National Committee accused the gay Brigadistas of showing "a greater interest in finding out about Cuban homosexuals than Cuban culture." Citing the long history of U.S. interference and Cuban resistance, the National Committee also charged GLFers with "imposing North American gay culture on the Cubans."[69]

The gay liberationists had allegedly attempted to reeducate Cubans, "assuming that the situation in Cuba must be the same as in the U.S.," the policy statement continued. Examples of imposing gay culture included "parading in drag in a Cuban town" and "acting in an overtly sexual manner at parties." Ultimately the gay Brigadistas were found guilty of "a lack of understanding of [their position] as guests of the Cuban Revolution" and of joining "a cultural imperialist offensive against the Cuban Revolution, carried out by U.S. imperialism in an attempt to discredit the Revolution and alienate North Americans from it." The statement interpreted criticism of state policy as failure "to affirm the Cuban peoples' right to self-determination." Defining the Cuban people to exclude anyone engaging in same-sex relations, the committee concluded that "only the Cuban people have all of the essential elements to analyze and solve their problems correctly." Hereafter only "gay North Americans [with] a clear understanding of revolutionary anti-imperialist priorities" — that is, those who would not criticize Cuban policies and would stay closeted while visiting the island — remained welcome on the Venceremos Brigades.[70]

By advocating Cuban "self-determination," U.S. Brigade organizers absolved themselves from questioning their own antigay assumptions, engaging any critiques of the revolution, or even recognizing alternate systems of organizing sexual desire and gender norms. Steadfast in their ideological certitude, they did not comprehend how their defense of the Cuban state's antigay policies reinscribed colonial notions of tropical sexualities. Even for the Brigadista leadership, Cuba assumed the position described by the literary critic Anne McClintock in her analysis of sexuality and European imperialism: the "porno-tropics for the European [including Soviet Russian and, by extension, North American] imagination—a fantastic magic lantern of the mind onto which Europe projected its forbidden sexual desires and fears."[71]

This, then, is the agonizing irony that befell the gay and lesbian Brigadistas: the homophobia they encountered in trying to support Castro's revolution, homophobia that the Brigade organizers justified as a defense against further North American cultural imperialism, recommitted the remnants of the New Left to the sexual ideology of empire. In the long run, the exclusionary policies and the subsequent controversies not only deprived the Venceremos Brigades of many experienced and devoted activists, but also produced a split between supporters of the revolution on the one hand, and gay and feminist critics on the other, that over time alienated more and more North American progressives from the Cuban cause.

Yet even as gay liberation activists condemned state homophobia in Cuba, they did so within a framework not unlike that of their straight comrades from the United States. Discussions of the oppression of gays in Cuba, couched in the day's language of personal and political liberation, took for granted the existence of such a clearly defined category of persons. Most GLF criticism grew out of encounters with Cuban gay and lesbian administrators and artists, individuals whose social roles and self-definitions most closely resembled the GLFers' own North American identities and whose work tied them most firmly to international political, cultural, and economic networks. In the 1970s, relatively few Cubans understood homosexuals as a discrete category of persons, instead drawing the line between normal and queer in terms of public gender behavior and sexual acts. They saw no contradiction between friendly, supportive encounters with GLF Brigadistas doing the work of revolution and defending state policies designed to rid las locas of pathological behaviors and reform them into productive men. This analysis is not offered to mitigate the GLF condemnations of Cuban abuses, or to uphold the National Committee's charge of "imposing North American gay culture on the Cubans," but instead to point out how gay liberation activists were as deeply implicated in their North American perspectives as their counterparts on the National Committee.

Throughout the rest of the 1970s, Venceremos Brigade recruiters continued to interpret the proclamations of the 1971 National Congress as a mandate to exclude gay men and lesbians. In 1974 the Philadelphia regional committee rejected Jim Green, an organizer for the local Chile Solidarity Committee, from the Seventh Wave for purportedly not knowing "how to work with Third World people" — despite the future Brazilian historian's established record of solidarity organizing with Latin Americans.[72] Green's cousin, then a member of the Venceremos Brigades National Committee, later admitted to him that homophobia had motivated the rejection. Similarly, western Massachusetts organizers cited bureaucratic technicalities to deny Leslie Cagan a spot on the Tenth Brigade contingent later in the 1970s.[73] In Berkeley, a Brigade organizers committee rejected the veteran organizer Amber Hollibaugh twice, the second time after a 1978 controversy over the singer Holly Near's scheduled appearance at the Eleventh World Festival of Youth and Students. The women's music icon's lesbianism made Near unpalatable to the CPUSA-led festival organizers, and her invitation to Cuba was rescinded, making Hollibaugh's own participation in the Brigades problematic. As Hollibaugh later recalled, "It was really a 'don't ask don't tell.' If you're prepared to shut up, we're prepared to not *remember* that you're a homosexual. But if you're asked, and you tell, you can't go. You just have to say nothing." Hollibaugh was not prepared to lie and never participated in the Venceremos Brigades.[74]

Despite these exclusions, the lessons learned by returned lesbian and gay Brigadistas informed and inspired their organizing efforts in various progressive movements for many years to come. Many Brigade veterans, including Cagan, spent many more years organizing in support of Cuba and other Latin American liberation movements throughout Latin America. Notwithstanding the antigay limits of both the U.S. New Left and the Cuban state, the island's revolution offered what Cagan deemed incontrovertible proof to a most quintessentially American notion, that "not just in my head but in my heart . . . people can actually change the course of history."[75] Like Cagan, many women returning from the cane fields and citrus groves threw themselves into feminist labor once they returned home. One member of Bread and Roses, an early socialist-feminist group in Boston, explained that the "only time [she] felt competent and confident was on [her] return from Cuba," while younger women involved with the group cited Brigadista veterans as their role models for female activism. Returned Brigadistas from the Second and Third Waves proved pivotal to creating a lesbian-feminist community in Atlanta, according to Saralyn Chesnut and Amanda Gable.[76]

While the Venceremos Brigades had originally sought to shore up SDS factionalism, one of their most important and unforeseeable legacies was the boost that returning Brigadistas gave to gay and lesbian activism.[77] This outcome was facilitated by the emergence of a national gay liberation movement made up heavily of veteran New Leftists more broadly. By the spring of 1970, communicating through personal networks, their own newspapers, and an increasingly gay-friendly underground press, gay liberation activists could articulate their own critique of Cuban state policy in a way not possible for the few isolated lesbian and gay male Brigadistas in the first two contingents. Over the course of the 1970s, the Venceremos Brigades forced heterosexual activists to directly address the challenge posed by gay liberation far more systematically than happened anywhere else in antiwar and anti-imperialist organizing on the mainland. First, no self-respecting stateside New Leftist would align himself or herself with antigay government authorities to justify his or her own prejudice; after all, "faggot" was one choice epithet flung at "the pigs," Nixon, and other representatives of "the Man." Second, the Brigades remained a coherent project covered nationally by the underground press during years when antiwar politics shifted sharply toward local organizing after SDS's demise.

Most importantly, the logistics of the Brigades differed dramatically from one-time marches, sit-ins, and other protest tactics where participants went home at the end of the day. The communes sprouting up all across the land came closest to replicating the personal and political intimacy of the Brigades but differed in their small household size and in their highly decentralized nature. Through the personal relationships generated over two months of discussions on never-ending bus and boats rides, living in the close quarters of tent bunks and work camps, and while out cutting sugar cane or picking fruit, many heterosexual Brigadistas did in fact reject their own homophobic assumptions. But as with the sectarian cadres at home, those critical thinkers did not set the tone or the policy for the Venceremos Brigades. Through the experiences of GLF Brigadistas in Cuba, the American gay liberation movement rebelled against the virulent homophobia of some of their comrades and, in doing so, confronted the enormous challenge of working for social change without sacrificing their personal integrity.

In 1981 Allen Young published his definitive comment on the Cuban issue. In *Gays under the Cuban Revolution*, he attacked the abuses of the Castro government and assailed "leftists, gay and straight, for grasping at anything to avoid forthright, angry condemnation of the persecution of gays in Cuba, and more generally, to avoid coming to grips with the left's historic role in reinforcing and creating antigay prejudice." He rebuked "leftists within the gay movement [who] have, more often than not, been toadies to their straight 'comrades.'"[78]

On the Venceremos Brigades, some New Leftists interpreted Cuban homophobia from their own American cultural and political framework and, by harassing and eventually excluding lesbians and gay men, applied that understanding to confirm their credentials as revolutionaries. Leslie Cagan and Clint Pyne, among others, found in the work of the Brigades the room to negotiate the traumatic contradiction between the promise of a better way to live, on one hand, and the antidemocratic means to that end that precluded reaching the beloved community, on the other. For Allen Young, his passions so inextricably intertwined with Cuba, personal and political heartbreaks proved too painful to settle for a severely imperfect revolution. He moved on, as ex-lovers do, finding comfort with new friends and new causes not bound by the rigidity of old comrades in arms.

Notes

Earlier versions of this essay were presented at the 1999 annual meeting of the American Studies Association, the Duke University History Department's Clioquium lecture series, and the 2005 Tepoztlán Institute for the Transnational Study of the Americas. Special thanks are due to Henry Abelove, Vincent Brown, William Chafe, Derek Chang, Jessica Delgado, Jay Driskell, Steve Estes, Greg Grandin, James N. Green, Ramón Gutiérrez, Lisa Hazirjian, Victor Macias González, Teresa Meade, Bethany Moreton, Horacio Roque Ramírez, Susan Thomas, Susan Thorne, Heidi Tinsman, Sharon Ullman, Pamela Voekel, and the anonymous referees for their helpful suggestions during the writing and revisions, and to Milo Pyne for all his active support of this study.

1   Sandra Levinson and Carol Brightman, eds., *Venceremos Brigades: Young Americans Sharing the Life and Work of Revolutionary Cuba* (New York: Simon and Schuster, 1971), 13–14; Kirkpatrick Sale, *SDS* (New York: Vintage Books, 1973), 517.

2   Jonathan Black, "A Happy Birthday for Gay Liberation," *Village Voice*, July 2, 1970, 2, 58. As recently as January 1970, the New York gay liberation newspaper *Come Out!* had published a pro-Cuba spread of photos and text excerpted from Elizabeth Sutherland's *The Youngest Revolution*. "Cuba: The Sexual Revolution, a Beginning," *Come Out!* January 10, 1970, n.p.

3   Allen Young, "The Cuban Revolution and Gay Liberation," in *Out of the Closets: Voices of Gay Liberation*, ed. Karla Jay and Allen Young (1972; New York: New York University Press, 1992), 206–28; interview with Allen Young, Athol, Mass., March 15, 1998. For details of the material developments under socialism in Cuba, see Marifeli Pérez-Stable, *The Cuban Revolution: Origins, Course, and Legacy*, 2nd ed. (New York: Oxford University Press, 1999), esp. chap. 4.

4   Allen Young, "Out of the Closet: A Gay Manifesto," *Ramparts*, November 1971, 57–58.

5   Young, "The Cuban Revolution and Gay Liberation," 216–17; interview with Leslie
     Cagan, New York, January 15, 1999; interview with Jim Fouratt, New York, Decem-
     ber 15, 1999; Allen Young, email to the author, November 15, 1999.

6   Thanks are due to Ramón Gutiérrez for his helpful comments regarding the discur-
     sive use of machismo. Ramón A. Gutiérrez, "Mexican Masculinities: A Diversity
     of Histories," unpublished paper in the possession of the author.

7   My analysis of the relationship between metropole and colony, especially regard-
     ing sex and race, draws on Anne McClintock, *Imperial Leather: Race, Gender, and
     Sexuality in the Colonial Conquest* (New York: Routledge, 1995); Sherry B. Ortner,
     "Borderland Politics and Erotics: Gender and Sexuality in Himalayan Mountain-
     eering," in *Making Gender: The Politics and Erotics of Culture* (Boston: Beacon
     Press, 1996), 181–212; Mrinalini Sinha, *Colonial Masculinity: The "Manly English-
     man" and the "Effeminate Bengali" in the Late Nineteenth Century* (New York: St.
     Martin's Press, 1995); Ann Laura Stoler, *Race and the Education of Desire: Fou-
     cault's History of Sexuality and the Colonial Order of Things* (Durham: Duke Uni-
     versity Press, 1995); and Susan Thorne, *Congregational Missions and the Making of
     an Imperial Culture in Nineteenth-Century England* (Stanford: Stanford University
     Press, 1999).

8   Louis A. Pérez Jr., *Cuba and the United States: Ties of Singular Intimacy*, 2nd ed.
     (Athens: University of Georgia Press, 1997), xviii–xix.

9   Van Gosse, *Where the Boys Are: Cuba, Cold War America, and the Making of a New
     Left* (New York: Verso, 1983).

10   Gosse, *Where the Boys Are*; Timothy B. Tyson, *Radio Free Dixie: Robert F. Williams
     and the Roots of Black Power* (Chapel Hill: University of North Carolina Press,
     1999). On race and the Cuban wars for independence, see Ada Ferrer, *Insurgent
     Cuba: Race, Nation, and Revolution, 1868–1898* (Chapel Hill: University of North
     Carolina Press, 1999). The Second War for Cuban Independence (1895–98), or the
     1898 Spanish-American War from the U.S. perspective, was preceded by the Ten
     Years' War (1868–78) and La Guerra Chiquita (1879–80), the Little War.

11   Gosse, *Where the Boys Are*, 46.

12   Michael Schumacher, *Dharma Lion: A Critical Biography of Allen Ginsberg* (New
     York: St. Martin's Press, 1992), 160; Allen Young, *Gays under the Cuban Revolution*
     (San Francisco: Grey Fox Press, 1981), 9–13. Also see Rosalie Schwartz, *Pleasure
     Island: Tourism and Temptation in Cuba* (Lincoln: University of Nebraska Press,
     1997). Todd Anders's report, reprinted in Young's volume, does not refer explicitly
     to "Superman's" race or color, though his language is consistent with the vast body
     of European and North American accounts attributing spectacular sexual powers
     to colonized peoples in the Americas, Africa, and Asia. "Superman" does make a
     brief appearance in Francis Ford Coppola's *The Godfather, Part II* (1979), where the
     Italian American protagonists watch in amazement as the Latino showman reveals
     his enormous endowment to a woman tied onstage to a stake.

13   Gosse, *Where the Boys Are*; Ian Lumsden, *Machos, Maricones, and Gays: Cuba and
     Homosexuality* (Philadelphia: Temple University Press, 1996).

14   Lee Lockwood, *Castro's Cuba, Cuba's Fidel* (1967; Boulder: Westview Press, 1990), 360; Louis A. Pérez Jr., *Cuba: Between Reform and Revolution*, 2nd ed. (New York: Oxford University Press, 1995), 339–40.

15   Levinson and Brightman, *Venceremos Brigades*, 13–14; Sale, *SDS*, 517.

16   Margot Adler, *Heretic's Heart: A Journey through Spirit and Revolution* (Boston: Beacon Press, 1997), 264; Levinson and Brightman, *Venceremos Brigades*, 14; Elizabeth [Sutherland] Martinez, "The Venceremos Brigade Still Means 'We Shall Overcome,'" *Z Magazine*, July–August 1999, 56–62.

17   Levinson and Brightman, *Venceremos Brigades*, 14.

18   "The Reminiscences of Carol Brightman," December 12, 1984, in the Collection of the Columbia University Oral History Research Office, 67. Interviewed by Ronald J. Grele. Hereafter cited as Brightman-Grele interview.

19   Interview with Milo Pyne, Durham, N.C., September 12, 1999. Born George Pyne Jr., Milo took the name Clint Pyne while in college, renamed himself Milo Guthrie in the 1970s, and legally renamed himself Milo Pyne in the early 1990s.

20   "Venceremos!" *Detroit Fifth Estate*, October 30, 1969, 24.

21   David Wheeler, "Cuba Sí!" *Detroit Fifth Estate*, April 16, 1970, 11.

22   "The Reminiscences of Robbie Skeist," December 8, 1984, in the Collection of the Columbia University Oral History Research Office, 57. Interviewed by Ronald J. Grele. Hereafter cited as Skeist-Grele interview.

23   Donn Teal, *The Gay Militants: How Gay Liberation Began in America, 1969–1971* (New York: Stein and Day, 1971), 200–203; "Ten Million," *Detroit Fifth Estate*, February 19, 1970, 17; "Eight Weeks in Cuba," recorded in February 1970 at radio station KPFA (Berkeley: Pacifica Tape Library, AP 1186, 1970). Testimony before the Committee on Internal Security of the U.S. House of Representatives in 1972 reports participation for the first five waves as follows: first contingent (November 28, 1969–February 12, 1970), 216 participants; second contingent (February 13–April 28, 1970), 687 participants; third contingent (August 25–October 29, 1970), 405 participants; fourth contingent (March 22–May 29, 1971), 221 participants; fifth contingent (March 6–May 4, 1972), 138 participants. Levinson and Brightman's 1971 anthology documenting the first two Brigades reports 409 participants on the Third Wave; its figures for the first two waves are consistent with those found in the House testimony. The source of the discrepancy is unknown, though the lists of participants printed in the House report are marked by omissions and misspellings. Another possibility includes the slippery use of "Americans" and "North Americans" in accounts of the Venceremos Brigades. There may have been a handful of Canadians on the Brigades; how often "North Americans" refers to residents of both the United States and Canada, and how often it is simply the English equivalent of the Spanish word *norteamericano*, which usually refers to U.S. residents, is unknown. Congress, House, Committee on Internal Security, *The Theory and Practice of Communism in 1972 (Venceremos Brigade)*, pt. 2, 92nd Cong., 2nd sess., October 16–19, 1972, 7825; Levinson and Brightman, *Venceremos Brigade*, 14–15.

24   "The Venceremos Brigade—Agrarians or Anarchists?" remarks by Senator

James O. Eastland, Mississippi, *Congressional Record–Senate*, March 16, 1970, 7462–67.

25   Committee on Internal Security, *The Theory and Practice of Communism in 1972 (Venceremos Brigade)*, especially 7949. According to the testimony before the House Committee on Internal Security, Deputy Sheriff Dwight Crews infiltrated the Venceremos Brigades, as well as the New Orleans Peace Action Center and Vietnam Veterans against the War, not through any federal agency but on a mission originating from the Jefferson Parish Sheriff's Office.

26   "On the Venceremos Brigade: A Forum," in Jay and Young, *Out of the Closets*, 228–44; "Third Contingent of Venceremos Brigade Given Enthusiastic Welcome," *Granma* (English ed.), September 6, 1970, 1; interview with Milo Pyne, September 12, 1999.

27   "On the Venceremos Brigade," 235.

28   Ibid., 235–37.

29   Martin Duberman, *Stonewall* (New York: Dutton, 1993), 240; interview with Jim Fouratt, December 15, 1999.

30   "The Reminiscences of Teresa Meade," April 13, 1984, in the Collection of the Columbia University Oral History Research Office, 76–82. Interviewed by Ronald J. Grele. Hereafter cited as Meade-Grele interview.

31   Adler, *Heretic's Heart*, 265–66; interview with Leslie Cagan, January 15, 1999.

32   Adler, *Heretic's Heart*, 272–74; Teal, *The Gay Militants*, 202; Brightman-Grele interview, 65.

33   Levinson and Brightman, *Venceremos Brigades*, chaps. 3–6; the quotes are from pp. 174 and 260–61, respectively.

34   Educational Commission, Venceremos Brigades, "The Venceremos Brigade 1974: Four Years Building Solidarity with Cuba," Pamphlet 9706, Labadie Collection, University of Michigan Special Collections Library, 5.

35   Pérez, *Cuba*, 339–42, 348; Lockwood, *Castro's Cuba, Cuba's Fidel*, 360–61.

36   La Isla de los Pinos was renamed La Isla de la Juventud (the Isle of Youth) in 1978.

37   Committee on Internal Security, *The Theory and Practice of Communism in 1972 (Venceremos Brigade)*, 7928; Meade-Grele interview, 79–83; email, Teresa Meade to the author, January 13, 2003. Evelyn Maddox was an African American student at the City College of New York when she and her then fiancé Edward Chatters participated in the Third Wave in 1970. Mr. Chatters was an activist in New Orleans involved with the Black Legionnaires and the Republic of New Africa. In her interview with the House Committee staff, Mrs. Chatters estimated the gender demographics of the Third Wave at "60/40 in favor of women" and the age range at "16 to 45, with most people being mostly from 20 to 30." Whites comprised a plurality of the participants, followed by Latinos (primarily Chicanos and Puerto Ricans), African Americans, Asian Americans, and Native Americans (7921). When asked if there were "any other groups that were not of ethnic label," she inquired back, "Are you referring to the gay?" and then confirmed, "There were some gay people; yes. That's the only other one" (7916).

38   Dos Brigadistas de N.C., "Cuba: Venceremos; Revolutionary Greetings from Cuba," *Carolina Plain Dealer* 1, no. 7 (January 1971): 4. Milo Pyne confirmed he co-authored this article; email to the author, September 14, 1999.

39   Teal, *The Gay Militants*, 202.

40   Ibid.

41   "On the Venceremos Brigade," 234; on Newton's August 21, 1970, "A Letter from Huey to the Revolutionary Brothers and Sisters about the Women's Liberation and Gay Liberation Movements," see Teal, *The Gay Militants*, 151–53.

42   Skeist-Grele interview, 60.

43   Young, *Gays under the Cuban Revolution*, 31; "On the Venceremos Brigade," 242; interview with Milo Pyne, September 12, 1999.

44   Pérez, *Cuba*, 340. On Guevara and the New Man in Cuba, see Ernesto Che Guevara, "Socialism and Man" (New York: Young Socialist Alliance, 1968). On the Soviet New Man, see Karen Petrone, *Life Has Become More Joyous, Comrades: Celebrations in the Time of Stalin* (Bloomington: Indiana University Press, 2000).

45   Lumsden, *Machos, Maricones, and Gays*, 30. Almost every work on sex between men in Latin America addresses this distinction, as do various works in American queer studies. See, for example, Tomás Almaguer, "Chicano Men: A Cartography of Homosexual Identity and Behavior," *differences: A Journal of Feminist Cultural Studies* 3, no. 2 (1991): 75–100; Joseph Carrier, *De Los Otros: Intimacy and Homosexuality Among Mexican Men* (New York: Columbia University Press, 1995); George Chauncey, "Christian Brotherhood or Sexual Perversion? Homosexual Identities and the Construction of Sexual Boundaries in the World War One Era," *Journal of Social History* 19 (1985): 189–211; George Chauncey, *Gay New York: Gender, Urban Culture, and the Making of the Gay Male World, 1890–1940* (New York: Basic Books, 1994); Cathy J. Cohen, *The Boundaries of Blackness: AIDS and the Breakdown of Black Politics* (Chicago: University of Chicago Press, 1999); James N. Green, *Beyond Carnival: Male Homosexuality in Twentieth-Century Brazil* (Chicago: University of Chicago Press, 1999); and Roger N. Lancaster, *Life Is Hard: Machismo, Danger, and the Intimacy of Power in Nicaragua* (Berkeley: University of California Press, 1992), esp. chap. 18.

46   See Reinaldo Arenas, *Before Night Falls*, trans. Dolores M. Koch (New York: Viking, 1993), for a discussion of the lexicon of homosexual practice and a vehement denunciation of Fidel Castro's government.

47   For further details of Stalin's recriminalization of sodomy in 1934, see Ian Lekus, "Queer and Present Dangers: Homosexuality and American Antiwar Activism during the Vietnam Era" (Ph.D. diss., Duke University, 2003); and Igor S. Kon, *The Sexual Revolution in Russia: From the Age of the Czars to Today*, trans. James Riordan (New York: Free Press, 1995), 70–74.

48   Lumsden, *Machos, Maricones, and Gays*, 60. For more on masculinity and the war of 1898, see Kristin L. Hoganson, *Fighting for American Manhood: How Gender Politics Provoked the Spanish-American and Philippine-American Wars* (New Haven: Yale University Press, 1998).

49   Lumsden, *Machos, Maricones, and Gays*, 58–59.

50   Ibid., 68.

51   José Yglesias, *In the Fist of the Revolution: Life in a Cuban Country Town* (New York: Pantheon Books, 1968), 275.

52   Arenas, *Before Night Falls*; Lumsden, *Machos, Maricones, and Gays*, chap. 3; Yglesias, *In the Fist of the Revolution*, esp. chap. 10; Young, *Gays under the Cuban Revolution*, chaps. 1–2; Néstor Almendros and Orlando Jimenez-Leal, *Mauvaise Conduite* [Improper Conduct], New Video, 1984.

53   Paul Julian Smith, "Cuban Homosexualities: On the Beach with Néstor Almendros and Reinaldo Arenas," in *Hispanisms and Homosexualities*, ed. Sylvia Molloy and Robert Irwin (Durham: Duke University Press, 1998), 251.

54   Lockwood, *Castro's Cuba, Cuba's Fidel*, 107. On youth and the Cuban Revolution, see Sutherland, *The Youngest Revolution*.

55   Arenas, *Before Night Falls*, 69–70; Lumsden, *Machos, Maricones, and Gays*, 65–76; Pérez, *Cuba*, 349; B. Ruby Rich, "Bay of Pix," *American Film*, July–August 1984, 57. Arenas claims the existence of the UMAPs as early as 1963, charges not corroborated by other accounts. Cuba scholars agree that the camps began in 1965, but disagree about whether they were terminated in 1967 (Pérez) or 1968 (Lumsden).

56   Young, *Gays under the Cuban Revolution*, 72.

57   Young, "The Cuban Revolution and Gay Liberation," 220–22.

58   Young, *Gays under the Cuban Revolution*, 71.

59   Young, "The Cuban Revolution and Gay Liberation," 207.

60   Allen Young, "Red Diaper Baby: From a Jewish Chicken Farm in the Catskills, to the Cane Fields of Cuba, to the First Gay Protests in New York City," *Vietnam Generation* 7, nos. 1/2 (1996): 29–30.

61   Young, *Gays under the Cuban Revolution*, 73.

62   Interview with Allen Young, March 15, 1998.

63   Martha Shelley and Guy Nassburg, "Homosexuals in Cuba: An Exchange from Gay Liberation," *Detroit Liberator*, August 1970, 5–6.

64   Shelley and Nassburg, "Homosexuals in Cuba"; "Gays in Cuba: A Detroit Socialist Responds," *Detroit Gay Liberator*, September 1970, 4–5; KW [Konstantin Berlant], "The Flaming Faggots," *Detroit Gay Liberator*, September 1970, 8–9; Young, "The Cuban Revolution and Gay Liberation," 216.

65   "Cuba Sí? Gayness and the Cuban Revolution," *Fag Rag* 1 (June 1971): 12. The full text of the declaration of the First Congress on Education and Culture can be found in English in the *Granma Weekly Review*, May 9, 1971, 1–6 (the proclamations regarding homosexuality are published on p. 5).

66   Skeist-Grele interview, 61, 72.

67   Editorial footnote to "Out! Out! Damn Faggot!" *Great Speckled Bird*, August 7, 1972, 8. See, for example, the anonymous letter, the LNS article explaining the controversy, and the sharp exchange of letters originally printed in *RAT* that ran in *Fag Rag* 2 (fall 1971): 16.

68   Allen Ginsberg with Allen Young, *Gay Sunshine Interview* (Bolinas, Calif.: Grey Fox Press, 1974), 27.

69 "Venceremos Brigade Policy on Gay Recruitment," published in Young, *Gays under the Cuban Revolution*, 98–100.

70 Ibid.

71 McClintock, *Imperial Leather*, 22.

72 James N. Green, "Feathers and Fists: Socialists and the Brazilian Gay Liberation Movement in the 1970s," unpublished essay in the possession of the author; letter to the author, September 15, 1999.

73 Interview with Leslie Cagan, January 15, 1999.

74 Interview with Amber Hollibaugh, New York, December 21, 1999. On the incident involving the youth festival, see Holly Near with Derk Richardson, *Fire in the Rain... Singer in the Storm: An Autobiography* (New York: William Morrow, 1990), 155–56; and Young, *Gays under the Cuban Revolution*, 84.

75 Interview with Leslie Cagan, January 15, 1999.

76 Interview with Leslie Cagan, January 15, 1999; Saralyn Chesnut and Amanda C. Gable, " 'Women Ran It': Charis Books and More and Atlanta's Lesbian-Feminist Community, 1971–1981," in *Carryin' On in the Lesbian and Gay South*, ed. John Howard (New York: New York University Press, 1997), 253; Ann Hunter Popkin, "Bread and Roses: An Early Moment in the Development of Socialist-Feminism" (Ph.D. diss., Brandeis University, 1978), 35–36, 146.

77 Committee on Internal Security, *The Theory and Practice of Communism in 1972 (Venceremos Brigade)*, 7824–25.

78 Young, *Gays under the Cuban Revolution*, 86–87.

Dislocations of Cold War Cultures

Exile, Transnationalism, and the Politics of Form

Rebecca M. Schreiber

> We visited the museums and had just a wonderful year—the best year of
> my life. . . . The year there [in Mexico] strengthened me in more ways than
> one—not only artistically, but morally and intellectually—so that when I
> came back to Chicago I was in a fighting mood, and I decided to fight the
> reactionaries who were trying to run me out of my job as a teacher in the
> Chicago public schools.
>
> —Margaret Taylor Goss Burroughs, interview with Anna M. Tyler,
> November 11 and December 5, 1988

The onset of the Cold War precipitated a distinct and extensive formation of
political exile, made up of U.S. writers, artists, and filmmakers who left the
United States during the 1940s and 1950s for political reasons. Although many
of these individuals relocated to Western Europe, including England, France,
and Italy, among the most crucial and least studied of this exodus were the communities that developed in Mexico. The communities of U.S. artists, writers,
and filmmakers in Mexico developed in stages. The first to arrive were a group
of Spanish Civil War veterans, including writers and musicians, who were welcomed by the liberal administration of Lázaro Cárdenas (1934–40) in the late
1930s and early 1940s. They were joined by visual artists, many of whom were
African American, who went to Mexico City to study art or to work alongside
Mexican artists at the Taller de Gráfica Popular (Popular Arts Workshop), a
graphic arts collective, in the late 1940s and early 1950s. The largest group of
Cold War cultural exiles, those blacklisted from the Hollywood film industry,
started migrating to Mexico City and Cuernavaca during the early 1950s. Following the filmmakers were writers, poets, editors, and agents who had been
blacklisted from the publishing industry.

This essay focuses on the work of African American artists in Mexico including Elizabeth Catlett, John Wilson, and Margaret Taylor Goss Burroughs. For these artists, the Mexican context of production, collaborations with Mexican artists (as well as with political exiles from Spain and Germany), and the address of their work to a local, Mexican audience significantly influenced their cultural production both thematically and aesthetically. In particular, the work of Elizabeth Catlett and John Wilson demonstrates how African American artists who relocated to Mexico during the Cold War chose to depict the experiences of African Americans in the United States through Mexican-derived cultural forms, techniques, and modes of production. Within this political context, the work of Elizabeth Catlett in particular provides an example of transnational artistic production that was in opposition to dominant U.S. art production (especially the work selected by the U.S. State Department for promotion internationally). While both of these artists interpreted the experiences of African Americans in the United States through Mexican-derived cultural forms, they drew on different sources for inspiration in the artwork that they produced in Mexico. Catlett's collaborations with artist members of the Taller de Gráfica Popular (TGP) changed both the form and content of her work. Specifically, her work was substantially transformed by the collective working environment of the printmakers in the TGP. Although Wilson worked at the TGP for many years, it was his interest in, and exposure to, the work of the muralist José Clemente Orozco that most influenced Wilson's work in Mexico.

Throughout this essay, I use the term "exile" to describe a form of coerced migration.[1] Exile is significant to the particular historical moment examined here because U.S. national belonging during the early Cold War era was rigidly policed in both symbolic and coercive terms that essentially abrogated the citizenship rights of specified individuals and forced them out of the country. In the case of these individuals who fled the United States to avoid harassment or arrest during the early Cold War period, their relocation to Mexico was a response to an explicitly U.S. national project, which excluded those who did not meet the politically normative terms that policymakers established for national belonging. This contributed to a narrowed realm of acceptability within cultural expression in the United States. It also led to the policing of the category of citizenship as a means to consolidate the Cold War political project. For the artists who left the United States for Mexico during the early part of the Cold War, migration was a direct consequence of these cultural and political proscriptions.

The artistic work of these U.S. artists in Mexico should be understood as a counterhegemonic transnational mode of cultural production. Michelle Stephens has argued that transnational approaches have examined the "heterogeneous character of migrants and the way in which they disrupted the integrity of the state as a homogenous, nationally imagined community."[2] Within Mexico, Catlett, Wilson, Burroughs, and others became members of international communities of artists, made up of antifascist exiles from Spain and Germany, as well as Mexican nationals. The context of art production in Mexico influenced the content of their work, influencing artists to represent specific aspects of African American life in the United States. These images challenged the ways that the U.S. State Department promoted artistic and musical forms, such as jazz, as both "universal" and uniquely American in order to associate the United States in the eyes of the so-called third world with concepts such as "artistic freedom" and "individual liberty." (As Penny von Eschen has discussed, it is important to note that the U.S. State Department's presentation of jazz was predicated on the promotion of one specific interpretation of this musical form.)[3]

I first examine how the work of these African American artists developed in Mexico, and how this context influenced their visual art and their production process. I then explore the work of Catlett and John Wilson in Mexico, looking specifically at the influences of the Mexican muralists, as well as artists at the TGP, on the content and aesthetic qualities of their work. While both Catlett and Wilson were influenced by Mexican artists, their portrayals of African American figures were also of interest to Mexican muralists, such as David Alfaro Siqueiros, and printmakers in the TGP. Finally, I analyze the effect of the Mexican context on African American artists in Mexico and how it enabled them to imagine ways both to distribute their work to African Americans and to aid other African American artists once they returned to the United States (either temporarily or permanently). Their experiences demonstrate how working in Mexico contributed to a transnational perspective that was in opposition to the U.S. Cold War ideology.

Revolutionary Associations

In *The Cultural Front*, Michael Denning has argued that the culture of the Popular Front "transformed the ways people imagined the globe." Artists affiliated with the Cultural Front in the United States drew inspiration from "international stories," as well as from artists in other parts of the world. As Denning describes it, "the romance of the Revolution was manifested not only in the popularity of the Soviet films of Eisenstein and Pudovkin, but also in the romance of the Mexican Revolution, embodied in the grand murals of Diego Rivera and José Clemente Orozco."[4] These artists were influenced by the Soviet's Prolcult movement and by the work of Mexican artists creating public art, such as making murals or working in a collective context on printmaking projects.

One of the earlier forums for this "left internationalism" within the United States was the John Reed clubs, developed by artists and writers in the late 1920s and early 1930s. In forming the clubs, these artists and writers attempted to implement the Soviet model of workers' collectives, the Prolecult program, in the United States.[5] The John Reed clubs organized exhibitions comprising the work of artists from around the world; exhibited the work of U.S. and other artists abroad; invited filmmakers such as Sergei Eisenstein, and artists including David Alfaro Siqueiros and Diego Rivera, to speak on occasion to members of the John Reed clubs; and brought these individuals and others to speak at conferences they organized, including the American Artists' Congress in 1936.[6]

The Mexican muralists and graphic artists were some of the most significant "international" influences on politically concerned U.S. artists during the 1930s. By this time, the work of *los tres grandes* (the big three), Orozco, Rivera, and Siqueiros, was well known and influential within avant-garde art circles in the United States. The Mexican muralists were also influenced by the proletarian cultural movement that emerged within the Soviet Union following the Russian Revolution. While "the Big Three" held distinct ideological viewpoints, all took up the call for the establishment of art from the point of view of the working class. As a member of El Sindicato Revolucionario de Obreros Téchnicos y Plásticos (Revolutionary Union of Technical and Plastic Workers), Siqueiros edited a manifesto for Mexican artists, which was signed by Rivera, Orozco, and others and published in the union's paper *El Machete* in June 1924. In it, Siqueiros stated that "the art of the Mexican people . . . is great because it surges from the people; it is collective, and our own aesthetic aim is to socialize artistic expression, to destroy bourgeois individualism."[7] Not only was it important for these Mexican artists to think about producing work collectively; they were also interested in the relation of the artwork to their audiences, whom they imagined as the poor, working-class, and indigenous populations of Mexico. They wanted to create public art that would be located in the environment of these groups, rather than easel painting, which was available only to the elite classes who visited museums and galleries.

However, as is evident from the manifesto, Siqueiros and others believed that their art should take up not only a *working-class* perspective but a specifically *Mexican* perspective as well. Siqueiros's viewpoint emerged in part from the context of the Mexican Revolution. He had been part of a congress of "soldier-artists," who decided in 1919 to send him abroad. In 1921 Siqueiros wrote a manifesto in Barcelona in which he argued for a new revolutionary art "based on the constructive vitality of Indian art and decrying outworn European ideals."[8] During the same year, Rivera painted his first mural in Mexico. According to the art historian Shifra Goldman, Rivera was primarily concerned with two issues in his work at this time: "the need to offset the contempt with which the conquistadores had viewed the ancient Indian civilizations, and the need to offset the anti-mestizo and anti-Indian attitudes of the European-oriented ruling classes during the porfiriato (the dictatorship of Porfirio Díaz)."[9] Goldman further explains:

> Mestizo and Indian peasants formed the basic fighting forces of the Revolution, and their economic needs were to be addressed on the political plane. The role of the arts was to restore understanding of and pride in a heritage and culture that the concept of Spanish superiority had subverted. Post-revolutionary *indigenista* philosophy appeared in the work of writers, musicians, filmmakers, sculptors, and painters as a facet of Mexican nationalism.[10]

During the early 1920s, Mexico was beginning to experience an "artistic renaissance" underwritten in part by José Vasconcelos, the secretary of education from 1921 to 1924. Vasconcelos believed that the government should fund public art — and specifically public murals "characterized by an emphasis on indigenism, folk characters, and historical epics; solidarity with the dispossessed; dramatization of class conflicts, mockery of egotism and hypocrisy of those in power; and a celebration of traditional rites and myths," according to the art historian Raquel Tibol.[11] It was Vasconcelos who, in the wake of the revolution, called on artists to "remake" Mexico by creating and reconstructing forms of popular art, drawing from the pre-Hispanic and colonial periods, to Mexican independence and later the revolution.[12]

While the work of the muralists was influenced by notions about art and art production that were developing in the Soviet Union, social realism in Mexico can be distinguished from socialist realism. The art historian David Shapiro provides a useful differentiation between the two genres, noting that "Socialist

Realism, as developed in the Soviet Union, supports the ruling class in the form of government. It selects as its subject matter the positive aspects of life under socialism: happy, cooperating workers, the beauty of factory and countryside, well-fed, healthy children, and so on."[13] He describes Mexican social realism as demonstrating "both the struggle of the people to gain control of the means of production and some of the fruits of that power."[14] Mexican artists drew from other aesthetic traditions as well, which included Renaissance classicism, expressionism, fauvism, and cubism.[15] Shifra Goldman has argued that "the language the Mexicans introduced . . . was the pictorial dialect of social realism, which they raised to the highest level of artistic development—in contrast to the visual clichés of Soviet Socialist realism."[16]

By the mid-1930s, the influence of the Mexican muralists had gone beyond avant-garde circles into broader U.S. culture, the outcome of the relief projects developed during the first New Deal. Simultaneously, as the U.S. Communist Party launched the Popular Front in 1935, many of the John Reed clubs disbanded. This had a two-pronged effect. First, members of John Reed clubs became involved in the Federal Art Project. Many viewed their participation in its programs as an opportunity to create "art for the people." Second, members of the John Reed clubs channeled their energies into Popular Front organizations such as the American Artists' Congress, which was established in the fall of 1935. The congress featured the first exhibition of El Taller de Gráfica Popular in the United States, which was attended by Orozco and Siqueiros, as well as the African American artist Hale Woodruff.[17]

Romare Bearden argued that there were mainly three groups of artists whose work interested African American artists during the 1930s and 1940s. The first group consisted of "regionalist" artists, including Grant Wood and Thomas Hart Benton, whose work could be characterized by its "realism" and attention to American subject matter. The second group consisted of "socially conscious" representational artists, such as Ben Shahn and Philip Evergood. The third group consisted of Mexican muralists and printmakers. Bearden suggested that African American artists were drawn specifically to the work of Mexican muralists because of the "Mexican concept of aiding uneducated, impoverished peasants by depicting their revolutionary past."[18] He further remarked that "this approach seems applicable to their own relationship to their own poor, oppressed people," and the artists' interest in representing African American history.[19] Other artists, such as Käthe Kollwitz and George Grosz, also appealed to African American artists because of their social commentary, but as was the case with artists like Jacob Lawrence, it was the content of the Mexican artists' work that "most excited and influenced" them.[20]

"No Racist Laws in Mexico"[21]

By the late 1940s and early 1950s, redbaiting in the United States contributed to an exodus of politically progressive artists, many of whom were African American. Anticommunism only further compounded the everyday effects of racism on African Americans following World War II, and the decline in support for African American art during the 1940s. Elizabeth Catlett recalled that she chose to go to Mexico in part because it was "the nearest place without racism and segregation."[22] During World War II, Catlett and other left-wing African Americans recognized the hypocrisy of African Americans fighting a war against race hatred while they experienced discrimination in the United States. Furthermore, in the postwar period, African Americans grew increasingly critical of their position within the United States owing to a sense of frustration and anger that there still existed incidences of brutality toward them, as well as Jim Crow laws.[23] This critical perspective can be seen in their work, including that of Catlett's husband, Charles White, whose painting entitled *Freeport* (1946) represented the murder of a black soldier and his brother in Freeport, Long Island.

The demise of the WPA in the late 1930s and early 1940s, which led to the elimination of federal funding for artists during the 1940s, also made it difficult for African American artists to support themselves. After the federal government withdrew its funding from the Federal Art Project in the early 1940s, many artists again became reliant on support from the private sector. In an interview, Charles White argued that "private patronage almost makes the artist completely dependent on taste."[24] He continued by suggesting that the artist "doesn't always shape the taste of his patrons. The patron sometimes exerts a kind of influence through his financial power."[25] The art historian Lisa Farrington has noted that while the WPA's Federal Art Project funded "social realist imagery that lionized the New Deal, American history, the working-class, (and) political activism" during the 1940s and 1950s, corporate and individual patrons tended to support artwork that did not demonstrate explicit political and social content.[26] These patrons had less of an interest in collecting the work of African American artists, which, as the art historian Lizzetta LeFalle-Collins has argued, "presented alternative voices that challenge[d] dominant cultural representation."[27]

This change in patronage had a significant effect on the artists who had been involved with the Federal Art Project, as well as the institutions that supported them. African American artists were marginalized within the mainstream art world, in part due to their association with the Federal Art Projects. If their work was figural, rather than abstract, they might be shut out of galleries.[28] As a result, a significant number of African American artists chose to leave the country. Some received funding from the Julius Rosenwald Foundation and the John Hay Whitney Foundation to study and work outside the United States.[29] Most African American artists who received this funding traveled to Mexico or to France.[30]

It was during this time that Elizabeth Catlett, Charles White, John Wilson, and Margaret Taylor Goss Burroughs left the United States for Mexico.[31] The scholar Bill Mullen has argued that by the early 1950s Mexico City "had become a haven and refuge for African-American artists seeking an alternative to the repressive political environment at home."[32] Most of these artists chose to go to Mexico because of difficulties they were experiencing in the political context of the United States during the Cold War era. Catlett decided to move to Mexico after she found herself unable to focus on her artwork in New York in 1946 while working as a promotion director and fundraiser at the George Washington Carver School. By that time, the Carver School, a community school in Harlem, was under attack as a "Communist front." In an interview in 1999, Catlett recalled that difficulties ensued at the school during a power struggle between the white educators and African American leaders on the board, including Ben Davis and Adam Clayton Powell Sr. Eventually the African American leaders took over. In response, a white member of the board contacted a journalist for the *New York Herald Tribune*, who wrote an article in which he referred to the Carver school as a "Red" institution. As a result, the school lost support from the black middle-class and upper-middle-class communities in Harlem.[33]

In 1952 Margaret Taylor Goss Burroughs took a sabbatical leave from her position as an art teacher at a Chicago high school, in large part to escape the harassment she experienced because of her progressive politics. Burroughs described years later in an interview that "during the McCarthy period . . . there was a lot of pressure put on anybody who was the least bit militant. They'd claim you were a communist and would try to take your job away from you."[34]

The decision to go to Mexico was also based on these artists' interest in, and familiarity with, the work of Mexican muralists and printmakers. Charles White and Elizabeth Catlett went to Mexico together in 1946 after Catlett's Rosenwald

Fellowship was renewed. Both became guest members of the TGP. There they joined other U.S. artists like Pablo O'Higgins, who had settled in Mexico during the 1920s and cofounded the TGP with the Mexican artists Luis Arenal and Leopoldo Méndez. John Wilson, who received a John Hay Whitney Fellowship in 1950 to study art in Mexico, knew Catlett and Charles White and like them had met a number of Mexican artists in the United States, including José Gutierrez, who encouraged Wilson to come to Mexico.[35] Mexico was also appealing because unlike in the United States, Wilson commented in an interview, "There were no racist laws in Mexico."[36] Furthermore, he noted in another interview with Lizzetta LeFalle-Collins that he went to Mexico because "they were doing in Mexico what [Wilson] wanted to do in the United States."[37]

Itinerant Modes of Cultural Production

Elizabeth Catlett's relocation to Mexico in the mid-1940s had a profound impact on her art practice. Her artwork changed significantly through her collaborations with Mexican artists at the TGP, and by her training at the Escuela de Pintura y Escultura de la Secretaría de Educación Pública (National School of Painting and Sculpture), known as La Esmeralda, in Mexico City with sculptor Francisco Zúñiga.[38] Not only did Catlett incorporate the techniques employed by artists at the TGP, but the culturally nationalist focus of these artists strengthened her interest in portraying both the history and contemporary life of African Americans in the United States.

In 1945, while working at the Carver School, Catlett applied for a grant from the Rosenwald Foundation to create a series of prints on the "role of Negro women in the fight for democratic rights in the history of America," which she planned to show to African American audiences throughout the United States.[39] In an essay she wrote years later, "Responding to Cultural Hunger," Catlett describes how her concept for "The Negro Woman" series was shaped by her experiences at the Carver School, where she interacted with women who were of a different class background from herself. Her conversations with working-class women inspired Catlett to include not only well-known African American female figures in her series, but also to show the contributions of working-class African American women.[40] When her grant was renewed for another year, Arna Bontemps, a committee member, told Catlett to leave New York so that she could complete the work.[41] Catlett left in part because she believed that "the New York art scene offered no opportunities for a black woman."[42] She chose to go to Mexico after meeting some artists from the TGP while they were in New York exhibiting their work. These artists, including José Chavez Morado, encouraged Catlett to come to Mexico and join their collective. Chavez Morado had in fact given Catlett the contact information for the muralist David Alfaro Siqueiros's mother in-law, who ran a rooming house in Mexico City. After hearing that there was a room available, Catlett made plans to go to Mexico. She and White arrived in Mexico City in 1946, where they both became guest members of the TGP.[43]

Catlett's decision to go to Mexico was related to her interest in, and knowledge of, the work of Mexican artists, including the muralists and those involved with the TGP. She knew, for example, that the TGP artists produced inexpensive reproducible art for the people of Mexico, and she was intrigued by the idea of working in the context of a collective. Catlett also wanted to create public art. The immediacy and accessibility of printmaking allowed the TGP artists to address current events in their work, and thus they took on more specific subject matter than did the Mexican muralists.

The TGP developed out of the Liga de Escritores y Artistas Revolucionarios (League of Revolutionary Writers and Artists, or LEAR). LEAR was founded in the 1930s at the beginning of the administration of Lázaro Cárdenas (1934–40) as an activist organization that included politically concerned artists, writers, and intellectuals in Mexico City. While the leadership of LEAR had ties to the Mexican Communist Party, it was not a requirement that those who joined be members. However, as the art historian Deborah Caplow has noted, when the organization was established in the early 1930s, members "followed the directives of the 1928 6th Congress of the Communist International, which emphasized the class struggle and encouraged the working classes in all countries to rise against the ruling classes, with the slogan 'class against class.'"[44] The organization developed ties with groups of artists, writers, and intellectuals in different countries, including the John Reed clubs in the United States, making LEAR an international organization. By the mid-1930s, tensions developed in LEAR as a result of a decrease in government support for the league and because of conflicts between LEAR members. Luis Arenal, Pablo O'Higgins, and Leopoldo Méndez left the organization to found the TGP in 1937.

The LEAR artists who established the TGP brought a new model of artistic practice to the group, creating prints primarily for the poor and working-class communities of Mexico. In their turn to printmaking, artists at the TGP drew on a tradition of Mexican printmaking that dated back to the nineteenth century, specifically to the work of the printmaker José Guadalupe Posada (1851–1913). Posada's work consisted in part of illustrated *corridos*, epic ballads that were sold all over Mexico. The sheets, printed on cheap paper, were the primary way that people who were illiterate became exposed to current events.[45] Posada was known for his *calaveras*, a uniquely Mexican form of popular art that featured skeletons representing the living. Through his calaveras, Posada satirized both politicians and other prominent figures in Mexican society.

While the cofounders of the TGP were all influenced by Posada, it was Leopoldo Méndez whose work most emulated his politically engaged printmaking style.[46] Méndez started publishing satirical prints in *Frente a Frente*, the newspaper published by LEAR, in the 1930s. These images both referenced and reworked Posada's style and imagery in response to contemporary political concerns, which, as Caplow has argued, produced "a new genre in Mexican art" — the "Mexican political print."[47] Caplow suggests that like the work of Leopoldo Méndez, the prints that the TGP produced drew on both Mexican and international sources, which included the work of Posada, but also that of German expressionism and Russian constructivism.[48] However, artists working in the TGP agreed to limit their work to realistic portraits of the themes that concerned them. Their work was also largely figurative, with a focus on social issues.

Arenal, O'Higgins, and Mendez organized the TGP as an artists' collective, similar to that of LEAR, with a central membership of about twelve to fifteen artists. In addition, there were between twenty-five and thirty artists who were affiliated with the TGP at any one time.[49] Artist members met every Friday to discuss new projects, as well as those in progress. Elizabeth Catlett described the process by which artists created work at the TGP:

> People would come to the workshop if they had problems: if students were on strike; or trade unions had labor disputes, or if peasants had problems with their land, they would come into the workshop and ask for something to express their concerns. We would then have collective discussion about what symbolism would be effective in expressing those concerns. The artists at the Taller would volunteer to do the work together or individually; after the preliminary sketches were made they were put up for more collective discussion.[50]

Members of the TGP created art that engaged issues concerning the working-class population of Mexico, as the collective produced much of its work for trade unions, student organizations, and the government's anti-illiteracy campaign.[51] Their artistic work consisted of prints for these groups, as well as portfolios and illustrated books.

Catlett joined the TGP during a period of intense productivity. Between the late 1930s and the late 1940s, when Catlett became a full member, artists in the TGP created a number of portfolios, as well as countless prints that addressed both national and international issues. Mexican subject matter included historical events such as the Mexican Revolution, the expropriation of petroleum in Mexico in 1938, and holidays such as the Day of the Dead. The main international issue that the TGP artists addressed in their work was fascism in Europe — both in Germany and in Franco's Spain.[52] During the 1930s and 1940s, the TGP artists exhibited their work internationally and published numerous portfolios, such as *450 años de lucha: Homenaje al pueblo Mexicano* (450 Years of Struggle: An Homage to the Mexican People), and books, including *El Taller de Gráfica Popular: Doce años de obra artistica colectiva* (The Workshop for Popular Graphic Art: A Record of Twelve Years of Collective Work), which was published in 1949. As a result of publishing these portfolios, the influence of the TGP grew significantly throughout the world, especially in the United States, Czechoslovakia, Italy, Brazil, Ecuador, and Guatemala.[53]

Susan Richards, in her dissertation on the first twelve years of TGP activity, covering the years 1937–1949, argues that there was a significant shift in the work of the collective during the 1940s, due in large part of the political environment of Mexico, which moved dramatically to the right following the administration of Lázaro Cárdenas. This occurred at a time when members of the TGP increasingly had to search outside the organization for financial support, leading them to funding sources supplied by the Mexican government. Richards suggests that the TGP shifted from "artistic production that addressed smoldering Mexican social issues" in the 1930s to "a graphic art that celebrated Mexican history and society" in the 1940s.[54]

When Catlett started at the TGP in 1946, members were at work on *Estampas de la Revolución Mexicana*, a portfolio of eighty-five linocuts focused on the Mexican Revolution. On the one hand, the TGP's decision to create a series about the Mexican Revolution at this historical moment was a critical response to what these artists saw as the "imperialistic pressure on Mexico," mainly from the United States, during the post–World War II era.[55] On the other hand, this project was less critical of the Mexican state as compared with much of the TGP's work of the late 1930s. Richards has argued that the TGP's decision to base their images on photographs of the revolution taken by Agustin Casasola also demonstrates the group's alignment with "official histories" of the Mexican Revolution.[56]

In creating this portfolio, the TGP artists worked to represent the specific experiences of the Mexican people during the revolution.[57] In part due to the high illiteracy rate in Mexico, and the interest of TGP artists in addressing their art to a working-class audience, their graphic work tended to be based on photographs and other reproductions that would be familiar to a majority of Mexicans. The portfolio included numerous portraits of leaders of the Mexican Revolution, drawn from well-known photographs by Agustin Casasola. In addition to the portraits of "heroes," the portfolio also contained images that acknowledged the contribution of "ordinary" Mexicans, such as Fernando Castro Pacheco's *La huelga de Rio Blanco: Los obreros textiles se lanzan a la lucha, 7 de Enero de 1907* (The Strike of Rio Blanco: The Textile Workers Launched the Struggle, January 7, 1907) and Leopoldo Méndez and Alfredo Zalces's *Mexico en la guerra: Los braceros se van a Estados Unidos* (Mexico in the War: The Braceros Go to the United States).[58]

As members of the collective were working on the portfolio, Catlett developed her own series of linocuts on the subject of African American women in the United States. As the art historian Melanie Herzog has remarked, the TGP's *Estampas de la Revolución Mexicana* suggested to Catlett "the means to envision her epic celebration of the historic opposition, resistance, and survival of African American women."[59] Similar to the TGP portfolio that included images of heroes of the Mexican Revolution and of Mexico's rural and urban working people, Catlett's "The Negro Woman" series included images not only of well-known African American women but also of ordinary individuals such as union organizers, musicians, and domestic workers, based on the women she met at the Carver School. While scholars such as Richards have criticized the work of the TGP in the late 1940s, including *Estampas de la Revolución Mexicana*, for portraying an "official" history of the Mexican Revolution, Catlett's "The Negro Woman" series challenged dominant accounts of U.S. history that had diminished or erased the contributions of African American women within the United States.

The aesthetic style of Catlett's "The Negro Woman" series reflected her exposure to new artistic techniques that she learned while making linocuts (prints made on linoleum) for the *Estampas de la Revolucíon Mexicana* portfolio. According to Catlett, collaborating with members of the TGP not only affected her general way of working but introduced her to new techniques such as working with linoleum prints.[60] The prints that Catlett produced soon after she came to Mexico for her "The Negro Woman" series, such as "In Phyllis Wheatley I Proved Intellectual Equality in the Midst of Slavery," reflect the aesthetic influences of Mexican artists on Catlett's work, in part by her choice of linocuts as her medium, but also, as Melanie Herzog has suggested, in Catlett's use of line and composition (figure 1).[61]

In looking at the project as a whole (images and text), one can also see how the explicit narrative content demonstrated in the work of the TGP portfolio on the Mexican Revolution influenced Catlett's series. The accompanying text reads as follows:

> I am the Negro woman. I have always worked hard in America . . . In the fields . . . In other folks' homes . . . I have given the world my songs. In Sojourner Truth I fought for the rights of women as well as Negroes. In Harriet Tubman I helped hundreds to freedom. In Phyllis [sic] Wheatley I proved intellectual equality in the midst of slavery. My role has been important in the struggle to organize the unorganized. I have studied in ever increasing numbers. My reward has been bars between me and the rest of the land. I have special reservations . . . Special houses . . . And a special fear for my loved ones. My right is a future of equality with other Americans.[62]

Each of the images is accompanied by one of these statements. For example, "I have always worked hard in America" is written beneath an image of domestic workers, and "In the fields" is the text for the image of a fieldworker. As in the TGP's portfolio on the Mexican Revolution, Catlett also used narrative to link these images in service of the larger project, which is a history of African American women's contributions.

In her "The Negro Woman" series, Catlett moves from portraying domestics and fieldworkers to a woman blues singer to the historical figures Sojourner Truth, Phillis Wheatley, and Harriet Tubman. Like artists at the TGP, who based their work on well-known, realistic images of their subjects, Catlett developed her portrait of Phillis Wheatley from an engraving of the poet created by the artist Scipio Moorhead in the eighteenth century. Similar to TGP artists who visually related their heroes to "ordinary" Mexicans by situating them within crowds, Catlett, in her portrait of Wheatley, reworked Moorhead's version by positioning three female African American figures in chains behind the image

1 Elizabeth Catlett, "In Phyllis Wheatley I proved intellectual equality in the midst of slavery" (1946–47). Art @ Elizabeth Catlett/Licensed by VAGA, New York, N.Y. Collection of Hampton University Museum, Hampton, Virginia.

of Wheatley. In so doing, she not only references the institution of slavery but also situates Wheatley, a former slave, within that historical context.

Catlett exhibited the work that she completed in Mexico in a show entitled "Paintings, Sculpture, and Prints of the Negro Woman" at the Barnett-Aden Gallery in Washington, D.C., from December 1947 to January 1948.[63] While Catlett had initially intended for the show to travel throughout the United States to "alternative" gallery spaces such as schools and churches in African American communities, it was shown only at the Barnett-Aden Gallery. Around the time of the exhibition, Catlett decided to relocate permanently to Mexico. In an interview, she said that "she never felt very patriotic in the States, growing up around Washington D.C. where blacks didn't have the vote." She did not feel discriminated against in Mexico—as she proclaimed years later, "I feel like an ordinary human being in Mexico."[64]

In addition to Elizabeth Catlett, other African American artists such as John Wilson came to Mexico to study and to participate in the TGP, where he became a guest member. Wilson chose to go to Mexico because of his interest in public art—both in murals and in printmaking. While Wilson had a strong interest in printmaking, he was in fact more interested in developing his skills in mural painting while in Mexico. As he noted in an interview, he "wanted to emulate the Mexicans and paint murals . . . to change people through the . . . environment of the community."[65] Of "the Big Three," Wilson most admired José Clemente Orozco, with whom he hoped to study after receiving the John Hay Whitney Fellowship that brought him to Mexico. Unfortunately, Orozco passed away before Wilson arrived in Mexico City in September 1950. However, Wilson met and befriended other Mexican and U.S. artists in Mexico, including the muralists David Alfaro Siqueiros and Diego Rivera, as well as printmakers associated with the TGP—Pablo O'Higgins, Francisco Dosamantes, and Ignacio Aguirre.

Even though Wilson did not get to study with Orozco, he did have the opportunity to view a significant amount of Orozco's work while in Mexico. Since Orozco's murals were primarily painted on public buildings, it was necessary to travel around Mexico City and other cities and towns in Mexico to view them. Wilson visited many of the sites of Orozco's work and purchased dozens of photographs taken by an individual who had documented Orozco's drawings and studies for his murals.[66]

Both the style and content of Orozco's work appealed to Wilson. While he learned something about new materials from Siqueiros and met Rivera, for Wilson, neither matched his engagement with Orozco's work.[67] What seemed especially significant about Orozco's work for Wilson was his political iconoclasm and, as he noted in an interview years later, "not taking into account whether it's going to be fashionable, whether it's going to come across, whether it's becoming recognized."[68] The art historian Dawn Ades has argued that Orozco's work "sets up an internal dialectic between the power and the dangers of the traditional icons and political myths of the revolution."[69] While Rivera's murals in particular celebrated Mexico, it seems fitting that Wilson, who found the United States to be profoundly undemocratic, especially in its treatment of its African American citizens, would be drawn to the more critical perspective of Orozco.[70] Through the model of Orozco, Wilson, as he put it, found a "form through which I could use my art skills to create convincing images of black people."[71]

In Mexico Wilson started to think about ways to visualize the specificities of the experiences of his Mexican subjects. Years later he commented that "I may have gone to . . . Mexico and painted Mexicans, but . . . I didn't just paint Mexican landscapes. I didn't paint, 'the colorful Mexican peon with his big hats.'" Wilson recalled that he "identified with the kind of reality that Orozco found . . . but I was identifying with it through my own experience in the United States as a black person."[72] Over time Wilson began to portray images of African Americans, as well as Mexicans. As Wilson notes about his work of the 1950s, he tried to be "much more specific" in his attempt to find "a way to make a visual statement, a meaningful visual statement, about the reality of life for blacks in the United States."[73]

One of the most important works that Wilson produced in Mexico, and one that demonstrates the influence of Orozco, was a fresco mural entitled *The Incident*, which portrays an African American family inside a house watching members of the Ku Klux Klan after they had lynched an African American man.[74] In 1951, with letters of recommendation from Pablo O'Higgins and Diego Rivera, Wilson applied for and received a grant from the Institute of International Education, which enabled him to remain in Mexico. With this funding, Wilson took classes at La Esmeralda, the National School of Painting and Sculpture in Mexico City, including a class on techniques of fresco painting with Ignacio (Nacho) Aguirre. While he was enrolled in Aguirre's class, Wilson painted *The Incident* (figure 2). In this mural, Wilson positions the African American father figure as actively and defiantly taking up arms against the KKK to protect his family. Orozco's influence on Wilson's mural is exhibited both formally and the-

2   John Wilson, *The Incident* (1952). Art @ John Wilson/Licensed by VAGA, New York, N.Y. Image Courtesy Sragow Gallery, New York City.

matically. Wilson distorts the figure of the lynched man, in part by elongating his fingers and feet, suggesting the violence to, and violation of, his body. The exaggeration of the menacing hands of the KKK member holding a whip and the enlarged hands of the African American father holding his gun underscores the brutality and visceral tension of the confrontation. In this image Wilson draws on Orozco's work as well as more broadly what Michael Denning has referred to as the genre of the "proletarian grotesque."[75] Denning argues in *The Cultural Front* that the proletarian grotesque is "an attempt to wrench us out of the repose and distance of the 'aesthetic.'"[76] While the original plan was to paint over the mural as soon as it was completed to allow another student the space for his or her work, Aguirre let Wilson's mural remain after Siqueiros, who had heard about the mural and was then head of the Department for the Protection and Restoration of Murals, requested that it be preserved.[77]

Siqueiros's response to Wilson's mural was just one example of the interest of Mexican artists in the work of African American artists. Mexican artists in the TGP were also enthusiastic about participating in the production of a print series of well-known figures in African American history, entitled *Against Discrimination in the United States*, conceived of by Elizabeth Catlett in the early 1950s. This series was a means for Catlett, Burroughs, and other TGP artists to interpret the experiences of African Americans in the United States using techniques drawn from Mexican art traditions and to direct this work to an African American audience. The project included images of Crispus Attucks, Blanche K. Bruce, George Washington Carver, Frederick Douglass, W. E. B. Du Bois, Paul Robeson, Sojourner Truth, Harriet Tubman, Nat Turner, and Ida B. Wells. Unlike her "The Negro Woman" series, Catlett had envisioned this series as a collective project. Although she picked the figures she wanted to include, she let other TGP members choose which individuals they wanted to portray.[78] In preparing the artists, Catlett provided the group with preexisting images of the subjects and information about their historical background. Similar to the TGP's portfolio of the Mexican Revolution, many of the images were modeled on well-known photographs or engravings.[79]

Catlett's hope for the project was that it would challenge dominant accounts of U.S. history that had diminished or erased the significant contributions of African Americans. Drawing on the example of the extensive distribution of the TGP's work, she also thought that it would reach a wide audience. The series was addressed to African Americans, as Catlett had intended for these images to be printed in *Freedom*, a newspaper published by Paul Robeson in Harlem. However, after the series was completed and the prints mailed to New York, editors from *Freedom* informed the TGP that they would have to strengthen the image of Frederick Douglass for it to be included in their publication. True to the ethos of the TGP, members refused to submit another print, as the work had already been approved by the collective. However, this meant that the series remained unpublished in the United States. While this must have disappointed Catlett, four of the images were reproduced for Mexican audiences and included in an issue of *Artes de México* published in 1957 that celebrated the twentieth anniversary of El Taller de Gráfica Popular, and included in TGP exhibitions throughout the world.[80]

While Catlett had originally intended that her series would inform an African American public about important historical figures in African American history, the end result of decisions made by the editors of *Freedom* and the TGP meant that it was in fact audiences outside the United States who were educated about the contributions of these African American heroes and heroines. Although Catlett regarded audiences outside the United States as secondary in the distribution of *Against Discrimination in the United States*, during the late 1950s and early 1960s she increasingly became interested in directing her work toward audiences in Latin America, Africa, and Asia.

Back in the U.S.A.: African American Artists, Action Painting, and Redbaiting

In 1961 Elizabeth Catlett gave the keynote speech at a meeting of the National Conference of Negro Artists (NCNA) held that year at Howard University. Her attendance at the meeting was to be the last time she traveled from Mexico before being barred from entering the United States because of her affiliation with the TGP, which the State Department considered a "front" for the Communist Party.[81] In her talk, which was later published under the title "The Negro People and American Art," Catlett asked her audience to consider the following questions:

> What is this great goal of being an accepted artist in the art movement of the United States? Of the hundreds of millions of human beings in our world, who reaps the cultural benefits of United States art in 1961? We all know who reaps the economic benefits. But what is the great United States contribution in the graphic and plastic arts to world culture? This question must be investigated and answered before the Negro artist can make his decision. I say that if not, he is doomed to a minor position in a minor contribution that is of little importance to our changing world.[82]

Catlett cautioned her audience of African American artists not to be swayed by the pressure exerted on them by the art establishment in the United States. Instead she encouraged them to think more broadly about the significance of their artistic production and its relevance not just within the confines of the United States but also within the context of the entire world.

In her speech, Catlett implicitly questioned the importance of the dominant aesthetic style of art production during the early Cold War era, namely, abstract expressionism. David and Cecile Shapiro argue that at the time of Catlett's speech, abstract expressionist artists "were so strongly promoted and dispersed by the art establishment that to an unprecedented degree . . . they effectively routed other stylistic and philosophical expressions in American painting."[83]

Furthermore, the Shapiros note that "large numbers of artists swung over to Abstract Expressionism during the 1950s, thus contributing to the force of the movement they were joining because they could not beat it."[84] In addressing her audience of African American artists, Catlett directly challenged the production and circulation of abstract expressionism, which agencies of the U.S. government promoted during the early Cold War era.[85] The historian Francis Stonor Saunders has argued that abstract expressionism "spoke to a specifically anti-Communist ideology, the ideology of freedom, of free enterprise. Nonfigurative and politically silent, it was the very antithesis to socialist realism."[86]

African American artists who returned to the United States from Mexico during the late 1940s and 1950s entered an environment that was both dismissive of, and hostile to, the work of "socially conscious" representational artists. Their marginalization was further compounded by institutionalized racism within the gallery system, and they were largely ignored by leading art critics. The content of their work as much as their aesthetic style appeared in stark contrast to the otherworldly metaphysics of abstract expressionism. As Romare Bearden and Harry Henderson have written in the case of Charles White, this work "ran directly counter to Abstract Expressionism."[87]

Due to racial discrimination, their left-wing politics, and the fact that their work diverged from the aesthetic style dominant in the United States during the 1940s and 1950s, Charles White, John Wilson, Elizabeth Catlett, and other African American artists found that they had limited opportunities for exhibiting their work in the United States.[88] During the early 1950s, White exhibited at the ACA (American Contemporary Art) Gallery in New York, one of the few venues that still featured the work of "socially conscious" representational artists. (Other artists who exhibited their work at the gallery included William Gropper, Jack Levine, Moses and Raphael Soyer, Philip Evergood, Anton Refregier, and Robert Gwathmey.) While John Wilson had been represented by a gallery in Boston before he left for Mexico, he could not find gallery representation in the 1950s.[89] At that time, his work was only included in group shows. Following her solo exhibition at the Barnett-Aden Gallery in 1947, Elizabeth Catlett was unable to exhibit much of her work in the United States during the 1950s.

One of the few places where Catlett and these other artists could exhibit their artwork consistently was the Atlanta University Annual, established by the artist Hale Woodruff, who had studied with Diego Rivera in Mexico during the 1930s. Margaret Taylor Goss Burroughs recollected what it was like for an African American artist to exhibit there:

For most of us, the Atlanta show provided the first memory, the first mention, and the first knowledge of the black arts presence. In those catalogs from Atlanta we first read the names of people like Hale Woodruff, Jacob Lawrence, John Wilson, Elizabeth Catlett, Charles White, Aaron Douglas, William Artis, and many, many others. Many were unknown, but through this cultural vehicle . . . Atlanta University became an oasis in the Southern desert, not only for the black artist of the South, but for those also in the East and West as well.[90]

The Atlanta Annual remained one of the few outlets for these artists to exhibit their work during the 1950s, especially painting and sculpture. Printmaking proved to be a slightly different matter, perhaps because once removed from the original gesture of painterly genius and tainted by its association with mechanical reproduction, it was already relegated to a lower artistic status in the art market.

While abstraction dominated in painting and sculpture, the art historian Eva Cockcroft has argued that "social content was more acceptable in the graphic arts than it was in painting."[91] Confronted with the limitations of the U.S. art market, White, Wilson, and Burroughs drew on their printmaking experiences working at the TGP as a model for the kind of art production process that they wanted to continue in the United States. They did this by working collectively with other artists in groups such as the Printmaking Workshop in New York, by producing print portfolios to distribute the work of African American artists to African American audiences, and by creating organizations that fought against racial discrimination and segregation in the arts. Thus with printmaking these artists were able to find a limited but still receptive market for their work.

Charles White retrospectively observed that in Mexico he "saw artists working to create an art about and for the people. This has been the strongest influence in my whole approach. It clarified the direction in which I wanted to move."[92] Upon his return, White became involved with the Printmaking Workshop in New York. The workshop was founded by artist Bob Blackburn, who purchased a lithographic press and opened his own studio in New York in 1948.[93] In many ways, the workshop was a continuation of the WPA art programs, but without government funding. Blackburn himself had been involved in the Harlem Community Arts Center, where he learned lithography, in addition to the "306," the Harlem Workshop and the Uptown Arts Laboratory.[94] The Printmaking Workshop fostered the artwork of African American artists in particular, including White, John Wilson, Jacob Lawrence, and John Biggers.

The art historian Alison Cameron notes that the workshop took on "the Taller's collective organizational structure and its ethos of producing socially useful art."[95] The collective art projects taken up by the workshop soon after White arrived in New York were two print portfolios — *Yes, the People* (1948) and *Negro USA* (1949). The workshop included two prints, "Mexican Boy" and "Mexican Woman," that White had produced at the TGP in 1946 in their first print portfolio. For their next portfolio, White produced a print entitled "Our War," in which he portrayed the bravery of an African American soldier. While the emphasis of the first portfolio was on everyday "people," the second portfolio, *Negro USA*, focused specifically on the contributions of African Americans.

As can be attested to by the epigraph at the outset of this chapter, Margaret Taylor Goss Burroughs's year in Mexico served as a respite from the increasingly politically hostile atmosphere of the United States during the early Cold War years and also provided renewed energy to overcome the impasses that she would encounter upon her return. For example, upon her return, Burroughs found that her membership to the South Side Community Art Center, an organization that she had helped found, had been terminated due to her radicalism.[96] Residence in Mexico helped inspire her to establish institutions and organizations whose goals were to build a sense of community for African American artists nationally and internationally, as well as to provide a forum for them to exhibit and sell their work.[97]

One of the most significant of these organizations was established by Burroughs and two other artists, Burroughs's ex-husband Bernard Goss and Marian Perkins. In 1959, after receiving an invitation from Atlanta University to attend its annual exhibition of African American art, Burroughs, Goss, and Perkins decided to use the Atlanta Annual as a platform to launch an organization tentatively called the National Conference of Artists. The group who assembled at this first meeting decided to change the organization's name to the National Conference of Negro Artists (NCNA) and established that their mission was "to encourage black artists in every way — to exhibit and sell their work."[98] Similar to Charles White's portfolios with the Printmaking Workshop in New York, artist members of the NCNA also created print portfolios. Unlike the work of the TGP or the Printmaking Workshop, the production of these portfolios was a means for the organization to support the work of its members, which it helped to distribute and sell.[99]

As mentioned earlier, Catlett gave the keynote address at the NCNA in 1961, held that year at Howard University. In her speech, "The Negro People and

American Art," Catlett recommended ways that African American artists could take up the methods of the TGP, both technically and in terms of a collective production process, as a means to circumvent the gallery system that excluded them. Early on, Catlett asked her audience to redefine what it meant to be a "successful" African American artist. She encouraged them to reevaluate their sense of what an "ideal" audience was for their work, and to redirect this focus from white gallery owners to blacks in the United States (especially in the South). She suggested that they do this by addressing the concerns of African Americans in their work, as well as exhibiting their work where African Americans congregated. Using the example of the TGP, Catlett encouraged these artists to take up printmaking, which could be easily reproduced, and was transportable, in order to exhibit their work to the largest number of people.[100]

In addition to directing their work to African Americans in the South and elsewhere, Catlett also encouraged her audience to exhibit their work outside the United States—in Latin America, Africa, and Asia. She emphasized the interest of citizens of these nations in the work of African American artists. Describing a 1960s visit by her husband Francisco Mora, on behalf of the TGP, to the Third International Educators Conference in the New Republic of Guinea, Catlett mentioned that of the large collection of TGP prints that Mora brought to give to the Teachers Federation of Black Africa, the work that most interested them was the series *Against Discrimination in the United States*. In her speech, she described why this work appealed to the teachers:

> The African teachers explained that their national culture had deteriorated under French colonialism for when a people must be dominated, first there is an attempt to destroy their culture. They spoke of their magnificent African sculpture[s] that now enrich the museums and cultures of other countries, and [have] even served as an inspirational source for modern art, but are lost to them, and that they were beginning again in these countries that had achieved national independence, to develop their artists and establish their own museums.[101]

Here Catlett highlighted the importance of the series for the African teachers, who understood the role of culture for groups of people who had previously been colonized.

African American artists who returned to the United States from Mexico, including White and Burroughs, drew on their experiences in Mexico as a means not only to survive the Cold War years but more importantly to create art, as

White once noted, "about and for the people," in this case African Americans.[102] Catlett, who remained in Mexico, not only directed her work to African Americans in the United States but also drew on her extensive work with the TGP in Mexico to develop a transnational perspective in which she envisioned links between the experiences of African Americans in the United States and people of color throughout the world.

Catlett, unlike most African American artists in Mexico, eventually became a Mexican citizen and was able to exhibit her work internationally during the early Cold War era as part of the TGP collective. Her artwork of this period referenced the history of slavery in the United States to the struggles of the Civil Rights Movement. Catlett's inclusion of individuals like Paul Robeson and W. E. B. Du Bois in her work was an important intervention during the Cold War, when U.S. government agencies attempted to silence these African American activists and others who spoke out against racism as the government simultaneously sent African American performers on tour as a "living demonstration of the American Negro as part of America's cultural life."[103] Catlett, who worked outside the context of the United States, produced artwork that was counter to how U.S. government agencies promoted other artistic and musical forms as both universal and uniquely American. Her representation of the experience of African Americans in the United States cut against the tenets of American exceptionalist ideology while also articulating a politically informed transnational and antiracist aesthetic.

Notes

1   I agree with the scholar Amy Kaminsky that "voluntary exile" is an "oxymoron that masks the cruelly limited choices imposed on the subject." Kaminsky, *After Exile: Writing the Latin American Diaspora* (Minneapolis: University of Minnesota Press, 1999), 9.

2   Michelle Stephens, "Black Transnationalism and the Politics of National Identity: West Indian Intellectuals in Harlem in the Age of War and Revolution," *American Quarterly* 50, no. 3 (September 1998): 592.

3   Penny von Eschen, *Satchmo Blows Up the World: Jazz Ambassadors Play the Cold War* (Cambridge: Harvard University Press, 2004).

4   Michael Denning, *The Cultural Front: The Laboring of American Culture in the 20th Century* (London: Verso, 1996), 12–13.

5   Other examples included the Workers Film and Photo League, known as the Film and Photo League after 1933, which was part of a cultural movement sponsored by the Communist International. Russell Campbell, *Cinema Strikes Back: Radical Filmmaking in the United States, 1930–1942* (Ann Arbor: UMI Press, 1982), 29.

6   As the art historian Patricia Hills has noted, "During their existence the John Reed clubs put on exhibitions, some of which traveled to workers' clubs and other John Reed clubs and even to the Soviet Union." Patricia Hills, *Social Concern and Urban Realism: American Painting of the 1930s* (Boston: Boston University Art Gallery, 1983), 15.

7   Quoted in Laurence E. Schmekebier, *Modern Mexican Art* (Minneapolis: University of Minnesota Press, 1939), 31.

8   Miguel Covarrubias, "Modern Art," in *Twenty Centuries of Mexican Art* (New York: Museum of Modern Art), 138.

9   Shifra Goldman, "Mexican Muralism: Its Influence in Latin America and the United States," in *Dimensions of the Americas: Art and Social Change in Latin America and the United States* (Chicago: University of Chicago Press 1994), 103.

10   Ibid.

11   Raquel Tibol, foreword to *In the Spirit of Resistance: African-American Modernists and the Mexican Muralist School*, ed. Lizzetta LeFalle-Collins and Shifra Goldman (New York: American Federation of Arts, 1996), 12.

12   Octavio Paz, "Social Realism in Mexico: The Murals of Rivera, Orozco and Siqueiros," *Artscanada*, December 1979–January 1980, 56. Leonard Folgarait has argued that "Vasconcelos's motives in directing the national cultures through education were to assist the government in creating a system of political control through the unification and classification of the masses, this by a means of a propaganda project of homogenizing purpose." Folgarait, *Mural Painting and Social Revolution in Mexico, 1920–1940: Art of the New Order* (New York: Cambridge University Press, 1998), 19.

13   David Shapiro, "Social Realism Reconsidered," in *Social Realism: Art as a Weapon*, ed. David Shapiro (New York: Frederick Ungar, 1973), 28n1.

14   Ibid.

15   As Miguel Covarrubias describes, "Rivera, who had labored in Paris through a three-year period as [a] cubist, returned to Mexico by way of Italy, where he saw the great frescoes, the Byzantine mural mosaics, and the Etruscan relics that recalled to him the plastic strength of ancient Mexican art" (Covarrubias, "Modern Art," 138).

16   Shifra Goldman, "The Mexican School, its African Legacy, and the 'Second Wave' in the United States," in *In the Spirit of Resistance: African-American Modernists and the Mexican Muralist School*, ed. Lizzetta LeFalle-Collins and Shifra Goldman (New York: American Federation of Arts, 1996), 70.

17   Siqueiros was a delegate for the Liga de Escritores y Artistas Revolucionarios (League of Revolutionary Writers and Artists, or LEAR) to the First American Artists' Congress.

18   Romare Bearden and Harry Henderson, *A History of African-American Artists, 1792-Present* (New York: Pantheon Books, 1993), 236.

19   Ibid.

20   Lizzetta LeFalle-Collins, "African-American Modernists and the Mexican Muralist School," in *In the Spirit of Resistance: African-American Modernists and the Mexi-*

can Muralist School, ed Lizzetta LeFalle-Collins and Shifra Goldman (New York: American Federation of Arts, 1996), 30.

21   "No racist laws in Mexico": John Woodrow Wilson, interview with Robert Brown, August 9, 1994, Archives of American Art, Smithsonian Institute, Washington, 343.

22   Elizabeth Catlett, interview with author, Cuernavaca, Mexico, June 8, 1999.

23   Mary Dudziak has written about how violence against African Americans increased in the postwar era: "In the years following World War II, a wave of violence swept the South as African-American veterans returned home. Lynchings and beatings of African-Americans, sometimes involving local law enforcement officials, were covered in the media in this country and abroad. The violence spawned protests and demands that the federal government takes steps to alleviate that brutality and other forms of racial injustice." Dudziak, *Cold War Civil Rights: Race and the Image of American Democracy* (Princeton, N.J.: Princeton University Press, 2000), 23.

24   Betty Lochrie Hoag, interview with Charles White, March 9, 1965, Archives of American Art, Smithsonian Institution, Washington, 22.

25   Ibid.

26   Lisa Farrington, *Creating Their Own Image: The History of African-American Women Artists* (New York: Oxford University Press, 2005), 96.

27   LeFalle-Collins, "African-American Modernists," 64.

28   Cecile Shapiro and David Shapiro, "Abstract Expressionism: The Politics of Apolitical Painting," *Prospects* 3 (1977): 203.

29   The Rosenwald Foundation gave money specifically to African American organizations, artists, and writers.

30   Tyler Stovall, "Life on the Left Bank," in *Paris Noir: African Americans in the City of Light* (New York: Houghton Mifflin, 1996).

31   Other African American artists who traveled to Mexico during this time included Sargent Johnson, John Biggers, and Harold Winslow.

32   Bill V. Mullen, *Popular Fronts: Chicago and African-American Cultural Politics, 1935–1946* (Urbana: University of Illinois Press, 1999), 191.

33   Elizabeth Catlett, interview with author, Cuernavaca, Mexico, June 8, 1999.

34   Margaret Taylor Goss Burroughs, interview with Anna M. Tyler, November 11 and December 5, 1988, Archives of American Art, Smithsonian Institution, Washington, 59. Here she is referring to how, thanks to Truman's anti-Communist executive orders, both government and private employers could fire employees based on their supposed "political disloyalty."

35   LeFalle-Collins, "African-American Modernists," 43.

36   Wilson, interview with Robert Brown, 343.

37   LeFalle-Collins, "African-American Modernists," 60–61.

38   In this essay I focus on the influence of Mexican artists on Catlett's early print work. However, it should be noted that Elizabeth Catlett learned much from Mexican sculptors at the National School of Painting and Sculpture, such as Francisco Zúñiga, who taught her about pre-Hispanic art-making techniques.

39   Letter from Mrs. William C. Haywood, acting director for fellowships, Julius Ro-

senwald Fund, to Elizabeth Catlett, April 25, 1945, Papers of Charles White, Archives of American Art, Smithsonian Institution, Washington.

40 Elizabeth Catlett, "Responding to Cultural Hunger," in *Reimagining America: The Arts of Social Change*, ed. Mark O'Brien and Craig Little (Philadelphia: New Society Publishers, 1990).

41 Camille Billops, "Interview with Elizabeth Catlett, October 1, 1989," *Artists and Influence* 10 (1991): 21.

42 Catlett, "Responding to Cultural Hunger," 246.

43 When Catlett returned to the United States in 1947 to divorce White, she realized that remaining in the United States might cause difficulties for her because of her political affiliations. Specifically, she was concerned that she could be subpoenaed by HUAC and questioned about her political activity, as well as that of her friends, some of whom had been members of the Communist Party. Melanie Herzog, *Elizabeth Catlett: An American Artist in Mexico* (Seattle: University of Washington Press, 2000), 70.

44 Deborah Caplow, "Leopoldo Méndez, Revolutionary Art, and the Mexican Print: In the Service of the People" (Ph.D. diss., University of Washington, 1999), 141. This position, in which the organization took a confrontational stance against the Mexican government, changed significantly after the emergence of the Popular Front.

45 Covarrubias, "Modern Art," 138.

46 See Caplow, "Leopoldo Méndez, Revolutionary Art, and the Mexican Print."

47 Ibid., 147.

48 Ibid., 148.

49 Elizabeth Catlett, interview with author, Cuernavaca, Mexico, June 1999.

50 Elizabeth Catlett, quoted in Samella Lewis, "Elizabeth Catlett," in *Elizabeth Catlett: Works on Paper, 1944–1992*, ed. Jeanne Zeidler (Hampton, Va.: Hampton University Museum, 1993), 9.

51 Goldman, *In the Spirit of Resistance*, 58.

52 This focus on international issues was in part related to the presence of exiles from Germany and Spain in Mexico in the TGP. One of these exiles was Hannes Meyer, who had been involved with the Bauhaus in Germany.

53 Dawn Ades, "The Mexican Mural Movement," in *Art in Latin America: The Modern Era, 1820–1980* (New Haven: Yale University Press, 1989), 188.

54 Susan Richards, "Imagining the Political: El Taller de Gráfica Popular in Mexico, 1937–1949" (Ph.D. diss., Department of History, University of New Mexico, 2001), viii.

55 El Taller de Gráfica Popular, *Estampas de la Revolución Mexicana* (Mexico: La Estampa Mexicana, 1947), 152. Hannes Meyer further elaborated on this statement in an essay he wrote for El Taller de Gráfica Popular, "Doce años de obra artística colectiva," which he edited in 1949: "The question of the TGP's future is in practice identical with that of the Mexican nation and of the revolutionary forces within. An art that is true to the life of the people is inseparably bound to their destiny. Mexico, along with the other Latin American countries, is exposed to eco-

nomic and cultural invasion from their 'good neighbors' to the north. 80 percent of Mexico's trade is with the United States. . . . This is a threat to the Mexican national economy on all fronts, to industry, education and art — to the entire achievements of the Mexican Revolution, in short." Meyer, "The Workshop of Popular Graphic Art in Mexico," in *El Taller de Gráfica Popular: Doce años de obra artística colectiva* [The Workshop for Popular Graphic Art: A Record of Twelve Years of Collective Work] (Mexico: La Estampa Mexicana, 1949), xxii.

56 Richards, "Imagining the Political," 170.

57 Floyd Coleman, *A Courtyard Apart: The Art of Elizabeth Catlett and Francisco Mora* (Biloxi: Mississippi Museum of Art), 13.

58 El Taller de Gráfica Popular, *Estampas de la Revolución Mexicana.*

59 Herzog, *Elizabeth Catlett,* 58–59.

60 Catlett, interview with author, June 1999.

61 Herzog, *Elizabeth Catlett,* 60.

62 Ibid. (From "Paintings, Sculpture and Prints of the Negro Woman," in the possession of Elizabeth Catlett.)

63 The Barnett-Aden Gallery was the first private gallery of African American art in Washington, D.C. It was founded in 1943 by Alonzo Aden and James Herring, who opened the gallery to provide a space for all artists, especially African American artists, to show their work.

64 Catlett, interview with author, June 1999.

65 Wilson, interview with Robert Brown, 301.

66 Ibid., 319.

67 Soon after arriving, Wilson met the U.S. exile Philip Stein, Siqueiros's assistant, who was experimenting with "fast-working" materials, such as paint used for automobiles and vinylite, a plastic for use in outdoor murals.

68 Wilson, interview with Robert Brown, 340.

69 Ades, "The Mexican Mural Movement," 170.

70 In his interview with Robert Brown, Wilson notes that he was "interested in some other social philosophy or direction" because "clearly capitalism or whatever I was living in wasn't working for me, it wasn't working for black people" (336).

71 John Wilson, "Biography" (1990), Papers of John Wilson, reel 4876, Archives of American Art, Smithsonian Institution, Washington.

72 Wilson had studied with Fernand Léger in Paris before moving to Mexico. Wilson, interview with Robert Brown, 342–43.

73 Ibid., 342.

74 The National Association for the Advancement of Colored People (NAACP) and the International Labor Defense (ILD) were involved in extensive anti-lynching campaigns during the 1930s. Although these organizations had proposed numerous bills to Congress and the Senate, federal anti-lynching legislation was not enacted owing to the intransigence of white politicians in the South. Marlene Park, "Lynching and Anti-lynching: Art and Politics in the 1930s," *Prospects* 18 (1993): 311–65.

75   See Mullen, *Popular Fronts*, 79. Drawing on the work of Kenneth Burke, Denning notes that "the arts of the 'cultural front' are better characterized as a 'proletarian grotesque' than as any kind of social realism." Denning, *The Cultural Front*, 123.

76   Denning, *The Cultural Front*, 123.

77   The Mexican government had established a law for the protection of national monuments. See Philip Stein, *The Mexican Murals* (Mexico City: Editur), 4.

78   Catlett picked Tubman, and although some confusion exists in the scholarship on the TGP, Burroughs, not Wilson, produced the image of Sojourner Truth. See Herzog, *Elizabeth Catlett*, 203nn60–61.

79   Herzog, *Elizabeth Catlett*, 103.

80   "Veinte años de vida del Taller de Gráfica Popular" [Twenty Years of the Taller de Gráfica Popular], *Artes de México* 3, no. 18 (1957).

81   See Karl Schmidt, *Communism in Mexico: A Study in Political Frustration* (Austin: University of Texas Press, 1965).

82   Elizabeth Catlett, "The Negro People and American Art," *Freedomways*, spring 1961, 76.

83   David Shapiro and Cecile Shapiro, "Abstract Expressionism: The Politics of Apolitical Painting," *Prospects: An Annual of American Cultural Studies* 3 (1977): 183.

84   Ibid., 203.

85   As opposed to the work of African American artists, it is interesting to note that the State Department promoted the music of (primarily) African American jazz musicians. See Penny von Eschen, *Satchmo Blows Up the World: Jazz Ambassadors Play the Cold War* (Cambridge: Harvard University Press, 2004).

86   Francis Stonor Saunders, *The Cultural Cold War: The CIA and the World of Arts and Letters* (New York: New Press, 1999), 254.

87   Romare Bearden and Harry Henderson, *A History of African-American Artists* (New York: Pantheon Books, 1993), 414. Peter Clothier has also suggested that White's work was "profoundly at odds with much of the art of its time, yet profoundly consonant with a history of a particular people at a particular time." Clothier, "Story of White's Art," *Freedomways* 20, no. 3 (1980): 141.

88   The United States Information Agency also limited the dissemination of their work abroad, as it would not exhibit the work of "avowed Communists, persons convicted of crimes involving a threat to the security of the United States, or persons who publicly refused to answer questions of congressional committees regarding connection with the Communist movement." William Hauptman, "The Suppression of Art in the McCarthy Decade," *Artforum*, October 1973, 49.

89   He had been represented by Boris Mirski's gallery in Boston. Lois Tarlow, "John Wilson," *Art New England* 19, no. 5 (August–September 1998): 21–23.

90   Margaret Taylor Goss Burroughs, lecture at the opening of "Highlights from the Atlanta University Collection of Afro-American Art," at the High Museum of Art in 1973. As quoted from Winifred Stoelting, "The Atlanta Years: A Biographical Sketch," in *Hale Woodruff: Fifty Years of His Art* (New York: Studio Museum in Harlem, 1979), 24.

91   Eva Cockcroft, "The United States and Socially Concerned Latin American Art: 1920–1970," in *The Latin American Spirit: Art and Artists in the United States, 1920–1970*, ed. Luis B. Cancel (New York: H. N. Abrams in association with the Bronx Museum of the Arts, 1988), 202.

92   Quoted in John Pittman, "He Was an Implacable Critic of His Own Creations," *Freedomways* 20, no. 3 (1980): 191.

93   John Wilson also worked with Bob Blackburn in New York in the late 1950s.

94   The "306," located in a former stable at 306 West 141st Street in New York, was a WPA-sponsored community art center established by the artists Charles Alston and Henry Bannarn.

95   Alison Cameron, "Buenos Vecinos: African-American Printmaking and the Taller de Gráfica Popular," *Print Quarterly* 16, no. 4 (1999): 364.

96   Mullen, *Popular Fronts*, 192.

97   Ibid. As a response to her rejection from the South Side Community Art Center, Burroughs helped found the Ebony Museum, later the DuSable Museum of African American history.

98   Burroughs, interview with Anna M. Tyler, November 11 and December 5, 1988, 64.

99   Ibid., 67.

100   Catlett, "The Negro People and American Art," 79.

101   Ibid., 78.

102   Quoted in Pittman, "He Was an Implacable Critic," 191.

103   Saunders, *The Cultural Cold War*, 291. Because of their association with the Communist Party or so-called Communist front organizations, Du Bois's and Robeson's passports were revoked by the State Department so that they could not travel outside the United States. Scholarly works about the U.S. government's treatment of African American activists associated with the Communist Party during the Cold War include Gerald Horne, *Black and Red: W. E. B. Du Bois and the Afro-American Response to the Cold War, 1944–1963* (Albany: State University of New York Press, 1986); Horne, *Black Liberation/Red Scare: Ben Davis and the Communist Party* (Newark: University of Delaware Press, 1994); and Kenneth O'Reilly, *Black Americans: The FBI Files* (New York: Carroll and Graf, 1994).

The Attributes of Sovereignty

The Cold War, Colonialism, and Community
Education in Puerto Rico

Alyosha Goldstein

During the early Cold War, as the terms of global conflict were displaced onto the so-called periphery, the U.S. State Department and the Partido Popular Democrático promoted Puerto Rico as an object lesson in market-directed popular sovereignty. In 1952, a U.S.-sanctioned islandwide plebiscite ostensibly liberated Puerto Rico from the colonial netherworld of "unincorporation" by designating the island an *estado libre asociado* (free associated state). According to governor of Puerto Rico Luis Muñoz Marín, the new commonwealth status provided "a dramatic refutation of the communist claim that the United States position is narrow, colonialistic, and reactionary." Moreover, asserted Muñoz, "the social and economic surge in Puerto Rico clearly demonstrates that a people of different historical background can find a way out of their former anguish and despair, in close association with the United States."[1]

Muñoz's vision of hemispheric relations provides a striking contrast to José Martí's classic 1891 portrait "Our America." Whereas Martí's text was an impassioned appeal for Latin American solidarity against U.S. imperialism, Muñoz presented a calculated celebration of Puerto Rico as a "bridge between two cultures" that could harmonize inter-American affairs. Martí warned against U.S. hemispheric machinations as the leviathan to the north bemoaned the closing of the continental frontier and began its frenzied course of "aberrant" colonial acquisition.[2] Sixty-five years later, U.S. Latin American policy promoted a stultifying constellation of covert counterinsurgency initiatives, trade-oriented banking and private investment operations, and increasing pressure for anticommunist hemispheric security measures.[3] In a 1955 memo to all U.S. diplomatic missions in Latin America, the cold warrior John Foster Dulles cautioned that "criticism of the proportional amount of United States aid to Latin America, as compared with economic assistance in other areas, especially Europe and the Far East, is so persistent as to constitute a serious factor in our good relations with other governments of this hemisphere."[4] It was within this context that Muñoz tactically endorsed an enhanced U.S. inter-American presence with Puerto Rico as its interlocutor.

This essay focuses on the political and social dynamics of the Muñoz administration's popular support and their place within the strategic expression of hemispheric cooperation. I argue that the political utility of "local community" as an articulation of populist reason was an integral component of Partido Popular Democrático hegemony. Community as a social and administrative category instantiated a collective popular identity intimately aligned with the PPD itself, as well as providing a tacit counterdiscourse to political nationalism that focused on community building as the essence of nation building and democracy as local community participation. Community as such served as an indispensable supplement to capitalist modernization precisely because it held out an implicit critique of imperialist subordination while rendering localized inequality a synecdoche for imperial expropriation.[5] Moreover, by localizing imperatives for self-determination and building economic capacity in cooperation with mainland capital, the PPD garnered both popular Puerto Rican allegiance and U.S. approval. The shift from political nationalism to cultural nationalism evident in the development of the PPD platform between the 1930s and the 1950s was contingent not only on reformist policies that produced tangible material outcomes for working people and the rural poor—most importantly through land redistribution—but on the simultaneous mobilization and containment of local community as the grounds of politics as such. The localized circumstances of the early Cold War conjuncture, and the specific constellation of political utilities that spoke in the name of community during that time, cast the idea of "community" through the historical intersection of competing political imaginaries.

Puerto Rico was of course not unique in being a U.S. colony. Rather, it was among a carefully policed constellation of "unincorporated territories" and "dependencies" whose existence belied the living history of U.S. colonialism. Hawai'i, Micronesia, the Philippines, the U.S. Virgin Islands, and Alaska each represent distinct historical trajectories of U.S. colonial policy. In each instance, the specific conjuncture of economic, military-strategic, symbolic, and geo-political U.S. interests, as well as the degree of organized anticolonial insurgency, during the post–World War II period contributed to a distinct course of U.S. action aimed at consolidating its global hegemony.[6]

My argument begins with a brief account of the ways in which ideas about local community—and community development in particular—mattered for U.S. Cold War policy. I then focus on Puerto Rico's División de Educación de la Comunidad (Division of Community Education, or DIVEDCO) during the 1950s and 1960s as a means to analyze the dynamics of Partido Popular Demo-crático hegemony on the island during this time. My central argument is that this hegemonic formation was built on localization and an operative tension between popular mobilization and containment overdetermined by Cold War geopolitics. I am not suggesting that Puerto Rico's "showcase" status was taken as a model by other Latin American countries and "third world" nations, but rather that PPD hegemony required this Americas or third world referent in its negotiation of U.S. colonial rule during an era of decolonization and super-power polarity. Popular identification with, and support for, the PPD required a delicate balance between the party as what Muñoz called a *nacionalismo pueblo* (people's state) discernible in the details of everyday life, and the party as the most advantageous mediator of U.S. colonial rule.

Puerto Rico and the Multiple Horizons of "Community"

Beginning in the late 1940s, community provided a localized scale of everyday life through which to insinuate the seemingly epic proportions of the Cold War. It was during this period that policymakers and social scientists formalized "community development" as an administrative model for state-assisted collective self-help purportedly intended to maximize and stimulate democratic participation and community action. This model drew on earlier community-based organizing paradigms from the U.S. settlement house movement, rural reconstruction in India, the Tennessee Valley Authority, British colonial administration, the United Nations Economic and Social Council, and President Truman's Point Four technical assistance programs.[7]

By the 1950s, community development was commonly articulated with liberal ideologies of economic growth that sought to emphasize democratic process as central to economic progress. Poverty, as perceived by policymakers, was a problem for modernization in terms of the potential disorder it posed to political stability and for impeding the socialization of the largely agricultural rural peasantry of the "underdeveloped" world. By aiming to retrieve community through development and to stabilize development through community, social scientists and policymakers insisted on a particular definition of community. This definition emphasized locality, social homogeneity, and common culture while advocating particular forms of collective action as the method and means of restoring and reinvigorating attenuated social bonds.[8]

Community development marshaled the "natural resource" of human labor in concert with the goal of increased productivity for development. A 1955 U.S. Foreign Operations Administration policy statement foregrounds this connection in its definition of community development: "Community Development is a technique for stimulating organized self-help undertakings through the democratic process. It aims to mobilize the principal resource of most underdeveloped areas — their manpower and their interest in improving their own lot — once they have become aware that improvement is possible."[9] Combined with an emphasis on fostering political and economic stability through participation and inclusion, the focus on cultivating labor as an underutilized raw material had a definite appeal to policymakers as a disciplinary mechanism.

In Puerto Rico, the terms through which the Partido Popular Democrático secured its standing as the embodiment of a "nacionalismo pueblo" changed over time. The PPD emerged from a particular fraction of elites, personified by Muñoz, who, in the context of 1930s Depression-era U.S. colonialism, embraced land redistribution and held as the party's symbol the *jíbaro* (rural peasant) with the motto of "Pan, Tierra y Libertad" (Bread, Land, and Liberty). The rise of the PPD during the 1930s and early 1940s was predicated on disaggregating the hold of the semifeudal foreign-owned sugar plantations and affirming the "traditional" values and interests of the rural poor. The PPD-sponsored 1941 Land Act, which provided *agregado* (squatter) families with small parcels of land arranged in planned rural communities and established an institutional infrastructure for enforcing the breakup of the *hacendado* (large landowner) controlled system of rural labor peonage, secured an enduring political loyalty among the rural poor.[10]

The PPD coupled its populist veneration of the jíbaro with efforts to promote a program for industrial modernization amenable to U.S. business interests. The *populares* initially advanced state-owned industry and locally run cooperatives only to jettison such ideas in favor of an agenda acquiescent to private capital. At the center of the island's economic transformation was "Operation Bootstrap" (Operación de Manos a la Obra), a PPD-devised plan for export-driven industrialization that vigorously courted U.S. private capital and industry with the help of tax-abatement arrangements and the promise of a no-strike, no-union pledge for factories.[11]

The sociologist Angel Quintero Rivera has underscored the significant shift in PPD ideology between the 1930s and the late 1940s. Although the party came to power through a reformist and populist platform, "the emphasis changed from the state as representative of the demands of the masses, to the state as an instrument which could regulate conflicting interests." The PPD espoused a liberal populism still ostensibly in the name of "the poor," even as the party sought to contain and manage "the poor." According to Quintero Rivera, "The transformation of the PPD, then, was the genuine response of a class, still in the process of formation, which saw itself as destined to rule, and which was being shaped through its populist political style and the myth of the 'People's State'—a state that was non-partisan and above class interests. It was a class which sought, nonetheless, to control the state, and to be the natural leader of the society."[12] The political hegemony of this class further depended on a delicate negotiation of the island's status with regard to U.S. colonial policy.

In 1944, the PPD gained control of both houses of the legislature, defeating the Republican-Socialist coalition. They proceeded to launch a concerted attack on the radical labor union Confederación General de Trabajadores (General Federation of Labor) and purged the pro-independence faction within the PPD, which had formed the Congreso Pro-Independencia. Muñoz became the island's first elected governor in 1948, after the United States granted Puerto Ricans the right to gubernatorial elections. The Muñoz administration's ruthless suppression of the October 1950 Nationalist uprising and subsequent persecution of Nationalist Party leaders made it clear that Puerto Rican anticolonialism would be treated by the PPD as politically subversive.[13] Following its 1952 political makeover as an estado libre asociado, Puerto Rico was vigorously promoted as a model for "emerging" nations to emulate despite its continued status as a U.S. territory.

In January 1953, five months after Puerto Rico's new constitution was ratified, the United States formally petitioned the United Nations to remove the island from its list of non-self-governing territories. By a narrow margin made more ambiguous by the number of abstentions, the UN General Assembly concluded the following December that Puerto Rico had the "attributes of political sovereignty which clearly identify the status . . . as that of an autonomous political entity." Puerto Rico was removed from the list, and both the PPD and the U.S. State Department collaborated in publicizing the island as a "showcase of democratic development," a "middle road to freedom," "America's answer to communism," and, later, a crucial counterexample to Castro's Cuba.[14]

U.S. propagandists also sought to win support from former colonies by drawing a parallel between the American War for Independence and mid-twentieth-century decolonization. Such a comparison extended the United States as a model for emulation, a colony liberated through democratic revolution and industrial capitalism, as well as interjected the United States as a patron and partner in a universal struggle against tyranny. According to one 1954 U.S. agency report, "The U.S., as the first colony in modern history to win independence for itself, instinctively shares the aspirations for liberty of all dependent and colonial peoples. It is U.S. policy to help, not hinder, the spread of liberty. The U.S. has in the past and will continue in the future to sponsor the development of political independence."[15]

It was precisely the highly visible character of Puerto Rico's poverty that enabled its transformation into a "showcase of development." The sociologist Earl Parker Hanson's Cold War boosterism clearly expressed the importance of this tension. Describing the State Department–sponsored tours of the island, Hanson recalls:

> One visitor in 1957 was a newspaper publisher from Indonesia. He told me that he had come to see the island because in his own country the politically strong Communists were constantly pointing to Puerto Rico as a suffering, starving, demoralized victim of the United States' imperialistic greed. He wanted to see for himself, and he did see. He saw many poor people, but he also saw them striving with hope and in freedom to improve their lives. When he returned to Indonesia, he published articles in his paper refuting the Communists' claims. Such articles, pointing to Puerto Rico as the refutation of imperialistic charges against the United

States, are beginning to appear by the dozens in Latin America, in Africa, in Asia, and in Europe.[16]

While the PPD may have wished to foreground the dramatic successes of economic development on the island, a persistent image of poverty-in-transformation was necessary for U.S. State Department efforts to depict the island as an object lesson for the third world.

Thus statehood for the island was also out of the question. To fully incorporate Puerto Rico into the United States would upset the delicate balance between the advantages of "association" with the United States and an appeal to sovereignty. Puerto Rico could serve as a model for other "underdeveloped" nations to emulate only if the island maintained a degree of formal independence. Similarly, the unseemly questions of racial and linguistic incorporation actually worked to the advantage of U.S. policy with the island's population as clearly autonomous from the U.S. polity. As distinct from the United States, Puerto Rico could appear closer to those for whom it was being "showcased" rather than becoming another front on the domestic battle over civil rights. For U.S. policymakers, black and brown people speaking a language other than English were best subsumed into a global image of, as Hanson put it, "many poor people . . . striving with hope and in freedom to improve their lives." From this perspective, association with the United States provided the hope, freedom, and democratic ethos but appeared to have no direct relationship to the condition of poverty.

The authority of the island's modernizing elite (e.g., Muñoz administration appointees Teodoro Moscoso, Arturo Morales-Carrión, Rafael Picó, and Jaime Benítez) was intimately linked to the highly visible role of U.S. social scientists on the island. This legitimating association extended from the Junta de Planificación de Puerto Rico (Planning Board) to the University of Puerto Rico to the implementation of programs such as División de Educación de la Comunidad. A major vehicle for the burgeoning of social science fieldwork and analysis conducted on the island in the post–World War II period was the founding of the University of Puerto Rico's Social Science Research Center. The center's staff succeeded in attracting a remarkable number of high-profile U.S. scholars, such as the economist John Kenneth Galbraith, the sociologist Melvin Tumin, the political scientist Carl J. Friedrich, and the anthropologists Julian Steward, Sidney Mintz, and Eric Wolf. Accentuating Puerto Rico's value as a "research laboratory" with a unique combination of Latin American and U.S. cultures, the center effectively promoted the island as "one of the most fruitful places in the world to study development, swift social change, and the culture fusion of a border society."[17]

Community Education and the Insularities of Democracy

Puerto Rico's División de Educación de la Comunidad (DIVEDCO) was a program for civic education piloted in 1947 and subsequently established as an agency within the Department of Education in 1949. To engage the island's rural poor, many of whom were illiterate, DIVEDCO produced motion pictures and graphic pamphlets, books, and posters. Pamphlets were distributed and films screened in rural communities by field organizers whose aim was to use the material as a catalyst for group discussion and collective self-help. Legislation defined DIVEDCO's mission as teaching the tenets of self-governance and inspiring among local Puerto Rican communities "the wish, the tendency, and the way of making use of their own aptitudes for the solution of many of their own problems of health, education, cooperation, [and] social life through the action of the community itself."[18] Local meetings served to identify collective concerns and mobilize community participation to address these concerns through government-supported small-scale education, social service, and infrastructure projects.

The inspiration for community involvement undoubtedly followed from budgetary restraints as much as any rhetorical claims. Part of the appeal of community development for Muñoz and the PPD was its low cost to government. With severely constrained financial resources historically depleted by the dispossessions of colonialism and compounded by the tax-abatement tariff-free strategies of Operation Bootstrap's efforts to attract private investment, the means of backing such projects were limited. Self-help ideology offered both the pretense and the possibility of working with such scarcity.

Whereas Operation Bootstrap was characteristic of the elite-driven centralized approach typically associated with the modernization agenda, DIVEDCO translated the demands of liberal capitalism into everyday, locally initiated democratic practices crucial to anticommunist discourse. As one education scholar summed up more broadly: "The Free World . . . is developing a new approach to community education, which depends on the understanding and acceptance of the desirability of change by the people who will be affected, so that their conscious and enthusiastic participation in making the change is assured."[19] Not only did modernization require a labor force inclined and adapted to the new industrial regime, but it could substantially benefit from a political order that passionately affirmed the requisites of popular consent.

DIVEDCO was a cornerstone of the PPD's hegemonic project because of its capacity to officially associate the daily life of the rural poor with state policy while championing the economic independence and self-initiated enterprise of "the people." Furthermore, the substance of this independence to an extent operated as a surrogate for the elusive and ever deferred possibility of Puerto Rico's political sovereignty. Small-scale local cooperation and mutual aid, of course, existed long before the introduction of state-sponsored programs such as DIVEDCO. Despite intermittent claims to the contrary, the rural poor did not have to be taught such forms of collective support and reciprocity. Thus DIVEDCO field organizers were instructed to be "aware of the history of the 'juntas'" and to locate existing "centers where community activity is already underway."[20] What was significant about PPD programs — and DIVEDCO in particular — was that they established a formal link to the state through such activities and institutionalized these localized mechanisms for survival within the state itself. Thus, although not new as such, local cooperation and mutual aid assumed an unprecedented significance. The political and administrative recognition of these activities valorized them as expressions of the state. Because they were associated with the tangible gains of redistribution and employment, the incorporation of such activities had the effect of confirming the everyday instantiation of the PPD as embodying the "nacionalismo pueblo."

This impression was possible to provisionally maintain because of the limited but perceptible material benefits for non-elites that resulted from the infusion of U.S. private capital, industrial wages, and labor migration to the U.S. mainland. In his 1949 legislative message, Muñoz contended that "we must ask ourselves: Production for What? Production to serve what class of life? . . . People do not exist for industrialization. Industrialization exists for the people."[21] DIVEDCO's community development programs fostered political consent and participation because of their association with material improvements and social infrastructure that had a marked impact on the everyday life of the rural poor. The annual per capita income in Puerto Rico increased dramatically from $150 in 1940 to $723 in 1960. Adjusting for inflation, real per capita income increased by almost 200 percent over this twenty-year period with a yearly growth rate for average personal income of 5.6 percent. Relative income inequality increased between the wealthiest 10 percent of the population and the poorest, but all income groups experienced growth. Between 1953 and 1963, the income of the poorest 10 percent grew by 25 percent, and that of the next 10 percent grew by 52 percent. In 1960, 78 percent of families were earning annual incomes of more than $1,000, compared with only 2.9 percent in 1940. In just ten years, life expectancy at birth in Puerto Rico leaped from an average of forty-six years in 1940 to sixty-one years in 1950.[22] These material improvements, however, were only significant for PPD hegemony because they were part of the more comprehensive popular structure of feeling embodied in the fieldwork of the División de Educación de la Comunidad.

Popular identification with the insular government was grounded in a sense of the state as the people's advocate, even when this became manifest in localized antagonisms that suggested a disjuncture between municipal authority and insular programs. Interviews conducted by the anthropologist Ismael García Colón provide a sense of the localized activities through which the rural poor came to identify with the state. Describing the process of neighborhood meetings and film screenings, Práxedes Collazo Ramos, a DIVEDCO group organizer in the town of Cidra during the 1950s, observed that "this program motivated neighbors to discuss their problems. In this way, many community projects emerged through the [DIVEDCO] movies." His colleague Francisco Zayas recollected that "as neighbors became more knowledgeable, began holding meetings, and discuss[ed] their problems . . . we began to help them and inform them on how to seek assistance from the government." According to neighborhood resident Concepción Rivera Santiago, this led to the creation of formal committees to petition the Municipal Hall for assistance. "We would discuss our needs," recalled Rivera, "and then we would head to the Mayor's Office. There, they would tell us whether or not they could help us. If they couldn't help us, they would give us some help for the moment and tell us to continue forward doing the rest on our own." Moreover, another resident, Monserrate Reyes Ramos, recounted that when demands for access to potable water and improved roads so that the ambulance could transport people in need of emergency assistance were not addressed, neighbors went to protest at the Municipal Hall.[23] Even when such conflicts challenged local authority, they had the effect of reinforcing a broader identification with the PPD-directed state, under whose auspices the "community" had mobilized to begin with.

Ostensibly directed by the needs of local communities, DIVEDCO was also unmistakably marked by the presence of imported expertise. The agency itself was designed by Muñoz, his wife Inés Mendoza de Muñoz, the former U.S. Farm Security Administration photographers Edward Rosskam and Jack Delano, and the graphic artist Irene Delano. Fred Wale, another former member of the Farm Security Administration, was brought in to serve as the division's director. Even as efforts were made to gradually replace mainland Anglo staff with Puerto Rican counterparts, a certain dynamic of colonial tutelage persisted. Wale's appointment as director further substantiated this sense of colonial overdetermination. Amilcar Tirado, one of Jack Delano's early recruits to the Division of Cinema and Graphics and the first director of DIVEDCO's Cinema Section, recalled, "I was very opposed [to] bringing in a North American to develop the Division of Community Education, something we had worked out and developed. . . . [Director Fred Wale] tried to do his best, but could never understand that basically we were not Evangelical."[24] The division's contract with the University of Michigan's Institute of Social Research to provide "objective" data on target populations and evaluate the reception of DIVEDCO educational materials to the Analysis Unit reiterated this outside presence.

DIVEDCO's films and graphics registered similar tensions between the local and the colonial metropole. Just as one author has described Jack Delano's FSA photographs of Puerto Rico as "a biographical sketch of imperial power reformed by New Deal policies," the extended body of the Division's filmic production was overtly shaped by New Deal documentary aesthetics and modes of address.[25] As with the increasing popularity of motion pictures for education during the 1940s and 1950s, DIVEDCO productions registered the influence of John Grierson, the Film and Photo League, and Pare Lorentz, as well as the technological advances and experiments in training developed by the U.S. military during World War II. The presence of U.S. educators, technicians, artists, and filmmakers not only linked the division to the North but also contributed to the greater visibility of its work. DIVEDCO films were distributed internationally by the United States Information Agency and UNESCO.[26] This required a balancing act such that even as DIVEDCO films were feted at international festivals in Edinburgh, Venice, and Melbourne, Wale and others repeatedly insisted that local Puerto Rican communities were the primary audience for the films.

Targeting the local poor, DIVEDCO sought to reform what were diagnosed as their paternalistic and fatalistic tendencies. Kalevro Oberg, a cultural anthropologist and consultant for the U.S. State Department, alleged that when poor rural people in Puerto Rico resisted the liberating overtures of community education, "this resistance is rooted in the traditional paternalistic type of rural society in which the community does little or nothing for itself but expects everything from the government through the intercession of its formal leaders,

such as political bosses, large land-owners, priests, and even school teachers."
Oberg contended that DIVEDCO could bring these recalcitrant peasants into
the fold of the nation, better harmonizing their aspirations with those of the
larger polity: "The rural folk are intellectually isolated, they are in the nation
but not really part of it. . . . With a properly oriented community education
program the people will be brought to a cultural level in which the national objectives are their objective, in which action and self-help will originate among
the rural masses."[27] On the one hand, there was a concerted effort to destabilize
locally entrenched political paternalism. On the other hand, the persistence of
such monopolization of political power was held to be a failure of enlightened
self-interest on the part of the peasants themselves.

Community initiative and local participation were the prescribed antidotes
to this failure of resolve. Each component of the División de Educación de la
Comunidad was intended to serve as a heuristic device informed by community concerns. The Production Unit made films and illustrated booklets geared
to problems articulated during community discussions organized by DIVEDCO
group organizers. Films were produced on location, often with nonprofessional
actors recruited from the surrounding community. The production process
itself, both in film and in graphics, served as a training ground for local technicians and artists, many of whom would subsequently assume leadership in
DIVEDCO projects. The Field and Training Unit recruited local community
members to serve as group organizers and functioned through ongoing community discussion and planning sessions. Writers working in the Editorial Unit,
who not only drafted DIVEDCO's pamphlets but were responsible for providing
screenplays for the Production Unit, lived in the communities they were writing about for a period of several days or several weeks for each project.[28] The
Analysis Unit gauged the efficacy of DIVEDCO materials by surveying community reaction and measuring changes in attitude toward the subjects addressed.

DIVEDCO's compulsion for localization was paralleled by a drive for remedi-
ating the conduct and consciousness of individuals. The division substituted a
concern for establishing conduits for collective mobilization and inclusionary
policymaking with a focus on producing the democratic citizen as a normative political subject. In its programs, an understanding of democracy as a form
of state power was essentially replaced by concerns for internal psychological
transformation. To a certain extent this focus on individual mental and emotional adjustment as a political end in and of itself was indicative of the ubiquity
of psychological vocabulary and truth-claims following World War II.[29] It also

fit well with the psychological diagnostics of Oscar Lewis's "culture of poverty" thesis, which, although not codified until 1959, provided a convenient phrase for an already widespread social-science belief in the family as the culpable agent for social inequality and intergenerational poverty.

As with the community development model more generally, DIVEDCO emphasized process over outcome. The accent on process privileged the normative ambitions of community development. The prominent advocates William and Loureide Biddle defined the value of community development as a "social process by which human beings can become more competent to live with and gain some control over local aspects of a frustrating and changing world. . . . The essence of process does not consist in any fixed succession of events . . . but in the growth that occurs within individuals, within groups, and within the communities they serve."[30] The sociologists Stephen B. Withey and Charles F. Cannell reiterated a theme evident throughout published accounts of DIVEDCO when they wrote that "the Division centers its work on the community—its perception of itself and its own potential. . . . The problems are the community's own; the motivations and processes by which the community grows as it solves these problems are the concerns of the Division."[31] Fred Wale further stipulated the terms of this process, stating that "material facilities must be accompanied by internal growth for community well-being and . . . this cannot be accomplished without the use of democratic methods in all matters effecting [sic] the related lives of those within the community."[32] The process of introspection is facilitated through group discussion and culminates in an emergent "democratic" consciousness.

In typical descriptions of DIVEDCO fieldwork, problems were detached from the broader social context and individualized. Social, economic, and political dilemmas were construed as an issue of community self-esteem and confidence. Individuals must overcome their own internalized sense of resignation and inferiority to begin to work collectively. Moreover, most DIVEDCO narratives did not include any significant discussion on the outcome of collective efforts other than to note that a milk station (a government-funded facility that provided poor children with free breakfast), bridge, or road was built. For instance, the field organizer Zacarías Rodríguez reported that "for more than a year the people of Cuyón talked and worked together, individually and in groups, seeking a solution to a problem common to all." Rodríguez recounts triumphantly that "through many disappointments but with even greater accomplishments, through sickness and poverty, often delayed by rain and mud, the community finally reached the place where today . . . the community is building its own milk station."[33] Reports such as this accentuated the protracted duration of the process, as well as persistent poverty and struggle. Of course, these forms of collective discussion were not inherently "therapeutic" narratives of personal psychological catharsis and could also potentially lead to more extensive and overtly political mobilizations. However, the administrative organization of DIVEDCO discouraged this by maintaining the closely circumscribed and assertively local character of the program.

Whereas activities within the communities themselves continually threatened to exceed the procedures of introspection, the selection and training of field organizers demonstrated to an even greater degree the therapeutic imperative. In describing the training design, Wale and Field Program director Carmen Isales reflected that "we believed that democracy began with the stimulus given each individual to search into his innermost resources."[34] Group organizers were selected on the basis of criteria that included the following questions: "Was he a man of the people?" "Could he work in his own community?" "Was he a happy man at home?" "What were his attitudes towards authoritarian behavior?" "Was he a secure person?" "Was he a static personality or did he possess the capacity for growth?"[35] Here a candidate's psychological profile was translated into a quantifiable political value. Democracy was an internal capacity, a propensity for a distinct set of moral values grounded in a stable and secure emotional foundation. Thus democracy in practice became a process of liberating oneself from neurotic disorders and interiorized constraints.

Both training and supervision also appear as a process of confronting and overcoming inherited attitudes. Wale and Isales insisted that "to assure the fulfillment of the aims of the program, attention must be given to the field man as a personality. His whole life is a subject that comes often into discussion during supervisory conference."[36] While this approach certainly replicated social work training and supervision, it also projected the distinctly social and economic struggle of local communities into purely psychological dimensions. The connection between training and the frame of community action is clearly articulated in the reflections of field organizer Higinio Rivera:

> I could not have been more surprised. There were no lectures on how to build roads or latrines, or how to rotate crops. We were told government technical people would help when they [the local community] needed such aid. Instead the instructor threw open to discussion such problems as— can a poor, uneducated jíbaro without any land do much to affect the wel-

fare of his community? We spent three months discussing such questions. I had to dig deep into my own attitudes to find the answers. . . . What it did was to prepare me to go into a community that lacked even the minimum facilities and to recognize that the tragedy was not that the people lacked latrines or paved roads or even pure water, but rather the spiritual isolation in which they lived.[37]

The material conditions of poverty and deprivation were thus reduced to being symptoms of "spiritual isolation." DIVEDCO organizers were taught to bypass the apparent complexities of such symptoms in order to concentrate on the more profound process of spiritual transformation.

The political scientist Henry Wells has noted that the budgetary support for DIVEDCO was insufficient to achieve any significant impact on the island's social conditions. Moreover, the early decision to shift the bureaucratic mechanisms for small-scale "self-help" community projects to the Social Programs Administration of the Department of Agriculture and Commerce only further diminished DIVEDCO's ability to marshal resources to provide for community-generated endeavors.[38] It was precisely this reticence toward fiscal sponsorship and long-term structural change, however, that propelled the community development model to begin with. Rather than merely embodying such grand and unrealized aspirations, community development and DIVEDCO specifically approached the ethical substance of democracy in the details of everyday life with little concern for systemic change.

This limited scope also translated into the representational framework of the division. The new forms of labor, new relations of production, and the social consequences of the accelerated programs for industrialization and modernization initiated under Operation Bootstrap were peculiarly absent from DIVEDCO's depictions of peasant life. While local communities were indeed prompted to organize and work collectively, and were even assisted in their efforts to challenge entrenched local leadership based on landed and mercantile power, the agency's work remained localized and rarely addressed the profound effects of the collapse of agriculture and new realities of industrial production and urbanization on the island.[39] Indeed, this could be said of community development programs generally. In this sense, even as community development forced local contingency and specificity upon the universalized abstractions of modernization theory, the salience and utility of local community lay precisely in its clear circumscription as local. DIVEDCO's stubborn myopia did little to address in image and narrative how Puerto Rico's broader socioeconomic circumstances changed over time. Apart from single projects on the issue of women's rights and migration—which reflected little concern for the realities of Puerto Rican public policy on sterilization and economic opportunities on the U.S. mainland—the narratives and stylistics of DIVEDCO films and pamphlets, as well as the division's objectives for fieldworker organizing, remained static. However, especially as industrialization and urbanization threatened to overwhelm "traditional" farming and local peasant culture, DIVEDCO's representational frame must not be reduced to mere sentimentalism. This resistance to the realities of massive social dislocation and modernization by recourse to images of "traditional" Puerto Rican life resonated strongly with multiple currents of cultural nationalism on the island at the time.

Indeed, the expansive resonance of Muñoz's cultural agenda allowed him to weather the various contradictions of his political and economic platforms. As the anthropologist Jorge Duany has argued, over the course of the 1940s, Muñoz gradually disavowed political nationalism in favor of an assertive and advantageous cultural nationalism. That the legacy of the División de Educación de la Comunidad has been almost entirely its role in Puerto Rican cultural history, and not in the expansion of local political and economic power, reaffirms precisely this turn to cultural nationalism. For the island's elite, cultural nationalism affirmed an autonomous national identity still conducive to the strategic compromise with U.S. colonial rule. It momentarily suppressed the political implications of championing a distinct national identity and thus also held appeal for pro-statehood advocates.[40]

Cultural nationalism, however, did not definitively displace political nationalism. The entreaty to a shared cultural heritage valorized the traditional and local as fixed and intrinsic attributes but did not guarantee a uniform or static political consent. Instead cultural nationalism provided the appearance of a shared identification that in fact remained manifestly heterogeneous. Its multiple trajectories—particularly the way in which it could in fact serve as a latent expression of class contradictions—undermined its capacity to serve as a stable ground for PPD hegemony. As the external factors that bolstered PPD preeminence became increasingly precarious during the 1960s, the difference of what cultural nationalism meant for elites and for urbanized, proletarianized, and displaced (emigrated) former peasants became increasingly volatile. The widespread labor unrest and wildcat strikes of the late 1960s and early 1970s made it abundantly clear that the days of the PPD-brokered class compromise were past.

The writing of René Marqués, a renowned playwright and longtime director of DIVEDCO's Editorial Unit, provides a striking example of the complexity of a cultural nationalism elevated through the symbol of the jíbaro. In his influential 1962 essay "The Docile Puerto Rican: Literature and Psychological Reality," Marqués presents a critique of internalized colonial rule and the outward passivity he believes characteristic of the Puerto Rican "personality." Often considered a sequel to *Insularismo*, Antonio S. Pedreira's seminal 1934 portrait of the Puerto Rican character, Marqués's essay abandoned Pedreira's quasi-historico-geographic racial analysis in favor of psychological explanation. Against the grain of the colonial imaginary, both writers deliberately assert a distinctive Puerto Rican national identity. Marqués's disparaging narrative of docility was simultaneously underwritten by a sentimentalized understanding and valorization of "traditional" peasant culture. As in his famous 1950 play *La carreta* (The Oxcart), it is the conditions of colonial modernity that corrupt jíbaro virtue and enable the protracted subordination of the Puerto Rican nation. "The Docile Puerto Rican" was in fact partially a critique of the PPD and U.S. colonialism veiled in rhetorical democracy, and yet Marqués casts the dilemma in definite psychological terms.[41] Nevertheless, his opposition between the "traditional" jíbaro and the modernizing dictates of PPD policy suggests that popular identification with cultural nationalism cannot be understood simply as the substitution of culture for politics. Rather, a popular cultural nationalism preserved an antimodern and class-based framework of belonging articulated through cultural politics.

On the Conditions of Association

The División de Educación de la Comunidad's political utility for the PPD was its capacity to convey an intimate and compelling sense for the rural poor of themselves as extensions of the state. This popular identification was also closely attached to the figure of Luis Muñoz Marín to the extent that he was in many ways perceived as indistinguishable from the PPD itself. This attachment was strong enough to mean that popular confidence in Muñoz often trumped potential dissatisfaction with PPD policies. Muñoz himself recognized the potential liability that this fusion of leader and party posed for sustaining PPD hegemony, and this contributed to his decision to step down as governor in 1964, with the intention of effectively passing the mantle to a chosen PPD successor. During the decade following Muñoz's gubernatorial retirement, social, economic, and political factors converged to fragment and destabilize both DIVEDCO's function as a legitimating force for the PPD and the PPD as a persuasive interlocutor of colonial power.

The Partido Popular Democrático's precipitous decline rendered the purpose and function of DIVEDCO increasingly uncertain. Efforts to depersonalize and institutionalize the PPD after Muñoz stepped down in 1964 foundered on internecine party politics, petty rivalries, and ineffectual leadership. The PPD's decisive electoral defeat in 1968 did not end its political life on the island, but the party would never again regain the complete dominance that it once had. Between 1944 and 1964, the PPD's share of the vote never fell below 58 percent, its strength residing in the rural districts, where it often received 70 to 80 percent of the total vote. PPD-sponsored industrialization and migration to the U.S. mainland, as well as largely unpopular urban resettlement programs during the early to mid-1960s, contributed to the erosion of the party's traditional base and made the rural orientation of its populism appear antiquated. Moreover, even rural electoral support for the PPD declined notably in the 1968 election. During its preceding twenty-four-year monopoly, the PPD had produced substantive material gains for poor and working people of the island. However, even before the global economic recession of the early 1970s, competition for the low-wage, labor-intensive production that was the hallmark of Operation Bootstrap had spread and lured business to other Caribbean, Latin American, and Southeast Asian sites. Even though economic growth persisted through the end of the 1960s, unemployment continued to be relatively high, and the promise of economic mobility eluded most Puerto Ricans.[42] Moreover, industrialization, urbanization, and emigration over the previous decade had substantially dispersed and diminished the island's rural peasantry—precisely the popular base of the PPD and the target group for DIVEDCO outreach.

Although the División de Educación de la Comunidad remained in operation until 1991, its heyday was undoubtedly the 1950s and early 1960s. At the height of DIVEDCO's popularity, its achievements were broadly publicized in scholarly journals, the popular press, UN publications, and U.S. State Department materials. Its most enduring legacy, as the anthropologist Arlene Dávila has argued, was its support for local cultural production and its influence on the founding of the Institute for Puerto Rican Culture.[43] Apart from this, by the late 1960s it had largely vanished from the international scene. During the 1970s, DIVEDCO was increasingly underwritten by direct U.S. federal funds, which by the decade's end made up more than 60 percent of the agency's budget.[44] This dramatic decrease in the insular government's fiscal sponsorship only further attenuated the sense of DIVEDCO as the everyday instantiation of the PPD as the "nacionalismo pueblo."

Ironically, President Kennedy's appointment of Teodoro Moscoso, the Muñoz-selected head of Puerto Rico's Economic Development Administration, to lead the Alliance for Progress both institutionalized and undermined the island's role as glorified hemispheric interlocutor. That the Kennedy administration recruited from among the upper echelons of the Muñoz administration to promote the kinder, gentler face of U.S. Latin American policy was evidence of the centrality it accorded Puerto Rican development during the 1950s. The Alliance for Progress initiative itself, the long awaited though ill-fated hemispheric corollary to the Marshall Plan, incorporated an apparent emphasis on social reform, economic redistribution, and self-determination that borrowed from the rhetoric of the Puerto Rican "social laboratory." Announcing the U.S. Latin American initiative in 1961, Kennedy proclaimed that "if our alliance is to succeed, each Latin nation must formulate long-range plans for its own development."[45] However, as Puerto Rican "talent" joined U.S. foreign policy agencies, their symbolic attachment to Puerto Rico became increasingly ambiguous. Rafael Picó led a diplomatic entourage to Santo Domingo not as a Puerto Rican emissary but as a Kennedy administration representative. Kennedy appointed Puerto Rican undersecretary of state Arturo Morales Carrión as the deputy assistant secretary of state for inter-American affairs.[46] By the time Muñoz announced that he would not seek reelection, the island's geopolitical significance was far less certain than when he championed its commonwealth status more than a decade earlier.

The recalcitrance of a Puerto Rican cultural nationalism that articulated class antagonisms contributed to the undoing of the localized terms of PPD hegemony. The worldwide economic crisis of the early 1970s heralded less a renunciation of U.S. colonial rule than growing disillusionment with PPD populism, which by then seemed incidental to, rather than essential for, the negotiation of U.S. colonial policy. Rather than evidence of popular acquiescence to colonial rule, continued popular support for "association" with the United States expressed a particular class politics. If anything, during the 1970s, the advantages of colonial "association" seemed more apparent to the poor and working class. Direct federal transfers to the Puerto Rican poor increased from $517 million in 1973 to $2.5 billion in 1980. Sixty percent of Puerto Rican families qualified for food stamps, compared with only 11 percent of all families on the U.S. mainland. Thus, during the 1960s and 1970s, a common saying among the Puerto

Rican non-elite was "To be independent like Haiti or the Dominican Republic, better to be a colony." As the sociologist Ramón Grosfoguel has argued, "Given the drastic differences between the situation of working classes in modern colonies and neo-colonial nation-states" of the Caribbean, it is not surprising that the Puerto Rican working class and poor preferred the benefits of colonial rule. Grosfoguel considers the class politics of independence and asks:

> On whose shoulders would the sacrifices required by the economic reconstruction for an independent state fall? Whose salaries and wages would be reduced for local and transnational industries to compete favorably in the world economy? Who would be affected by the reduction of state assistance (e.g., food stamps, housing subsidies) in favor of the republic's economic reconstruction?

Moreover, upon surveying the post-independence authoritarian regimes throughout the region — still themselves operating under the yoke of U.S. hegemony — why relinquish the social entitlements and economic assistance accorded by association, especially when political independence held the likely prospect of neocolonial domination without ancillary compensation?[47]

Disassociated from Muñoz, the División de Educación de la Comunidad's mission for community building as the focal point of nation building and local community participation as the foundation of democratic character lost its internal and external coordinates. Furthermore, the class contradictions of the colonial compromise proved unmanageable as both the localized and grand strategy contingencies of "community" shifted. By the end of the 1960s, the PPD's populist reason as embodied in DIVEDCO's localization could no longer bear the weight of organizing popular consent, and "community" appeared too internally antagonistic to serve as a definitive structuring absence.

The centrality accorded to Puerto Rico within early U.S. Cold War geopolitical machinations provides a means to critically reassess the dimensions and dynamics of U.S. imperial power. Without diminishing the often manifest orchestration of imperial domination, it remains essential to attend to the informalities and complexities through which the implementation of colonial governance and imperial geopolitics must be fashioned. Specifically, as the case of the División de Educación de la Comunidad and the Partido Popular Democrático demonstrates, to understand U.S. empire historically and concretely, it is necessary to consider the reciprocities between often elaborately localized dynamics of power and the more capacious and universalizing horizon of U.S. preponderance.

Notes

1   Luis Muñoz Marín, "An America to Serve the World," speech delivered at the Annual Convention of the Associated Harvard Clubs, Coral Gables, Florida, April 7, 1956 (Pamphlet Collection, Centro de Estudios Puertorriqueños, Hunter College, City University of New York), 9. Also see Luis Muñoz Marín, "Puerto Rico Refutes Charges of U.S. Colonialism by Cuba and U.S.S.R.," *U.S. Department of State Bulletin* 43 (October 24, 1960).

2   José Martí, "Our America," in *José Martí: Selected Writings*, ed. and trans. Esther Allen (New York: Penguin Books, 2002), 295.

3   See, for example, Alonso Aguilar, *Pan-Americanism: From Monroe to the Present* (New York: Monthly Review Press, 1968); David Green, *The Containment of Latin America: A History of the Myths and Realities of the Good Neighbor Policy* (Chicago: Quadrangle Books, 1971); Barbara Stallings, *Banker to the Third World: U.S. Portfolio Investment in Latin America, 1900–1986* (Berkeley: University of California Press, 1987); Paul W. Drake, ed., *Money Doctors, Foreign Debts, and Economic Reforms in Latin America: From the 1890s to the Present* (Wilmington: Scholarly Resources, 1994); Ian Roxborough, "Cold War, Capital Accumulation, and Labor Control in Latin America: The Closing of a Cycle, 1945–1990," in *Rethinking the Cold War*, ed. Allen Hunter (Philadelphia: Temple University Press, 1998); and Greg Grandin, *The Last Colonial Massacre: Latin America in the Cold War* (Chicago: University of Chicago Press, 2004).

4   U.S. Department of State, "Instruction from the Secretary of State to All Diplomatic Missions in the American Republics" (February 15, 1955), in *Foreign Relations of the United States, 1955–1957*, vol. 6, *American Republics* (Washington: U.S. Government Printing Office, 1987), 300.

5   For more on the supplementarity of community to capital, see Miranda Joseph, *Against the Romance of Community* (Minneapolis: University of Minnesota Press, 2002), 1–29.

6   Among the texts essential for a comparative analysis of the U.S. colonial state and the differential conditions leading to the post–World War II status question are Déborah Berman Santana, "No somos únicos: The Status Issue from Manila to San Juan," *Centro: The Journal of the Centro de Estudios Puertorriqueños* 10, no. 1 (fall 1999); José Trías Monge, "Decolonization in the Caribbean and in Micronesia," in *Puerto Rico: The Trials of the Oldest Colony in the World* (New Haven: Yale University Press, 1997); Roxanne Lynn Doty, *Imperial Encounters: The Politics of Representation in North-South Relations* (Minneapolis: University of Minnesota Press, 1996); Julian Go and Anne L. Foster, eds., *The American Colonial State in the Philippines: Global Perspectives* (Durham: Duke University Press, 2003); Catherine Lutz, *Micronesia as a Strategic Colony* (Cambridge: Cultural Survival, 1984); Roger W. Gale, *The Americanization of Micronesia: A Study of U.S. Rule in the Pacific* (Washington: University Press of America, 1979); Huanani-Kay Trask, *From a Native Daughter: Colonialism and Sovereignty in Hawai'i*, rev. ed. (Honolulu: University of Hawai'i Press, 1999); Noel J. Kent, *Hawaii: Islands under the Influence* (New York: Monthly

Review Press, 1983); and Stephen Haycox, *Alaska: An American Colony* (Seattle: University of Washington Press, 2002).

7   For more on the extended history of community development, see Sugata Das-gupta, *A Poet and a Plan: Tagore's Experiments in Rural Reconstruction* (Calcutta: Thacker Spink, 1962); C. B. Mamoria, *Co-operation, Community Development, and Village Panchayats in India* (Allahabad: Kitab Mahal, 1966); British Information Services, *Community Development: The British Contribution* (London: Her Majesty's Stationery Office, 1962); Philip Selznik, *TVA and the Grass Roots: A Study in the Sociology of Formal Organization* (Berkeley: University of California Press, 1949); James Dahir, *Region Building: Community Development Lessons from the Tennessee Valley* (New York: Harper and Brothers, 1955); Neil Betten and Michael J. Austin, *The Roots of Community Organizing, 1917–1939* (Philadelphia: Temple University Press, 1990); and Robert Fisher, *Let the People Decide: Neighborhood Organizing in America*, updated edition (New York: Twayne Publishers, 1994).

8   On various classifications and common presumptions, see the sociologist George Hillery's often-cited contemporaneous essay "Definitions of Community: Areas of Agreement," *Rural Sociology* 20 (1955).

9   As quoted in Team Number II, *Report on Community Development Programs in Jamaica, Puerto Rico, Bolivia, and Peru* (Washington: International Cooperation Administration, November 1, 1955), 24.

10 While the sociologist Eduardo Seda has argued that the "success" of land reform was achieved in part because local PPD officials simply took the place of the expropriated hacendado, assuming the role of patron with little change in local structures of power, it is clear that such measures did cement widespread party loyalty among the rural poor, and thus the simple transposition of power fails to explain the dynamics of hegemony at work. See Eduardo Seda, *Social Change and Personality in a Puerto Rican Agrarian Reform Community* (Evanston: Northwestern University Press, 1973). Also see P. B. Vázquez-Calcerrada, "A Research Project on Rural Communities in Puerto Rico," *Rural Sociology* 18, no. 3 (September 1953).

11 The best studies on Puerto Rican development during this period include Emilio Pantojas-García, *Development Strategies as Ideology: Puerto Rico's Export-Led Industrialization Experience* (Boulder: Lynne Rienner, 1990); Richard Weisskoff, *Factories and Food Stamps: The Puerto Rican Model of Development* (Baltimore: Johns Hopkins University Press, 1985); and Gordon K. Lewis, *Puerto Rico: Freedom and Power in the Caribbean* (New York: Monthly Review Press, 1963). Uncritical but useful studies include A. W. Maldonado, *Teodoro Moscoso and Puerto Rico's Operation Bootstrap* (Gainesville: University Press of Florida, 1997); William H. Stead, *Fomento: The Economic Development of Puerto Rico*, National Planning Association Planning Pamphlet 103, March 1958; Harvey Perloff, *Puerto Rico's Economic Future: A Study in Planned Development* (Chicago: University of Chicago Press, 1950). For an economic analysis extending through the era following "Operation Bootstrap," see James Dietz, *Puerto Rico: Negotiating Development and Change* (Boulder: Lynne Rienner, 2003).

12   Angel Quintero Rivera, "The Socio-political Background to the Emergence of 'The Puerto Rican Model' as a Strategy for Development," in *Contemporary Caribbean: A Sociological Reader*, ed. Susan Craig (Maracas, Trinidad and Tobago: College Press, 1982), 41.

13   David M. Helfeld, "Discrimination for Political Beliefs and Associations," *Revisita del Colegio de Abogados de Puerto Rico* 25, no. 1 (November 1964).

14   Sherman S. Hayden and Benjamin Rivlin, *Non-Self-Governing Territories: Status of Puerto Rico* (New York: Woodrow Wilson Foundation, September 1954); W. Michael Reisman, *Puerto Rico and the International Process: New Roles in Association* (Washington: American Society of International Law, 1973); Surendra Bhana, *The United States and the Development of the Puerto Rican Status Question, 1936–1968* (Lawrence: University Press of Kansas, 1975), 174–75; Millard Hansen and Henry Wells, eds., "Puerto Rico: A Study in Democratic Development," *Annals of the American Academy of Political and Social Science* 285 (January 1953); Carl J. Friedrich, *Puerto Rico: The Middle Road to Freedom* (New York: Rinehart, 1959); and Earl Parker Hanson, *Puerto Rico: Ally for Progress* (New York: D. Van Nostrand, 1962).

15   Brief of Militant Liberty project, October 22, 1954, National Archives, Department of State, Lot 62 D 430, Records Relating to State Department Participation in the OCB and the NSC, 1947–1963, Box 8, Miscellaneous 1953–1956, as quoted in Scott Lucas, *Freedom's War: The American Crusade against the Soviet Union* (New York: New York University Press, 1999), 224.

16   Earl Parker Hanson, *Puerto Rico: Land of Wonders* (New York: Alfred A. Knopf, 1960), 16–17.

17   Social Science Research Center director Millard Hansen, quoted in Michael Lapp, "The Rise and Fall of Puerto Rico as a Social Laboratory, 1945–1965," *Social Science History* 19, no. 2 (summer 1995): 180.

18   From the preamble to Law no. 372 (May 14, 1949) that established DIVEDCO, quoted in *Un Programa de Educacion de la Communidad en Puerto Rico/Community Education Program in Puerto Rico* (New York: RCA International Division, n.d.), n.p.

19   Willard W. Beatty, "The Nature and Purpose of Community Education," in *Community Education: Principles and Practices from World-Wide Experience; The Fifty-eighth Yearbook of the National Society for the Study of Education*, ed. Nelson B. Henry (Chicago: University of Chicago Press, 1959), 11.

20   "Report of the Division of Community Education of the Department of Education: From July 1, 1949, to October 15, 1951" (San Juan, Puerto Rico: Department of Education), 35.

21   Luis Muñoz Marín, "Mensaje a la décimoséptima Asamblea Legislativa en su primera legislature ordinaria: 23 de febrero de 1949," in *Los Gobernadores Electos de Puerto Rico*, vol. 1 (San Juan: Corporación de Servicios Bibliotecarios, 1973), 27, quoted in Maldonado, *Teodoro Moscoso and Puerto Rico's Operation Bootstrap*.

22   Fuat M. Andic, "Changes in the Income of the Puerto Rican Labor Force, 1949–1959," in *The Caribbean in Transition: Papers on Social, Political, and Economic Development*, ed. Fuat M. Andic and Thomas G. Mathews (Río Piedras, Puerto Rico:

Institute of Puerto Rican Studies, University of Puerto Rico, 1965); Rafael Picó, "The Experience of Puerto Rico," in *Community Development: Theory and Practice* (Mexico City: Inter-American Development Bank, April 1966), 83; Dietz, *Puerto Rico: Negotiating Development and Change*, 1–23.

23   Ismael García Colón, "Hegemony, Land Reform, and Social Space in Puerto Rico: Parcelas, a Land Distribution Program for Landless Workers, 1940s–1960s" (Ph.D. diss., University of Connecticut, 2002), 126–27.

24   Interview with Amilcar Tirado in Waldemar Perez Quintana, "An Oral History of the Division of Community Education of Puerto Rico from 1949 to the Present" (Ph.D. diss., Pennsylvania State University, 1984), 104–5.

25   Edgardo Rodríguez Julia, "Memories of Underdevelopment," review of Jack Delano's book of photographs and essays *Puerto Rico Mio: Four Decades of Change*, *Afterimage* 18, no. 7 (February 1991): 17.

26   *Films with a Purpose: A Puerto Rican Experiment in Social Films* (New York: Exit Art and El Instituto de Cultura Puertorriqueña, 1987).

27   Kalervo Oberg, "Community Development Programs in Puerto Rico," *Community Development Review* 1 (January 1956): 59.

28   René Marqués, "Writing for a Community Education Programme," UNESCO Reports and Papers on Mass Communication 24 (November 1957).

29   On the centrality of psychological thought as a normative framework in the mid-twentieth-century United States more broadly, see Donald S. Napoli, *Architects of Adjustment: The History of the Psychological Profession in the United States* (Port Washington, N.Y.: Kennikat Press, 1981); Joel Pfister and Nancy Schong, eds., *Inventing the Psychological: Toward a Cultural History of Emotional Life in America* (New Haven: Yale University Press, 1997); and Steven C. Ward, *Modernizing the Mind: Psychological Knowledge and the Remaking of Society* (Westport: Praeger, 2002).

30   William W. Biddle and Loureide J. Biddle, *The Community Development Process: The Rediscovery of Local Initiative* (New York: Holt, Rinehart and Winston, 1965), 78–79.

31   Stephen B. Withey and Charles F. Cannell, introduction to "Community Change: An Action Program in Puerto Rico," ed. Charles F. Cannell, Fred G. Wale, and Stephen B. Withey, special issue, *Journal of Social Issues* 9, no. 2 (1953): 2.

32   Fred Wale, "The Division of Community Education — an Overview," *Journal of Social Issues* 9, no. 2 (1953): 12.

33   Zacarías Rodríguez, "A Village Becomes a Community," *Fundamental and Adult Education* 5, no. 2 (April 1953): 63.

34   Carmen Isales and Fred Wale, "The Field Program," *Journal of Social Issues* 9, no. 2 (1953): 23.

35   Fred Wale and Carmen Isales, *The Meaning of Community Development: A Report from the Division of Community Education* (San Juan, Puerto Rico: Department of Education, 1967), 7–8.

36   Ibid., 26.

37   Quoted in Marjorie Page, "Out in the Field with an Organizer," *Island Times*, January 5, 1962, 7.

38   Henry Wells, *The Modernization of Puerto Rico: A Political Study of Changing Values and Institutions* (Cambridge: Harvard University Press, 1969).

39   Antonio Lauria-Pericelli, "Images and Contradictions: DIVEDCO's Portrayal of Puerto Rican Life," *Centro: The Journal of the Centro de Estudios Puertorriqueños* 3, no. 1 (winter 1990–91).

40   Jorge Duany, *The Puerto Rican Nation on the Move: Identities on the Island and in the United States* (Chapel Hill: University of North Carolina Press, 2002). On the Creole propertied elite's construction of "cultural nationalism" with respect to the dispossessed majority, see also Kelvin A. Santiago-Valles, "The Unruly City and the Mental Landscape of Colonized Identities: Internally Contested Nationality in Puerto Rico, 1945–1980," *Social Text* 38 (spring 1994).

41   René Marqués, *The Docile Puerto Rican: Essays*, trans. Barbara Bockus Aponte (Philadelphia: Temple University Press, 1976). Also see Juan Flores, "The Insular Vision: Pedreira and the Puerto Rican Misère," in *Divided Borders: Essays on Puerto Rican Identity* (Houston: Arte Público Press, 1983).

42   Robert W. Anderson, *Party Politics in Puerto Rico* (Stanford: Stanford University Press, 1965); Kenneth R. Farr, *Personalism and Party Politics: Institutionalization of the Popular Democratic Party of Puerto Rico* (Hato Rey, Puerto Rico: Inter-American University Press, 1973); Jorge Heine, *The Last Cacique: Leadership and Politics in a Puerto Rican City* (Pittsburgh: University of Pittsburgh Press, 1993); Ramón Grosfoguel, "Puerto Rico's Exceptionalism: Industrialization, Migration, and Housing Development" (Ph.D. diss., Temple University, 1992).

43   Arlene M. Dávila, *Sponsored Identities: Cultural Politics in Puerto Rico* (Philadelphia: Temple University Press, 1997).

44   "Evaluation of the Community Education Division of the Department of Education of Puerto Rico" (San Juan, Puerto Rico: Department of Education, November 1980), complete document reproduced as appendix E in Perez Quintana, "An Oral History of the Division of Community Education."

45   As quoted in Hanson, *Ally for Progress*, 10.

46   Maldonado, *Teodoro Moscoso and Puerto Rico's Operation Bootstrap*; Jerome Levinson and Juan de Onís, *The Alliance That Lost Its Way: A Critical Report on the Alliance for Progress* (Chicago: Quadrangle Books, 1970); Stephen G. Rabe, *The Most Dangerous Area in the World: John F. Kennedy Confronts Communist Revolution in Latin America* (Charlotte: University of North Carolina Press, 1999).

47   Ramón Grosfoguel, "The Divorce of Nationalist Discourses from the Puerto Rican People: A Sociohistorical Perspective," in *Puerto Rican Jam: Rethinking Colonialism and Nationalism*, ed. Frances Negrón-Muntaner and Ramón Grosfoguel (Minneapolis: University of Minnesota Press, 1997), 67–70.

All Cumbias, the Cumbia

The Latin Americanization of a Tropical Genre

Héctor Fernández L'Hoeste

Cuando un pueblo cae en desgracia, escucha cumbia.

— Pappo, Argentine rocker

The epigraph above, "When people despair, they listen to cumbia," is a working-class Argentine rocker's comment on a musical genre. But his is only one interpretation among many, and, in fact, one that might not resonate particularly well in Colombia, where cumbia first originated. Cumbia is an important example of how cultural genres associated with national authenticity become transnational and are themselves transnational products from the start. Transnational flow, however, does not imply homogeneity. In Colombia, cumbia began as a form linked to Afro-Caribbean cultures on the northern coast and became a national genre only through its reification as folk music, or through processes of cultural whitening and *mestizaje*. In other places, such as Argentina, Peru, Mexico, and the U.S.-Mexico border, cumbia became associated, in different ways, with the racialized urban poor.

Music has long been a particularly fruitful site for scholarship on transnationalism, for its illumination of the ways that the local is produced through global (or hemispheric) cultural circulation. Yet Latin American music was for many years curiously marginal to the conversation.[1] One of the most

famous works on transnational music—Paul Gilroy's *The Black Atlantic*—
ignored Latin America altogether.[2] More recent scholarship has sought to address this void but has often told the story of Latin American music in terms of
distinct national experiences. This essay considers cumbia's travels across the
Americas, largely in the 1980s and 1990s, and through a variety of locales and
social-political conditions, to consider the nature of diasporic form. Central to
this inquiry are fundamental questions about cultural transformation, about
origins and mutations, and about how we understand what is "old" and what
is "new."

In musical terms, cumbia can be identified through its rhythmic structure. Despite the profoundly different ways in which cumbia has been played
throughout time and place, some very unlike the Colombian versions, it is
possible to hear a common beat (*golpe*) reverberating across styles. Two ensembles, the *conjunto de cumbia* and the *conjunto de gaitas*, accompany traditional cumbia. The first plays five instruments, four of which involve percussion: *tambor mayor*, a leg-held drum, played with both hands; *llamador*, a
knee-held drum, played with one hand; *bombo*, a two-headed drum, played
with sticks; and *guaches* (rattles). The only other instrument is the melodic *caña
de millo*, a modified version of the millet-cane clarinets of the Sudanese regions
of Africa. In the second ensemble, there are two *gaitas* (duct flutes), a tambor
mayor, a llamador, and a maraca.[3] In both groups, the importance of percussion is evident. The cumbia exported from Colombia, beginning in the 1950s
and 1960s, was already a stylized, simplified form, with orchestral arrangements
enhancing the musical structure but preserving the central rhythmic pattern.
The relative simplicity of cumbia as a musical genre—which tends to emphasize percussion above other components, in particular, those pertaining to the
Afro-Amerindian and Amerindian aspects of the music—proved remarkably
open. Cumbia provided an ideal template for experimentation and could be
imitated easily and even augmented by local bands throughout the Americas.
In this way, an apparent lack of musical complexity became key to cumbia's
ability to move and change form.

Moreover, cumbia's ability to travel was enhanced, paradoxically, by its comparatively weak association with Colombia, or at least with a robust Colombian nationalism. Unlike music exported from the United States, Mexico, Cuba,
Brazil, or Argentina during the twentieth century, cumbia did not openly emphasize its country of origin or aggressively celebrate "Colombianness." Cultural industries elsewhere in the Americas actively worked to promote images

of modernity associated with specific national projects (the Mexican Revolution, U.S.-style capitalist democracy) or a national essence (*cubanía* or Brazilian *tropicalismo*). In contrast, Colombian nationalism was, during most of the century, organizationally and ideologically fragmented, traumatized by the vicious midcentury civil conflict of La Violencia, which profoundly questioned Colombia's viability as a nation and haunted its politics thereafter. Yet for cumbia as a musical form there were certain advantages to being less nationally marked. Part of its ability to travel, and to be rearticulated in multiple national forms elsewhere, was precisely because its origins seemed more vague, less tied to precise locations and political projects. From the beginning of its migration, cumbia invited others to claim it as their own.

Cumbia also traveled well because it was recognizable, even in its novelty. While cumbia stands independently as a genre, it belongs to the greater body of music known as "tropical music," which emerged from the dance band arrangements of Afro-Colombian music styles on the Atlantic coast in the 1930s and 1940s.[4] More colloquially, *música tropical* defined any music with a "tropical" flavor and was identified as "coming from the tropics." Música tropical was similar to the ballroom rumba popularized throughout the Americas and Europe during the same period and, by the 1950s, was well established in social circles throughout Latin America. In Colombia, tropical music dominated clubs and ballrooms, posing as a national musical style. In Argentina, tropical music was more associated with dance subgenres, while in Peru it encompassed a vast array of musical styles associated with the Caribbean rim. In Mexico, with its huge variations of *música regional mexicana* (regional Mexican music), tropical music meant different things in different places. In the United States, on the other hand, música tropical tended to signify Latin American music not associated with Mexico.

Thus cumbia had multiple incarnations. Its very association with música tropical made it problematic in Colombia for elite and aspiring middle-class sectors eager to present themselves as having transcended tropical stereotypes. Conversely, in Argentina, Peru, and Mexico, it was the very association of cumbia with the racialized tropics that held so much appeal, albeit in very different ways. In the United States, revealingly, where cumbia crossed borders via Mexico and into areas where Latinos were most associated with Mexico, it was characterized as "Mexican regional music."[5] Conversely, in places where Mexicanness did not dominate definitions of the Latino (New York, Miami, etc.), cumbia was characterized as tropical music and associated with the Caribbean

Rim.[6] Regardless of its various styles and how they were characterized, cumbia was (and is) a best-selling genre with mass appeal. It is cumbia's very popularity and fluidity throughout the Americas that raise important questions about how transnational flows mediate difference, identity, and national popular culture.

Colombia: Carlos Vives and the Mestizoization of Cultural Whitening

Ironically, perhaps, throughout much of the twentieth century, cumbia in Colombia was more narrowly developed as a national musical genre than it was elsewhere in Latin America. Despite, or precisely because of, its origins on the Afro-Caribbean coast, cumbia was popularized throughout Colombia only where it could present itself as folk tradition or where it appeared sufficiently whitened in style to appeal to Colombia's middle and upper classes. As Peter Wade has noted, Cuban and U.S. music exerted enormous influence on the development of *costeño* music — music from Colombia's Caribbean coast, including cumbia — and its eventual acceptance by the more powerful middle and upper classes of the Andean regions of the country, eventually rising to power as the favored national music form.[7] After the 1970s, cumbia was limited to highly stylized enactments, such as choreographies by the Ballet Nacional de Colombia, headed by Sonia Osorio. A few important cultural actors, such as the Bazanta family, champions of the Afro-Colombian tradition, held on to cumbia in a more folkloric form. At a grassroots level, cumbia survived in the form of a local variety: the *chucu-chucu*, a monotonous, highly commercialized music favored by the Colombian recording industry. After the arrival of salsa, merengue, and reggaeton in Colombia in the 1970s, 1980s, and the early years of the twenty-first century, respectively, cumbia remained largely in the hands of musicians dedicated to its celebration in a traditional format, such as Delia Zapata Olivella or Totó La Momposina, who disregarded electronic instrumentation and embodied a return to acoustic arrangements. For the most part, by the late 1970s, cumbia was relegated to the music store corner assigned to folklore, where it represented the national musical tradition in an almost essentialist form. The 1980s witnessed the rise of *rock en español* as a popular cultural form in Colombia, but its many local versions still lacked the hybrid, autochthonous content later embraced by most bands. Hence, until this point in time, musical tradition and commercial innovation were at odds.

In the 1990s, cumbia's fortune changed, thanks in large part to the musical innovations of Carlos Vives. Under Vives, cumbia emerged in new and dynamic forms that became central to Colombia's national popular music scene and became hugely popular as "Colombian music" in the United States and elsewhere in Latin America. Initially famous as a teenage heartthrob and soap opera star, Vives made several attempts at a music career inspired by the production of Argentine rocker Charly García. Eventually, thanks to his starring role in the soap *Escalona*, based on the life of a legendary folk composer, Vives had an epiphany. Though Vives is originally a middle-class white man from Santa Marta, a port on the Colombian Caribbean, his coming-of-age was impacted by life in Bogotá, the Colombian capital, where costeños are traditionally viewed as outsiders. The filming and success of *Escalona*, with a soundtrack including Vives, brought the actor-singer in touch with his roots. As a result, he discovered that he felt more comfortable with the lyrics and arrangements of Colombian country music than with the riffs and cadences of rock emulating the Anglo tradition. To an extent, Vives incarnated what his many followers, the scions of the Colombian urbanized middle class, eagerly awaited: someone who would combine tradition and modernity successfully, giving voice to an entire generation bred concurrently on rock and folk genres.

Certainly Carlos Vives was not alone responsible for cumbia's resurrection in Colombia—icons such as Joe Arroyo, Juan Carlos Coronel, and "Checo" Acosta also recorded new styles of cumbias. But Vives was arguably the most important force in cumbia's transformation, and his particular style is emblematic of the contradictions implicit in this change. Vives both rescued cumbia from its reification as folk tradition and, in many ways, continued the tradition of cumbia's cultural whitening in a more hybrid form. Vives, too, succeeded where others had failed, in popularizing cumbia at home and abroad as an expression of Colombian national unity. While his vision was in many ways radically inclusive of marginalized sectors of Colombian society, his uses of hybridity and appeals to nationalism remained problematic. Vives's ability to repopularize cumbia owes a great deal to his successful reinterpretation of the Colombian musical genre *vallenato*, an accordion-centered Colombian country music, to which Vives added instruments and rhythms more closely associated with cumbia proper.

Vallenato emerged out of the same sensibilities that first created cumbia, and was, in Vives's hands, always inseparable from cumbia. In vallenato's conventional form, three instruments—*guacharaca*, *caja*, and accordion—combine to generate a self-consciously hybrid form. The guacharaca is an elongated wooden instrument of indigenous descent that is played by scraping it with a metal fork. Allegedly, earlier versions of the guacharaca involved the use of a cane (in the place of wood) and a bone (to brush and create the sound). Its name is an indigenous word for a wild turkey, whose call is comparable to the sound of the instrument. The caja, or drum, represents an African component and dates back to colonial slavery. The accordion was brought by German immigrants to the Colombian Atlantic coast (and many other places in the Americas) at the beginning of the nineteenth century. In musical terms, then, vallenato, like cumbia, combined the heritages of the three main cultures that made up the Americas, a quality of potentially great appeal to societies like Colombia's, which eagerly sought expressions of national identity.

Like many other musical genres that moved easily, vallenato was born in a border culture, from the interaction between people from the Sierra Nevada de Santa Marta and the Caribbean savannas. In 1934, Antonio Fuentes, influenced by his time in Cartagena, Colombia's tourist port, recorded artists like Alejandro Durán and Leandro Díaz in his studios in Medellín.[8] Vallenato also benefited from the tradition of the great tropical music bands of the 1950s and 1960s, whose repertoire, thanks to a cosmopolitan disposition (the emphasis on wind instruments à la Glen Miller and Benny Goodman, as well as many of their visual cues), opened the doors to cumbia and *porro*, vallenato's sister form. In the 1970s, vallenato traveled to the center of the country, championed by members of the Bogotá elite attracted to its verve as a form of popular culture. Its fans included the former president Alfonso López Michelsen, first governor of the young province of Cesar, birthplace of vallenato; the Santos family, owners of Colombia's largest daily, *El Tiempo*; and the columnist Daniel Samper Pizano, a well-known defender of popular culture. The annual contest of the Festival of the Vallenato Legend, started in the 1970s, also contributed to its appeal to a national market. In the 1980s, vallenato's popularity was enhanced by the popularity of *casetas*, large commercial establishments for open-air dancing, and the growing profile of the drug trade, which, having started on the Caribbean coast—thanks to the marijuana boom—sought opportunities for increased social relevance. Electric instruments were added and a more commercial sound established. Yet it was not until the arrival of Carlos Vives in the 1990s that vallenato—and, along with it, cumbia—came to have a cross-class cosmopolitan appeal. Vives's great innovation was to more thoroughly fuse vallenato and cumbia, or rather to make cumbia's foundation for vallenato much more explicit.

Vallenato traditionally has four basic patterns: *puya*, merengue, *paseo*, and *son*. While puya is the most frenetic, paseo can be just as fast and includes, additionally, pauses, punctuating the narration of sentimental lyrics. Vallenato's versions of merengue and son are stylish variations, bearing little resemblance to Dominican merengue and Cuban son. To this mix, Vives added the gaita, an instrument of Amerindian origin, proper of cumbia, which had the effect of fortifying and accentuating vallenato's relationship with its musical precursor. Vives also added the electric guitar, a decisive move away from folk traditions and one that explicitly identified with a younger Colombian generation brought up on a steady diet of international pop and rock. In fact, Vives has referred to his discovery of the rhythmic pattern of cumbia in the electric guitar as a key moment in the development of his musical orientation—thanks largely to his guitarist, Ernesto "Teto" Ocampo, who, like Vives, is originally from the Colombian Caribbean.[9] Vives's self-conscious fusion seeks a connection between two historically antagonistic entities: the city and the country, between the eminently white urban middle and upper classes and the racialized ranks of the working class and rural poor. This hybridity is also reflected in Vives's dress: his mix of the leather jackets of rockers with the sandals, hats, and improvised jean-shorts of a working farmhand. Here Vives interrogates and refuses the dichotomies of barbarism and civilization—rural backwardness versus urban modernity—that have been especially long-lived in Latin American political discourses and policy.

In a way, Vives's reworkings of cumbia and vallenato propose something akin to what Jesús Martín Barbero describes as a recontextualization of cultural practice in which music, though conscious of its past, transcends myth and consolidates a new musical memory, surpassing what was previously glorified as a national form.[10] Certainly, Vives aspired to invent a more inclusive and multitemporal national musical identity. In recent years, Vives has moved away from recording material authored by other composers. This change, notable in the marked shift from the 1993 *Los clásicos de La Provincia* (Classics of The Province) to his 2004 album *El rock de mi pueblo* (My People's Rock), is no doubt promoted by his record label's pursuit of new audiences, but it also reflects Vives's own increasing commitment to experimentation.[11] At the same time, Vives habitually stresses the cultural authenticity of his music: that "la mamá cumbia está detrás de todo esto" (mother cumbia is behind everything) and "el vallenato me ha enseñado que es hijo de la cumbia" (vallenato has taught me that it is the son of cumbia).[12]

Whatever Carlos Vives's musical creativity and committed egalitarianism, the success of his music lies, in part, in the ways his persona and style operate to elide issues of racism, historical and contemporary, and to reinvigorate

Colombian fantasies of national unity. While Vives has expanded the notion of who is included in "the national," his brand of syncretism profoundly romanticizes Colombian mestizaje. Nowhere does he explicitly comment on his own entitlement to represent Colombia's hybridity or the extent to which many in Colombia would consider him "white." While his music has brought the Afro-Caribbean and indigenous traditions of cumbia and vallenato to more people, his innovations also contribute to the erasure of important aspects of these genres. In some ways, Vives's version of vallenato unwittingly ratifies the exclusion of blackness from the national imaginary. Whereas cumbia more broadly underwent an explicit whitening of its African roots in order to gain mass popularity in Colombia, vallenato was more often seen as eminently mestizo, a genre in which the influence of Africa was attenuated, yet acknowledged.[13] To come to the point, Vives's reassertion of cumbia within the modernized vallenato that he represents attenuates such African heritage still further. Indeed, Colombian upper- and middle-class sectors do not relate rock or other genres influencing Vives to black culture. Black musical forms such as hip-hop have a base in Colombia, but they are more associated with the lower classes. Whatever Vives's conscious intentions, his success reflects and contributes to a continued whitening of Colombian popular music, albeit in more populist and mestizoized forms. Perhaps sensing these contradictions, the journalist Celeste Fraser Delgado noted in a 2002 article for the *Miami New Times* that Vives was similar to Elvis, "a white man who sings with black feeling."[14]

Yet there is something more, too. Vives's music is popular in Colombia because it has attained enormous success internationally, and this international celebrity has firmly associated him with "Colombian popular music." In fact, in many ways, Vives's celebrity is greater outside Colombia than it is inside; to Colombians in exile and at home, his version of cumbia cum vallenato incarnates a romanticized form of the nation. This has, in turn, led to problematic displays of nationalism within Colombia. During a Vives concert in Bogotá in June 2002, the stage displayed signs of an exacerbated patriotism, with yellow, blue, and red lighting. Other artists with nationalist propensities, like Juanes and Andrea Echeverri, the vocalist of Aterciopelados, appeared onstage, joining Vives to sing "La tierra del olvido." Egidio Cuadrado, his admirable accordionist, covered himself with the flag. Even Juan Pablo Ángel, a member of the Colombian soccer squad, whose fans are rabidly nationalist, appeared during the show. In Colombia, amid social injustice, political repression, and general violence, nationalism can be viewed in an uncritical manner as something good, as a naive and festive negation of the current situation of the country. It is obvious: Vives's artistic workmanship praises a comprehensive, more flexible version of nationality. It pretends to recover the normative potential of the idea of nation but, in the end, pays scant attention to the deficiencies that, to this day, make a utopia of the thought of peace in his country.

Argentina: Los Negros and the Meaning of Class

In Argentina, cumbia emerged as a national musical form in the 1990s as a direct result of economic crisis, wherein its original association with the urban poor came to also represent the grievances of an increasingly beleaguered middle class. Though many forms of cumbia have existed in Argentina since its arrival from Colombia in the 1960s, the one that interests me is *cumbia villera*, which emerged from the *villas miseria* or shantytowns of Greater Buenos Aires during the late 1990s and the beginning of the twenty-first century. Musically, cumbia villera takes cues from Colombian cumbia (the beat) as well as from Argentine folk genres such as *cuartetazo*, an Italo-Spanish music from the interior of the country, and even from working-class rock. Villera also belongs to the greater genre of tropical music in Argentina. Minimally interested in acoustic fidelity, villera musicians rely heavily on synthesizers to reproduce arrangements that more traditional big bands would create with a full brass section. Yet what most marks villera is its celebration of the cultural codes of life in the slums, in many cases glamorizing illegal activities and gang lifestyles. Some critics have dismissed villera as a form of crass commercialism, in which its main performers reinforce and benefit from the same principles of radical individualism and entrepreneurialism promoted by Argentina's neoliberal policies under the Menem government.

In contrast, I argue that villera is a primary example of how a local variety of cumbia, initially associated with the racialized poor, transforms into a national form that speaks to a broad cross section of society. In Argentina, villera was (and is) associated with *los negros* (the blacks) of Buenos Aires' working and under classes but has also appealed to sectors of Argentina's Europeanized middle class. "Blackness" in Argentina is a tag for the working-class and impoverished, rather than a marker of acknowledged African ancestry or identity. In this way, Argentine society validates the racist construct that blacks are meant to belong, economically, to bottom of the ladder. By the twentieth century, the memory of Argentina's very significant African and Afro-Argentine presence during colonial times had been largely erased amid aggressive state policies and mythologies of whitening. Yet the link between blackness and servitude persisted, a connection bolstered by the reality that the bulk of Argentina's huge immigrant working classes after 1880 came from southern and eastern Europe, as well as the Middle East, and included large numbers of Jews. During the mid-twentieth century, Juan and Eva Perón thrust Argentina's symbolically unwashed and darker-skinned working classes to center stage and proclaimed *los cabecitas negras* (the black-headed ones) and *los descamisados* (the shirtless ones) the soul of the nation.[15] However, during the long, bloody efforts by the military to rid Argentina of Peronism in the 1960s and 1970s, the "blackness" celebrated by Perón became once again profoundly derogatory, if not treasonous. Cumbia villera took this racialized hierarchy and turned it on its head. It celebrated the daily heroism of los negros and contrasted it with the immorality of a selfish and corrupt elite. As Argentine society became more economically polarized in the 1990s and plunged into crisis after 2002, cumbia villera's message resonated beyond the slums as the livelihood of middle- and even upper-class Argentines became increasingly precarious.

As was true elsewhere, cumbia in Argentina had long been associated with the lower classes. Argentine tropical music more broadly dates to the *cuartetos* of the 1940s (Leo, Berna, Cuarteto de Oro). After the 1960s, with the arrival of the Colombian band El Cuarteto Imperial, cumbia gained a firm presence, which, in the 1980s, was made even more visible by acts such as Ricky Maravilla, Las Panteras, and Alcídez.[16] As a working-class genre, consisting of a series of simple arrangements and sugary lyrics, cumbia invaded the *bailantas*, the popular ballrooms along the industrial beltway of the Greater Buenos Aires. Nevertheless, it wasn't until the appearance of hugely popular acts like Green, Sombras, and Comanche that cumbia's potential to cross over into other social milieus was evident. While these bands endorsed more traditional forms of Argentine cumbia, they certainly prefigured the success of the villera variety. In the late 1980s, despite scandalously high inflation, sales of cumbia recordings reached seven digits, with an ever larger share of popular music being produced from within Argentina.[17]

Ironically, despite the widespread hardship caused by the Menem administration's policies of stiff monetary control and the privatization of public enterprises, the neoliberal reforms of the 1990s inadvertently helped propel working-class musical production, both rock and cumbia, to the center of the national music scene. Dramatic tariff reductions made it easier to import the latest recording equipment, improving sound and lowering overall production costs. Accelerated migration from nearby countries, where unemployment was even higher than in Buenos Aires, swelled the ranks of working-class audiences in poor neighborhoods. Within the slums, marginal musicians began developing a more politicized form of cumbia that more directly addressed issues of deprivation and class outrage. The first villera groups were Flor de Piedra (slang for drug in a solid form), with Pablo Lescano, and Guachín, with Gonzalo Ferrer. Later other acts surfaced: Damas Gratis (Free Ladies, with Lescano as composer), Yerba Brava (Tough Weed), and Los Pibes Chorros (Young Thieves). The repertoire of such groups annoyed the traditional *porteño* bourgeoisie as well as respected figures of the folkloric music scene such as Víctor Heredia.[18] With titles like "Discriminado" (Discriminated), "El Súper Cheto" (The Super Snob), and "Sos un gobernado" (You Are the Government's Accomplice), villera spoke frankly about poverty, sex, unemployment, and drugs in a language aimed straight at the corrupt ruling class, and combined politics and dance, to the bewilderment of the Latin American *nueva canción* (political song), which relied heavily on the separation of these two cultural practices. While Los Pibes Chorros introduced themselves in "Llegamos los pibes chorros" with "Aunque no nos quieran, somos delincuentes / Vamos de caño, con antecedentes / Robamos blindados, locutorios y mercados / No nos cabe una, estamos re jugados / Vendemos sustancia, y autos nos choreamos" (Though nobody wants us, we're felons / We're armed and with criminal records / We rob armored trucks, cybercafés, and supermarkets / We're up for anything and have nothing to lose / We sell drugs and steal cars), to the lilting beat of "Industria argentina," a song by Damas Gratis, the villera star Pablo Lescano proclaimed, "La bruta que te parió / Devolvé la plata que te llevaste al exterior / Políticos de porquería / Se robaron lo poco que quedaba en la Argentina" (The beast who gave birth to you / Return the money you took abroad / Damn politicians / You stole the little that was left in Argentina). The presentation and language of Yerba Brava's first album, titled *Cumbia villera* and released by the Argentine label Leader in 2000, acknowledged the music's commercial focus with an irreverent flair; the cover, which celebrates graffiti and cartoons, displays the image of a child urinating on an old Ford, much like the iconic imagery of stickers on pickups in U.S. highways. Not unlike the criticism of rap and hip-hop in the United States, cumbia villera was widely condemned for its celebration of substance abuse, be it alcohol, glue, or pot, in its lyrics. The main hero of its songs was the marginal youth from the slums, who was portrayed in a festive light.[19] Likewise, there was widespread grumbling about the impact of music labels like Leader and Genoma on the integrity of "Argentine" music. In a sense, the impression generated was that as soon as these companies realized the sales potential of villera, they rushed in and launched improvised recordings seeking to profit immediately.[20] Thus villera's popularity spread rapidly throughout Argentina as well as to Chile, Paraguay, and Uruguay. Between 2000 and 2002, sales of villera skyrocketed; in fact, by 2000, Leader was selling around 150,000 units per month, a remarkable sum considering the condition of Argentina's economy.

More recently, cumbia villera has been prominent in a variety of visual culture forms in Argentina. In 2000, the director Marcelo Piñeyro included "Cumbia bendita," an extemporized form of villera, in the soundtrack of *Plata quemada*, his controversial adaptation of the novel by Ricardo Piglia, set in the 1960s. Cumbia villera also appeared in the motion picture *La ciénaga* (2001), by Lucrecia Martel, to highlight the opposition between a decadent upper middle class and mestizo sectors of Argentine society. In 2002 multiple events ratified the genre's increased profile: the villera group Damas Gratis was included in the soundtrack of *El Bonaerense*, the film by Pablo Trapero, which debuted at Cannes; Los Pibes Chorros appeared in the comic strip *Son amores*; Universal released the soundtrack for the television series *Tumberos*, with music by Yerba Brava; and Lescano was awarded a prize in the category of testimonial song by the prominent Argentine newspaper *Clarín*. The lyrics and appearance of these groups were repeatedly equated with U.S. gangsta rap and condemned for transgressing boundaries of the socially and morally acceptable. During the Duhalde administration, which succeeded Fernando de la Rúa's brief stint as president in 2002, the government took concrete steps to regulate and censor villera music and issued official guidelines for evaluating villera lyrics, criteria published in July 2001 by the Comité Federal de Radiodifusión (COMFER).[21] By February 2003, as a result of official censorship, several radio programs previously dedicated to cumbia stopped broadcasting it.[22]

But censorship could not stop villera's wide appeal, which had already clearly reached a middle-class audience at home and abroad. Middle-class students and aspiring professionals alike saw in cumbia villera an expression of their own anger and doubt about the future and their sense of betrayal by their leaders. During the 1990s, thanks to the ailing economy, the Argentine middle class was able to experience disenfranchisement from the state in a manner comparable to the experience of the inhabitants of the slums, as it saw its standard of living slip further and further. In 2002 the Argentine economy collapsed; overnight, per capita income plunged from US$7,474 to $2,720, and the number of people living in acute poverty soared to 60 percent, a figure almost unknown in modern Argentine history.[23] Villera was already being widely discussed within middle-class artistic, journalistic, and academic circles, but by 2003 it became reflective of the entire national mood. Take, for instance, the best-selling chronicle by the Chilean journalist Cristian Alarcón, *Cuando muera quiero que me toquen cumbia*, first published in Argentina in 2003. Based on the life and death of Víctor Manuel Vital (aka El Frente), a young Robin Hood from the slums who became a national legend when Alarcón recorded his assassination by the Buenos Aires police, the story narrates how the urban *pibes chorros* (the young thieves) come to have an iconic expression of *argentinidad* (Argentineness). Throughout his text, Alarcón, a former writer for the Argentine daily *Página/12*, employs musical references to villera to represent El Frente's mythification and import to the nation. Here villera becomes a signifier for neglected segments of Argentine society, which now included not only the working class and poor, but the middle class as well.

Villera cumbia both chides and welcomes middle-class listeners. Its lyrics poke fun at the national media's alarmist warnings about the end of the Argentine middle class, answering back that they, the long-ignored poor, are well equipped to assist the downwardly mobile in crash courses on governmental indifference, social discrimination, and state repression. Mocking the chauvinism that sees "poverty" as "new," because it is only now happening to the middle class, villera argues that the "real" Argentina has always been there— poor, angry, and *negra*. Yet villera is simultaneously conscious of its new national standing as a voice for conditions and frustrations suffered widely across Argentina. In this sense, it extends a hand down to its alleged superiors to help them up to "reality" and hints at the possibilities of cross-class solidarity.

The prospect that cumbia's incarnation as villera offers Argentine "blackness" as a basis of national authenticity and political action is a meaningful expansion of Argentina's racial imaginary and a definite assertion of urban class militancy. This is a brand of cumbia quite distinct from the forms lionized in Colombia, including the one reinvigorated by Carlos Vives's easy take on mestizaje. Furthermore, villera's political militancy and racial overtones depart from the orthodox leftism and folkloric invocations of the "ethnic" that predominate in South American and Cuban genres of the nueva canción and *nueva trova* (protest music). Villera is certainly a protest, and a protest well conscious of class, but it is a protest less ideologically mediated, or more ideologically elastic, than that of other protest music, and its condemnations of neoliberalism are not unfriendly to individual aspirations for money and personal fulfillment. Villera's claims to "national authenticity" are based not on a reinvention of rich national or regional "traditions" (as is Vives's) but instead on the "realness" of contemporary experiences of poverty, drug economies, and racialized discriminations.

Peru: Exclusionary Mestizaje

As in Argentina, cumbia in Peru has been closely associated with urban modes of racial representation. However, in Peru, cumbia's racialized claims are not first and foremost about African heritage, or even about "blackness" as a signifier of class. Rather, Peruvian cumbia—which, by the 1980s, had evolved into a hybrid electronic genre known as *tecnocumbia*—was most associated with Peru's urban, working-class Indian migrants and mestizos of Indian descent. Tecnocumbia drew its cues from tex-mex rhythms emanating from U.S. Latino populations and pointedly avoided styles associated with African American rap and hip-hop. Peruvian cumbia's lack of interest in African and black styles is especially remarkable given that, unlike Argentina, Peru has a significant minority of self-identified Afro-Peruvians concentrated on its Pacific coast. Their exclusion from cumbia's articulation as a national genre within Peru underscores the limits of mestizaje and the ways that its national forms have worked to exclude people of African descent from the nation.

Cumbia first developed in Peru as a genre known as *chicha* (a name for a popular alcoholic beverage). Cumbia had been growing in popularity in urban areas and their outskirts since the 1960s, the beginning of an accelerated migration of indigenous people from the Andean highlands to Lima and other cities. According to Jaime Bailón, almost all music arriving from Colombia, regardless of its style, was at this time interpreted as cumbia.[24] Peruvian groups such as Los Demonios del Mantaro mixed Afro-Colombian percussion and melodies of the *huayno*, the quintessential genre of the Inca highlands. To give their production a dash of modernity—after all, their fans were mainly provincial migrants, eager for progress—they also included electric instruments, hoping also to appeal to the youth orientation toward rock and pop. By the early 1980s, *chicha cumbia* was well established and enjoyed substantial popularity. Its degree of acceptance was such that then president Alan García and the APRA,

Peru's dominant populist political party, frequently introduced chicha acts such as Los Shapis and Alegría during political campaigns. Chicha's capacity to tap working-class electoral support was not lost on politicians. In Lima's working-class neighborhoods, huge storehouses with cement floors and powerful sound systems, called *chichódromos*, served as centers of social gathering for urban youth. By 1985, Los Shapis were so popular that they recorded fashionable television commercials, among them one in which the band invited all *cholitas* (young urban women of Indian descent), their main constituency, to benefit from the services of the local banking sector. Although chicha did not enjoy a following among the upper and aspiring middle classes, its huge commercial success guaranteed it cross-class exposure: it filtered into Peruvian homes through radio and television and could be heard in buses, taxis, and public facilities of all kinds.[25] A decade later, in the 1990s, in a notorious display of chicha's appropriation by politicians, president and authoritarian strongman Alberto Fujimori started his speeches with a song titled "La cumbia del chino" (literally "The Chinese Cumbia," but *chino* had multiple references, including to people of Asian descent, as well as to Indians and laborers, significant numbers of whom were historically from China and Japan).

In the late 1980s, Peruvian cumbia underwent a decisive shift. Harsh inflation and the dire economic climate of the decade made apparent the need for a more innovative version of cumbia. To make a long story short, if consumers were to dispose of their hard-earned cash for music, a novelty was mandatory. Whereas chicha combined cumbia and huayno, a younger generation of musicians looked north for inspiration to the tex-mex styles of Mexico and the U.S. Southwest. Acts like the Bio Chips, with Tito Mauri and Nilo Segura, began to mix what they knew from Colombia with the jumpy, upbeat sound of tex-mex bands like Bronco, ornamented with electronic instruments and synthesizers. Thus, as in Argentina, Peruvian musicians added electronic percussion to the mix. The singer Rosa Guerra Morales (known as Rossy War), who joined Mauri, overtly emulated the style of the Tejano singer Selena, in a move that transformed the Peruvian music scene.[26] Without a doubt, the influence of tex-mex can be traced to the increased contact of the Peruvian community abroad (mainly in the United States) with music strongly favored by Mexican Americans. In addition, the lineage of tex-mex, essentially a country-like genre consumed by newly urbanized folks, replicated the migratory experience of the Peruvian population: they both traveled to find work and improve their life, leaving behind rural tradition, which was sorely missed in the city.

In 1995, Rossy War released her first major recording, made in Chile, and soon launched international tours in the United States and Europe, where her brand of tecnocumbia was celebrated by audiences (which included many Peruvian expatriates) as the very incarnation of *peruanidad* (Peruvianness).[27] Thanks to Rossy War's success, other acts such as Agua Marina, Agua Bella, Néctar, Ruth Karina, and Armonía 10 soon joined the tecnocumbia scene.[28] Although the bubble of novelty surrounding it burst by 2003, tecnocumbia remains one of Peru's most popular musical genres. Recently it has shown up in the story lines of successful soap operas such as *La Hechicera*, in which the main star plays the role of a tecnocumbia singer. What began as a subgenre has gained social acceptance and gone mainstream.

Most musicians and fans of cumbia celebrate its obvious cultural hybridities. But in Peru, perhaps more so even than in Colombia and certainly more than Argentina, cumbia functions not only to include cultural otherness but to exclude it. The "Peruvianness" associated with tecnocumbia is that of a Peruvian mestizaje that imagines the national assimilation of Peru's majority indigenous population through processes of modernization and all but ignores the place of Peruvians of African descent. While tecnocumbia's firm link to, and celebration of, the urban working class *cholos* (and *cholas*) counters the enduring racism of Peru's European-identified elite, it accepts and actively perpetuates the idea that Africanness lies outside Peru's national essence.[29] Such prejudice and racial division date to the labor systems of colonial times but were reinvigorated by twentieth-century cultural movements of *indigenismo*, which idealized Inca civilization as the basis of Peru's modern national identity. Nonetheless, not unlike the ways mestizaje has worked in postrevolutionary Mexico and twentieth-century Nicaragua, Peruvian mestizaje imagined a unique blend of the European and the Amerindian, a mythology that worked well to erase or marginalize other heritages (Asian, Jewish, and Muslim, as well as African).[30] In Peru, where visions of mestizaje more heavily weighted the indigenous quotient and where the presence of people of African descent was, in fact, never "erased" from society, tecnocumbia's refusal to acknowledge the centrality of African heritage to cumbia flows directly from its creators' and fans' investment in a certain racial differentiation and superiority. If tecnocumbia has succeeded in representing a national Peruvian cultural form, purportedly inclusive of the popular classes, its pointed exclusion of blackness reinscribes Afro-Peruvians as something less than full members of the nation.

This logic also extends to tecnocumbia's cultural borrowings from the United States. Tex-mex music references the Indo-European mestizaje of Mexico, which also excludes blackness from the mix and updates it through association with elements of the U.S. Southwest. Conversely, the rap or hip-hop styles common to cumbia's renditions in Argentina and the Afro-Caribbean accents of Carlos Vives's music in Colombia are seen as entirely unrepresentative of, if not threatening to, tecnocumbia's version of Peruvian national identity. That in multiracial Peru, with its significant black minority, Africanness could be successfully expunged from the history of cumbia's foundations is not merely ironic. It goes to the heart of how myths of mestizaje can reinvent and uphold racial hierarchies.

Mexico: The Revival of Blackness

In Mexico, cumbia has developed more along the lines of the case in Argentina, to the extent that it has validated black styles and sensibilities in a country that negates its African heritage. Mexican cumbia has integrated the aesthetics of black rock, rap, and hip-hop and has stressed cumbia's Afro-Caribbean essence. This has been especially evident in northern Mexico, where the rapid industrialization and migratory flows that have characterized the U.S.-Mexican border in the last several decades have brought issues of urban poverty, drug-related violence, and social displacement to the fore. Cumbia's ability to interrogate these issues is reminiscent of cumbia villera's class-based claims. At the same time, Mexican cumbia's greater elaborations of cultural syncretism and use of regional music traditions echo the Colombian vallenato's celebration of hybridity. While Mexican cumbia audiences do not identify themselves as "Afro-Mexican" or even as negroes in the Argentine sense of the term, their eager embrace of African American and Afro-Caribbean styles and thematics through cumbia has challenged the official national-revolutionary version, Mexico's *raza cósmica* (cosmic race), purportedly born of the fusion of Aztec greatness and European know-how. In sharp contrast to the ways cumbia has functioned in Peru to erase African heritage from national forms, Mexican cumbia interrogates the limits of official mestizaje and recasts them in more inclusive and class-specific ways.

Mexican cumbia is perhaps the form of cumbia best known in the United States, given the porousness of the U.S.-Mexican border. Cumbia began in Mexico in the early 1960s with the arrival of Colombian bands such as La

Sonora Dinamita (to the Mexican heartland) and Los Corraleros de Majagual (to northeastern Mexico) and soon led to adaptations of Colombian music in other parts of the country. From the beginning, Mexico's incarnations of cumbia took multiple forms, given its already hugely varied and regionally distinct musical forms. Colombian cumbia, itself, also traveled in different forms. While La Sonora came from Medellín, bringing a polished, commercial sound, Los Corraleros came from the Caribbean coast, emphasizing a less urbane, more autochthonous tradition. According to Juan José Olvera's notable research on Colombian music in Mexico, Mexican cumbia took on four distinct forms: tropical cumbia, dispersed around the Mexican coasts and heartland; Monterrey cumbia, allied to the *norteño* ensembles and *conjuntos*; a purist version of nationwide consumption, which attempted to preserve a sound akin to original Colombian arrangements; and cumbia bands from central Mexico, which adapted their repertoire to various Colombian and Venezuelan bands (Pacho Galán, Lucho Bermúdez, Billo Frómeta). According to Olvera, the first place to play cumbia was the area of the Texas Valley, in cities on both sides of the border, like Nuevo Laredo, Tamaulipas, Nueva Rosita, Kingsville, Alice, and San Antonio. Thus he argues that the area around Monterrey plays a crucial role in the success of cumbia in Mexico. He also names Beto Villa y los Populares de Nueva Rosita as the first representatives of the northern Mexico variety of cumbia.[31]

Many factors contributed to cumbia's spread in Mexico. With the arrival of television, many musicians unable to find work in the new medium migrated to the north, where the more mobile, urban spaces of border cities offered greater opportunities. Additionally, the *sonideros*, who played music at parties and traditionally exposed their audiences to new musical forms, had a key role. Radio, with its long-standing border tradition of broadcasting music to the United States from south of the Rio Grande since the 1930s, also contributed to the process. Like the Colombian tropical music bands of the 1960s, Mexican cumbia eliminated the llamador and added a beat. In its Mexicanization, cumbia experienced something similar to what happened in Colombia, in particular in Medellín, where, thanks to rock and electric instrumentation, groups passed from ten or more members to only five to seven members. Cultural communication between Colombia and Mexico happened through various channels, one of the most important of which was the drug trade. Music from the Caribbean coast traveled easily with the many illicit loads passing from Colombia through Mexico on their way to the United States. It was through these routes that Colombian vallenato became popular in Mexico, especially in the northern state of Nuevo León, where its fans proudly labeled themselves *colombianos.* These colombianos were mainly youths from working-class sectors of Monterrey. They frequently belonged to neighborhood gangs, and their level of occupation ranged from unemployment to the lower rungs of economic productivity.[32] As in the case of villera, it was precisely the allure of an association with the drug trade — in this case, Colombian — that spoke so directly to these Mexican youths' own feelings of marginality. Vallenato styles flourished in a more general way within Mexican cumbia elsewhere but were most concentrated in, and associated with, the urban industrialism, slums, and gangs of the north. Vallenato's overt use of the accordion also helped its spread in northern Mexico, where the accordion had long played a starring role in Mexican *corridos* and polkas. However, cumbia's evolution in northern Mexico was also heavily influenced by U.S. styles brought by Mexican migrants who continually traversed the border. Indeed, Mexican migrants were crucial to changing musical genres on both sides of the Rio Grande. Migrants carried cumbia's influence to places as diverse as Jalisco, Tamaulipas, Mexico City, Texas, and California and, in turn, brought influences to bear on new interpretations of cumbia. In addition, while Mexicans contributed to the distribution of genres like tex-mex, they occasionally made inroads into U.S. Latino communities that favored a predominantly Caribbean repertoire (like the Northeast and Florida) and served as vehicles for communication between markets. The Texas-based Selena incorporated cumbia into her arrangements, and following her tragic death, the glamorization of her life in a Hollywood movie created a surge in Anglo interest in Latino music associated with the border. It is no accident that Selena's brother has since prospered and appealed to wide audiences as leader of the band Kumbia Kings. Today artists such as Aniceto Molina, a former member of Los Corraleros de Majagual, and Brenda Mejía, once linked to Selena, tour Mexico and the United States and even share the stage with community favorites such as Los Tucanes de Tijuana and the El Recodo band.

Mexican cumbia has also looked to Afro-Latin and African American musical styles for inspiration. The Cuban salsa star Celia Cruz once alluded to Brenda Mejía as "la princesa de la cumbia," a title Mejía formally won at one of the first renditions of Manzanillo's International Carnival of Cumbia, Salsa, and Merengue in the first years of the twenty-first century. The contest's very name, and Cruz's flattering endorsement, squarely situated Mexican cumbia within the tropical music traditions of the Caribbean Rim and their explicit celebration of African influences. Mexican bands such as the Kumbia Kings, Los Chicos de Barrio, and El Gran Silencio have fused cumbia styles with African American hip-hop, soul, and rock. In the case of the Kumbia Kings and Los Chicos de Barrio, the appropriation of hip-hop aesthetics, as in the case of Argentine *villeros*, was evident in their attire, colorful barrio garments, and the covers of their CDs (albums like *Amor, familia y respeto* . . . [1999], *La Lola* [2000], and *4* [2003]), which display A. B. Quintanilla and the members of Los Chicos gesticulating like rappers with open hands and a square stance, or glorify graffiti as a ghetto expression.[33] Of course, commercial incorporations of African American musical styles by Mexican artists were not new. Since the 1950s, with the growing popularity of the Eastside Sound, one of the seminal movements in the musical history of Los Angeles, and the rise of bands such as Thee Midniters and Hannibal and the Headhunters, Mexican popular music has drawn on black music traditions from the United States. Although groups such as the California-based Los Lobos del Este de Los Ángeles, which emerged in the 1960s, marked a distancing of Mexican popular music from African American styles, black music remained a central influence. Carlos Santana, who in 1968 was the first Mexican rocker to truly conquer U.S. charts, embraced the lavishness of Afro-Caribbean rhythmic structures in his music, blending in Haight-Ashbury's acid zest and Latin flair. More recently the regionally based productions by Kumbia Kings and Los Chicos de Barrio have reached out to Mexican youth through an Afro-Colombian musical style, already Mexicanized, and ornamented it with codes from the African American audiovisual lexicon (gestures, jewelry, and clothing). As such, their production remains within the mainstream of the Mexican regional repertoire but exhibits a distinctly internationalist and youthful flavor that is represented by the hip-hop trappings. While some critics have dismissed such *pocho* dress style as little more than U.S. commodification, the bands' heterogeneous uses of various African American and Afro-Caribbean styles from across the Americas nonetheless invite Mexican youth to identify with cosmopolitan modernity through blackness.

In the case of bands such as El Gran Silencio, blackness takes an even more central place on the stage as its renditions of cumbia and vallenato more thoroughly fuse with hip-hop. El Gran Silencio is closely associated to the norteño rock scene, yet its version of rock is highly hybridized. Hence it more explicitly interprets Colombian cumbia styles in terms of recent developments within international rock and hip-hop, as well as reinvigorated folkloric traditions. It also casts itself much more frankly as a political voice for the underclass. In their debut CD, *Libres y locos* (1999), El Gran Silencio referred to their musical movement as the "Frente Vallenato de Liberación Musical" or FVLM (the Vallenato Front for Musical Liberation), a whimsical but intentional gesture to the acronyms of Latin American guerrilla groups, especially perhaps the Zapatista EZLN and the Nicaraguan FSLN. The CD also listed a vast number of musical groups relevant to El Gran Silencio's style: Rafael Escalona, Lisandro Mesa, the Binomio de Oro, Carlos Vives, Los Tigres del Norte, Los Cadetes de Linares, Run-DMC, Pink Floyd, Björk, Led Zeppelin, and the Black Crowes. Although such variety intentionally underscored the band's claims to international cosmopolitanism, the mention of several Colombian groups, and especially of Carlos Vives, stressed El Gran Silencio's central engagement with vallenato. In addition, the presence in the list of Run-DMC, a staple of the world of hip-hop, underscores the significance of African American influence. El Gran Silencio can be a rock en español fusion band, but its heightening of the profile of *chúntaros*, the hillbillies of Mexico, while mixing raga, reggae, ska, cumbia, vallenato, world beat, R&B, and rap does wonders for the profile of African descent in their production. At times, their call-in shouts over percussion recall 1980s icons like the Sugarhill Gang.

As Olvera has noted, the "Frente Vallenato de Liberación Cultural" [*sic*] spoke directly to and about youth from working-class neighborhoods. El Gran Silencio uses cumbia and vallenato to underscore an inclusive modernity while also paying homage to musical legacies from regional Mexico, the border, and tropical music. Thematically, its lyrics insist on the centrality of the urban barrio and the claims of the disposed.[34] Not unlike Argentine villera, El Gran Silencio openly criticizes the Mexican establishment and claims to be a voice of resistance for Mexico's lower classes. Additionally, the group's outspokenness against the cultural and political establishment fits well within the narrative of societal and cultural resistance of the lower sectors in Mexico. Quite recently, the group has enjoyed increased popularity in parts of the country that display evident affinities toward Afro-Caribbean styles, like the state of Veracruz, better known as the Mexican gateway to Cuba and a link to Afro-Caribbean culture.[35]

Not all Mexican renditions of cumbia that center on working-class barrio life emphasize blackness. The longtime veteran of Mexico's cumbia scene Celso Piña has recently attained great success in three albums: *Barrio Bravo* (2001), *Mundo Colombia* (2002), and *Una visión* (2003). An article in the *Austin Chronicle* dated October 18, 2002, related Piña's triumph with no small degree of sarcasm, noting that it had taken the overweight musician more than two decades to become an overnight success. Nonetheless, as if in evidence that old dogs can learn new tricks, the paper attributed the mass appeal of Piña's recent work to the singer's considerable talent for musical experimentation and even went so far as to suggest that Piña's home barrio by the mountain overlooking Monterrey might be considered a Graceland for a new Mexican musical form. Piña's style is not unlike that of Carlos Vives, in that it draws heavily on traditional regional genres and combines and modernizes them. Yet unlike Vives's middle-class origins and message, Piña's grassroots sensibilities come from his profoundly working-class background. He has been far more interested in representing working-class perspectives rather than in ennobling them for middle-class consumption—though certainly his music has a solid following among the Mexican middle class. Not surprisingly, then, Piña has been a favorite of Monterrey's colombianos, whose interest in cumbia has been more bound up in working-class alienation. Piña's influence has been enhanced by his collaboration with celebrity musicians such as Alejandro Rosso (Plastilina Mosh), Alejandro Marcovich (ex-Caifanes), Julieta Venegas, Flavio Cianciarullo (Fabulosos Cadillacs), Toy Hernández (Control Machete), "Flaco" Jiménez, and the Kronos Quartet. Yet Piña's music remains committed to the idea that cumbia is fundamentally a genre of the popular classes, and that its societal views and styles should not be whitewashed for middle-class audiences.[36] While race is not central to Piña's message, his class focus echoes the agendas of Argentine villera and Mexican norteño bands and thereby puts the hybrid traditions of cumbia vallenato to very different uses than those in Colombia.

Coda: Listening to Cumbia

The variety of cumbia styles encountered while moving through the Americas pushes us to think about the tensions within diasporic culture and to acknowledge multiple forms of "authenticity" and newness. Almost simultaneously, cumbia has been variously associated with processes of cultural whitening, racialized class militancy, and invocations of mestizaje, both inclusive and exclusive in nature. In each of the regional spaces visited in this essay, cumbia came to embody a national cultural form that easily made cumbia a "Colombian," "Argentine," "Peruvian," or "Mexican" representation, each quite distinct and itself internally heterogeneous. Such plasticity is, of course, not unique to cumbia and characterizes other cultural forms as well. But cumbia's articulation across the Americas is specific to its particular histories. Cumbia has proved to be especially adaptable to popular nationalism in various nation-states, a vivid illustration of how transnational flows create local meanings. At the same time, cumbia's foundational articulation as a multicultural form has made issues of difference—race and class, in particular—obvious themes for its expression, albeit with dramatically different political meanings.

Notes

1   For more recent coverage on the impact of globalization on Latin American music, see Charles Perrone and Christopher Dunn, *Brazilian Popular Music and Globalization* (Gainesville: University Press of Florida, 2001); and Deborah Pacini Hernández, Héctor Fernández L'Hoeste, and Eric Zolov, *Rockin' Las Americas* (Pittsburgh: Pittsburgh University Press, 2004).

2   Paul Gilroy, *The Black Atlantic: Modernity and Double Consciousness* (Cambridge: Harvard University Press, 1993).

3   "Colombia," *Grove Music Online*, ed. L. Macy, http://www.grovemusic.com.

4   Ibid.

5   In the U.S. Latino market, the Recording Industry Association of America (RIAA) would come to distinguish between Mexican regional music, with almost 60 percent of the Spanish music market, and tropical music, with less than 20 percent. http://www.riaa.com.

6   *Hispanic-American Almanac*, DISCovering Multicultural America (Gale, 1999).

7   Peter Wade, *Music, Race, and Nation* (Chicago: University of Chicago Press, 2000), 106–212.

8   Nate Guidry, "A Vallenato Revival," *Pittsburgh Post-Gazette*, April 7, 2002.

9   Alberto Abello Vives, "Por debajo todas las raíces del árbol están conectadas," *Aguaita*, no. 7 (July 2002).

10   Jesús Martín Barbero, *De los medios a las mediaciones* (Barcelona: G. Gili, 1987).

11   Daniel Samper Pizano, "Carlos Vives, de Paraguachón a Miami," *Aguaita*, no. 7 (July 2002).

12   Liliana Martínez Polo, "Carlos Vives regresa a la ceremonia de los Premios Grammy Latinos," *El Tiempo*, September 18, 2002.

13   Peter Wade, *Music, Race, and Nation*.

14   "Vives, más vallenato que nunca," *El Tiempo*, May 1, 2004.

15   Though grammatically incorrect in terms of gender agreement, the use of the male article for *los cabecitas negras* ratifies the construction of the working class as eminently male. For the time, the movement integrated women in a significant fashion, yet it was still viewed in the light of Argentine society's patriarchal order.

16   For a summarized account of the history of Argentine cumbia, see http://muevamueva.com/mimusica/cumbia_argentina.htm.

17   Starting in the early 1990s, data by the International Federation of the Phono-

graphic Industry (IFPI) show constant growth of domestic product in the Argentine music market. Whereas domestic product represented only 34 percent of the market in 1991, by 2002 it had climbed to 47 percent, peaking in 2000 with 50 percent of the market. Without a doubt, the peak can be associated with the growing popularity of the local brand of tropical music, in particular, with cumbia villera. This shift in the origin of music production came largely at the expense of international and regional music, which shrank from 63 percent in 1991 to 50 percent in 2002. Remaining segments, like classical music, remained untainted by market shifts, representing 3 percent of the market. During the decade, other shifts in the Argentine music industry show the effects of economic volatility. In 1999, sales of 30,000 and 60,000 units represented gold and platinum awards, respectively. By 2003, figures had shrunk to 20,000 and 40,000 units. In addition, the level of piracy increased from 10 to 25 percent in 1997 to over 50 percent in 2002. See *The Recording Industry in Numbers* (London: IFPI, 1999), 92; idem (London: IFPI, 2000), 98; idem (London: IFPI, 2001), 114; idem (London: IFPI, 2002), 121; idem (London: IFPI, 2003), 116.

According to the Cámara Argentina de Productores de Fonogramas y Videogramas (CAPIF), 53 percent of the local music market is illegal. For more information, see http://www.capif.org.ar. According to IFPI, 9 percent of the market in 1999 and 2000 was covered by bailanta/tropical/cuartetos. The only genres with higher participation were Latin and international pop (20 percent and 12 percent, respectively), and Spanish and international rock (12 percent and 10 percent, respectively), all categories combining local production with regional and international product. More recent data by IFPI do not show sales by genre. Yet, according to Juan Costa and José Nosal, executives at Leader Music and Magenta Records, the two leading labels of the tropical music market, current sales of tropical music cover 50–60 percent of the domestic market, followed by rock at 30–40 percent, and folklore at 10 percent. Costa, in particular, confirms the peak level of sales in 2000, when Leader sold up to 150,000 units per month. Though Magenta does not release sales figures, Nosal sets the peak of cumbia villera at a later time, in 2002 (from phone interviews with Costa and Nosal, March 24 and 26, 2004, respectively). Aside from these two brands, only Genoma (a label distributed by Distribuidora Belgrano Norte [DBN] Records), BMG, and some other smaller labels cover the Argentine tropical music market. To a large extent, Leader and Magenta are the mainstays of the genre.

18 Chris Moss, "The people Will Be Heard," *Guardian*, October 4, 2002.

19 See the interview with Lescano in *Clarín*, February 16, 2003.

20 Hernán Iglesias, "La cumbia combativa encandila a los bonaerenses," *El Pais*, sección internacional, April 25, 2001.

21 The guidelines are available at http://www.comfer.gov.ar/pdf/pubvenezuela/villera .pdf.

22 Ernesto Martelli, "La encrucijada de la cumbia villera," *Clarín*, February 16, 2003.

23 *The Recording Industry in Numbers* (London: IFPI, 2003), 116.

24   Liliana Angelica Martínez and Jimmy Arias, "La cumbia y sus hijas," *El Tiempo*, March 18, 2001.

25   Thomas Turino, "Somos el Perú [We Are Peru]: 'Cumbia Andina' and the Children of Andean Migrants in Lima," *Studies in Latin American Popular Culture* 9 (1990): 15–37.

26   See Rossy War's official website, http://www.peru.com/rossywar.

27   According to Marco Collazos, Rossy War's manager from 2001 to 2004, she was able to sell over 200,000 units through press promotions, an enormous quantity in a market as small as Peru. Rosita Productions, her main distribution company, sold well over 60,000 units. The sale of her music through IEMPSA, the only locally managed and owned recording house, went double platinum, reaching over 20,000 units. At her peak, War charged up to $20,000 per show. Collazos also argues the total number of sales must be at least twice as large, given that piracy in Peru stands at well over 50 percent, a fact confirmed by IFPI. He suggests 80 percent as a more realistic figure (phone interview with Collazos, May 21, 2004).

In Peru, as in Argentina, IFPI data show an increase in the domestic portion of the music market from 30 percent in 1991 to 42 percent in 2001 (no data are available for 2002). In turn, international product dropped from 68 percent in 1991 to 58 percent in 2001, then peaked at 82 percent in 1998. This spike in international product was ephemeral. Consumption of domestic product increased to 29 percent in 1999, while international product dropped to 70 percent. See *The Recording Industry in Numbers* (London: IFPI, 1999), 108; idem (London: IFPI, 2000), 115; idem (London: IFPI, 2002), 136; idem (London: IFPI, 2001), 132; idem (London: IFPI, 2003), 129. In other words, legal consumption of domestic product dropped sharply in 1998, a fact that can be explained by many aspects, economic instability, political transition, worldwide patterns of music consumption, even the rise of tecnocumbia in itself. The increase in sales of international product in 1997–98 is consistent with the overall peak of music sales in Latin America during the same period, a development evident in most national markets of the region. After 1998, music sales across Latin America dropped consecutively. Moreover, the succeeding increase in the sales of domestic copyrighted music confirms the mainstreaming of tecnocumbia, given that its popularity peaked from 1997 to 2000. For more on Rossy War's eventual decline, see "El caso War: La moda pasa factura," *El Comercio*, December 30, 2003.

Still, it is important to consider that as domestic genres become more popular, so does piracy. In terms of genre, IFPI data show tropical music representing 20 percent of the market as early as 1999, a figure only surpassed by Spanish pop/rock (30 percent), a multinational and transregional category. In 2000, tropical music accounted for 9 percent of the music market and remained the second largest domestic segment, only surpassed by domestic pop/rock (15 percent), once again a mixed category. Recent IFPI data do not include figures for sales by genre. Nonetheless, the nature of the success of tecnocumbia in the late 1990s and after 2000 is unquestionable.

28 According to Collazos, these groups sold over three million units. IFPI data for 2000 confirm the great success of the genre: within the top ten spots for albums, only three were not held by Rosita Records (Shakira's *MTV Unplugged*, Iempsa's anthological *Las más bailadas, volumen 1,* and Mega's *Lo mejor y lo nuevo de Los Gaitán*). Néctar appeared thrice, taking up the third, seventh, and eighth slots, and Armonía 10 occupied the sixth. See *The Recording Industry in Numbers* (London: IFPI, 2001), 133. Collazos questions these data (probably passed to IFPI by its Peruvian affiliate, Coferp), arguing that, as far as he knows, Rosita Records lacks documentation for its sales. If anything, he claims, the list understates the success of tecnocumbia. The list does not account for groups like Agua Marina, which he estimates sold well over 50,000 units through the promotion with La República. Sales of tecnocumbia, he claims, were extremely high during this period (e-mail correspondence with Marco Antonio Collazos Gonzáles, June 6, 2004).

29 For discussion of mestizaje's fluid meanings for "indigenous" Peruvians, see Marisol de la Cadena, *Indigenous Mestizos: The Politics of Race and Culture in Cuzco, Peru* (Durham: Duke University Press, 2000).

30 Jeffrey Gould, *To Die in This Way: Nicaraguan Indians and the Myth of Mestizaje, 1880–1965* (Durham: Duke University Press, 1998); Alan Knight, "Racism, Revolution, and Indigenismo: Mexico, 1910–1940," in *The Idea of Race in Latin America, 1870–1940*, ed. Richard Graham (Austin: University of Texas Press, 1990).

31 Juan José Olvera, "Al norte del corazón: Evoluciones e hibridaciones musicales," proceedings of the III Congreso Latinoamericano de la Asociación Internacional para el Estudio de la Música Popular, http://www.hist.puc.cl/historia/iaspmla.html.

32 Juan José Olvera, "Continuidad y cambio en la música colombiana en Monterrey," proceedings of the IV Congreso Latinoamericano de la Asociación Internacional para el Estudio de la Música Popular, http://www.hist.puc.cl/historia/iaspmla.html.

33 For a more detailed coverage of the influence of hip-hop in Chicos de Barrio, see "Chicos Add Hip-Hop to Cumbia Mix," *Billboard*, September 8, 2001, 51.

34 A key article on this subject is Jon Pareles's "Beyond Borders, without Boundaries," *New York Times*, July 12, 2001.

35 Juan Arenas Acosta, "El PRI te roba y también te deja robar," *Milenio*, February 25, 2004.

36 IFPI figures for Mexico show a decline in the domestic component of the music market from 65 percent in 1993 to 49 percent in 2002. The increased internationalization of the market, resulting from an opening national economy, is evident, going from 30 percent of international-regional (in the Latin American sense) origin in 1993 to 49 percent in 2002. Yet traditional/popular music, the rough equivalent of the RIAA's regional Mexican/Tejano, accounts for 45 percent of the sales by genre in 2002. Given the extent of hybridity and intergeneric production of the Mexican market — Piña is just an example — the data do not reflect sales by genre to a more precise level. In addition, the IFPI 2003 report states that "sales of local

repertoire experienced a small increase, although competition in this segment is fierce with the pirate market." See *The Recording Industry in Numbers* (London: IFPI, 2003), 127.

Piracy in the Mexican music market stands at over 50 percent, targets music of domestic nature, and is increasing rapidly. In the RIAA's report for 2003 mid-year statistics for Latin music, regional Mexican/Tejano accounts for 66 percent of sales, in almost direct proportion to the population of Mexican origin within the U.S. Latino population. Though regional music is clearly the best-selling genre in both markets, the difference can be explained by the increased buying power of Mexican Americans (hence purchasing legal product), in contrast to lower sectors of Mexican society.

"Panama Money"

Reading the Transition to U.S. Imperialism

Victor Bascara

Ya no podemos ser el pueblo de hojas, que vive en el aire, con la copa
cargada de flor, restallando o zumbando, según la acaricie el ca-
pricho de la luz, o la tundan y talen las tempestades; ¡los árboles se han
de poner en fila, para que no pase el gigante de las siete leguas!

[We can no longer be the people of leaves up in the air, tree-
tops heavy with flowers, creaking or rustling at the whim of car-
ing light, or thrashed and uprooted by the tempests: the trees must
close ranks to keep the over-developed giant from passing!]

—José Martí, "Nuestra América"

Writing in 1891, José Martí imagines, to his horror, an America that is a brushy
throughway waiting for the United States to clear it and pass through. Panama
would eventually be created as the point of least resistance, where the phalanx
of trees *did not* "close ranks to keep the over-developed giant from passing." In
such an image, we might discern a possible reference to the long-desired trans-
isthmian conduit at Mesoamerica, but Martí is also, of course, being poetical.
He invokes an agency, perhaps associated with Shakespeare's Ariel, that can
marshal forces of nature to resist overdevelopment, vividly figured as a "giant
with seven league boots" who presumably possesses an appetite that explains
his size.[1] Today, in an age of myriad antiglobalization movements and a proliferation of green values in mass culture, it is not difficult to see how Martí's
words resonate with contemporary discontents over a world that the subsequent
"American century" of the United States has created.[2] To translate Martí's "de
las siete leguas" from American Spanish in 1891 to "overdeveloped" in American English today is to assert a potentially anachronistic but compelling reading of Martí's prescience about the role that the idea of development played in

365

the United States' ascendance in the twentieth century. That is, we can see how Martí anticipates the ways in which the overdevelopment of the United States would be made possible by American underdevelopment. And in making such a zero-sum relationship visible, "Nuestra América" not only conveys the problematic terms of unity of the Americas under rising U.S. hegemony but also perhaps figures the geopolitical relations of the overdeveloped and underdeveloped worlds that would emerge so clearly a century later. "The time is near at hand," Martí writes, "when our America will be approached by an enterprising and booming nation demanding close relations, although it does not know our America and, indeed, despises it."[3]

At the dawn of a new millennium, it could well be asserted that the problem of the twenty-first century is the problem of the development line, that is, the relation of the underdeveloped to the overdeveloped in Asia and Africa, in America and the islands of the sea.[4] Such a line can exist within the borders of a nation-state and even within a family, particularly an immigrant one. It is not only a geographical line, as implied by terms such as "global north" and "global south," but also a line drawn between those who can exist primarily and sustainably as consumers and those who cannot. Under contemporary globalization, consumer-centered culture has become so much the rule that remembering the labor that was necessary to make a grape, a college sweatshirt, or the infrastructure of the modern world, such as the interstate highway system or the Panama Canal—the subject of this essay—becomes an act of pious revisionism. We eat sugar, and, as the abolitionists exhorted us to, we taste blood.[5] That is, remembering the history of a commodity's production often means remembering a process for legitimating exploitation. And so the development line gets critically drawn.

To examine how a line between overdeveloped and underdeveloped becomes visible, this essay analyzes how the building of the Panama Canal comes to be forgotten and then remembered as a passage across a development line for the laborers who built the canal, or at least for their relatives. These stay-at-home relatives, not unlike other labor migrants in transnational family structures, clearly benefited from remittances, sums that can become quite sizable when transferred into the economy of the sending country.[6] The first part of this essay broadly considers the ways in which the canal functions and functioned as a symbol of a triumphant new modernity for the United States. The second half looks at a specific revision of that triumph from a minority perspective on the building of the canal. Specifically, that perspective comes from the Barbadian American writer Paule Marshall's short story "To Da-duh: In Memoriam." This much-anthologized story, first published in 1967, concerns a 1930s trip to Barbados taken by a second-generation immigrant from Brooklyn. The story obliquely offers an account of the ways in which "Panama money" enabled an early-twentieth-century Barbadian diaspora to move both horizontally (from Barbados to New York City) and vertically (into the middle class of the United States). An appreciation of "Panama money" makes possible a critical rereading of the canal as a passage across the development line, to help us better see the material conditions that it made possible, as well as the ideas for which it was, is, and could be a symbol.

The Panama Canal is certainly well remembered for its great cost, its creative and innovative engineering, even its being a high watermark for modern sanitation methods, and certainly for its symbolic significance for an ascendant world power at an early point in that nation's rise. That the canal zone was — and could be — returned to the Panamanians in 1999, safely and with little anxiety, is a testament to the confident hegemony of the United States. The canal can be remembered for the ways in which it transformed the lives of its builders, not just the Roosevelts and Goethalses of the world, but also the throngs of migrant laborers who went to a quasi-frontier location. Because of this transposition of their bodily labor to a risky and high-growth region, they were able to transform their labor into alienable property and remit it to their families throughout the world.

In an address at Bridgetown, Barbados, in 1994, Paule Marshall reminds her audience of this way of reading the Panama Canal:

> I should hope that knowledge of former customs and traditions like the tea-meetings, as well as an awareness of facts about emigration, Panama money and other important events in Bajan life over the generations is being passed on to the younger people today. That this wealth of local history is being included in the curriculum. Not only are these former customs and events part of the character and cultural memory of the Barbadian people, they are critical elements in shaping a more complete and authentic national identity in the continuing realization of true independence.[7]

Marshall hopes that the institutionalization of these "facts about emigration" will lead to the "realization of true independence." In affirming the ideal of "true independence," Marshall echoes Edouard Glissant's provocative assertion, "We are shown . . . the advantage of large groupings; and I still believe in the future of small countries."[8] To shape "a more complete and authentic national identity," historical knowledge of Barbados must, Marshall contends, reckon with the history of emigration, the history of the conditions that demanded that Bajans leave Barbados for sites of greater opportunity. Rather than look directly at the canal, this essay turns to a curious moment when its history is remembered in a piece of immigrant literature. Paule Marshall animates the process by which a second-generation Barbadian American learns and becomes discontented with her place vis-à-vis the development line. Marshall's 1967 story "To Da-duh: In Memoriam" narrates a trip to Barbados taken by a young, Brooklyn-born-and-bred second-generation Barbadian American in the 1930s. On her trip she fundamentally disidentifies with the underdeveloped site from which she came. At the end of the story, at a much later moment in her life, the grown-up girl ambivalently realizes the extent to which she was formed as a champion of development. This essay thus offers not a labor history but an examination of the challenges facing the remembering of labor when the fruit of that labor seems to be the next generation's apparent achievement of the status of middle-class consumer. The point at which the unlearning of that status begins turns out to be the Panama Canal, or to be more specific, remembering the dangerous labor that made it possible, as well as the "Panama money" that enabled migration from Barbados to Brooklyn.

El Mundo Unido

A casual glance at any globe will show that the Panama Canal connects the Atlantic and Pacific Oceans. These two great bodies of water become one when they flow through the locks of the canal and become Gatun Lake. Opened in 1919, the canal was the realization of a long-awaited dream — in the words of the historian David McCullough, "a thirty-year dream, a fifty-mile shortcut, a timeless achievement."[9] Yet, as Paule Marshall infers, the canal also connects Barbados and Brooklyn; the labor necessary for its building helped generate the capital necessary to make the move from the Caribbean to the United States. For Bajans, the Panama Canal has historically served as a means for crossing the development line.

But first it is instructive to remember how and why the canal was a more broadly celebrated achievement. It is not altogether obvious why the canal was so difficult to build, and why its building would be an event so exceptional it would enable mass migrations. In the history of urbanization, the bridge and the elevator had been the great symbols of modernization; they are the sine qua non of development. The Panama Canal is both an elevator and a bridge, as its main engineering feat is not just the actual fifty-mile span—such a length is not particularly impressive. Indeed, much of the canal is actually Gatun Lake. Rather, the great feat is one of verticality: the eighty-five feet that ships must be elevated to get to the lake. Contending with this elevation eventually bankrupted the French team led by Ferdinand de Lesseps, the celebrated engineer of the Suez Canal, who persisted in the idea that the canal must be built at sea level.

As a cultural icon, the canal was a ripe symbol of man's conquest of nature. Posters for the 1915 World's Fair in San Francisco displayed an image of Hercules, pushing apart the continents at midpoint to allow a sea lane. As Bill Brown notes, the 1915 fair was an opportunity to show how the East and the West were closer than ever.[10] Despite the outbreak of the Great War, the fair was profitable.[11]

Theodore Roosevelt's frustrations during the Spanish-American War led him to determine that the Panama Canal must be built. By 1903 he would declare, "I took the isthmus." By 1906, he would visit the work site, being the first sitting president to leave the country while in office, albeit to visit a site of insular status: the canal zone. And by 1919, Roosevelt's dream of a two-ocean navy was realized as American warships passed through the canal. For much of the twentieth century, the canal zone was essentially a military base.[12]

The official website for the canal begins with animated maps and the slogan, in both English and Spanish, "Una tierra divida/El mundo unido" (The land divided/The world united). As the animation proceeds in both languages, the viewer's perspective moves closer and closer to the isthmus until it reaches an animated rendering of one of the famous locks opening.

In addition to the large-scale vertical challenges of the canal, the other great impediment was microbial. Until the Americans took over the project, the sickness and death rate among the workers was staggeringly high. The death rate from disease among the French team made progress on the construction ultimately impossible. Seventy-five percent of those hospitalized did not survive. The Americans managed to eradicate yellow fever. The many deaths came from ordinary work site accidents, not uncommon when working with large machinery and high explosives, as with arguably the greatest engineering feat of the nineteenth century: the building of the transcontinental railroad.

And through the work of cultural activism and revisionist scholarship, it has become important to remember the forgotten Chinese laborers who made that feat possible, an "indispensable enemy" famously omitted from the ceremonies in Utah in 1869.[13] As Leland Stanford swung and missed the golden spike at Promontory Point, the telegraph operator nonetheless tapped out a signal to simulate the contact of hammer and head. New York, London, and San Francisco were all listening for the sound of the hammer simultaneously, in one of the earliest known efforts at worldwide broadcasting. Thus a new era of the information age began with misrepresentation. This simultaneity is the key innovation of new information technologies, as space and time are being annihilated.[14] Chinese immigrant labor is absent from the record of that moment, and through revisionism, that absence is now more conspicuous.[15] The emergence of new media has been strategically absent from narratives of the development of modernity and indeed postmodernity.

In the span of about twenty-four hours in 1903, with the help of the U.S. Navy, a coup against Colombia creates the nation-state of Panama. U.S. construction of the canal begins in 1904. A point of pride was that more dynamite was used in the excavation of the canal than was used in all the wars the United States had fought up to that moment. Technological triumphs in communication, transport, and munitions have facilitated the development of globalization, in both material and ideological terms. The canal is considered the last great project of its kind, that is, a project that sought to transform the material world. It is highly unlikely that a project of this magnitude (i.e., environmental impact) would be undertaken or approved today.

Not since the completion of the transcontinental railroad in 1869 had there been an American achievement of its magnitude, scope, ambition, and environmentally destructive consequences. It may be odd to think that a three-thousand-mile railroad, over arid deserts and through the thin atmosphere of permafrost mountaintops, would predate a fifty-mile canal through the tropics by more than four decades. These two developments are linked both materially and ideologically. What these two events clearly have in common is the linking of the Atlantic and Pacific, the rendering of the New World as an isthmus. Both projects involved massive mobilizations of labor forces and the pacification of local resistance. Both diminished the need to reckon with the peninsula of South America; its austral extremities could be left to the penguins of Tierra del Fuego in the westward thrust of the United States.

In geological and geographical terms, an isthmus is a strip of land that bisects a body of water and bridges land masses. The road to the "space-time compression" of globalization can be characterized by an isthmian epistemology, both conceptually and historically. In comparing the discourse of the transcontinental railroad (traditionally an object of analysis for Asian American studies) and the isthmian canal, as it was called until Panama was created (traditionally an object of analysis for Latin American and Caribbean studies), we can discern the material and ideological conditions that linked the world for globalization, and the histories of the making that had been occluded until the desires of new social movements realized conditions for remembering those forgotten pasts. Culture then emerges as the site for that remembering.

I turn now to Paule Marshall's short story "To Da-duh: In Memoriam," to read for the ways in which it dramatizes the drawing and crossing of the development line. In considering the various canonical functions and dysfunctions that the story performs, we can see how it is both a dramatization of historical change and a case study of it.

"Panama Money"

Ada Clement immigrated to New York from Barbados in the early 1920s. In 1929, in Brooklyn, she gave birth to a daughter, Paule Burke, who would grow up to be the acclaimed author Paule Marshall. On November 28, 1994, Marshall returned to the Barbadian capital city of Bridgetown to deliver the Nineteenth Sir Winston Scott Memorial Lecture, titled "Language Is the Only Homeland: Bajan Poets Abroad." This august event was sponsored by the Central Bank of Barbados. Considering this sponsorship, it is altogether fitting that Marshall would identify and describe the financial conditions that occasioned and enabled her mother's emigration to the United States, namely, "Panama money."

> More often than not, when the time came, their passage was paid with Panama money—the money sent back to the island by the hundreds of Bajans who helped build the Panama Canal around the turn of the century—an important chapter in the economic and social history of the island. For example, my grandmother, Alberta Jane Clement, a widow from St. Lucy, shrewdly used the Panama money remitted by her oldest son Joseph, to accumulate land, then later, sold small portions of it to send her other children to the States. My mother left Barbados a pampered, tearful 18-year-old who didn't know how to braid her own hair—

it'd always been done for her. "I saw New York rise shining from the sea,"
is the way she used to describe her first glimpse of the city from the deck
of the ship.[16]

The image of her shipboard mother in the period following the end of World
War I, floating past Lady Liberty in New York Harbor, is the stuff of the sepia-
toned "epic story" of "uprooted" immigrants.[17] But actually, on closer scrutiny
of the quotation, we notice that her mother describes herself as a fixed point
while a mobile New York emerges from the watery depths. That is, rather than
describe herself as a picaresque protagonist moving through a stationary world,
Marshall's mother strategically inverts convention by figuring herself as a stable
standpoint around which the rest of the world revolves.

Such a seizure of subjectivity and epistemological centrality demands a reck-
oning with the complex of histories that converge at such a site. Her epic story
may indeed invoke that of the immigrant, as some conservative accounts of a
West Indian model minority seek to assert.[18] And many of the events and details of her socioeconomic ascent from cleaning houses as a domestic to "buying house" bear out the American dream. But the story of Mrs. Burke also
merges with histories of slavery, genocide, colonialism, and the multidirectional migrations of labor and capital. Marshall, in offering this narrative of
her mother's coming to America — and America coming to her mother — as-
sembles a palimpsest of memories, about the Brooklyn-based Barbadian immigrant communities in which she was born and raised, and the memories of
Barbados that she inherited from the generation of women who traveled the
circuit between the Caribbean and the outer boroughs in the interwar period.

These women, whom she calls "the poets in the kitchen," filled her childhood
with a unique perspective, at once local and worldly: "Using everyday speech,
the simple commonplace words — but always with imagination and skill — they
gave voice to the most complex ideas."[19] Her talk, and indeed her entire literary
career, celebrate "the Mother Poets" who taught her the usefulness of verbal
creativity:

> I call them the Mother Poets — and with a capital M and capital P to under-
> score their importance. Now they didn't look like poets. Whatever that
> breed is supposed to look like. . . . Indeed, as if to disguise their call-
> ing as poets, they insisted on wearing — much to my embarrassment be-
> cause one of them happened to be my mother — they insisted on wearing
> those bargain basement housedresses, which they themselves described

as "cheap cheap come from Fogarty" alluding to the former department store on Broad Street—and those long dismal winter coats and always dowdy hats planted "heap me on"—a term I'm borrowing from them—on their heads.[20]

She describes how the language of everyday life among Barbadian immigrant women in Brooklyn, especially the conversations she listened to in the kitchen, inspired much of her own creative output: "My mother and her poetry circle would sit around the large oilcloth covered table in the middle of the kitchen and talk endlessly, passionately, brilliantly."[21]

Through this acknowledgment of debts and origins, Marshall situates her own emergence and output. She also performs a by now familiar, but still important, act of revision that shows how the private, the personal, and the local are always already suffused with the public, the political, and the globally significant. By calling these women "poets," she both dignifies their virtuosity with language to the world that respects poets and dignifies the calling of the poet as relevant and vital to a world that needs such poets. Organic intellectuals, these women discoursed on "the state of the economy" and on wars, politics, and politicians. This language made intelligible and speakable histories and subjectivities at the nexus of race, class, gender, nation, and empire from the 1920s through World War II. Like these Mother Poets, Marshall herself is a liminal figure, caught between and within occasionally incommensurable paradigms: postcolonial, immigrant, diasporic, cosmopolitan, postemancipation, feminist, third world, Caribbean, Bajan, bourgeois, working-class, to name a few. This liminality has been something of a problem for readers and scholars of her work, but now it is a site of possibility and linkage. As Barbara Christian noted in the early 1980s, Marshall was a relatively underappreciated writer, as her writing, especially her early work, was "a literary anomaly." Marshall is such an anomaly that Christian has to defend Marshall's novel against criticism by Nikki Giovanni of its being "too elegant, too white."[22] Published in 1969, *The Chosen Place, the Timeless People* is a highly prescient novel that examines the promise and pitfalls of a development project on a fictional Caribbean island. We can reconstruct these alternative histories and subjects at the sudden emergence of an arresting detail, what Walter Benjamin would refer to as a "seizing hold of a memory . . . flash[ing] up at a moment of danger."[23] Marshall's own origins were made possible by Panama money and are now made visible by means of her remembrance of it, the significance of which the future is now more ready to appreciate.

The 1994 Central Bank lecture was not the first time Marshall invoked the significance of Panama money in relation to the formation of diasporic Barbadian communities. About halfway into "To Da-duh: In Memoriam," we find her description of a piece of property, a plot with a small orchard and a "good-sized canepiece" that Da-duh had purchased with the Panama money sent by her eldest son, Joseph.[24] Marshall's story is a first-person autobiographical account of a child visiting her maternal grandmother in 1930s Barbados.[25]

This chapter examines how occluded genealogies of the present emerge from a seemingly offhand reference to social and economic history in a literary text.[26] This detail reveals, by its very appearance, the inescapable material history of the story, and, by its offhandedness, the conditions and interests that betray a will to escape that history and all that it entails. It embodies what Edward Said called the "material that paradoxically cannot be overlooked but systematically has been."[27] What is the systematicity that makes a crucial detail like Panama money get routinely and paradoxically overlooked? Ultimately I would argue that the legacies and genealogies of such a detail emerge in frank and subtle ways to help us envision a genealogy of globalization that needs to account for material conditions that have been forgotten.[28] Marshall's story wistfully presents a sassy "brown girl" from New York visiting her sassy grandmother in Barbados in the 1930s. In this story we see how the history of the building of the Panama Canal figures in the circuits between the British colonial marginality of Barbados and the ascendant imperial centrality of New York City, a centrality already apparent by 1967 and certainly undeniable today.

Marshall's story is a narrative of the transition to the new world order out of the old. It is a story of the pointed remembrance of a waning colonialism, that of Barbados in the late 1930s. Her story dramatizes a return of the repressed, as the memories of Da-duh continue to haunt the grown-up narrator decades after the visit. But it also shows us how within that return of the repressed, other repressed histories are given an arena in which to emerge into intelligibility. That is, Marshall's story, ostensibly and in its historical moment, serves the needs of what would come to be called multiculturalism. "To Da-duh: In Memoriam" shows the Americanization of a second-generation immigrant, connected to a sending country of the past but still an active and affirming participant in modern America.

It is also a document of the waning of the era of high imperialism. It shows us a moment of transition, through three generations of one family: grandmother, mother, and narrating-protagonist daughter. These generations function as a schematic for tracing the decline of British empire, the triumph of

America, and the barely recognized seeds of resistance to U.S. imperialism. Unlike Caribbean narratives that follow a protagonist to quasi exile in Mother England, the circuits of migration in Marshall's story more directly implicate and animate American ascendance in the twentieth century. While Afro-Caribbean immigrants to London said, "We are here because you were there," the narrator of Marshall's story can say, "We are here (in the United States) because they (British colonizers) were there." In other words, the United States, with its putatively noncolonizing relationship to Barbados, can be seen as a destination away from territorial colonialism.

That older order of colonialism has by now been thoroughly disparaged. It has become almost too easy to look to territorial, extractive, administrative colonialism as the great evil that the current world order has overcome. Yet, while local sovereignty is in theory compelling, it is often more illusory in practice. This is not necessarily to assert that Marshall is being ironic in her invocation of "true independence" in her 1994 lecture. Rather, she may be calling for a reimagining of the meaning of independence under the globalization that emerged through events such as the building of the Panama Canal, the emigration of West Indians to metropolitan destinations such as New York and London, and the transformations of colonial dependencies through postcolonial underdevelopment, even in the face of nominal independence. Frantz Fanon knew well the pitfalls of national consciousness if a "slightly stretched Marxism" were not applied. That stretched Marxism would theorize the ways in which the new hegemony is fundamentally built on the old.[29] Decolonization has often meant recolonization by other means. While the critical study of colonial discourse is a necessary critique of the fallacies of high imperialism's civilizing mission and its Manichaean order, Fanon and other insightful commentators have also focused on the imperialisms of the present, postcolonialism notwithstanding.[30]

U.S. imperialism has not only managed to emerge in the face of anticolonialism; it has in practice risen to dominance because of it through ostensibly reluctant interventionism in anticolonial struggles in locations such as the Philippines and Cuba. In the face of all the skillful wordplay to describe American interventionism as liberating rather than occupying and colonizing, a few isolated events have developed a reputation for having been forgotten. The history of the Panama Canal is, like U.S. colonial adventures on islands in the Caribbean and the Pacific, the story of the tardy imperialist fashioning an empire on the troublesome cast-offs of more established powers.

In Marshall's story, the legacy of the building of the Panama Canal unleashes a flood of associations that critically express how the canal can be understood as both a missing link and an anomaly in the evolution of globalization. The reference is fleeting but significant, and significant in its fleetingness. The narrator has just arrived in Barbados, and she is taking in her surroundings with the help of her grandmother.

> "Yes, but wait till you see St. Thomas canes," Da-duh was saying to me. "They's canes father, bo," she gave a proud arrogant nod. "Tomorrow, God willing, I goin' take you out in the ground and show them to you."
>
> True to her word Da-duh took me with her the following day out into the ground. It was a fairly large plot adjoining her weathered board and shingle house consisting of a small orchard, a good-sized canepiece and behind the canes, where the land sloped abruptly down, a gully. She had purchased it with Panama money sent her by her eldest son, my uncle Joseph, who had died working on the canal.[31]

In multiple ways, this description links Barbados to the modern world. Interestingly, it is not clear whether the narrator is telling this detail for the reader's edification or if she is paraphrasing something Da-duh tells her at that moment. The form of cultural and historical transmission remains ambiguous, but the content is nevertheless clear. The capital generated from the construction of the canal is transformed into productive property for Da-duh: Panama money. The fact of property ownership for Da-duh is not a given fact but a condition that must be literally and historically accounted for. And she owns income-generating property, as it is a means of production. That is, the property she owns is a business, a cane field. Cane is the crop that made the island significant to modern history.[32] This fact is not lost on Da-duh as she jousts with pride at the comparisons between the narrator's New York and her Barbados.

> "Tell me, have you got anything like these [cane plants] in that place where you were born?"
>
> "No."
>
> "I din' think so. I bet you don't even know that these canes here and the sugar you eat is one and the same thing. That they does throw the canes into some damn machine at the factory and squeeze out all the little life in them to make sugar for you all so in New York to eat. I bet you don't know that."
>
> "I've got two cavities and I'm not allowed to eat a lot of sugar." (2068–69)

Da-duh is proud of her connection to her granddaughter's world. Indeed, it is literally a pride of ownership made possible by her son's lethal labor on the canal. Da-duh has become a capitalist. She seems to have lived out the classic story of Marx's M-C-M (money-commodity-money': Panama money becomes commodified sugar cane, which becomes money plus profit. As we might interpolate from Marshall's 1994 lecture, that "shrewd[ly]" handled surplus value enables an expansionist moment: the sending of Da-duh's daughter to New York in the early 1920s.

Ownership makes Da-duh something of an anomaly. She has ascended to the propertied class, but also under waning colonialism. She is resolutely colonized; appropriately, she views this status with pride, as a connection to her granddaughter's world in the core of the modern world system. She even feels a sense of embarrassment at how parochial some of the relatives are upon meeting the narrator and her family:

> Da-duh, ashamed at their wonder, embarrassed for them, admonished them the while. "But oh Christ," she said, "why you all got to get on like you never seen people from 'Away' before? You would think New York is the only place in the world to hear wunna. That's why I don't like to go anyplace with you St. Andrews people, you know. You all ain't been colonized." (2067)

Yet Da-duh eventually succumbs to the mesmerizing wonder of modernity. For much of the story, we watch Da-duh and the narrator spar over what is more impressive: Barbados or New York City. At first Da-duh wins the battles, as the vegetation on the island is unlike anything in the Big Apple.

> "No," I said, my head bowed. "We don't have anything like this in New York."
> "Ah," she cried, her triumph complete. "I din' think so. Why, I've heard that's a place where you can walk till you near drop and never see a tree."
> "We've got a chestnut tree in front of our house," I said.
> "Does it bear?" She waited. "I ask you, does it bear?"
> "Not anymore," I muttered. "It used to, but not anymore." (2069)

The tide turns as the unparalleled scale — and perhaps unparallelable scale — of New York becomes the narrator's greatest weapon in belittling Da-duh's homeland. The tallness of the recently completed Empire State Building is her trump card, as it is taller than the tallest trees and hills of Da-duh's universe.

Da-duh watched me a long time before she spoke, and then she said very quietly, "All right, now, tell me if you've got anything this tall in that place you're from."

I almost wished, seeing her face, that I could have said no. "Yes," I said. We've got buildings hundreds of times this tall in New York. There's one called the Empire State Building that's the tallest in the world. My class visited it last year and I went all the way to the top. It's got over a hundred floors. I can't describe how tall it is. Wait a minute. What's the name of that hill I went to visit the other day, where they have the police station?"

"You mean Bissex?"

"Yes, Bissex. Well, the Empire State Building is way taller than that."

"You're lying now!" she shouted, trembling with rage. Her hand lifted to strike me.

The grandeur of nature has been displaced by man-made constructions, and Da-duh is reduced to mute rage on the brink of violent manifestations. The young protagonist continues:

"No, I'm not," I said. "It really is, if you don't believe me I'll send you a picture postcard of it soon as I get back home so you can see for yourself. But it's way taller than Bissex."

All the fight went out of her at that. The hand poised to strike me fell limp to her side, and as she stared at me, seeing not me but the building that was taller than the highest hill she knew, the small stubborn light in her eyes (it was the same amber as the flame in the kerosene lamp she lit at dusk) began to fail. (2071)

Even before this, the noncolonial status of the United States creates a racial order with which Da-duh is unfamiliar: "Beating up white people now! Oh, the lord, the world's changing up so I can scarce recognize it anymore" (2070). The narrator's own ability to use violence serves as further evidence of her being more socially integrated across the color line in the United States.

Yet at the end of the story, the narrator is haunted by the memory of her first and only visit to her maternal grandmother. In the late 1960s, as she paints in a loft above a factory in New York, she looks back on the events of the late 1930s. She characterizes her brief life as an artist in the garret as the life of "one doing penance." Like a penitent—from which we get the term "penitentiary"—she stands apart from the day-to-day productive life of the world and reflects on her (former) place in it.

She died and I lived, but always, to this day even, within the shadow of her death. For a brief period after I was grown I went to live alone, like one doing penance, in a loft above a noisy factory in downtown New York and there painted seas of sugar-cane and huge swirling Van Gogh suns and palm trees striding like brightly-plumed tutsi warriors across a tropical landscape, while the thunderous tread of the machines downstairs jarred the floor beneath my easel, mocking my efforts. (2072)

She is an embodiment of cultural hybridity as she draws inspiration from Western art icons like Van Gogh and her non-Western ancestors. And yet, rather than blithely celebrate her creative output as a postmodernist pastiche, the story ends with the revealing and almost defeatist remark that the factory was "mocking my efforts."

As a woman artist of Afro-Barbadian descent in the 1950s or 1960s, her relationship to the factory is one of ostensible antagonism. It appears to be the humanist confrontation between mechanized, dehumanizing industrialization on one hand, and the liberatory world of art, nature, creativity, and resistance on the other.[33] She offers a glorification of a landscape as her productive output as she stands atop a thundering, vibrating factory. For a person of her race and gender, she is more likely to be considered as cheap labor for the factory than as its critic. And yet the story ends with her feeling that her efforts are being mocked, with the factory seeming to get the last word.

Viewed in the context of the entire story, this image may not convey her antagonism to the world of the Fordist factory—something that seems so quaintly nineteenth-century for downtown New York. Rather, this image conveys her complicity with that industrialized and deindustrializing world so far from, yet so connected to, Da-duh's Barbados. Living in a converted loft, the protagonist lives in the decline of an industrial age in the metropole that occasions the material conditions of her creative labor. The factory, then, is "mocking [her] efforts" in the sense of making fun of them, but also mocking in the sense of imitating them. She is, to use the language of Walter Benjamin, a worker in the residual "aura" of the work of art, while the factory is her mechanical reproduction. She remembers how she was modernity's champion as a child, and in the final irony, she may still be.

As the narrator says, "She died and I lived, but always, even to this day, in the shadow of her death." In the structure of the story, that day is a present that inexplicably finds itself in the shadow of Da-duh's death. The narrator lives in the shadow of Da-duh's death, not Da-duh's life, but her *death* specifically.

Marshall herself has said of the historic Da-duh: "It was as if we both knew, at a level beyond words, that I had come into the world not only to love her and to continue her line but to take her very life in order that I might live." That death, we are told, is the product of the last gasps of British imperialism in the Caribbean.

> By the time I mailed her the large colored picture postcard of the Empire State Building, she was dead. She died during the famous '37 strike which began shortly after we left. On the day of her death England sent planes flying low over the island and in a show of force—so low, according to my aunt's letter, that the downdraft from them shook the ripened mangoes from the tree's in Da-duh's orchard. Frightened, everyone in the village fled into the canes. Except Da-duh. She remained in the house at the window so my aunt said, watching as the planes came swooping and screaming like monstrous birds down over the village, over her house, rattling her trees and flattening the young canes in her field. It must have seemed to her lying there that they did not intend pulling out of their dive, but like the hardback beetles which hurled themselves with suicidal force against the walls of the house at night, those menacing silver shapes would hurl themselves in an ecstasy of self-immolation onto the land, destroying it utterly.
>
> When the planes finally left and the villagers returned they found her dead on the Berbice chair at the window. (2072)

Cause of death might well be called shock and awe. Da-duh died in her Berbice chair in a home of her own, an ownership both made possible and haunted by the labor and *death* of her son in the building of the Panama Canal. The narrator states that she lives in the shadow of Da-duh's death, while Da-duh can be said to live in the shadow of her son's death. Theodore Roosevelt may have "[taken] the isthmus," but the isthmus took Uncle Joseph. For the narrator of the story, that watershed event lives on in a postwar moment in a loft in New York City. She then reapprehends a moment from the 1930s as a moment of transition, from frontier expansionism and territorial colonialism to our current globalization, via the Panama Canal. The profound irony and pathos of that closing moment is, as in many a well-constructed short story with a twist ending so emblematic of the genre, a call to go back and retrace the steps to that point to see why that moment strikes the protagonist and the reader with simultaneous identification and alienation. By 1994, Marshall, speaking to a Barbadian audience, calls on the present, postindependence Barbados to remember and institutionalize that history, for that is the history that she and they share as participants and creators of the new world order.

Conclusion: Learning and Unlearning an Isthmian Epistemology

Embodying a new frontier, an outpost of uneasy empire, and a crucial component of the infrastructure for incipient globalization, the Panama Canal takes its place in the formation of U.S. modernity.[34] At the fractious convergence of American, African American, Barbadian, Caribbean, and third world, Marshall's writing makes visible sites of contradiction as well as convergence. And it is the late realization of that contradiction that makes the narrator of "To Da-duh" uniquely positioned to question her place in the drawing of the development line. Her story dramatizes the transition from zealous advocacy of modernization to ambivalent resistance to it. It contributes to the awakening of what Martí called "the octopus in its sleep." Her story allows us to grasp the interplay of the discourses of empire, frontier, and globalization. Specifically we can register a transition between colonialisms: out of territorial colonialism and into the conception of empire that Michael Hardt and Antonio Negri simply called "world order."[35]

To these three prominent discourses of modernity—empire, frontier, globalization—can be added a fourth that has not enjoyed as much attention: an isthmian epistemology. An isthmian epistemology imagines a new relationship to territory and territoriality that is emerging as (1) the frontier gets closed, (2) empire is losing its legitimacy, and (3) space is being annihilated through the simultaneities of globalization. The isthmus can be seen as a structuring trope for the changing relationship of the core and the periphery, of the "overdeveloped giant" and the underdeveloped "trees" that did not "close ranks." The periphery is a site not for creolized settlement but for passage at a point of least resistance and maximum impact. No longer is space seen as necessarily radiating from a center, but rather as traversing points of least resistance without the privileging of a particular direction. What matters more is mobility itself, which will lead to modernity's dream of the annihilation of space. One could even read the old palindrome that emerged with the idea of the canal—a man, a plan, a canal, Panama—as an embodiment of that back-and-forth idea.

The canal was a dream of Goethe as early as 1827,[36] among others, and a challenge to colonial powers throughout the nineteenth century and well before, as the Spanish explorers had envisioned a canal as far back as the early sixteenth century. Yet it would not be until the early twentieth century that the project was realized. The long-awaited realization of this dream is one of the last great components of a unified world, "el mundo unido." Marshall's story concerns the relationship of a Barbadian American girl in the 1930s who visits her grandmother in the era of the waning of the British empire and the ascendance of the United States, what Martí had called "the formidable neighbor." By examining the meaning of the canal from an apparently unrelated Caribbean location, we can uniquely appreciate how, in Martí's conception of "Nuestra América," "difference in origins, methods, and interests between the two halves of the continent" curiously reside in the history of worldly Bajans, migrating not only to Panama and to Brooklyn but from colonialism to property ownership.[37]

Marshall's story provides us with a way of seeing the significance of pasts that the present has yet to learn how to use. To come to terms with the uneven development of modernity is to abide by Walter Benjamin's oft-quoted lines: "To articulate the past historically does not mean to recognize it 'the way it really was' (Ranke). It means to seize hold of a memory as it flashes up at a moment of danger."[38] A continuing challenge, therefore, to committed scholarship on empire in the United States is to discern when and how empire emerged, and how it came to flash up after having been lost or otherwise misrecognized. In other words, we need to come to terms with what the transition to U.S. imperialism looks and feels like. For the narrator of Marshall's story, that transition feels like a passage across the development line. U.S. imperialism, as a new formation that has historically found former models of empire an ill-fitting garment, demands to be recognized through evidence that emerges not as grand narratives of a succession of power, but rather as fragments and eruptions. These eruptions manifest as the extraneous, even anomalous, details that come to prove significant for a future newly ready to recognize itself as connected to formerly occluded pasts.

Notes

1   Enrique Sacerio-Garí provocatively chooses to translate "el gigante de las siete leguas" as "over-developed giant" instead of "giant in seven league boots," which has been the usual translation of the phrase. See *Our America: Writings on Latin America and the Struggle for Cuban Independence*, ed. Philip Foner (New York: Monthly Review Press, 1977), 85. Thanks to Courtney Johnson (Department of Spanish and Portuguese, University of Wisconsin, Madison) for pointing out to me some of Martí's productive linguistic idiosyncrasies in this passage.

2   Henry Luce coined the term "the American century" in early 1941 to approvingly

describe U.S. hegemony. Luce, *The American Century* (New York: Farrar and Rinehart, 1941).

3   José Martí, "Our America," trans. Enrique Sacerio-Garí, in *The Heath Anthology of American Literature*, vol. 2 (New York: Houghton Mifflin, 2002), 885.

4   In *The Souls of Black Folk* (1903), W. E. B. Du Bois famously declared that the problem of the twentieth century is the problem of the color line, as he eloquently narrated how it feels to be a problem in an era of both racial uplift and constitutionally sanctioned racial segregation. Any myths of equality and national unity are contradicted by the fact of Jim Crow. The development line carries on that tradition of exclusion and exploitation alongside visions of advancement.

5   Sidney Mintz, *Sweetness and Power: The Place of Sugar in Modern History* (New York: Penguin, 1985), 68.

6   In this way, the canal resonates with the building of the railroad, as well as the waves of overseas contract workers of globalization, migrating to the developed world, as well as within it, to work in oil fields, to make sneakers in the metropolis, or to change diapers of other people's children or parents in private homes. Recent work has offered histories and sociologies from below by looking at Filipino migrant workers in the American century. For example, see Rhacel Salazar Parreñas, *Servants of Globalization: Women, Migration, and Domestic Work* (Stanford: Stanford University Press, 2001); Catharine Ceniza Choy, *Empire of Care: Nursing and Migration in Filipino American History* (Durham: Duke University Press, 2003); and Dorothy Fujita-Rony, *American Workers, Colonial Power: Philippine Seattle and the Transpacific West, 1919–1941* (Berkeley: University of California Press, 2003).

7   Paule Marshall, *Language Is the Only Homeland: Bajan Poets Abroad* (Bridgetown, Barbados: Central Bank of Barbados, 1995), 12.

8   Edouard Glissant, *Caribbean Discourse: Selected Essays* (Charlottesville: University Press of Virginia, 1989), 3.

9   David McCullough, "A Man, a Plan, a Canal, Panama," *Nova*, 1987.

10 Bill Brown, "Science Fiction, the World's Fair, and the Prosthetics of Empire," in *Cultures of United States Imperialism*, ed. Amy Kaplan and Donald Pease (Durham: Duke University Press, 1994).

11 Burton Benedict, *Anthropology of World's Fairs* (Berkeley: Scolar Press, 1986), 31.

12 In the wake of Operation Just Cause, General Manuel Noriega bluntly stated why such an invasion took place: "The Panamanian isthmus is of strategic importance to the United States! For that reason we see interest in it, and the phobia against Panama rather than Peru or Paraguay or Argentina or Venezuela or Guatemala; because none of them are either the passageway or the focus of geopolitical strategy, they don't have an interoceanic canal, and they are not the geographic center of intercontinental routes." Independent Commission of Inquiry on the U.S. Invasion of Panama, *The U.S. Invasion of Panama: The Truth behind Operation "Just Cause"* (Boston: South End Press, 1991), 121.

13 Alexander Saxton, *The Indispensable Enemy: Labor and the Anti-Chinese Movement in California* (Berkeley: University of California Press, 1971).

14   The Suez Canal was also completed in 1869.

15   For an insightful analysis of the visual politics of this famous photograph, see David Eng, "I've Been (Re)Working on the Railroad: Photography and National History in *China Men* and *Donald Duk*," in *Racial Castration: Managing Masculinity in Asian America* (Durham: Duke University Press, 2001), esp. 35–45.

16   Marshall, "Language," 14.

17   See Oscar Handlin, *The Uprooted: The Epic Story of the Great Migrations That Made the American People*, 2nd rev. ed. (Boston: Little, Brown, 1973). The first edition won the Pulitzer Prize for history in 1951.

18   Most notably, see Thomas Sowell's *Ethnic America: A History* (1981), esp. 216–28. Sowell writes: "West Indians were much more frugal, hard-working, and entrepreneurial. Their children worked harder and outperformed native black children in school. West Indians in the United States had lower fertility rates and lower crime rates than either black or white Americans. As early as 1901, West Indians owned 20 percent of all black businesses in Manhattan, although they were only 10 percent of the black population there. American Negroes called them 'black Jews' " (219).

19   Paule Marshall, "The Making of a Writer: From the Poets in the Kitchen," in *Reena and Other Stories* (Old Westbury, N.Y.: Feminist Press, 1983), 6.

20   Marshall, "Language," 12.

21   Ibid., 8.

22   "Paule Marshall," *Dictionary of Literary Biography*, vol. 33 (Detroit: St. James Press, 1984), 162. See "The Race for Theory," in *The Nature and Context of Minority Discourse*, ed. Abdul JanMohamed and David Lloyd (New York: Oxford University Press, 1990), 44. More recently, book-length studies of Marshall's writing have emerged, including Joyce Pettis, *Toward Wholeness in Paule Marshall's Fiction* (Charlottesville: University Press of Virginia, 1995); and Dorothy Hamer Denniston, *The Fiction of Paule Marshall: Reconstructions of History, Culture, and Gender* (Knoxville: University of Tennessee Press, 1995).

23   Walter Benjamin, "Theses on the Philosophy of History," in *Illuminations* (New York: Schocken, 1971), 126.

24   Paule Marshall, "To Da-duh: In Memoriam," in *The Norton Anthology of African American Literature*, ed. Henry Louis Gates Jr. and Nellie McKay (New York: W. W. Norton, 1994), 2068.

25   While the story is fictional, Marshall refers to her maternal grandmother, Alberta Jane Clement, as "Da-duh" in her dedication to her novel *Praisesong for the Widow* (New York: G. P. Putnam, 1983): "For my grandmother, Alberta Jane Clement ('Da-duh')."

26   In her chapter on Marshall's short stories, Denniston notes that "Panama money" in "To Da-duh: In Memoriam" is a significant detail: "Marshall inserts this information to record a common experience for workers in the Caribbean who, of economic necessity, traveled outside their homelands to earn livelihoods for themselves and to support their families" (*The Fiction of Paule Marshall*, 171n19).

27   Edward W. Said, *Culture and Imperialism* (New York: Vintage, 1993), 114.

28 For a recent example of the premature declarations of the "end of geography," see the geographer Neil Smith's *American Empire: Roosevelt's Geographer and the Prelude to Globalization* (Berkeley: University of California Press, 2003).

29 Frantz Fanon, *The Wretched of the Earth* (New York: Grove Press, 1963).

30 In the conventional narrative of its emergence, postcolonialism as a field of study in the developed world rose on the paradigmatic, but still rather exceptional, example of the rise and fall of the British Empire in South Asia. Closer scrutiny of much of this canonical scholarship reveals an embedded critique of the current empire. For example, Gayatri Spivak's "Three Women's Texts and a Critique of Imperialism" examines the limits of Anglo-American feminism in a global frame. Yet that article's opening sentiments — that it would be impossible to read nineteenth-century British literature without understanding the immanence and importance of the civilizing mission — are not so much a critique of imperialists in the nineteenth century as a critique of literary critics in the late twentieth. The titular question "Can the Subaltern Speak?" is that, under the hegemony current at its moment, the subaltern is a form of subjectivity that is useful for its ability to imagine the limits and alternatives to epistemologies of the non-West. Edward Said's *Orientalism*, for all its magisterial erudition, is a project committed to mapping a genealogy of "Orientalism today." To call Cromer and Balfour imperialists is presumably not something we need a scholar like Said to help us see. Nor would that be an effective use of his status as public intellectual. Rather, when he reads contemporary culture, such as psychology studies or the words of Henry Kissinger, as resonant and related formations, we understand the breaks and continuities between the old empire and the new. *Culture and Imperialism* is the suitable sequel, for it spends much of its later sections dissecting U.S. imperialism today as built on older British and French colonialisms the world over.

31 Marshall, "To Da-duh," 2068. Hereafter cited parenthetically in the text.

32 For example, see Mintz, *Sweetness and Power*. As early as 1944, Eric Williams's insightful study *Capitalism and Slavery* described how the intense profit margins offered by growing sugar cane with slave labor made the appeal of self-sufficiency through a more diverse agricultural base and economy quite weak. Williams quotes Adam Smith: "The profits of a sugar plantation in any of our West Indian colonies are generally much greater than those of any other cultivation that is known either in Europe or America." Williams, *Capitalism and Slavery* (1944; Chapel Hill: University of North Carolina Press, 1994), 53.

33 Ambivalence over machines is a recurrent theme in Marshall's writing. In her debut novel, *Brown Girl, Brown Stones* (1959), Deighton Boyce, the rascally but beloved father, gets an arm ground up in a factory accident. In *The Chosen Place, the Timeless People* (1969), Vereson Walkes dies tragically in an automobile race. And Da-duh herself is both dependent on, yet frightened of, "some damn machine at the factory [that] squeeze out all the little life in [the canes]" (2069).

34 The great articulation of this frontier's end is Frederick Jackson Turner's "The Significance of the Frontier in American History" (1893). On the uneasy U.S. empire

Victor Bascara

emerging at the time, see Amy Kaplan, *The Anarchy of Empire in the Making of U.S. Culture* (Cambridge: Harvard University Press, 2003); and Matthew Frye Jacobsen, *Barbarian Virtues: America Encounters Foreign People at Home and Abroad, 1876– 1917* (New York: Hill and Wang, 2000). For a discussion of the contours of globalization, see David Harvey, *The Condition of Postmodernity* (London: Blackwell, 1989); Saskia Sassen, *Globalization and Its Discontents: Essays on the New Mobility of People and Money* (New York: New Press, 1998); and Joseph Stiglitz, *Globalization and Its Discontents* (New York: W. W. Norton, 2002). Sassen had the prescience of using that title *before* the epochal demonstrations in Seattle in late 1999; Stiglitz, a 2001 Nobel laureate in economics, references Seattle, as well as 9/11, near the outset of his book.

35 Michael Hardt and Antonio Negri, *Empire* (Cambridge: Harvard University Press, 2000).

36 Noted by Marshall Berman in *All That Is Solid Melts into Air: The Experience of Modernity* (New York: Penguin, 1982), 73.

37 Martí: "But our America is facing another danger that does not come from itself but from the difference in origins, methods, and interests between the two halves of the continent. The time is near at hand when our America will be approached by an enterprising and booming nation demanding close relations, although it does not know our America and, indeed, despises it. And since potent countries, self-made by shotgun and law, love strong countries, only strong countries; since the time of unbridled recklessness and ambition (from which North America could perhaps be freed by the predominance of what is purest in its blood, or on which it may be thrown by its vengeful and sordid masses, its tradition of expansion, or the interests of a clever leader) is not so near at hand even to the most startled eye that there is not time to put it to the test of continuous and discreet dignity that could approach and dissuade it; since its honor as a republic in the eyes of the world's attentive nations places a restraint on North America that would not be eliminated even by the puerile provocation, or ostentatious arrogance, or parricidal discourse of our America, the urgent duty for our America is to show itself as it is, one in soul and purpose, swift defeater of a suffocating tradition, stained only by the copious blood sapped from hands by the struggle to clear away ruins, and dripping from our veins, cut by our masters. The scorn of the formidable neighbor, who does not know our America, is the greatest danger for our America. It is imperative, since the day of the visit is at hand, for our neighbors to know our America, and to know it soon, so they stop disdaining it. Through ignorance, they might go so far as to covet it. Out of respect, once they know us, they would remove their hands. One must have faith in the best in men and distrust the worst. One must promote the best so that it be revealed and prevails over the worst. Otherwise, the worst prevails. Nations should have a pillory for whoever arouses useless hates and another one for whoever does not tell the truth in time" ("Our America," 885–86).

38 Benjamin, "Theses on the Philosophy of History," 126.

Contributors

Rachel Adams is an associate professor of English and American studies at Columbia University. She is the author of *Sideshow USA: Freaks and the American Cultural Imagination* (2001). Her current research is on cultures of the North American continent.

Victor Bascara is an associate professor of Asian American studies and English at the University of Wisconsin, Madison. He is the author of *Model Minority Imperialism* (2006).

John D. Blanco teaches comparative literatures of the Americas and the Philippines and cultural studies at the University of California, San Diego. His published work includes articles on the intersections of colonialism and modernity in the Philippines, Spain, and the Americas. He has also translated *Divergent Modernities of Latin America: Culture and Politics in the Nineteenth Century*, by Julio Ramos. His current work focuses on the generative relationship between modern Philippine culture and the juridical, politico-economic, and administrative contradictions of late Spanish colonialism.

Alyosha Goldstein is an assistant professor of American studies at the University of New Mexico. He is presently completing a book entitled *Worlds Within: Democracy, Poverty, and the Politics of Belonging*, which examines the political utilities of poverty in the United States during the 1950s and 1960s in the context of the Cold War and decolonization.

Héctor Fernández L'Hoeste is an associate professor at Georgia State University, Atlanta. He specializes in Latin American cultural studies. His publications include *Narrativas de representación urbana* (1998) and *Rockin' Las Americas* (2004). His articles on Latin American cinema, literature, and media theory have appeared in journals such as *Hispania*, *National Identities*, *Chasqui*, and *Film Quarterly*. He is currently working on a volume on Latin American comics and national identity.

Ian Lekus is a Franklin Postdoctoral Fellow in History at the University of Georgia, where he also holds affiliate faculty status in the Institute for Women's Studies and teaches during the summer at the university's Costa Rica campus. He is currently revising his dissertation into two books, titled *Queer and Present Dangers: Masculinity, Sexual Revolutions* (forthcoming from the University of North Carolina Press) and *Out of the Sixties: The New Left Origins of Gay Liberation*. He has published in the journals *Radical History Review*, *Peace and Change*, and *OAH Magazine of History*; and is a contributor to *The New Left Revisited* (2003), *Modern American Queer History* (2001), and *The Encyclopedia of Lesbian, Gay, Bisexual, and Transgender History in America*.

Caroline Levander is a professor of English and the director of the Humanities Research Center at Rice University. She is the author of *Voices of the Nation: Women and Public Speech in Nineteenth-Century American Literature and Culture* (1998) and *Cradle of Liberty: Race, the Child, and National Belonging from Thomas Jefferson to W. E. B. Du Bois* (Duke University Press, 2006), and co-editor of *The American Child: A Cultural Studies Reader* (2003) and *Hemispheric American Studies: Essays Beyond the Nation* (forthcoming from Rutgers University Press). Her articles have appeared in *American Literature*, *American Literary History*, *Prospects: An Annual Journal of American Cultural Studies*, and *Studies in American Fiction*.

Susan Y. Najita is an assistant professor of English and Asian–Pacific Islander American studies, Program in American Culture, at the University of Michigan, Ann Arbor. She writes about the literatures and cultures of the Pacific Islands. She is the author of *Decolonizing Cultures in the Pacific: Reading History and Trauma in Contemporary Fiction* (2006).

Rebecca M. Schreiber is an assistant professor of American studies at the University of New Mexico. She is the author of *The Cold War Culture of Political Exile: U.S. Artists, Writers, and Filmmakers in Mexico, 1946–1966* (forthcoming from the University of Minnesota Press). Her current research examines contemporary representations in photography and film/video of the transnational movement of workers from Mexico and Central America to the United States.

Sandhya Shukla is an associate professor of anthropology and Asian American studies at Columbia University. She is the author of *India Abroad: Diasporic*

Cultures of Postwar America and England (2003) and is currently completing a book entitled *Cross-Cultures of Twentieth/Twenty-first Century Harlem.*

Harilaos Stecopoulos is an assistant professor of English at the University of Iowa. He has edited (with Michael Uebel) *Race and the Subject of Masculinities* (1997) and is currently finishing a book-length manuscript entitled *Colored Spaces: Southern Strategies of U.S. Empire from Thomas Dixon to Richard Nixon.*

Michelle Stephens is an associate professor of English and of American and African American studies at Mount Holyoke College. She is the author of *Black Empire: The Masculine Global Imaginary of Caribbean Intellectuals in the United States, 1914 to 1962* (2005) and has published pieces on Bob Marley's and Harry Belafonte's mix of political radicalism and incorporation by the market, and on the black modernism of diasporic figures such as Eric Walrond and Richard Wright. She is currently at work on two projects, one concerning issues of black masculinity and performance across the diaspora, and another exploring the intersecting histories of women of color.

Heidi Tinsman is an associate professor of history at the University of California, Irvine. She is the author of *Partners in Conflict: The Politics of Gender and Sexuality in the Chilean Agrarian Reform, 1950–1973* (2003) and has published widely on issues of gender, labor, and military rule in Chile. She is currently finishing a book on consumer culture and table-grapes in Chile and the United States during the 1970s and 1980s.

Nicholas Turse works in the Department of Epidemiology at Columbia University and is the associate editor and research director of the Nation Institute's TomDispatch.com. He has written for the *Los Angeles Times*, the *San Francisco Chronicle*, the *Nation*, and the *Village Voice*. His book on the new military-industrial complex in America, *The Complex*, is forthcoming from Metropolitan Books/Henry Holt.

Rob Wilson is a professor of literature at the University of California, Santa Cruz. His published works include *Reimagining the American Pacific* (Duke University Press, 2000), *Waking in Seoul* (1988), and *American Sublime* (1991), and the coedited collections *Global/Local* (Duke University Press, 1996) and *Asia/Pacific as Space of Cultural Production* (Duke University Press, 1995). He has a study of conversion and counter-conversion titled *Henry, Torn from the Stomach* forthcoming from Harvard University Press; and he has coedited (with Christopher Leigh Connery) a collection of cultural criticism titled *Worldings: World Literature, Field Imaginaries, Future Practices — Doing Cultural Studies in the Era of Globalization* (2006).

Index

Mori, Yoshiro, 174
Morley, Morris, 104, 110 n. 68
Morris, Charles, 67, 84 n. 8
Morrow, Prince A., 143–44, 157, 163 n. 34
Morton, Oliver, 91
Mosquito (Gayl Jones), 226–29
Mouritz, Arthur, 149, 151–53, 154, 156,
    160, 162 n. 19, 162 n. 22, 163 n. 37, 164
    n. 53, 165 nn. 65–66, 165 nn. 72–76, 165
    nn. 79–83, 166 nn. 85–86, 166 n. 90, 166
    n. 99, 166 n. 102
"Movement," 25
Mufti, Aamir, 33 n. 45
Muir, Ernest, 162 n. 26, 163 n. 36, 163
    nn. 42–43
"Mulatto" histories, 200–201, 203
Mullen, John, 289, 308 n. 32, 311 n. 75, 312
    nn. 96–97
Multiculturalism, 374
Muñoz, Marín, Luis, 313–17, 320–22,
    328–32, 333 n. 1, 335 n. 21
Murayama, Milton, 24, 111, 113–30, 134
    n. 9, 134 n. 11, 135 nn. 15–18, 135 nn. 22–
    26, 135 n. 28, 137 n. 45
Musgrave, George Clarke, 108 nn. 42–44
Música regional mexicana, 340
Música tropical, 340, 346–47, 355
Muthyala, Walter, 22, 33 n. 51

Naisbett, John, 178, 188 n. 45
Najita, Susan Y., 24–25
Napoli, Donald S., 336 n. 29
Narrative of the Life of Frederick Douglass,
    94
Nash, June, 30 n. 22
Nassburg, Guy, 280 nn. 63–64
Nation, 2–3, 6, 10, 20, 22, 66, 76–77
National Afro-American Party, 102
National Association for the Advance-
    ment of Colored People (NAACP), 39,
    57
National Conference of Negro Artists
    (NCNA), 301, 304

Nationalism, 1, 4, 17, 66, 75
Nation-states, 1, 5, 7, 10, 16, 17
Native Americans, 49, 73, 192–93, 200,
    203; decimation of, 67, 80
Natives, 111
Natural History of Afro-Mexico, A (Word-
    law), 228
Nearing, Scott, 59 n. 3
Néctar, 353
Negri, Antonio, 174, 381, 386 n. 35
Negritude, 193, 233
Negroes, 48, 81, 91, 97, 265–66
Negro USA, 304
Neocolonialism, 332
Neoliberalism, 2, 4
New Deal, 287, 288, 323
New Left, 249, 250, 252–54, 257–58,
    260–70, 274
"New Man," 265–66
"New Negro," 48
New World, 140, 193, 197, 210, 219, 226–
    27, 370; cultural mixing in, 203, 207;
    epics and metanarratives of, 205; ex-
    propriation of, 195–98; plantation
    culture in, 40; populations of, 200
Newton, Huey, 263
Neylan, T. C., 162 n. 18
Nicaragua, 17, 19, 35, 37–40, 56–57, 227
Noble savages, 193
Noli me tangere (Rizal), 63, 70
Nonini, Donald, 187 n. 39
Norris, Frank, 173, 178, 185 n. 23
Norteño, 356, 359
North American Free Trade Agreement
    (NAFTA), 168
Novales Brothers, 72
"Nuestra America" (Martí), 4, 47, 65,
    68–69, 74, 76, 78–81, 111, 168, 214–15,
    313–14, 365–66, 382
Nugent, Daniel, 31 n. 24

O. Henry, 34, 58 n. 2
Oberg, Kalevro, 323–24, 336 n. 27

Sandhya Shukla is an associate professor of anthropology
and Asian American Studies at Columbia University. She is
the author of *India Abroad: Diasporic Cultures of Postwar
America and England* (2002).

Heidi Tinsman is an associate professor of history at the
University of California, Irvine. She is the author of
*Partners in Conflict: The Politics of Gender, Sexuality, and
Labor in the Chilean Agrarian Reform, 1950–1973* (2002).

Library of Congress Cataloging-in-Publication Data
Imagining our Americas : toward a transnational frame /
edited by Sandhya Shukla and Heidi Tinsman.
p. cm. — (Radical perspectives)
Includes bibliographical references and index.
ISBN 978-0-8223-3950-2 (cloth : alk. paper)
ISBN 978-0-8223-3961-8 (pbk. : alk. paper)
1. America—Civilization. 2. Multiculturalism—America.
3. Transnationalism—Social aspects—America.
4. Globalization—Social aspects—America. 5. America—
Race relations. 6. America—Ethnic relations.
7. Cross-cultural studies.
I. Shukla, Sandhya Rajendra. II. Tinsman, Heidi
E20.143 2007
305.80097′0904—dc22   2007000159

\ \